W9-CLJ-007

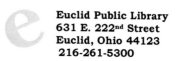

FLEETWOOD MAC
ON FLEETWOOD MAC

FLEETWOOD MAC
ON FLEETWOOD MAC
INTERVIEWS AND ENCOUNTERS

EDITED BY SEAN EGAN

CHICAGO
REVIEW
PRESS

An A Cappella Book

Library of Congress Cataloging-in-Publication Data

Names: Egan, Sean, editor.
Title: Fleetwood Mac on Fleetwood Mac : interviews and encounters / edited by
    Sean Egan.
Description: Chicago, Illinois : Chicago Review Press Incorporated, [2016] |
    Includes index.
Identifiers: LCCN 2015038135 | ISBN 9781613732342 (cloth : alk. paper)
Subjects: LCSH: Fleetwood Mac (Musical group)—Interviews. | Rock
    musicians—Interviews. | Fleetwood Mac (Musical group)
Classification: LCC ML421.F57 F54 2016 | DDC 782.42166092/2—dc23 LC record
available at http://lccn.loc.gov/2015038135

A list of credits and copyright notices for the individual pieces in this collection can
be found on pages 417–420.

Interior design: Jonathan Hahn
Interior layout: Nord Compo

Printed in the United States of America
5 4 3 2 1

CONTENTS

INTRODUCTION

In 1968 Fleetwood Mac's eponymous debut—colloquially known as *The Dog and Dustbin LP* in reference to its cover photograph—was the United Kingdom's bestselling album. Although it boasted fine musicianship, its success was surprising because its music mainly consisted of hardcore blues at a point when the UK blues boom was considered long over.

There was more to the original Fleetwood Mac than blues, however. Their string of classic, groundbreaking singles over the next couple of years—"Black Magic Woman," "Albatross," "Man of the World," "Oh Well," and "The Green Manalishi (with the Two Pronged Crown)"—covered the waterfront of popular music. This was clearly a remarkable band on more than one level.

Those hits were written by vocalist and virtuoso guitarist Peter Green. Green's colossal talent, though, was like a butterfly—here and gone. By the end of 1970, he was an acid casualty and an ex-member. With fellow guitarist Jeremy Spencer's involvement in a cult rendering him also lost to the group, it would seem Fleetwood Mac was finished. Some viewed with skepticism or even contempt the decision by John "Mac" McVie and Mick Fleetwood to keep the show on the road. The band might have been named after the pair, but only through a moment of whimsy on the part of Green. They were merely bassist and drummer, respectively, and neither wrote songs. In the early seventies, such brand-name-oriented behavior rendered people nothing less than uncool breadheads.

However, the rhythm section laughed all the way to the bank. More-over, they eventually turned the band into something arguably even more artistically valid than the original lineup. In 1977 a Fleetwood Mac of which only McVie and Fleetwood were original members released an album called *Rumours*. The album didn't quite match the debut's feat of becoming Britain's biggest-selling long-player of its year of issue, but it was up there. More important for the band's finances, it was America's top album and a bestseller in a host of other countries. Moreover, it was hailed as a cast-iron classic, one of those select records that remain in the charts for years and public affection forever.

Indivisible from the quality, success, and high profile of *Rumours* is the internal trauma that gave rise to its songs. The band's latest lineup, unusually for the time, was mixed-gender. Keyboardist and songwriter Christine McVie was the wife of John McVie. Guitarist, vocalist, and songwriter Lindsey Buckingham and vocalist and songwriter Stevie Nicks were lovers. In the calendar year preceding the release of *Rumours*, both couples split. The songs subsequently written by Christine McVie, Nicks, and Buckingham understandably dripped with heartbreak and recrimination, made worse by their obligation to continue to work together—and indeed play with their ex-partners on songs that were postmortems on their relationships.

As if the band's recordings weren't already like diary entries, the Fleetwood Mac members sometimes seemed to use the press like a therapist's couch. The ethereal Californian Nicks, the tormented, frustrated punk rocker Buckingham, the dignified English rose Christine McVie, the blunt-speaking John McVie, and the loquacious Fleetwood all regularly had their say and were all astoundingly candid.

Miraculously, the band did not allow their troubles to undermine their career, and this despite an ill-starred affair between Nicks and the married Fleetwood. Instead, for the next decade they continued to release fine music in their thoughtful, melodic style. Double LP *Tusk* (1979) was perceived as their expensive folly but continues to be highly listenable. *Mirage* (1982) was a solid mellow effort. *Tango in the Night* (1987) was burnished adult-oriented rock that constituted a beacon of soulfulness in an emotionally and musically sterile decade.

Buckingham's departure in '87 seemed to bring to a close the era of the *Rumours* Five. However, he has returned, as have Nicks and Christine

McVie despite their own later never-again declarations. Releases by any configuration of the band have become few and far between, and perhaps even irrelevant to large parts of the audiences who flock to the tours Fleetwood Mac continues to mount. However, 2013 and 2014 brought news that made millions ecstatic: the reassembling of the *Rumours* Five and talk of a new album.

Through interviews across the decades, *Fleetwood Mac on Fleetwood Mac* examines the group's long, tortured journey: their initial joyous rise; the tragedy of Peter Green's mental deterioration; their struggle to find a new voice with transitory members like Bob Weston, Dave Walker, and Bob Welch; the emotionally troubled but commercially triumphant years of the *Rumours* lineup; the successive departures of Buckingham, Nicks, and Christine McVie and their respective returns; and the ensemble's glide into the twin statuses of senior citizens and Heritage Artists.

It is a saga described in more than one of the features included herein with the ambiguous phrase "rock's greatest soap opera." One thing about Fleetwood Mac's remarkable history is not ambiguous: this soap opera has the greatest soundtrack of them all.

—Sean Egan

PETER GREEN—THE GUITARIST WHO WON'T FORSAKE THE BLUES

Norman Jopling | August 19, 1967 | *Record Mirror* (UK)

This is one of the earliest pieces of Fleetwood Mac press exposure, published before "Peter Green's Fleetwood Mac" had even released a record and before the name of the band had impressed itself on the consciousness of even those who knew about them: Jopling refers to them as "Fleetwood Wing."

An example of just how early is provided by the revelation that it's inconceivable to their lead vocalist/lead guitarist/guiding spirit Peter Green that the group might ever abandon the blues. Herein, he virtually accuses Eric Clapton of selling out on that score—rather ironic considering that Clapton famously left the Yardbirds two years previously over the alleged abandonment of their blues roots.

ANYONE who in a year has built up the reputation of being Britain's best blues guitarist, must have some interesting things to say, and therefore be interesting to write about and read about. That's what I figured and indeed Peter Green is very interesting.

He made his reputation as John Mayall's lead guitarist when he replaced Eric (then "slowhand") Clapton. It is necessary to know that Peter Green really and truly lives for the blues and with the blues, everything from his East End upbringing (he was a shy and reticent child) to his natural talent has contributed to his present reputation.

When he replaced Clapton after a series of auditions by John Mayall in which Peter won hands down, he was taunted on nearly every date by cries of "We want Clapton" from some of the audience.

"They weren't the kind of things which made me play better," said Peter, "they would just bring me down. For a long time with John I wasn't playing at my best, as good as I was able. Only in the last few months with him could I really feel uninhibited."

Peter first became interested in the blues when he heard a Muddy Waters' record when he was fourteen. At that time he was playing bass, but after hearing more and more blues he felt he could play blues guitar and switched instruments. From playing Shadows material he has changed to playing real blues—he is on the new Eddie Boyd LP and in a private letter to a record producer Eddie said that Peter could play Blues guitar better than anyone else he had heard—a truly fine compliment.

Peter's guitar playing has made him into one of the most highly-rated musicians in the country, but does Peter think that his very specialist form of music can be truly appreciated by the audiences?

"No, no, only by a few. I think this is demonstrated by the applause I get when I play very fast. This is nothing, it doesn't mean a thing, playing fast—it's something I used to do with John when things weren't going too well. But it isn't any good. I like to play slowly, and feel every note—it comes from every part of my body and my heart and into my fingers, I have to really feel it. I make the guitar sing the blues—if you don't have a vocalist then the guitar must sing.

"Only a few people in this country can really do this. Clapton could. I would watch him and think how great he was. But he sat in with us the other week and he isn't the same, he's lost the feeling. Mind you he could, I think get it back—but he's so easily influenced. He sees Hendrix and thinks 'I can do that, why don't I?'. But I'll always play the blues."

A while ago Peter wanted to go to Chicago, because he felt that the blues scene in Britain wasn't wide enough. But he has abandoned the project now and formed his own band, Peter Green's Fleetwood Wing. Why did he leave John Mayall's band, which has the reputation of being the country's most successful blues outfit?

"Various reasons. But the most important was that I didn't agree with the kind of material which was being played. It was becoming, for me, less and less of the blues. And we'd do the same thing night after night. John would say something to the audience and count us in, and I'd groan inwardly."

Peter's group will record for the Blue Horizon label, a specialist label which will soon be distributed nationally.

If you appreciate blues, and real blues guitar, don't miss them.

ROCK'N'BLUES VIA PETER GREEN

The Big Beat Bug Bites
Bluesman Peter

Norman Jopling | March 9, 1968 | *Record Mirror* (UK)

Only half a year after his blues purist interview with Norman Jopling, Peter Green was justify-ing to the same journalist the incorporation of mainstream rock oldies into Mac's set. Even so, the band's just-released first album cleaved to that blues purism. Green waxes strangely lukewarm about it, but the record proceeded to eclipse the sales of the contemporaneous likes of *The White Album* by the Beatles and *Beggars Banquet* by the Rolling Stones.

THE BIG BEAT Rock'n'Roll bug is biting everywhere.

Think of the most unlikely place for it to bite. No, not Des O'Connor. Not even warm. Think of a dedicated musician NOT in the rock'n'roll field who has spent a long long time building up a reputation as a blues guitarist . . . you got it, baby—Peter Green.

If you go and see Peter Green's Fleetwood Mac and you hear "Jenny Jenny" or "Keep A Knockin'," don't run away and grab your bicycle chain to hit them with. Stay and listen and you'll hear Peter and the boys play some pure blues numbers. Then the similarity between the two kinds of music will be apparent to you—and you'll be able to see how the early primitive rock'n'roll developed from the blues. And remember that the Sun studios (who first recorded Elvis, Jerry Lee, Carl Perkins,

Johnny Cash and Roy Orbison) were recording blues artistes—some of the best—many years before the rock'n'roll craze started.

"I've always liked rock", confessed Peter to me, while he was sipping a glass of Mackeson. "And it's a pity in a way that everyone is going on about the rock thing because it seems as though we're just being 'in'. Actually I've always wanted to do this kind of thing on stage—but it doesn't mean we'll be neglecting the blues.

"We're still doing the same kind of numbers as we always did—but I'm playing more to the audiences nowadays. For instance—when we started we used to play to please ourselves, and didn't bother too much about the audience. Now—I play numbers that are requested—like 'Going Down Slow' for instance which they like because of the guitar sounds we can get into it. Funny about guitar playing—the people in the audience think you're great if you play fast but that just isn't so. Now I only play fast when I want to, which isn't THAT often."

On stage—if you've ever seen the Fleetwood Mac—they wear no stage clothes, amble on stage, and tune up before the audience. A necessary part of the "white blues" stage ritual perhaps, but effective. It makes them seem dedicated. And when the group starts playing the audience really get into the music.

Peter talked about his new LP out on the CBS label Blue Horizon.

"It really represents what we first started doing when the group was together. I think that ultimately we will think all the time in LP's, but of course I'd like a hit single."

I told Peter that I thought it was difficult for a British studio to get the "hard" sound that blues studios in America get—take Howlin' Wolf or Elmore James records for instance.

"Yes, that's true", admitted Peter. "I asked our producer Mike Vernon if we could do a 'live' LP but he said no. I've always wanted to play straight through the LP—no stopping for mixing and reductions etc. On a new LP we've just recorded with Eddie Boyd we've done almost just that. It's all recorded in mono but it is played just how I wanted it to be. I'm very excited with it. Our own LP I'm not fully satisfied with, but I don't think I'd ever be satisfied with our records—it's already sold quite well so I'm keeping my fingers crossed.

"Talking about studios I was talking to Marshall Chess who was over here and he said that if we were ever in America we could use his Chess studios. I'd love to take him up on that offer.

"Some of the tracks on our LP are very exciting—'Shake Your Moneymaker' for instance and I think that the echo effect and the dropped voice used on 'I Loved Another Woman' is very effective."

BIG MAC

Two All Gold Albums Special Songs Let-ups Cheesecake Pickles Divorce on a Star-Crossed Success Run

John Grissim | November 1976 | *Crawdaddy* (US)

At the point in time covered by the first entry in this book, the lineup of Fleetwood Mac was Peter Green (guitar, vocals), Jeremy Spencer (guitar, vocals), Bob Brunning (bass), and Mick Fleetwood (drums). By the time of the second entry, John McVie had replaced Brunning. Between then and December 1974, the following people joined the band:

> Danny Kirwan (vocalist, guitarist)
> Christine McVie (keyboardist, vocalist)
> Bob Welch (guitarist, vocalist)
> Dave Walker (vocalist)
> Bob Weston (guitarist, vocalist)

And the following people left:

> Peter Green
> Jeremy Spencer
> Danny Kirwan

Bob Welch
Dave Walker
Bob Weston

This sort of wholesale change was then not only uncommon in rock but—for many—ludicrous. Losing Peter Green, the band's original guiding voice, was bad enough, but to rapidly also suffer the departure of fellow guitar hero Jeremy Spencer was, on the face of it, untenable. It seems reasonable to conclude that only the serendipity of the band's name being a conflation of the surnames of its extant rhythm section prevented the group suffering a terminal validity crisis.

In January 1975 came some personnel news bizarre even by the standards of Fleetwood Mac. A duo called Buckingham Nicks who had released an album on Polydor Records were to abandon their own career to be subsumed into Fleetwood Mac. For those not keeping up with the group's revolving-door membership, it now constituted Fleetwood, McVie (J), McVie (C), Buckingham, and Nicks—an ensemble with an almost equal division between the genders, then remarkable. Moreover, the new double appointment was in step with the soap-opera intrigues established by the McVies' married status and Bob Weston's notorious affair with Mrs. Fleetwood: Lindsey Buckingham and Stevie Nicks were a couple.

For the first time, though, the upshot of adding new members was something more than workmanlike music and the impression of a mercenary attempt to return to past commercial heights. The craftsmanship of Buckingham (guitarist, vocalist, and songwriter) and Nicks (vocalist and songwriter) was injected at the precise same time that Christine McVie was blossoming as a composer. As if to underline this genuine rebirth, the group made their first album with that lineup another eponymous one. *Fleetwood Mac* (July 1975) was sheened, melodic soft rock graced with multipart harmonies but shot through with an unusual emotional grit. It would be this lineup's defining style. The album slow-burnt its way to number one in the US charts.

This feature—written as the band was recording an album that would be called *Rumours*—is suffused with the group members' euphoria over their newfound success, although there is also a tinge of sorrow: the couples in the group have split. (Strangely, Christine McVie never went back to the sweet maiden name that made her, literally, Miss Perfect.)

Note: For "Lindsay" read "Lindsey."

"What does it feel like to have won? You couldn't have put it better." Mick Fleetwood laughed contentedly in the back of the limousine headed for the soundcheck at the San Diego Sports Arena one afternoon late in August. John McVie, sitting in front in aviator shades and a white cotton longshoreman cap, had an answer. "Well," he said, throwing an elbow over the seatback, "in terms of going down to the bookstore and looking at boating magazines and drooling, which, I have for five years—I can now buy one. And I just did."

Mick unlimbered his 6'6" frame from what a moment earlier had been an attempted nap and curled up sideways like a praying mantis in hibernation. "Winning on our own personal charm is the most important. I mean the money is great, but in a lot of ways it has nothing to do with money. The thing is we are all tremendously pleased with ourselves."

He removed his blue felt-brim hat and tossed his head back, revealing a tarnished brass pendulum earring. It is one of several fashion accoutrements which, like the old *I Ching* coin around his neck and the narrow rectangular heirloom wristwatch, possess the same well-seasoned character of their owner.

Fleetwood sat up now, seeming more intense. "But right now we are so completely involved in what we are doing that it's hard to relate to any of it. The number one item on everyone's mind is the album. We absolutely *have* to finish the album."

"Chris, I think we should go for one more take to get a little brighter mood." The pleasantly modulated voice flowing through the studio talk-back speaker belongs to Richard Dashut, Fleetwood Mac's sound engineer and production assistant. He is standing at the console, his finger pressed on the talk button while he gropes for a helpful description. "This is really more of . . . a cocaine song . . . than it is an alcohol song—if you know what I mean."

After several seconds of silence, Dashut peers through the double glass windows. "Uh . . . Chris?"

Sitting behind a mammoth Steinway grand facing the far wall of the darkened studio, Christine McVie ponders the situation without looking around or moving her hands from the keyboard. A single directional spot overhead highlights her mopsy blond hair and the bottle of Blue Nun on the piano.

"Well," she drawls laconically, rocking ever so slightly to one side. "I *am* drunk."

Dashut falls back into his armchair laughing as everyone in the control room cracks up. Mick Fleetwood's grim countenance vanishes. Stevie Nicks, sitting cross-legged in a reclining chair embroidering a pair of denim pants, stands up for a near-sighted glimpse of Christine, whose own laughter percolates through the monitors.

The comic relief, however inadvertent, is desperately welcome; especially at 4:30 a.m., near the end of another in a series of intense all-night sessions at the Record Plant's studios in Sausalito. For some time, there hadn't been much to laugh at. Here it was, early March, and Fleetwood Mac, after nearly a month in the studio, was way behind schedule in finishing the thirteenth album in its kaleidoscopic nine-year career. The group was feeling the strain of heavy recent-success pressure with too little time off. Part of the delay had been mechanical: pianos (three in succession) had failed to stay in tune; and a tape machine, nicknamed "Jaws," had acquired an appetite for eating fresh takes.

Then there was the night some delicious grass cookies showed up with the food prepared by Andrea and Robin, the Record Plant's caterers. Pooh-poohing the advertised potency, the band gobbled freely. There followed what had come to be known as the "thousand-dollar cookie" session. The band spent most of the night in an exceedingly bent condition and the engineer went home early. All John McVie remembers is spending hours sitting with Stevie while the two of them giggled over a copy *of Playboy.*

Of greater consequence was the plethora of soap opera scenarios that dominated the band members' personal lives, playing havoc with the album's progress. John and Christine were struggling to go their separate ways after seven years of marriage. The Buckingham-Nicks non-marital five-year coupling was also lurching towards an end, accompanied by occasional tears and ill-concealed arguments. And Mick was broodingly preoccupied with what seemed the end of his 12-year partnership with ex-model wife Jenny, the mother of his two daughters. More soap flakes had appeared in the person of Sandra, John McVie's silently svelte English girlfriend (as well as one-time companion of Fleetwood Mac's former lead guitarist Peter Green).

"We were all in pretty bad shape," Stevie Nicks would later observe from a much happier perspective. What was remarkable about the group's handling of the situation was the consideration its members seemed to show for each other's hurt feelings; an attitude, they'll tell you, that had more to do with a collective sense of family than any wish to keep together an act that was on the brink of becoming enormously successful.

No one in Fleetwood Mac was ashamed of the romantic turmoil, but one might have questioned their wisdom in allowing an observer access to the studio during those hectic weeks. To an outsider, the band appeared to be dangerously directionless, operating without management and governed only by some vaguely functional group mind.

Complicating matters was the surrounding social scene that grew more intrusive in direct proportion to the weekly chart position of the band's unkillable lp, *Fleetwood Mac.* By the time the album turned platinum in February, the secondary sanctums inside the Record Plant—the lobby, recreation room and carpeted dining nook—were populated by aloof, fashionable men and women with purposeful expressions that suggested they were there for *serious* reasons that had nothing to do with vamping on the excitement of their proximity to Studio B. There seemed to be a stream of trendy strangers passing by band members in the corridor with hardly a side-long glance—a two-way procession like some kind of weird unbonded double helix. "Hey, who *are* all these people?" Lindsay whispered in the kitchen one midnight while scrounging in the refrigerator for cold chicken. He was less irritated than curious. No one had a clue.

Inevitably the ersatz entourage developed its own hierarchy, the top rung of which could be found within a cigarette haze in the semi-privacy of the sunken lounge room. By unspoken agreement, the role of host was reserved for whichever nameless calfskin-coated stage door heavy was tapping the glass.

In the meantime the band stayed sequestered, working long hours, doing its best to ignore the phone calls from Warner Bros. Records and the pressure to come up with a brilliant follow-up to its most successful album ever. Fleetwood Mac would do the best it could, driven by necessity and sustained by a lot of freefloating creative tension.

Stevie Nicks, physically the most fragile, exemplified that drive. The night she recorded the vocal track to her "Gold Dust Woman," she did the first take standing up in a fully-lit studio. The song required a lot of power and an equal measure of feeling. As take followed take, Stevie gradually withdrew. The lights were turned down; a chair was brought in for her, and she wrapped herself in an oversized cardigan to keep warm. Forty minutes later she was barely visible in the darkness—a mere waif wearing flight-deck earphones, huddled in a chair while next to her on a stool sat a convalescent stash of Kleenex, a Vicks inhaler, a bottle of Calistoga mineral water and a box of throat lozenges. Stevie had achieved an astonishing command of the material and on the eighth take she sang the song straight through, nailing it perfectly.

As tempestuous as the Sausalito sessions were (the group returned home to Los Angeles in mid-March with only the basic tracks completed), there was one major compensation that made life a lot easier to bear: their ship was coming in. Fleetwood Mac, a transplanted British band with a good, albeit low-profile reputation and a solid cult following, was at last achieving mass acceptance. The change in fortunes was little short of phenomenal. Quite possibly no group in contemporary music had been around so long as a durable second-line attraction and then made an almost quantum jump to become one of the hottest acts in America.

The transformation began early last year when the British nucleus of the band—Mick Fleetwood (drums) and John and Christine McVie (bass and keyboards, respectively)—asked Americans Lindsay Buckingham and Stevie Nicks to join the band, replacing guitarist Bob Welch. The singer-songwriter duo, who had recorded one much underrated album (*Buckingham-Nicks*) agreed, and within days the five of them went into the studio to record, having never performed together in public. They were pleased with the resulting album, *Fleetwood Mac* (titled to reemphasize the band's continuity despite line-up changes) but hardly suspected it would remain on the charts for more than a year.

For nearly six months following the lp's July '75 release, Fleetwood Mac worked the road relentlessly. Things had clicked onstage from the beginning. The infusion of fresh voices with new songs added depth and variety to the repertoire. Buckingham's inventive guitar phrasing—at first restrained, then growing bolder—merged easily with the band's unpretentious but now punchier sound. And Stevie's powerful, distinctly nasal vocals blended beautifully with Christine's darker voice, notably on "Over My Head," a melodic hit single that soared into the top ten.

Months later, Stevie's haunting, ethereal "Rhiannon" (about "a schizophrenic Welsh witch," she claims) was similarly successful as a single. In concert, the song became the focal point of the set as Stevie, dressed in diaphanous black chiffon and a silk hat, would swirl and writhe across the stage in a stunning dance that was at once mystical, seductive and totally feminine. By the end of the year she was on her way to being heralded as the most vivacious woman in rock. Not bad for less than a year into a new gig.

Last summer, Fleetwood Mac toured for six weeks, sharing the bill several times with the Eagles and the Jefferson Starship before as many as 62,000 people. The band sizzled, the reviews were superlative, and Stevie Nicks—seen now as the blonde pixie with the hypnotic voice—grew even more magnetic and glamorous.

Paralleling the stage success was the rinsing off of virtually all the Sausalito soap: these days Lindsay, Stevie, Christine and John all seem happily single. And Mick and Jenny, while legally divorced, are again living in the couple's Topanga Canyon home.

Add to that *Fleetwood Mac* finally reaching Number One a year after release and it's easy to see why Mick is looking so chipper these days. This afternoon he's sitting on a couch in the lounge of the group's Hollywood offices, sipping a Heineken and discussing the recent past. A clear-eyed, spindly Englishman, he's a striking contrast to his sidekick, John McVie, who's scrunched into a beanbag chair on the floor. John's wearing a wrinkled cap, a slept-in sweatshirt, Levis and the hangover of a man accustomed to one. He suggests it's still a bit early in the day for someone who hasn't been to bed the night before.

"It was such a good tour," Mick says. "And after all the things that had gone down, it was doubly important. When we got back here we were all thinking, 'Shit, man, we did it! That's bloody good!' All the weirdness is gone."

The discussion turns to the flurry of rumors around Hollywood that Fleetwood Mac, having finally hit, will no longer continue to manage itself and will soon sign with an industry heavy. Fleetwood and McVie, who have shared the management responsibilities for two years, become splendidly animated.

"That's the hardest thing for people in this business to accept," John insists. "They can't believe that this band has achieved all this without professional help. Some people still think that Mick's just a dumb drummer and I'm a dumb bass player."

Mick grins. "Before, people would come up to us and say, 'You won't make it without us.' Now they say 'You *really* need our help now, you can't possibly keep it up without us.' But take this band six months ago with all the heavy emotional stress that was occurring—I doubt seriously if we'd had a manager that we'd be here today. It would have been fatal, because the band was totally responsible to itself. No one could take sides. Besides, there was no way of anyone even beginning to understand how the people in this band work. With the band managing itself—the fact is it's working, it has worked, and we've got the results to show it."

The two are obviously proud of their independent business stance; however their vindication is not without humor. They recently took out a full page ad in the trades that featured a doctored photo of the group gathered happily around a desk where John and Mick were sitting disguised as sleazoid fly-by-night scammers in black hats, pinky rings and suits with large bills stuck in breast pockets. The ad announced that Fleetwood Mac was proud to be signing with "Seedy Management."

There was a time when the group did have a manager, whose departure led to a bizarre episode that seriously threatened the band's credibility. In early 1974 Clifford Davis, insisting he owned the rights to the name Fleetwood Mac, hired several unknown English musicians, booked a national tour, and sent "the New Fleetwood Mac" on the road for three months. The real Fleetwood Mac quickly got a court injunction to prevent the use of its name, but in the meantime a lot of astonished fans were angrily demanding ticket refunds. The legal battle is heading for resolution at a hearing in London, and Mick is optimistic: "There's a chance it'll be settled out of court, which is entirely at our discretion. Up to now the other side has been totally stubborn but there's been a change of heart. Maybe it's because we've now got the money to continue paying lawyers."

Exactly why Fleetwood Mac has survived for nine years is hard to explain. So many musicians have come and gone that its identity should have long since been diluted beyond recognition.

In 1967, John McVie, a four-year veteran of John Mayall's Bluesbreakers, teamed with Mick Fleetwood (hence the group's name) to form a rock-oriented blues band with guitarists Jeremy Spencer and Peter Green, the latter also a former Mayall sideman and one of Britain's premiere blues stylists.

A third guitarist, Danny Kirwan, was added several months later and for a brief time the aggregation was billed as Peter Green's Fleetwood Mac. Within a year the group had the first of several hit singles on the British charts.

One admirer in particular was Christine Perfect, pianist and singer with the blues band Chicken Shack. "Whenever I had a night off," she recalls, "I'd always go hear Fleetwood Mac 'cause I adored them." Christine's own musical career had been circuitous. The daughter of a Birmingham music teacher, she hated studying classical piano until one day when she found a book of Fats Domino tunes in the piano bench. Her blues interest continued through four years of art school (from which she received "a completely useless degree in sculpture"). There followed a stint in London as a window dresser before she joined Chicken Shack and married John McVie.

For a while life was hectic. "I was in Chicken Shack for another six months and it worked out that John and I were meeting each other on the doorstep with suitcases in hand. He'd be coming back from a tour just as I was leaving—or vice versa."

After a half year of this hello/good-bye lifestyle, Christine left Chicken Shack to be a full-time wife. A year later she would join Fleetwood Mac but not before an abortive solo career. "It was a disaster. I hadn't written any material and didn't have a band. But I got one together and recorded the lp in about a month. The two or three songs I wrote weren't very good. I was such a novice."

That album, originally titled *Christine Perfect*, has recently resurfaced, having been reissued last August as *Christine McVie* and subtitled "The Legendary Christine Perfect Album." Predictably, she is "sort of offended and embarrassed" by the fast-bucks attempt to capitalize on her Fleetwood Mac success. "Anyway," she adds, "I'm too young to be a legend."

In the summer of 1970, following a European tour, Peter Green announced his retirement from rock, claiming he wanted to live as a Christian laborer. Shortly thereafter he left to become a cemetery gardener and later a hospital orderly. Christine has a theory: "On the European tour Peter had met a group of decadent German jet-set types who were into black magic and weird occult stuff. They put a couple of tabs of acid in his drink and I think he took a couple of pretty heavy involuntary trips that way. I think that did contribute to his later state of mind."

The band was at loose ends until a decision was made to find another instrument to fill out the sound. Christine McVie was perfect. A week after joining, she found herself playing her first gig with Fleetwood Mac at the Warehouse in New Orleans.

In Los Angeles a year later (1971) yet another band member became a rock 'n roll casualty for Christ. Guitarist Jeremy Spencer walked out of his hotel room to go shopping and got cornered on the street by some Children of God, a heavy-duty religious sect. He never made it back to the hotel. "When we found him," Christine says, "he was surrounded by about 400 kids chanting prayers. Fortunately he came out of it more or less OK. He's now living in South America, has a band and five children, and seems very religious."

Guitarist Bob Welch, a native of San Francisco, was recruited to fill the void left by Green and Spencer. *Bare Trees* was released in 1972 and reflected the shift in emphasis from blues to a mellower rock.

Many changes followed: Danny Kirwan, who had become increasingly nervous on stage, was reluctantly ousted in '73 (the only member of the band ever to have been fired). Replacing him was former Long John Baldry guitarist Bob Weston, who remained in the fold for two albums, *Penguin* and *Mystery to Me,* both of which sold respectably but lacked the old fire.

After the situation was made even more perilous by Clifford Davis' bogus band fiasco, Fleetwood Mac made a permanent move to Los Angeles, recorded *Heroes Are Hard to Find,* and went on tour, anxious to reestablish its credibility. Bob Welch left amicably around Christmas '74 to form the power trio Paris, but this time Fleetwood and McVie had anticipated the departure. They had a hunch that Angelinos Lindsay Buckingham and Stevie Nicks might be the right combination to finally set Fleetwood Mac's career a-buzzing.

The arrival of a second female band member was a nice change for Christine McVie. Despite many years on the road, and a reputation as a Blues Mama, she appears warm and easygoing. Her manner is that of a seasoned rocker, a mature lady, a scarred survivor.

"I think I *have* seen it all," Christine states unabashedly. "It's really not an easy life. You have to take reasonable care of yourself—and be adaptable. Before Stevie I was the only girl, and I was also with John 24 hours a day—for years—and that's exactly why everything went wrong. So I had to decide; either I'll be lonely or I'll damn well adapt enough to be like big sister, to be with the guys and still retain that respect. I mean I love to be with men, generally more so than women, but since Stevie's been with us, it's great, especially on the road. If you got a gripe about an old man or whatever, you can just sit down and rap and drink coffee."

How does she feel about Stevie's high voltage visibility on stage? Isn't the pretty upstart stealing her thunder?

"It's great," Christine counters, "because Stevie's a show woman and she loves it. I'm the keyboard player, which keeps me out of the limelight. I enjoy it because I'm not an extrovert. Nobody contrived for Stevie to be a foxy chick. It just emerged. She moves and dances purely because she likes dancing. But she has a split personality. Onstage she's the goddess of whatever, but offstage she's very often like a little old lady with a cold or a sore throat. Yet she's amazing—she can feel like shit before she goes onstage but then she goes out there and pulls out the stops."

———————————

Stevie, in fact, does have a slight cold one afternoon when she discusses life and love at the top. Barefoot, and wearing a patchwork shirt and white stretch-weave tube top, she is relaxed and pleasantly disheveled, her shag hair still streaked here and there with green highlights from the last gig.

Her surroundings are comfortable, the patio next to a black rock swimming pool at the Benedict Canyon home of Irving Azoff, the 28-year-old wizard manager of the Eagles, Minnie Riperton, Dan Fogelberg and Boz Scaggs. Stevie is staying there for two weeks while she looks for her own place. Azoff's digs are appropriately posh: a ranch-style home hidden at the top of a winding driveway protected by a remote-controlled gate. The game room, with its bar and billiard table, appears to have been installed roughly two #1 albums ago—but not used extensively. And scattered casually about the living room—on the floor, on bookcases and along the mantlepiece—are an overflowing array of framed gold and platinum records.

Stevie sits in an outdoor lounge chair spooning her way through a cup of low-cal apricot-flavored yogurt as she talks. Her voice even at conversational level is throaty and resonant.

"It's not like I just go onstage and sing every night," she begins. "I *scream*. And crash tambourine on my leg and dance around a lot. It's almost an athletic trip for me 'cause I've never been very strong. In fact, I'm like a snake all day, just grooving along slowly. Then for two hours onstage I have all that energy. Afterwards I'm a basket case. I've got to be practically carried away immediately.

"As for the dancing, it's nothing I haven't done my whole life. It's not a ploy to be sexy. I decided from the beginning that if I didn't have something visually interesting to do I wouldn't stand out there. I leave the stage when Lindsay or Mick has a heavy solo. 'Rhiannon' is the heavy-duty song to sing every night. Onstage it's really a mind tripper. Everybody, including me, is just blitzed by the end of it. And I put out so much in that song that I'm nearly down. There's something to that song that touches people. I don't know what it is but I'm really glad it happened."

There is a guileless—even girlish—enthusiasm here, but Stevie regularly mixes in punchy bottom liners: "I feel a lot older than when I joined this band. I'm 28 now—no breaks."

Stevie comes from a fairly wealthy background. Born in Phoenix, she was raised (successively) in Los Angeles, New Mexico, Texas, Utah and San Francisco while her father moved up in business, eventually becoming vice-president of the Greyhound corporation and president of Armour and Company. In 1968, while living in the Atherton-Menlo Park area of the San Francisco peninsula, Stevie joined Fritz, "a riff-oriented" quasi-acid rock band which had a bass player named Lindsay Buckingham. The group worked the area steadily for 3½ years before breaking up. After that, Stevie and Lindsay teamed together offstage as well as on, and moved to Los Angeles in 1972 to pursue a record contract.

The album that resulted, *Buckingham-Nicks,* was released on Polydor in late '73 and promptly stiffed despite its striking bare-skinned cover photo. After a frustrating year of turning down offers to become a Top Forty lounge act on the steak and lobster circuit, Stevie went to work as a waitress at Clementine's, a fashionable Twenties-style singles rendezvous in Hollywood. Lindsay held a somewhat shady job soliciting ads by phone for a non-existent business products directory. In their spare time the couple worked on a demo tape for a second album. Finally, on New Year's Eve, Mick Fleetwood (who had met Lindsay briefly in the studio and had heard the Polydor album) called with an invitation to join Fleetwood Mac.

If the Buckingham-Nicks addition to Fleetwood Mac was a natural, so was Stevie Nicks' emergence as the new flash fox in rock. One senses she hasn't deliberately created that identity, at least as a primary concern.

"Seriously, I'm not terribly aware of that image," Stevie asserts. "And I rarely see the things written about me. When it comes down to it, I'm pretty naive really, and gullible. Plus, I've always had the fear of walking up to another band, even since I've been in Fleetwood Mac and saying,

'Hi, I'm Stevie, I really like your music.' I'm so afraid they'll think I'm a glorified groupie.

"I hate that trip that's put on women in rock 'n roll. But I'd love to meet more people, especially now, since for the first time I'm independent. I haven't been in that position for *six years.*"

Gullible Stevie got her chance a few months back when the Eagles' Don Henley called out of the blue, asking to meet her. Both were touring at the time, so the sweet-talking titillation continued by phone for some time before the two groups ended up on the same bill.

"It was weird—and fun. We arrive and the Eagles are in the next dressing room, right? Now I would never go in there and say 'Hi, I'm Stevie.' Never. I would *die* first. So I go into our dressing room and here's this huge bouquet of roses with a card in it. So I open up the card and it reads 'The best of my love, dot dot dot. Tonight, question mark, Don.' And I said 'That's about the uncoolest thing I've ever seen in my whole life! I mean how could he possibly preconceive something like that?' And I'm *dying* right? My face is red and I'm *fuming.* And then, finally, Christine grabs me and takes me aside and says 'Don didn't send that. Mick and John did.' They were in hysterics."

Introductions were eventually made and a fast friendship was born. Despite the inevitable gossip this star-crossing inspired, the relationship is pretty to look at but not, intimates advise, celestial.

Balancing any romantic attachments is Stevie's determination to firmly establish her autonomy, to which end she has acquired an apartment, a car and a roommate. A secure nest takes precedence over a rampantly exotic lifestyle. Moreover, she seems little disposed to play the role of rock siren and in fact, up close, does not exude a savvy sexual aura.

"The last thing I need is to hear one more person saying, 'Isn't Stevie Nicks cute.' I'm not responsible for the way I look, but I *am* responsible for what I do creatively. Nothing would make me happier than recognition as a songwriter."

There's an openness to Stevie, a disarming willingness to trust, that suggests: Here is a girl-woman to whom life has been kind. She seems vulnerable and yet her lack of conceit, coupled with an intuitive knowledge of who *can* be trusted, belies a deeper strength. She's been in rock nearly as long as Fleetwood Mac has existed as a group. That experience has enabled her to survive the uncoupling with Lindsay without damaging either the group or their close relationship.

"Splitting up has not been an easy thing for either Lindsay or me," Stevie confides. "I think we both knew deep down that it was the only thing we could do. We weren't creating, either of us. . . . It's much better now."

It was probably the last time it would ever happen to Lindsay Buckingham in his hometown. On one side of Sunset Boulevard was this giant billboard in lights, advertising Fleetwood Mac's four-day sold-out appearance at the Universal Amphitheatre in Los Angeles. And on the other side is the Rainbow Bar & Grill, Tinsel Town's rock 'n roll watering hole and disco body exchange.

Lindsay had decided he would drop into the Rainbow and make the scene and maybe meet some ladies—and *not* get recognized. But he didn't really try. As a bona fide star who'd recently played to more than a million people across the country, Buckingham instead was reminded of the grim years he spent romancing LA's bitch goddess success.

"I guess we've gotten there now, realized the dream, whatever the dream was," he admits afterward, driving his BMW back to his home in West Los Angeles. "I've thought about it, that this is everything I've ever wanted to do, to be, for the last ten years as a musician. But it's not as weird as I thought it'd be. I feel pretty normal. In a lot of ways I'm still working out a lot of insecurities. Being in this position hasn't automatically given me new confidence, nor am I necessarily getting a lot of validation. In fact I probably had more confidence five years ago than I do now. It's odd, but having been in LA for a while and having a lot of people tell you that you're shitty doesn't help.

"Stevie and I weren't ecstatic about Mick's offer to join Fleetwood Mac because we really believed in what we were doing with our second record. But when we went up to their house to meet them, that clinched it right there. You could just tell the five of us in that room that there was something happening."

At the time was he familiar with Fleetwood Mac's music?

"No, except for the *Then Play On* album. But they've always had good guitar players. So we just did it. Nobody knew what was gonna happen but that's the way Fleetwood Mac has always been—played everything by instinct; by feel rather than calculation. I've got to hand it to them—that's probably why they've been around so long."

Back at a spacious white stucco house (which he shares with sound man "Disco Dickie" Dashut and Curtis Brothers drummer Bob Agurra) Lindsay puts on a vintage Beatles record and pops a beer. He recalls one off-the-wall episode just after joining the band:

"Someone in Birmingham, Alabama called out of the blue and asked us to headline a show there. Stevie and I had gone there twice in the previous year to open shows, and apparently our album had sold very well there. So we went to Birmingham and discovered we'd sold out an auditorium. Just blew our minds because we were totally unknown in LA, couldn't get a gig at a club or anywhere. And here were 6,000 people out there going *nuts!* We played three dates around there, the great 'Buckingham-Nicks inaugural/ farewell tour.' We announced we were joining Fleetwood Mac and everybody went 'Whaa?' I dunno, we had no idea what we were getting into."

As the conversation turns to the recent past, Buckingham warms to the subject of how, with Fleetwood Mac, music and love didn't mix. Lounging on the couch, wearing faded denims and an Hawaiian shirt, he speaks openly, now and then nipping nervously at a cuticle.

"I came back from this tour feeling really cleansed," he offers. "All the things that had been happening between me and Stevie and between John and Chris mellowed into the situations they are now. And it was important that I met a lot of beautiful women who I like a lot because, y'know, with the exception of one intervening summer, for the past ten years I've been tied up with just two ladies. Now here I am at 26, re-realizing capabilities about myself and being a little more aggressive socially and having a good time.

"And for Stevie, someone like Don Henley is good for her. It's strange; it's one thing to accept not being with someone and it's another to see them with someone else, especially someone like Don, right? A big star in another group. I could see it coming and I really thought it was gonna bum me out, but it was really a good thing just to see her sitting with him. It actually made me happy. I thought there was something to fear but there wasn't. So the whole break-up has forced me to redefine my whole individuality—musically as well. I'm no longer thinking of Stevie and me as a duo. That thought used to freak me out but now it's made me come back stronger, to be Lindsay Buckingham."

———————

And what of the album? That soul-wrenching masterwork born in the heat of serious road fever and nurtured with giddy dope-laced cookies? That 24-track jewel which had survived knife-twisting jealousy and studio vamps bearing silver straws and Pouilly Fouisse?

"Well, it's changed from what it was originally," John McVie quips dryly, just before putting the finishing touches on it.

"It's *warmer,*" Mick adds. "I don't mean in a soft way. It means more personally to everyone in the band than the last album, which was executed, as it were, rather than felt out. There's been a lot more suffering with this one."

"The song lyrics are about things that went on in and around the band," Lindsay says. "They were all written since Stevie and I joined, so they hang together as more of a statement."

The new album offers as much variety as the previous release, and musically should be more consistent. Stevie's contributions include "Dreams" (an R&B cut with a strongly melodic bass line); a sad song about everyone's break-ups called "Silver Springs," and the powerful "Gold Dust Woman."

"It's about groupie-type ladies," Nicks explains. "About women who stand around and give me and Christine dirty looks but as soon as a guy comes in the room are overcome with smiles."

Rock on, ancient queen
Follow those who pale in our shadow
Rulers made bad lovers
You better put your kingdom
Up for sale

Lindsay's "Go Your Own Way" is punchy, acoustically-based rock 'n roll, currently being performed on tour as a first encore. The remaining two Buckingham numbers consist of a scintillating instrumental track with sharp guitar work and a real scorcher with vaguely pornographic lyrics.

Christine's four cuts include "Oh Daddy," a slow, sensual track with strong lyrics; an uptempo piano boogie number titled "Think About Tomorrow"; a blues/rock combo called "You Make Lovin' Fun," which features a stomping major chorus; and a reflective ballad tentatively titled "Songbird," which was played on a concert grand piano recorded in Berkeley's acoustically near-perfect Zellerback Auditorium.

"It's a personal song," Christine claims. "I don't like to hear it too much." In general she feels the new album is a natural follow-up to *Fleetwood Mac*. "It shows we know each other a lot better and I think we're playing better and singing better," she confides. "Everything is more cohesive."

San Diego gave Fleetwood Mac a tumultuous hero's welcome as the group walked to its stage positions in darkness, opening in a shower of lights with Christine's "Over My Head." "Station Man" followed immediately with John stepping forward to churn out the song's classic bass line as Mick grinned at him behind a formidable drum kit. Lindsay, looking very relaxed in jeans and white kimono jacket, grabbed the lead, layering in sparkling riffs and fills that drew applause. Halfway through, Stevie—a sultry witch in black suede boots and midnight chiffon—took center stage with "Rhiannon" and brought the arena to its feet in a screaming peak of excitement. Christine followed with excellent vocals on "Why" and "You Make Lovin' Fun." Then Stevie moved behind Mick's drum kit to play congas during a vintage favorite "Green Manalishi," as John and Lindsay worked out on a ballsy bass-guitar exchange.

On "World Turning," a sizzling highlight of the set, Christine moved out from the keyboards to play mariachis and power a three-voice chorus as Mick's drumming gradually gained solo domination with a crackling tempo shift. He polished off a beer with one hand, then leaned out from behind his kit holding an African talking drum beneath one arm. For the next minute this goateed beanpole in black vest and skinny plus-fours bounced amazing sounds around the arena, then rushed back to pump to a high-kicking finale. The 90-minute set closed to a roaring ovation after "Don't Let Me Down" and "Hypnotized," the two encores.

The backstage area after the set was crowded but orderly as roadies gently kept a lot of equally polite California girls away from the dressing room. Moments later, Stevie Nicks emerged and made her way to a waiting limousine, stopping several times to talk with admirers. One young woman pressed five turquoise stones into her hand ("For everyone in the band"); another slipped an over-sized bracelet on her wrist. Moments later, she was settled in the car's interior, and the crowd sounds were immediately replaced by the low *woosh* of conditioned air. The limousine, with only two passengers, sleeked up the ramp out of the arena, passed a clutch of waving fans and headed for a hotel on Harbor Island.

During the 20-minute ride, Stevie talked excitedly. "We've really got that set down, don't you think? And Mick's such a dynamic drummer, such a showman. I wish there was more room for Lindsay to open up more on his guitar solos; he's hot and getting so confident."

She settled back in the cushy seats, staring out the window for a moment. The glow of passing street lights bathed her face in a soft blue/white glow. "You know the part that always gets me? It's when you're standing there just as you're about to go onstage and the audience is cheering. There's this incredible excitement that just grabs you in the pit of your stomach. I know it's all very Hollywood and everything, but it's a fantastic high."

She shifted to the upcoming home stand in Los Angeles and the lavish party Warner Bros. was planning. "It's ironic. It's getting harder to meet people now because the people I'd probably really like are too cool to come up to me to introduce themselves. I sometimes feel people are afraid. . . ."

Stevie stared ahead for a few seconds, poised in profile. Tiny flecks of glitter on her left cheekbone sparkled in the half-light. Her green-streaked stage-tousled hair fell perfectly around her face. Her lips were slightly parted. Here was the visual apotheosis of a stone fox, a vixen in black gossamer. She turned now with a slight smile, her tone of voice wonderfully ambiguous. "The whole presentation has got to be dramatic," she confided. "I mean, we're talking about a little glamor here!"

RICH MAC, POOR MAC

Roy Carr | April 2, 1977 | *New Musical Express* (UK)

Despite securing the coup of an interview with Mick Fleetwood and Lindsey Buckingham, the *NME* opted not to feature Fleetwood Mac on its cover; that position was taken by a British band releasing its eponymous debut album that month by the name of the Clash. However, although musicologists' histories record 1977 as the Year of Punk, chart statisticians denote it the Year of *Rumours*, the LP that was about to become a sales phenomenon. As touched on in this feature, its songs were underpinned by emotional trauma that could hold its own with even the Sturm und Drang of the Clash's urban-wasteland tableaux.

Note: For "Danny Kirwin" read "Danny Kirwan."

SOME NEWSPAPERS employ scribes whose sole function is to regularly update the unpublished obituaries of prominent personalities—so as to be in-at-the-kill on their demise. Something of a dead-end job, as it were. However, it would take scores of full-time researchers to keep abreast of the fluctuating fortunes of Fleetwood Mac—the band that continues to exist despite itself.

In the 10 years since they debuted at the National Blues & Jazz Festival at Windsor, Fleetwood Mac have transmogrified from a star-crossed guitar hero-dominated cult blues band into Warner Brothers Records' biggest-ever album selling attraction.

But it has been a career continually fraught with impending disaster. Guitarists have quit under harrowing banner headlines, bogus line-ups have laid claim to the name, and those original members who've stuck it out have enacted more melodramas than a whole slew of soap-opera scriptwriters could have concocted in a lifetime. In truth, all aspects of human emotion are to be found in Fleetwood Mac.

Bands have broken up for much less, but Mac stubbornly refuses to roll over and expire. Call it masochistic, but the band appears to thrive on one Big Hurt after another.

Until the middle of last year, F. Mac had resigned themselves to the fact that they worked to live, lived to work, and weren't in a position to rest-up for a year or more to re-think or record. Their albums always got reviewed, made a brief, if not auspicious appearance in the best-sellers and received more air-time than that usually afforded albums enjoying much more commercial success on the charts. It may not have been La Dolce Vita but it was a fairly comfortable existence.

LET'S START in 1975: After a four year residency, American guitarist Bob Welch became yet another Mac statistic, being unceremoniously replaced by the highly attractive boy/girl team of Lindsey Buckingham and Stevie Nicks.

After just 10 days of routining new material, the refurbished line-up of Mick Fleetwood, Christine and John McVie and Buckingham and Nicks were in the studio recording a bunch of originals subsequently released under the unadventurous title, "Fleetwood Mac".

At first, nothing much happened and a six-months road tour ensued before (professionally) their fortunes were to take a turn for the better.

It was during this period that deep cracks began to appear in their personal stability, and almost on cue Fleetwood Mac went into yet an all-too-familiar emotional nosedive.

Christine and John McVie separated mid-tour, adding the cost of an extra hotel room to the band's travel budget; and after six years of being inseparable Buckingham and Nicks ceased cohabitating—and Mick Fleetwood, desperately trying to play piggy-in-the-emotion middle, realised that his own marriage had hit the skids.

Bands have broken up for much less. But not Fleetwood Mac.

Contrary to belief, pressure of success wasn't the cause. "Fleetwood Mac" had yet take off like an epidemic, sell in excess of four million albums Stateside and hatch three hit singles, "Rhiannon", "Over My

Head" and "Say You Love Me". Everyone just fell out of love with one another at precisely the same moment.

So . . . three broken homes for sale. John and his collection of penguin statuettes moved out of the McVies' Malibu apartment on to a 41-foot schooner, while Christine set up home overlooking the hustle and bustle of Sunset Strip.

Lindsey and Stevie established singles lifestyles, and Mick and Jenny Fleetwood divorced, though they were later to re-marry.

To add to their immediate problems, Mac were attempting to record tracks for what would eventually evolve into "Rumours".

"Being in Fleetwood Mac, is more like being in group therapy!" Who said that?

It was drummer and Mac manager elect Mick Fleet- [*Text was missing in feature when originally published—Ed.*] manager elect. He is trying to fight off a head cold as we sit jawing in the pleasant rustic atmosphere of Seedy Management, situated by the gates of the Columbia movie lot in the very heart of Hollywood Babylon.

It's a typical Californian spring morning. Warm, sunny, light to variable. Definitely not the kind of day to be feeling one degree under.

However, with typical British reserve, Mick Fleetwood has mastered the art of coping with any and every situation. And his resilience must be contagious because Lindsey Buckingham—en route to having his wisdom teeth yanked—shows no apparent signs of fear.

Over the last year Fleetwood Mac have supplied America's dirt-diggin' gossip columnists with more copy than the Burton's divorce-reconciliation-divorce marriage-go-round, to the extent that Mac's marital shenanigans have been likened to everything from *Peyton Place* to *Bob, Ted, Carol and Alice*.

AS IT transpires, it took a whole year to record "Rumours", the project being near completed long before "Fleetwood Mac" began to be pressed-up in platinum—the latter album having pursued an eccentric pathway towards success. According to Mr. Fleetwood it originally reached as high as No. 9 and dropped to 40 before it regained its upward curve.

"Fleetwood Mac"—the Californian Soundtrack of '76. Even Mick Fleetwood has long since given up trying to evaluate its phenomenal success in the Americas and its apathetic reception in the Old Country.

It's happened and he's thankful, but he's not about to go into deep analysis on the subject. Obviously, the introduction of two singer-songwriters had a great deal to do with it, but, as Mick points out, Fleetwood Mac has never conformed to one specific recognisable style.

"Nobody", he suggests in between sniffles, "who has ever joined this band has been forced to structure their music to conform. You've only got to flick through our mess of albums to see that." He emphasises the word mess.

"I can remember when Danny Kerwin joined. Peter (Green) turned round to him and casually said, 'Right lad, you've got half the album' and 'Then Play On' contains a lot of new things that nobody had ever heard on a Fleetwood Mac album before".

"Lots of bands," argues Fleetwood, "wouldn't take that kind of risk. We do. And, I think it's healthy."

As to the band's resurgence of popularity, both Fleetwood and Buckingham agree with my theory that primarily the present line-up is a singles band utilising an album formula.

"There's a lot of flexibility and versatility within the current set-up," Buckingham interjects before leaving for his dental appointment. "Even with three separate lead vocalists there's still this cohesive continuity, so it doesn't really matter if either Christine, Stevie or myself are taking the lead.

"As a contributor", he concludes, "I feel that much of Fleetwood Mac's strength is in the fact that only the very best material makes it on to an album. And, as there are three main writers, it makes competition that much keener".

Mick Fleetwood agrees "This way there's no strain on any particular writer. Nobody is constantly under extreme pressure to write *all* the material for the next album. So that's no problem."

Yet problems—the kind that floor you—have become an integral part of Mac's very existence.

Why have they always refused to throw in the towel?

"Over the years", says Fleetwood, "we've been so wrapped up in our destiny, that, though offers have been forthcoming, the idea of being somewhere else, playing in another band, has never really appealed to either, John, Christine or myself. It's as simple as that."

According to the drummer, nobody—with the exception of Danny Kerwin—has ever quit Fleetwood Mac due to the overall encompassing excuse of "difference of musical policy".

From his lofty vantage point as manager-performer and pillar-of-strength, he opines that being in the band may well bring out the weak points in a person's character, but by the very same token it strengthens others. He cites the recording of "Rumours" as testament.

"When the shit hit the fan everybody probably thought that this *really was* the end of Fleetwood Mac, and that it would be impossible to work under such intense conditions.

"Theoretically, it was a helluva bad time to try and record a new album, but in retrospect it proved to be the reverse. Because it all came out in the music."

As a result "Rumours" is an album of strong personal emotions, persistent soul-searching—and currently America's best-seller.

Still, it can't have been easy spending nine weeks incarcerated in the Record Plant's Sausalito studio with everyone falling apart at the seams and a recording desk that all but destroyed the original backing tracks?

"Things never got bitchy," says Fleetwood. Sure, the atmosphere was confused—to say the least—but it wasn't destructive.

"It may be difficult for someone outside of the group to understand what I'm saying, but we're a bunch of people before we're a bunch of musicians. What happened was that all five of us were going through exactly the same problem at the very same time. Only in Fleetwood Mac could that ever happen.

"So there we all were, trying to put down the basic backing tracks and all feeling so desperately unhappy with life. But somehow we created a mutual bond. We could all relate to each other's desperation. Despite ourselves, we didn't lose contact. It wasn't as though there wasn't anyone else we could turn to. Strange as it might sound, we had one another—so we went through shit to get to the point where we could still live and communicate as friends.

"I don't think anyone ever turn round and said, 'I don't need this, I'm splitting.' We all understood how we felt because we were all involved in each others lives.

"Sure, we laugh at it now . . . we even makes jokes."—a recent cover of *Rolling Stone* sports an Annie Leibovitz shot of all five in one bed: Christine cuddling Lindsey, Mick with his arm around Stevie and John off in a corner reading. "But believe me, it wasn't funny at the time."

"The thing that happened between Lindsey and Stevie and Christine and John wasn't that they suddenly took a dislike to one another, it was just that they realised they could no longer live together, and so there was no malice when they separated.

"For instance, the other evening John and I went round to Christine's place to have a drink with her and her boyfriend. So, if anything, the weird circumstances in which we decided to record 'Rumours' helped to make that much stronger than before.

"From the start to finish it took one year to complete 'Rumours'. We'd recorded the backing tracks in nine anxious weeks, but the emotions that we'd originally put down on the tape in Sausalito were so strong that we didn't want to be immature and insensitive towards those feelings. That's why we took such care in the dubbing and the mixing.

"We just went through our collective traumas head-on and it was then that we all revealed our true colours. In the past, both John and I have had to handle some really weird situations . . . Peter Green . . . Jeremy Spencer, but as far as Lindsey and Stevie were concerned, they didn't go like lambs to the slaughter, they just underwent a crash-course in maturity."

I wonder what these guys do for an encore?

THE TRUTH WILL TELL

Salley Rayl | March 31, 1977 | *Circus* (US)

Salley Rayl's 1977 *Rumours*-oriented feature was shrewdly spread across two issues by a *Circus* magazine cognizant of what a marquee name the group now constituted.

From this end of history, it's almost amusing to note that neither the band members nor Rayl have any inkling that they are discussing what will transpire to be a phenomenon. *Rumours'* self-absorption, mellow ambience, and alternative attitude made it the perfect soundtrack for the people who had come of age in the Me Decade, as would soon become clear from the sort of sales figures that made it an album seemingly owned by every household.

Rarely did a week go by last year when you could pick up a rock magazine or newspaper and *not* read something about Fleetwood Mac—a good percentage of which was all rumors. Now, Fleetwood Mac's got its own set of *Rumours* (WB).

"The outcome of the various separations and emotional upheavals in the band that caused so many rumors are in the songs," says Christine McVie, relaxing in front of a fire on this misty Los Angeles afternoon. "We weren't aware of it at the time, but when we listened to the songs together we realized they were telling little stories. We were looking for a good name for the album that would encompass all that *and* the feeling the band had 'given up' (the most active rumor flying about). And, I believe it was John, one day, who just said we should call it *Rumours*. He didn't *state* that, but rumors kept cropping up."

When Fleetwood Mac at long last finished *Rumours*, their ninth album, eager anticipation since its first scheduled release date last July had not begun to wane. "Go Your Own Way," the single released in December from the new album, was a partially-confirming testimonial that the last album, *Fleetwood Mac* (WB), was not just a fluke. After nine years of personnel changes (this LP is the second with Buckingham and Nicks) and a moderate, cultish degree of success, *Rumours* proves Fleetwood Mac could meet the expectations and is still, now more than ever, a rock and roll band.

After a two-week skiing jaunt in Aspen, Lindsey Buckingham came home to listen to the test pressing, get back to the business of the band and rest up for Mac's next six-month tour that began in January with a benefit concert for the Jacques Cousteau organization. "The last album had a very soft quality to it—somebody called it progressive M.O.R.—but this one," says Lindsey, sipping a cup of coffee, "is definitely more rock and roll. The last 11 months or so, we've gone through a lot of changes, a lot of head trips and made a lot of mistakes. Well, I don't know if they were mistakes or not, just things that we tried that didn't work so we tried something else. Nothing was safe on this album. We didn't go the safe route on any of the tunes." *Rumours'* 11 songs were written during those 11 months Fleetwood Mac was on the road and in the studio. "They're all about things that were going on in the band. The whole thing comes across more as a statement of who Fleetwood Mac is. The album has," says Lindsey, "a lot more *vibe* to it."

"*Rumours* is more cohesive in that it shows we've worked together," asserts Christine. "There's so much more warmth and it's showing a little bit more of our inside personalities—a little bit of unzipping, as it were. And I think it's a little bit more representative of Fleetwood Mac live. Fleetwood Mac's pretty rock and roll on stage."

After the July release date fell through, *Rumours* was officially rescheduled for January release, a deadline that was passed by in lieu of reshaping a couple of the tunes. But, the final February 4 date was good and 800,000 *Rumours* found their way into local record stores across the country.

"There was never a conscious delay," insists Lindsey, "in the releasing. We just assumed it was going to be easy like the last one. The *Rumours* album." Lindsey sighs: his face is transparent of the past-historyness of it all. "It was funny, the way we started the whole thing. We went into the studio after seven months of touring. We were tired. John and Chris had just broken up on the road; Stevie and I were on the verge of breaking up. We started cutting tracks, but everyone was going through so many weird personal trips on the side. For those two months in Sausalito (last July-August), the communication was very bad. It's not that anyone was fighting," Lindsey clenches his fists, "it's just that no one was quite together enough to get a really healthy start." After the Sausalito sessions, Fleetwood Mac packed up and went back on the road to return later to studio sessions in Los Angeles, North Hollywood and Miami.

If there was any danger of Fleetwood Mac losing its spontaneity, one of the group's more exceptional attributes, or its objectivity, that danger was, somehow, avoided. *"That's* the thing about this album," Lindsey says, "it's a lot more spontaneous. There was nothing specifically worked out when we went into the studio. We didn't have demo tapes like the last time. The whole thing—just happened."

"When we went into the studio to record," reminisces Christine, "I thought I was drying up. I was practically panicking, because every time I sat down at a piano, nothing came out. One day, in Sausalito, I just sat down and wrote in the studio, and the four or four and a half songs of mine on the album are a result of that." Christine's contributions on *Rumours* tend to be more optimistic than Lindsey's or Stevie's. "Partly because I was so thrilled I was able to write some songs and I wasn't necessarily talking through my own viewpoint. Rarely do I stand in my own shoes and write a song that is *that* personal. "Oh Daddy," for example, is not a song about me. It's a song about Mick and Jenny. And, "Don't Stop" was just a feeling. It just seemed to be a pleasant revelation to have that "yesterday's gone" and it might have, I guess been directed more toward John, but I'm just definitely not a pessimist."

"You Make Loving Fun" is probably one of the more upbeat tunes she's ever written, "because of the funky-funkiness I felt when I wrote it." But her most powerfully emotive tune, "Songbird," was recorded at seven in the morning in Zellerback Auditorium in Berkeley; to set the mood of really being alone she was secluded in the auditorium. "The vibe was so good on the original that we left it really raw and basic."

Probably never before in the history of rock and roll has there been a group so intertwined on a personal as well as business level that has not only overcome so many emotional heartaches and kept the desire to stay together, but, ironically, seem to actually been heightened by it all. "Everyone in the group feels that we have accomplished—aside from growing closer musically—something that's better for the hassles that we went through. It was a necessary thing," Lindsey explains, "when we were all bummed out and spaced out—in order to have a strong foundation. It's like something else, other forces I guess, that just keep taking you along. There's a lotta love in this band."

Though Lindsey describes the first side as "just a selection of songs," the lyrical interplay between Stevie Nicks and Lindsey is obviously revealing:

I know I got nothin' on you
I know there's nothing to do
When times go bad
And you can't get enough
Won't you lay me down in the tall grass
And let me do my stuff
     "Second Hand News" (Buckingham)
     Gentoo Music Inc./Now Sounds Music

Now here you go again
You say you want your freedom
Well who am I to keep you down
It's only right that you should
Play the way you feel it
     "Dreams" (Nicks)
     Gentoo Music Inc./Welsh Witch Music

If I could
Maybe I'd give you my world
How can I
When you won't take it from me
     "Go Your Own Way" (Buckingham)
     Gentoo Music Inc./Now Sounds Music

"That wasn't conscious either," says Lindsey. "I mean you just write about what's happening. All the songs, really, seem to relate to each other—they're all about each other."

"It *is* sort of strange," Christine says, "but the compulsion to succeed after 10 years of struggling exceeded the traumas we were going through. It would have been silly to throw it all away. We proved to each other that we had a pretty strong character, that we'd cope with the problems and surmount them, which we did. Now, John and me are friendly which, at a point we weren't, and Stevie and Lindsey are friendly, which at a point, they weren't. The bonds were just too great to sever just because there was an emotional ruckus going on."

"The Chain," a dynamic, relentless pulsating hard rocker, incorporates the moods and feelings of the Fleetwood Mac unit during those tumultuous times. The song was originally one of Chris' songs, "but it was just a melody and I couldn't find any words to it," she says. So they edited in Lindsey's bridge parts for use as the chorus and made up new verse parts. "The whole thing," Lindsey says, "is like a Brian Wilson, Good Vibrations and they just worked." Says Christine: "There's definitely a heavy connection with the "chain." In the end, the chain would keep us together.

"*Rumours* was 11 months of hard work and traumatic moments and we really feel we put everything we could into it. It represents a lot of blood, sweat and tears to all of us."

Unquestionably, the reason *Rumours* is more rock and roll oriented than *Fleetwood Mac* is Lindsey's bolder guitar playing. "Lindsey's guitar playing *has* changed on this album," says Christine. "On *Fleetwood Mac,* he was more laid back, not so sure of himself, still very good. But, on this album, his playing has come up much more forcefully. There's more power and dominance in the guitar and the aggressiveness of the guitar changes the characteristics of the songs." Says Lindsey, "We just wanted to get a ballsier thing on this album. We wanted to do something different and the next album we may do something mellower again. I don't really know, but I don't think we'll progress into Grand Funk." He laughs.

But, Fleetwood Mac doesn't intend to head right back into the studio. "Hopefully," Lindsey says, "we can take a month or two off after the next tour and just do nothing before going back to the studio." Lindsey then falls into a mocking fit of rage, clenching his fists in a Kong-like manner, almost cringing at the thought of going back into the studio so soon. "Again?" he snorts with a guttural, deep-toned voice, "please, not yet." He becomes serious again. *Rumours* is finally over. "I'll be glad," he says with a sigh of relief, "to hear something else on the radio."

OUIJA STILL LOVE ME TOMORROW?

Salley Rayl | April 14, 1977 | *Circus* (US)

Part 2 of Salley Rayl's *Circus* feature moves from discussion of the awkward genesis of *Rumours* to the band's future. Considering what we know now of the turbulence that lay ahead, the group members' optimism is simultaneously touching and poignant.

"It is what it is at the time. Whatever comes out is what Fleetwood Mac is," says John McVie, "and that's always been the way."

And, probably, it always *will* be the way. Fleetwood Mac has traveled the roads of rock and roll for almost a decade—spanning a musical range from electric blues to soft rock, surviving various personnel changes and a management burn that booked a bogus Fleetwood Mac on tour, and, finally, rising to "successdom" in the midst of some very heavy emotional difficulties last year. Lindsey Buckingham and Stevie Nicks joined Fleetwood Mac in 1975 after Bob Welch left the band to form his own group. The Buckingham/Nicks combination seemingly provided a refreshing impetus to Fleetwood Mac's ongoing longevity. A few short weeks later, Mick Fleetwood, John McVie, Christine McVie, Lindsey Buckingham and Stevie Nicks went into the studio to record.

The result was *Fleetwood* Mac (WB), the album that took the temperately successful Mac and catapulted them to the top of the charts, an album that was still on Billboard's charts after 90 weeks. But, there's a paradox in being successful in rock and roll. Once a rock band does meet with success, everytime they pass "GO" on rock's Monopoly board, they're attacked by critics for being commercial. "No one ever sits down and says 'This seems to be popular, so let's do this.' It's just whatever it is, which is really healthy and which, I think, has a lot to do with the longevity."

"I think we just had a product," says Christine, Mac's keyboardist, of the last album, "that everybody wanted at the time. It was a very versatile album and on stage the band projected a kind of exciting image—a new sort of image that's never really happened before. I think it was unique to have two women in a band who are not just back-up singers or just singers period. Stevie sings, sure, but she also does other musical-movement type things that are aesthetic. The five characters on stage definitely became five characters as opposed to just a band." *Rumours*, their ninth album, proves Fleetwood Mac could meet expectations.

The lawsuit over the Clifford Davis creation of a "new" Fleetwood Mac in 1973 without the consent or even the knowledge of the *real* Fleetwood Mac is still pending with a trial date set sometime this spring. Now, Seedy Management—Mick Fleetwood and John McVie—has taken over and hassles no longer exist. "We thought we knew ourselves better than the rest of them. We understand the vibe and the feeling of the music and the way it should be presented. When you get burned once, you don't do it again. It's a very human trip now," says John, noting that Mick is the more active half. "It may take longer to get things done, but they're done in a much nicer way."

For being a part of rock's multi-billion dollar conglomerate world, it's almost ironic that there's a very uncorporate feel to Fleetwood Mac and their Penguin organization. The end result of their approach stems from an attitude. "It all kind of fits into a pattern," says Lindsey. "There's no calculation happening. There's a lot of love involved with this band and there's a lot of energy, talent and creativity. It's all a family. We're just doing it and going along as we go and that's the way the music is and the way the business is run."

Last year's tumultuous triumph for Fleetwood Mac opened up their lives on a personal as well as business level; for more than a year the group was, and probably will continue to be, at the mercy of rock's gossip mongers. The break-ups of couples within the band developed into rumours of the band breaking up; a rumor that had Fleetwood Mac vying in some circles for 1976's top rumour with the Beatles are-they-going-to-get-back-together-again speculations. But, Lindsey analyses the emotional traumas last year as a sort of cleansing. "If Stevie and I, and John and Chris had remained as couples, the stability of the band would not have been very good. It was like that was a necessary thing to go through to eliminate all those weird vibes. And, we respect each other a lot more now."

Says Stevie, "That two hours on stage is beautiful and *always* was even in the midst of the worst times. And, really, each one of us was way too proud to and way too stubborn to just walk away from it. We like touring. We like making money. And we like being a band. But, it's like a marriage—you're married to five people—and sometimes you've just got to have some space."

Rumors seem to go hand-in-hand with the rise to the top and Stevie, usually singled out and labeled as the group's sex symbol, seemed to get the brunt end most of the time. For a while it was funny. "Then," Stevie says, "I really started to get angry. I mean I'm having all these relationships with all these guys that I don't know, that maybe I've met once, that I don't *want* to know and there's nothing I can do about it. All of a sudden I'm picking up these papers and I'm the Siren of the North." In reality, Stevie lives, as do Mick, John, Chris and Lindsey, on the other end of the spectrum. "In the last year," says Stevie, "I've begun to realize what a tremendous power trip rock and roll people are on. I don't *like* rock and roll stars. I especially don't like *men* rock and roll stars, mainly because they're just too egoed-out. And, I don't *need* it. I've gone through it and I didn't like it and I won't do it again. I'm really a very quiet lady and I love being at home and so does Chris."

Christine is spending most of her spare time these days remodeling her Hollywood Hills home and specifically transforming an outside guest room into an art studio loft for her artistic endeavors. "I'm enjoying the success," she says, "and the freedom it gives me. It's enabled all of us to realize a few dreams that we just never thought would happen. But, I think I've kept it pretty much in perspective. I mean life does not begin and end with Fleetwood Mac. Lately, I've been mixing with some people that are not involved with rock and roll, that know nothing about rock and roll and don't give a shit about rock and roll. That's been very stimulating—to meet people from other walks of life. There's only so much you can talk about in rock and roll and, sure, I get bored with it. Maybe that isn't a really wonderful thing to say, but at least it's realistic."

John says he enjoys being a musician. But he doesn't enjoy the name game. "People will ask 'What's it feel like to be a rock and roll star?' There's no rock and roll *stars*. They're all dead. Who makes people who play in rock bands non-human? It's the p.r. people, it's the managers, and that's the set goal. But, rock and roll is not the beginning and end of all life. It's 95 per cent bullshit. I mean rock and roll in the 70s is boring. It's not happening. In the 60s rock and roll was a change of attitude—a drastic change which I think the Beatles were hugely responsible for, praise the lord. Their influence was just phenomenal. In the history of going out and doing a gig, making money was the furthest thing from most minds. That's sort of true now with Fleetwood Mac. Of course we get paid and we play the game. I'm making more money, but then I'm spending more money too."

Money, as the saying goes, isn't everything. Stevie reflects on Mac's fan mail—baby announcements from people who've named their daughters Rhiannon (after Stevie's Welsh witch song) and letters of gratitude for their songs. "*That*," says Stevie, "is the sum total of why I write. It's so wonderful to know that something you wrote made a difference. These things that I say that meant so much to me seem really to mean a lot to other people. And it's just because it's *real*."

Stevie remembers seeing Janis Joplin (when a band she and Lindsey were a part of in San Francisco several years ago opened Joplin's show). "I walked away from that show saying, 'Okay, Stevie, there's your competition. If you ever, *ever* do anything good, then you're going to have to try and at least capture the feeling that she gave out.' I could never be *like* Janis and I wouldn't want to be like her. She was her own, unique self, but I do want to capture the charisma she had. And I think maybe I've touched the surface of it and I will continue—that *is* the goal. I want to make films on record. If I say 'I wish you were mine/I'll give you up even though I'll never hold you again' I want people to go 'Oh yeah, I *know* how that feels.' That's really all I want to leave behind. A little bit of a good memory in people's heads so they don't just write it off as something that went by."

The potential of Fleetwood Mac, says Christine, doesn't ever stop. "There's endless things we can do. Lindsey, Stevie and I all write individually, very different styles. Lindsey and I are just learning to write with each other—an exciting possibility that would be more of a rock and roll thing. Lindsey and I work very much alike. We'll fool around with chords first and work out the words later. Stevie's more of a poet. She'll write the words first—and it is poetry—and then struggle with the melody later. Fleetwood Mac's a very organic band and very songy. That's the way we write. This band will never digress from playing songs."

And, for some reason, Fleetwood Mac is one of the few bands that can get away with technical breakdowns and mistakes on stage. "I think a lot of people who go to see us," says Christine, "*hope* something goes wrong. It's a bit of a comedy show. There's no way you can look seriously at Mick grasshoppering around the stage with his African drum. That is not serious. You've gotta find that funny or you have no sense of humor at all."

"It's possible," says Lindsey, "we have just scratched the surface as far as potential goes for what these five people could do musically. The strength in this band is in the fact that there's a lot of talent and sometimes a lot of tension and it all works off of each other."

"It's amazing, 'cause sometimes when we're on stage," Stevie contends, "I feel like somebody's just moving the pieces. Lindsey'll move back I'll move forward, Christine will smile. Mick, then John, look over. I'm just going 'God, *we* don't have any control over this.' And that's magic. That is the appeal of this band and that is what will make this band never boring.

"If Mick and John can keep our work schedule to a point where Christine and I can live through it—that's where the crux of the matter lies—then we could tour for years. We'll never run out of songs. We've got libraries of songs. Musically as we do get to know each other, it can only get better. It's really a potential forever band."

Fleetwood Mac is successful. There's no question of that. "It'll probably be the most successful band in the world this year, I think," says John. "It's a good live band, it's a good recording band and it's got charisma. That's not ego. I hope it isn't."

It's only rock and roll. "And," says John, "in the scheme of things, rock and roll is so unimportant."

NATION GRIPPED IN MASSIVE FLEETWOOD MAC ATTACK!

Salley Rayl | July 1977 | *Creem* (US)

The feature goes intriguingly deeper into the way *Rumours* came together—and if any album is worth discussing at length, it's this one.

As the feature was published only a few months after Salley Rayl's similarly themed *Circus* pieces (with whose contents it has a little overlap), it's still a little too early for anyone to apprehend quite what an epoch-marking album they have on their hands. The only issue that had been resolved at this point was which of the new members was which: there had been some public confusion caused by the fact that "Stevie" sounded like a man's name and "Lindsey" a woman's.

"Sausalito was *the worst*," moans Stevie Nicks. Sinking into a corner of her cranberry velour sofa, a bowl of split pea soup in one hand, she recollects the first recording session for Fleetwood Mac's latest, *Rumours*.

It was February 1976 when Mick Fleetwood, John McVie, Christine McVie, Lindsey Buckingham and Stevie left Los Angeles for the Record Plant in Sausalito to record—rather *try* to record—material for a follow-up to the immensely prosperous *Fleetwood Mac* album. It was then that the pressures of the business and their new-found fame and fortune started to cast dark clouds on the romantic relationships within the band. When the thunderstorms let up, John and Christine, after eight years of marriage, and Stevie and Lindsey, after six years as roommates, had separated. Mick and his lady Jenny were in the middle of divorce proceedings—only to eventually remarry.

"Not only was it cold, what was happening," says Stevie, "but it was cold to leave and cold to come back. We were all trying to break up and when you break up with someone, you don't want to see him. You especially don't want to eat breakfast with him the next morning, see him all day and all night, and all day the day after and all night . . . Finally [after nearly two months] Mick said one day 'We're going home.' We took a couple days off, spent four days rehearsing and then went on the road for 10 days. At that point, we *needed* the feedback. We needed to hear the people say 'ok, we know you're having problems, but we still like you.'"

Fleetwood Mac then traveled to different studios in L.A., North Hollywood and Miami, in hopes of meeting their deadline for Warner Brothers. "I don't remember much of anything during that time, recording a little here and a little there," says Stevie. "It's like a dream sequence to me now."

One can't help but wonder why and, more significantly, *how* Fleetwood Mac could survive the romantic traumas and remain together on a business level. "Because," explains Stevie, matter-of-factly, "we basically really like each other, and once we go onstage all those problems, the fights, the arguments and disagreements, they all disappear. That two hours onstage is beautiful and always was, even when things were at their worst." Before joining Fleetwood Mac, Californians Stevie and Lindsey had released one album, *Buckingham/Nicks* (Polydor), but it quickly found its way into the cut-out bins ("We were tax write-offs," says Lindsey) and they were dropped from the label. Emotional entanglements or not, they weren't about to slam the door in the face of success. "Really, each one of us was way too proud and way too stubborn to walk away from it," Stevie recalls. "I wasn't going to leave. Lindsey wasn't going to leave. What would we have done? Sat around L.A. and tried to start new bands? Nobody wanted to do that. We like touring. We like making money and we like being a band. It was just grit your teeth and bear it."

Once the couples within the band split up, Fleetwood Mac was no longer groupie-proof; they became fair game for gossip writers and columnists in rock mags across the country. Rumors had Fleetwood Mac breaking up; Christine in the hospital; Peter Green, Jeremy Spencer (original FM members) and Danny Kirwan (the only guitarist asked to leave the band) re-joining the current lineup for a special 10th Anniversary tour this year; and Lindsey and Stevie the proud poppa and mama of a beautiful blonde baby girl (who actually belonged to Mick and Jenny). Rock magazines portrayed Stevie as the Farrah Fawcett-Majors of rock 'n' roll, and she, along with the other newly free members of the band, were seen everywhere locked in the arms of others, often rock musicians.

"For a while it was funny," Stevie says, "but then personally I really started to get angry, because I live a very quiet life. I'm either working or I'm home and all of a sudden I'm picking up these papers and I'm the Siren of the North." Seemingly attempting to set the record straight, she adds, "Don Henley [of the Eagles] are *friends*. We're not into a heavy romantic relationship. How can we be? We're always on the road. And Paul Kantner [of Jefferson Airplane/Starship fame]—I never went out with him. He called me a couple of times, but basically I wasn't interested. I don't even *like* rock 'n' roll stars," she groans. "I especially don't like men rock 'n' roll stars, mainly because they're just too egoed-out. And I *don't* need it. I don't need to go out with rock 'n' roll stars for their money. I've got my own money. I've gone through it and I didn't like it and I won't do it again. It's like that lady onstage—I can't hold a candle to her if that's what they want."

With one of the most distinct voices in the feminine arena of rock and a pair of pouty lips. Stevie evokes a raw, sensual-but-innocent power and, dressed in her black Rhiannon outfit, she cuts a surrealistic image onstage. But, really now, she's not a witch. "I'm not a heavy psychic weirdo. I just happen to love black and I love to dance. I hate seeing rock 'n' roll ladies that stomp across the stage and that are so hard core. It's so unfeminine. Being a sex symbol has never been my goal in life. I just happen to love beautiful flowing movements. You know," she continues, "Mick and I are definitely the entertainers. We *are* the hamburgers. Sometimes the rest of the band just can't believe us 'cause we love to do crazy things. It makes us laugh. But we've got three real shy people and two extroverts, so somewhere we have to arrive at a compromise. It's gotta be a group effort—and it is.

"You know," she continues without so much as a pause, "Fleetwood Mac is real loose. We're all aware that we're not virtuosos and that the world will survive without Fleetwood Mac. We don't take ourselves too terribly seriously because when you do, you start going down the tubes. So we just make our mistakes and continue on."

———————

"For some reason, Fleetwood Mac is one of the few bands that can get away with making mistakes." Christine, 33, has been with Mac since the blues days of late 1970. On this rainy Los Angeles afternoon, she's relaxing in front of a fire in her Hollywood Hills home. "This band is *unknown*," she laughs. "Like one time, I don't know where we were, but during a concert once we started up a song and something happened to Mick's drum and he said, 'There's no way. We gotta stop.' One of the roadies came up to fix the drum and John went up to the microphone and said, 'What do you think we are? A professional rock 'n' roll band?' The ice was instantly broken. The audience cracked up and we started the song again. But I think a lot of people that go to see us *hope* something goes wrong. It's a bit of a comedy show as well. When you look at Mick grasshopping around with his African drum, well, that is *not* serious. You've gotta find that funny or you will have no sense of humor at all."

Christine, who lived briefly with the band's lighting director, Curry Grant, after separating from John McVie, wouldn't term Fleetwood Mac's massive acceptance as being 'overnight' anymore than she would view her break-up with John as reason for Fleetwood Mac to call it quits. "As far as all this recent success, it was timing and a combination of all things connected with this band. All of a sudden we had the properties that maybe the public wanted at the right time. The band projected an exciting image onstage and I think it was quite unique to have two women in a band who are not just backup singers."

The compulsion to succeed inevitably exceeded the romantic traumas. Says Christine: "After 10 years of struggling, it would have been silly to throw it all away. We proved to each other that we had a pretty strong character, that we could cope with the problems and surmount them—which we did. John and I are friendly now, which at a point we weren't. The bonds were just too great to sever because there was an emotional ruckus going on."

When Mac's three songwriters; Christine, Stevie and Lindsey, finally got their songs together, that emotional ruckus produced the platinum follow-up to *Fleetwood Mac, Rumours*. Not so ironically for any songwriter, all three were writing about their crumbling relationships. "But," says Christine, "rarely do I stand in my own shoes and write a song that is *that* personal. 'Oh, Daddy' is not a song about me, it's a song about Mick and Jenny. 'Don't Stop' was just a feeling. It seemed like a pleasant revelation to have." She ponders that a minute and then adds with a snicker, "It would make a great song for an insurance company. But, I'm definitely not a pessimist. I'm basically a love song writer."

But even with the platinum success of *Fleetwood Mac* and now *Rumours*, Christine hasn't felt the pressure ease up. "I think we have a lot of proving to do. There'll still be pressure for another year or so, but the way we conduct the tours will be a lot nicer for sure. When you have the money to charter your own plane and stay in nice hotels, it makes life on the road infinitely easier."

Though Christine and John have no immediate plans for divorce, Christine is content for now to simply enjoy her freedom and the money success has piled up. "It's enabled all of us to realize a few dreams that we never thought would happen. But I haven't egoed out. I'm pretty much of a recluse as it happens. What this has done though, well . . . the doors have just opened. Now I have the money to get my sculpture studio together and the whole way of looking at my life has expanded over the last six months. Suddenly you realize 'To hell with it. Life does not begin and end with Fleetwood Mac.' Lately I've been mixing with some people that are not involved with rock 'n' roll and that aren't involved with the business, that know nothing about rock 'n' roll and don't give a shit—that's been very stimulating. I mean, there's only so much you can talk about in rock 'n' roll. Above and beyond that, it's a very big world. It just occurred to me quite recently that I was absorbing myself so much in Fleetwood Mac and all the problems that I wasn't having all that good of a time."

"'How does it feel to be a star?' People ask this all the time. Ughhhhh! Get out! Or people introduce you—'This is John McVie. He's a rock 'n' roll star.' It's embarrassing. You try to find something to crawl under." When it comes to discussing Fleetwood Mac's position in rock 'n' roll, John McVie's voice is unassuming, his volume soft and his tone far from narcissistic.

"There's no rock 'n' roll stars," he said adamantly. "They're all dead. Who makes people who play in rock 'n' roll bands non-human?" he asked, then answered, "It's the managers, the PR people, and that's the set goal. More sensible would be to put rock 'n' roll in its place. It's just part of being human. Rock 'n' roll is not the beginning and end of all life and in the scheme of things rock 'n' roll is so unimportant. It's 95% bullshit." Then why bother? McVie's answer is simple: "I enjoy being a musician." Beyond that he has no great ambitions except "to be happy and right now that's being a musician. A few years from now it might be something else. Fortunately, I've got the chance."

The mass acceptance of Fleetwood Mac doesn't seem to faze Mick or John much at all, though it has increased their business responsibilities in the band. With attorney Michael Shapiro, Mick and John form the management, which is nothing if not Seedy. When former manager Clifford Davis booked a bogus band with the same name on tour in 1973, Mick and John were granted a court injunction forcing the ersatz Mac off the road and into court—the outcome of which may be decided soon. With that, and the fact that the group's albums had only been selling mediocrely, Mick and John decided to take over the managerial duties. John, acknowledging that Mick is the "more active half," added, "We thought we knew ourselves better than the rest of them. We understand the vibe and the feeling of the music and the way it should be presented. Plus, we didn't trust anybody else. When you get burned once, you don't do it again. It's a very human trip now. Record companies respond to managers with briefcases, always barking at someone and it's not like that here. It's very low-key. It takes longer to get things done, but they're done in a much nicer way."

Through a gradual shift from British blues to a sound that has gripped the nation in a massive Fleetwood Mac attack; through *six* guitarists, Peter Green (who left the band to find himself and is now confined to a mental institution after brandishing a gun in his accountant's office in an attempt to stop royalties from early Fleetwood Mac albums), Jeremy Spencer (who left to join the Children of God), Danny Kirwan, Bob Weston and Dave Walker (the first Americans to join the band) and Californian Bob Welch (who left to form his own group, Paris), Fleetwood Mac has *adapted* and "It will probably be the most successful band in the world this year," says John. "It's a good live band," he adds. "It's a good recording band and it's got charisma. That's not ego . . . I hope it isn't.

"A lot of people have come up to us in the last year to interview us and they say 'Well, now that you guys have become a commercial success, did you just decide you were going to go commercial and make it that way?' and we say 'NO!'" For Lindsey Buckingham, being called "commercial" comes on like an insult. "Stevie and I joined the band and the way we write happens to be the way we write. We've never tried consciously to fit into anything or do anything like say 'OK, we gotta write a hit.'"

Although Stevie and Christine are thinking about solo albums in the future (ABC released a "Christine Perfect" album in England, "But," she says, "the less said about that, the better"), Lindsey isn't even considering it. "It's funny once you get successful, there's always a million people who'll offer you money to get away from the unit, like: 'Hey, man. Why don't you sign a solo deal?' Why should I do that?" he asks. "I'm not sure that we have just scratched the surface as far as potential goes for what these five people can do musically. So many groups break up because of egos and all that. Buffalo Springfield," he muses nostalgically, "imagine what they could have done if they'd stayed together."

How does Fleetwood Mac plan to approach that potential?

"Well," Lindsey sighs, "we'll never be a band like Tower of Power who goes into rehearsal and rehearses a song so that they can just go in and play the whole thing in one or maybe a few takes. The way we approach it is more the way the Beatles used to approach their things in the studio—having a general idea and then going into the studio and letting the spontaneity happen. That's where you capture the magic." Spontaneity and "letting it happen" all sounds wonderful and very true to the rock 'n' roll spirit, but unfortunately, record companies don't seem to care much. In the case of Fleetwood Mac, Warner Brothers was just a little bit, shall we say, *nervous* about the *Rumours* album.

"They didn't want us to release a single at all this time," Lindsey says, "because they were afraid that if it didn't go, it might hurt the album sales and 'Oh, wow man, the single bombed out.' They were really paranoid—understandably—because they hadn't heard the album. They didn't know anything about it for 10 months at that point and probably thought we were just in the studio helplessly flailing away. But Mick went down and met with Mo Ostin and the people down there and listened very calmly to all their reasons why we shouldn't release a single. Then he played "Go Your Own Way." That was it. They went 'Yeahhhhh!' and said 'Go ahead. You've got it!' They realize the last album wasn't just a fluke and I think they feel now that we know what we're doing."

Since the release of *Rumours,* Fleetwood Mac has met with its usual run of bad luck; fifteen shows were cancelled at the start of the 1977 world tour because Stevie, suffering from vocal strain, lost her voice and had to resort to lessons to help strengthen it. Then Lindsey had his wisdom teeth out and suffered the side effect of two black eyes, just in time to ruin their cover photo for *People* magazine. "We get bummed out at times," says Lindsey, "just like everybody else. But, it's only natural 'cause the only way to define the highs is to have the lows."

FLEETWOOD MAC

The Group as Group Encounter?

Chris Salewicz | January 19, 1980 | _New Musical Express_ (UK)

How do you follow up an album that epitomized gloss and domesticity? In Fleetwood Mac's case, with _Tusk_, a record released in October 1979 that juxtaposed easy-listening with sounds and sentiments that responded to the fractious punk zeitgeist.

There was, though, at least one thing about their new LP that remained on a continuum from the mid-seventies vibe of the previous record: decadence. Drugs references had dotted previous interviews, but the now megarich Fleetwood Mac members could afford to fully indulge not just their taste for stimulants but also their (probably not unrelated) grandiose conceits: _Tusk_ was a double set that cost an unprecedented million dollars to record. Some swear to this day it's the best thing they ever did, but that didn't translate into _Rumours_-level sales figures. Nor did their financial and conceptual extravagance and persisting easy-listening proclivities endear them to the New Wavers.

This feature finds the band, six months after the album's release, touring it hard, as was their wont, and still fielding questions about its troubled hinterland.

Chris Salewicz, a traditionally irreverent British music-weekly writer, was granted extraordinary access to the band. As well as smoking a joint with Buckingham, he elicits some extraordinary verbal offerings from Nicks about geopolitics and mysticism.

OF course, Fleetwood Mac _is_ The American Dream.

The band's success story is the stuff of which the mythology of modern day America is made: Mick Fleetwood, John and Christine McVie, down on their luck in the Oulde Country, make the decision to move to The Promised Land. Travelling as far west as possible these humble immigrants settle out on the most advanced technological frontier in the world, Los Angeles.

Operating within rock'n'roll's picaresque tradition, a surprise encounter teams the three English people up with two down-and-out American natives, Stevie Nicks and Lindsey Buckingham. Within a year, following closely the code of the WASP work ethic, their fortunes are changing for the better.

Within three years of moving to America they have become part of the aristocracy to which you are granted entry in the United States of America by virtue of your material rather than by virtue of your blood. When in Washington Fleetwood Mac are invited to the White House for social chitchat with President Jimmy Carter.

By now they are so rich that Mick Fleetwood tells a friend he knows he need never work again in his life.

Gosh, it's like a good made-for-TV movie!

'RUMOURS' was a musical soap opera detailing diary entries of the emotional chaos within Fleetwood Mac following the breakthrough of the 'Fleetwood Mac' album. The romantic traumas it dealt with, though, were those of wealthy Beautifully Tanned People. A very glamorous record really, a sort of musical *Dallas*.

Incorporating as many emotional buzz-words and buzz-areas as possible 'Rumours' rather simply discussed the romantic problems of many people in their late twenties or early thirties. By so doing it established once and for all the viability of what has now become known as AOR— Adult Oriented Rock.

In what seemed so apt in Me Generation, Self-fixated ("Buddy, from now on I'm looking after number one!") mid-'70s California, the state with the highest divorce rate in the world, Fleetwood Mac's position became something like the group-as-group-therapy. Easier than EST, safer than Synanon, 'Rumours' seemed as Californian as any of the new quasi-religious texts like *Zen And The Art Of Motorcycle Maintenance* or the collected works of L Ron Hubbard.

That was not the sole factor, of course, behind 'Rumours' selling close on twenty million copies. All that was just the in-depth back-up team, really. The real reason 'Rumours' sold so many copies was that it became bigger-than-life-itself was because, in the words of Warner Brothers' Derek Taylor: "It's just a very, very good double-sided pop record."

Fleetwood Mac's music is rock'n'roll—just the rhythm section alone would ensure that—but it's a very poppy rock'n'roll, closer to Abba than Elmore James, the inspiration of the band's original guitarist.

But can you imagine what the vibes must've been like in the studio during the making of 'Rumours'? Fleetwood Mac probably shouldn't be begrudged a single cent of their wealth.

Even now—perhaps more than ever—there is something indefinably sad about Fleetwood Mac, especially about the three English expatriates, or so it appears when I travel to San Francisco to see them play two dates at the Cow Palace at the end of their American tour.

Mick Fleetwood, for example, as well as apparently being still deeply in love with Jenny (sister of Patti) Boyd, his ex-wife of two divorces, suffers from both diabetes and a related condition that is the exact opposite of diabetes—i.e. Fleetwood mustn't eat sugar and must eat a lot of sugar. One wonders at the possible cause of such an imbalance within his body. Meanwhile, the re-married John McVie (the band's "Penguin" logo stems from the bassist's fascination for the bird—he even has one tattooed on his forearm), for many the definition of A Good Bloke, continues to seem happiest when he has a glass in his hand though most people have a favourite drug, of course. Christine McVie, who has taken up with recently fired Beach Boy Dennis Wilson, seems to epitomise the paradoxes scattered throughout all aspects of the group: a Cancer, with all its mother (Earth) implications (her pure, rich vocals can only be described by the word "fecund") she's had herself sterilised, a very Californian thing to do.

Really, though, the sadness of Fleetwood Mac has a very large responsibility for the band's popularity and for making so many people so happy.

THE regally named Lindsey Buckingham, the youngest group member at just thirty, is the one F Mac Person who is very much in sympathy with the newer ways of thinking. There's obviously a link between this and the fact he has nine songs on the new album, as opposed to the six of Christine McVie and the five of Stevie Nicks.

When we meet for a formal interview session he quizzes me about the English music scene and reveals a fair knowledge of such acts as Talking Heads and The Gang Of Four. By contrast the tapes playing in the suite of Stevie Nicks—a very '60s sort of person, really—are Derek And The Dominoes and Steve Miller. Her tastes, though, are probably more representative of what the band listen to than Buckingham's. Fleetwood Mac are essentially conservative in their musical outlook—not just in their music, either: John McVie has a bit of a hard time relating to my pink socks.

So at a time when most younger bands are seeking to destroy the once assumed divinity of the massive studio bill, it's hardly surprising that the production costs of 'Tusk', the 'Rumours' follow-up, should make it the first million dollar album. 'Tusk' seems closer to a mega-budget Hollywood movie production than to good ol' funky rock'n'roll . . . which is appropriate, really, because with their homes in Bel-Air, Beverley Hills and Malibu Fleetwood Mac are part of The New Hollywood.

Though no-one will admit it, part of the expense of 'Tusk' must've been (unconsciously, perhaps) justified internally within the band as a weapon to fight the uncertainty and insecurity that would've inevitably been present in trying to follow up as huge a success as 'Rumours'. Besides ivory's expensive. Ask elephants.

According to Buckingham, anyway, the cost of the record has become a little overstated. Basically, 'Tusk' cost so much because someone cocked up: Partially as an investment, no doubt, F Mac were going to have their own studio built, until they were strongly advised against it by people at Warner Brothers who told them costs would be absolutely prohibitive. Of course, if they'd listened to their own advice—a rare slip for the self-managed outfit—they'd have something more to show for all that money spent.

"In the context of the whole," Buckingham's high metallic voice tells me, "the 'Rumours' album took longer to make than 'Tusk'. One of the reasons why 'Tusk' cost so much is that we happened to be at a studio that was charging a fuck of a lot of money.

"During the making of 'Tusk' we were in the studio for about ten months and we got twenty songs out of it. The 'Rumours' album took the same amount of time. It didn't cost so much because we were in a cheaper studio.

"There's no denying what it cost, but I think it's been taken just a little out of context."

In addition, the much touted digital recording hardly affected the band at all, its real use being in preserving the quality of the master-tape and the records that are pressed from it.

Anyway, as Nick Kent wrote in his review of the double album, 'Tusk' is a pretty fine traditional pop/rock record. It's only when Fleetwood Mac play some of it onstage, that you become aware of its deficiencies: the band *did* spend too long in the studio. Live, the 'Tusk' songs have a freshness and vital spirit that has become muted during all that studio time. It's still a good record, though. "You've got to play it a lot," says John McVie. "It keeps getting better." Yeah, but if you keep doing that do you eventually reach saturation point, as happens with 'Rumours', a basically inferior record, incidentally, to the 'Fleetwood Mac' album that preceded it?

Warner Brothers, of course were anxious that the delay between 'Rumours' and its successor was too great. For a while they wanted to release the first record of the two record set as soon as it was completed. That was nixed. So was a heavy advertising campaign that the company had a New York agency present to the band. Mick Fleetwood: "The record company let this agency try something and when we saw it it was . . . . just *nothing* . . . It was scrapped immediately.

"I said I didn't think they'd be able to do it, because for pretty obvious reasons we're pretty preoccupied with *not* overselling ourselves. I think it's very unfortunate that someone like Peter Frampton let his music be cheapened by doing things like putting adverts for Peter Frampton watches in his albums. That just shouldn't happen. A record's supposed to be there to listen to. I think that's sick. I can't understand how people let that happen. I think it's real crass."

All this balance sheet stuff aside, it may interest fans of the original Fleetwood Mac to learn that none other than Peter Green himself plays on the album. "That's right," confirms Fleetwood, "he plays literally about eight notes at the end of one of Chris's songs—'Brown Eyes', I think it is. He just wandered into the studio whilst the track was being done.

"But," continues Fleetwood with sudden despondency, "I've given up with Peter. I've totally given up. *He's* just given up where anything to do with money is concerned. After a while it just wears me down." The drummer confirms what I'd heard, that on the recently released Peter Green solo album the guitar hero actually handles very little of the work on his chosen instrument: "A lot of the guitar is done by a friend of his. He told me that he'd handed over the guitar duties to someone else—*ridiculous.*"

It was Mick Fleetwood—a good-natured fellow who presumably wanted to hand some of his new fortune Green's way in the same manner that he's assisted former Mac guitarist Bob Welch—who set Green up with a contract with Warner worth nearly a million dollars: "The day he was supposed to sign it he freaked out. I looked a bit stupid. After all, who would believe that he didn't want to sign a contract because he thought it was with the Devil?"

(Well, quite a few chaps, actually . . .)

FLEETWOOD Mac may be part of the New Hollywood but they're not taken in by all the LA bullshit—three of them are *British* after all, and all three old lags in this rock'n'roll circus: they've seen it all before.

Buckingham, meanwhile, would far rather live in his native San Francisco than Los Angles. Stevie would probably favour living on a flying carpet.

"America is my home," says Fleetwood, "but I don't plan to live in Los Angeles much longer—none of us do, in fact. There is definitely going to be an earthquake. LA will be flattened. I'll have no regrets at all about moving."

He claims that the flakiness of Hollywood hardly affects him: "We work a helluva lot so we don't get much chance to think about it."

Fleetwood Mac tour a lot for a band of their status (and age). "Out of the next thirteen months," Mick tells me, "we're spending nearly nine months on the road. That is the sort of commitment to what we do. It's not that we just want to throw out an album and say, 'Oh, it'll do alright!'"

As the new royalty, of course, it's necessary for the band to occasionally hold court to meet local media dignitaries. These press conferences are fairly appalling affairs with—at the one I attended in San Francisco prior to the band's final three shows of their American tour, anyway—the local press and TV and radio fielding their questions with strained, reverential smiles, like forelock tugging supplicants come to beg for boons.

Held in one of the bland conference rooms at the San Francisco hotel in Union Square in the centre of the city, the event was strictly showbiz Presidential, with the band—except Buckingham who'd gone to visit his mother—sitting at a dais at one end of the room as questions of the weight of "Who is 'Sara?'" and "Mick, do you ever sneak out at night and go to clubs?" were put to the tolerant Mac. The killer was when some mutant got up and asked Stevie what she was doing for dinner that night.

In the middle of an hour and twenty minutes of this nonsense Mick Fleetwood's whole body appears to go into spasms. Christine McVie, sitting next to him, massages his shoulders and arms with thoughtful concern. Mick's having one of his diabetes attacks. He'd been late arriving at the press conference because he'd felt so lousy he thought he might have to blow it out altogether.

At times like this one wonders, "Is it worth it?"

ONSTAGE Fleetwood Mac are a great rock band.

Whatever Mick Fleetwood may say about attempting to step away from the LA soft-rock sound on 'Tusk' the band haven't gone far enough—or at least they probably did go far enough and then just stuck around for too long in that overpriced studio blowing their 'Rumours' bread on overdubs. Onstage, though, they really *burn,* with the new short-haired Buckingham—the somewhat camp shots of him on the 'Tusk' sleeve being only stage one of a metamorphosis into Beverley Hills New Waver that has now been completed—spurring the band on from his centre-stage stance. By the third number the sweat's running down his face and neck like a waterfall.

John McVie, who with Mick Fleetwood makes one of the hardest, most inventive rhythm sections in rock, adopts a most unusual stance for a bassist by moving about a lot and entering into duelling partnerships with Buckingham, himself a feisty rather than academic or soulful gui-tarist.

On stage right Christine McVie provides the Mother Earth image she is so keen to renounce, an anchor behind her keyboards.

Stevie Nicks has, as you might expect, six or seven dress changes (though, equally, Mick Fleetwood, who looks very late '60s and Jethro Tull-like in his boots and waistcoat, has a gong at the back of his kit (often the sign of a dodgy band) but, in fact, these are just part of the show, and Nick's real strength is her superb voice, deep—maybe deeper than Buckingham's, actually—(until I saw F Mac onstage in London I couldn't figure out which parts were sung by the chaps and which by the gels) and resonant and clear, as though she'd been gargling with redwood sap. Nicks is a bit of a clown sometimes but she's okay, really—think what you'd be like if you lived in California.

Each individual's instrumental and vocal accomplishments aside, however, what really makes this show work is that there are so many great songs in the set—since the release of 'Tusk' Fleetwood Mac have effectively twice as many songs at their disposal.

Backstage at this show promoted by Bill Graham (as featured in *Apocalypse Now)* at the Cow Palace (a mere twelve or thirteen thousand seater) there is a very good vibe. There is an undeniable elegance about the benchwood furniture and potted palms that fill the dressing-rooms. John McVie is very happy. Slumping around in an old army fatigue jacket looking to put something in his empty glass he seems pleased at my praising the show. "This is a *great* band," he nods to himself, and picks up a bottle of vodka.

Christine McVie and Dennis Wilson sit on a couch, canoodling and spooning like teenagers at a drive-in movie. Dennis seems pretty drunk, actually, or that's my interpretation of the near-total failure in communi-cation that we experience when we try and talk to each other. Maybe it's just a bad case of culture gap. Oh well, Surf's Out: Don't Make Waves. What seems like the entire Buckingham family tree is also present.

Mick Fleetwood and myself end up sitting round a tape recorder in the middle dressing-room, the one that has the urinals and toilets. It also has the F Mac oxygen cylinder and mask. This was a new one on me and didn't seem to work when I tried it. Presumably, though, if all you do is breathe air-conditioned air in hotels and limos all your life, maybe you need a drop of the bottled stuff now and then. Perhaps it's the sort of breathing equivalent of Perrier water. I can't see it catching on in Bradford, though.

MICK Fleetwood was the original founder of Fleetwood Mac in July, 1967, following his being kicked out of John Mayall's Bluesbreakers after only a couple of months for drinking too much. Apart from Mayall himself the line-up Fleetwood had been part of was completed by John McVie, who'd played with Mayall since the beginning of 1963, and Peter Green. Green followed Fleetwood shortly afterwards and an initially reluctant McVie joined in September of that year.

Prior to working with the Bluesbreakers, Fleetwood had been working as a decorator for a few weeks following the break-up of white soul roadshow The Shotgun Express, also featuring Rod Stewart. He is a man with a very absurd sense of humour that is rarely revealed in interviews when he seems keenest to play the political spokesman role that is presumably a development of his also managing the band, a position he took over following the notorious occasion when their former manager Clifford Davis, claiming to own the name "Fleetwood Mac" and to be able to use it as he saw fit, sent a bogus F Mac out on the road in America in January, 1974.

He loathes the idea of managers now, and thinks that no band or artist should need one: "A good accountant and lawyer and a good tour manager—an old roadie can do that—are all you need."

Along with John McVie, Fleetwood's the real backbone of Fleetwood Mac. He's a formidable drummer, which is why it's very puzzling that his actual drum solo—with hand-held "talking" drum—should be so duff. Maybe it's hexed by [Text was missing in feature when originally published —Ed.]

These days with his beard he can look a lot like Donald Sutherland, which is very confusing considering that Sutherland starred in the remake of Invasion Of The Bodysnatchers which was, of course, set in San Francisco.

I try not to think about that too much and make a general opening remark about the manner in which the music scene, in England anyway, has changed since the New Ascension of F Mac. I tell Fleetwood the F Mac don't appear to have the same amount of abuse hurled at them as the likes of The Eagles or Led Zeppelin.

"Well," he replies, in not too practised a manner, "we've never stayed one way for very long, and I don't think we ever will. When the band first started Peter was writing and then 'Albatross' came out and people said, 'What the *fuck's* that?'—though people stayed loyal.

"We've always changed a lot whether or not players have changed. We're actually afraid, I think, of getting into that rut, which can be very easy to do, and very awful, too. Especially when it's just so you can 'make a lot of money'. Doing a double album didn't make any business sense at all. But it meant a lot to us, artistically—whether we could still feel challenged. We really, really *are* pleased with it. We've also, I think, got enough discretion to know if the songs aren't up to standard, in which case we'd have just put out a single album.

"We've got a great advantage, though, in having three very different songwriters. We're very lucky. When Danny, Peter and Jeremy were in the band they all wrote and played very, very different stuff. So in a way we're back to that sort of situation—again we have the advantage of three very different styles. So it's come something like full circle."

WERE you aware of just how strong the punk/New Wave thing had become in England?

"No-o-o-o," Mick Fleetwood shakes his head, perhaps with no great passion, shrugging his shoulders as he continues in the slightly slurred, drawn-out syllables of the Home Counties rock'n'roll accent first popularised by such near-contemporaries of the drummer as Mick Jagger "because we're not physically there . . . But I know there's a whole social thing going on.

"The good musical things," he continues, more confidently, "will stay behind. Most bands that I know of didn't really have any great masterplan. They just started off listening to the blues and the Rolling Stones and Chuck Berry records, played the school dance or whatever and went on from there. Just went off and did it. And developed.

"It's not that evident over here. England's such a tiny place—all those great bands always come out of it. England brings out some kind of hardcore staying power. I don't think this country has that, because it genuinely isn't as hard here. I'm not saying people don't have a hard time here. Stevie and Lindsey certainly did . . ."

With Jungian synchronicity, or maybe just good timing, Stevie Nicks sticks her rather shattered-looking head round the door with all the experience of . . . someone who's done a lot of waitressing. "Cheeseburger fries, kidney pie, potatoes and starch . . . well, anyway, I'm sorry I broke in your little tea-party . . ."

She disappears. The door closes. Mick Fleetwood scratches his head, as though bewildered at this display of Rock Star Looning. "Gosh", he says, just like that.

Enough of this frivolity. On with the questions—of course, one of the reasons you left England in 1974 was because you were so pissed off with living there . . .

"We were just pissed off with the whole thing, because basically Fleetwood Mac didn't mean a shit then in Europe. The band had changed, whatever we played wasn't appealing—the *balls* of the band, namely Peter, had gone. At that point, anyway, we were playing more and more over here.

"Also, I thought England was very grey and full of depressed people. All those kids were just reacting to that. I know that. *We* just got out. But it can never have that same effect in terms of the nucleus effect here, simply because of the size of the country. You can go through the whole Mid-West and it's just not there."

Actually, when I was watching you onstage tonight I was thinking of the colossal sense of history in your songs . . .

"Yeah," agrees Fleetwood, pleased, "before I went on tonight I shouted out 'You know what this is? This is the last three gigs of the decade'. And then while I was playing I was trying to count the years I'd been with John. I thought, 'God! Not so long now and it'll be something like 20 years!' That's what I mean; there's a lot of feeling up there, of people that have developed together.

"There's a lot of waste of talent that starts up and just fizzles out. You just see the spark of something and then they all start throwing TVs out of windows and showing they're a load of bastards."

You had the Youth Success thing . . .

"Yeah. But we held it together as a band. We were lucky—because of the people in the band we became involved in the thinking process of what we were trying to do. For ourselves. *Selfishly,* if you like. And we're still doing that. It's not just a crank it out and let it roll in until it stops rolling in number: 'Oh, I'll just do it for a few years and clean up'. This is a career. This is what we *do.*

"It's just a question of having some integrity about what you do, and we definitely try to have that. And I suppose when we stop having that feeling then it will be time to stop altogether . . . Rather than just an 'Oh, we'll do a quick tour and rake it in'.

"There's a lot of that goes on."

I think for quite a while after 'Rumours' came out it was assumed that the next F Mac record would be a live album, after which you'd all retire . . .

"We've recorded some gigs on this tour. We do it every tour and they just get put away. They might be used sometime. Who knows?"

At one stage, though, wasn't there talk of this double album being one record live and one record studio?

"I don't remember that. I think we thought of the possibility of going into a concert hall and just cutting these songs literally *live.* Live these songs are very different. Without all the overdubs they really kick ass.

"I think it'd be an interesting thing to do to just go in an empty hall and just develop the number in the same way you have to play it onstage. We don't do a lot of the stuff onstage. You can't get all those little tinkles and cymbals and tom-tom overdubs. You play the gut of the number. To approach doing some new tunes in that way could well be an interesting thing to try.

"A good live album can be great, but it's often treading water a bit, and a very easy thing to do. People say we must be crazy that a band as big as we are haven't put out a live record . . . or a Greatest Hits in between 'Rumours' and 'Tusk'. But it takes the freshness away of what we're trying to do. Of course, there'll be a Greatest Hits sometime. One day. As a final curtain, perhaps.

"But certainly now the intention is to keep on recording new stuff. Hopefully the next album will be out a lot quicker than other people think. I think we'll just go for a quick one."

DID 'Rumours' do your heads in?

"Just the colossal success?"—very matter-of-fact—"we were working a lot of the time on the road. Again, I just think we're lucky."

But did you feel it was becoming just a commodity?

"No. Because we don't let that sort of thing happen. If we wanted to utilise all the marketing resources we could make 'A Lot More Money', a lot more cash-in stuff. But,"—derisively—"that's going for a real cheap one. You shoot your integrity out the window . . . Because we're internally very . . . well, we look after our own affairs for a start, so we don't have anyone feeding us a load of bullshit on how great we are . . . So we're constantly having to make our minds up ourselves, which keeps you open . . . And I think that's kept us relatively sane.

"Of course, there *is* pressure. And you just have to hang on to the same thing as you've hung on to for the last however many years it is. You just don't presume that you're anything special, ever. As soon as you do that, then forget it.

"There's a lot of natural energy in this group. Without it it wouldn't work. It's apparent to me that onstage there's just genuine rapport. We know what numbers we're going to play next, but in point of fact it *is* relatively different every night. We need the subtleties that go on between us onstage. We *need to* look at each other and know you're looking at someone and it feels good. I enjoy myself as much now as I ever have. It has *nothing* to do with how much money you've made or how well you're doing.

"I really don't think we'd be doing it if we weren't enjoying it. And equally I know there are lots of people that make the choice to continue doing it, presumably because they're making a lot of money.

"This band," he adopts a Mancunian accent, "has got *guts* in it!"

Warners presumably wanted to do a huge number on 'Tusk' to equal 'Rumours'? The advertising campaign, etc . . .

"I think with any record company you have to just acknowledge that they want to make the record successful. And their measure of success is *money*. It would be naive of me to say we're totally oblivious to how much money you can make. But the music comes first—everytime. Then maybe you make some money. A lot of people approach it with 'This is the sort of music we're going to do to make the money'. And I . . . *shit on that!*

"Because then the point of the music is lost. Gone. Totally. Because you're doing it just to make money. And people panic"—adopts drongo voice—'We've got to sell so many units'. Give yourself a break. Please yourself. You might not go on selling billions of albums . . .

"To me an artist with a huge amount of integrity is Neil Young. He's doing exactly what he wants to do, he's always done that, and—you know that?—he's still bloody successful, too. Because people acknowledge the fact that he has artistic integrity, period.

"He's still great, still pumping away up there, still interested, still looking to grow. I remember talking to him and he was absolutely intrigued—he'd even been to England—by all the punk rock things. You should use anything that comes past you. You should be open to all influences. And in turn you can then put out something which is really yourself—because everyone has influences: it doesn't just come from out of the sky. There are always reasons for everything.

"Music is a development of a whole load of things. As soon as you stop developing, then forget it. I mean, all the recent success has been very, very gratifying. And it's also really nice to know that you're not just jacking yourself off. First of all, we're pleased because it's happening just for us five people; then it's incredibly nice to know that other people really enjoy it, too, for however long they enjoy it.

"But, anyway, I'm repeating myself, but it means a lot to all of us."

AN hour or so later I'm sitting in the living-room of Stevie Nicks mock-Regency suite.

Stevie is drinking large Remy Martins and appears to have something of a bad head cold. I ought to tell you what she's wearing but I can't remember; I can't keep up with all these changes. Certainly the most loopy member of the band, she suffers from having lived for too long on the West Coast. Her patriotism and belief in America is quite absurd, though I'm sure she'll never see that, and wouldn't think of it in those terms anyway. She'll be good on chat shows in a few years time.

On the Buckingham-Nicks album, released by Polydor in 1973 to no great success, there is a dedication to "A. J. Nicks, the grandfather of country music". A. J. Nicks was also Stevie's grandfather.

"He was a country singer and songwriter," she explains, "very into it. He wanted to take me on the road when I was four. But my parents wouldn't let him and he wouldn't speak to them for years. We actually sang together when I was that tiny. He was definitely the one who first got me interested in music."

With her penchant for writing numbers like 'Rhiannon' and for Isadore Duncan-like stage moves Stevie Nicks is always, often not without irony, referred to as "the *mystical* member of Fleetwood Mac". No doubt, this is why—before we can begin the interview—she drapes all the lamps with antique shawls or scarves.

"But there's always been a very mystical thing about Fleetwood Mac," she responds, "when I first joined Fleetwood Mac I went out and bought all the albums—actually, I think I asked Mick for them because I couldn't possibly afford to buy them—and I sat in my room and listened to all of them to try to figure out if I could capture any theme or anything.

"And what I came up with was the word 'mystical'—that there is something *mystical* that went all the way from Peter Green's Fleetwood Mac straight through Jeremy, through all of them: Bob Welch, Christine, and Mick and John. It didn't really matter who was in the band—and it was always just there.

"And since I have a deep *love* of the mystical, this appealed to me, and so I said, 'Well, this might really be the band for me' because they *are* mystical and they play wonderful rock'n'roll and there's another lady so I'll have a pal.

"Not witchery. Not occult. Not turning into toads or anything like that. Just a *freedom* to be mystical."

It's the right of every human being . . .

"Because I *am* mystical, with or without Fleetwood Mac or Lindsey, and that's just *me*. And it's important for me to be free to do that. I'm a

Gemini: a Gemini has two very opposite personalities. I have the moving furniture, cleaning-up-the-room-quickly side and the cream-coloured chiffon personality.

"I majored in speech communication at college—and psychology—and it all seems to work. I am a communicator. I love to talk—as you can see—and I love to make people understand, and listen to them and understand."

A lot of good journalists are Geminis. . . .

"When I stop doing this I want to be a writer. I'm writing a book. I have a typewriter set up in there: a whole album and all the last tour are all typed up."

There has, of course, been talk for some time about the possibility of Stevie quitting Fleetwood Mac to make a solo album and film based on her 'Rhiannon' song on 'Fleetwood Mac', and she is said to have been made a number of highly lucrative offers. When I'd spoken to Fleetwood he dismissed the reports as nonsense with "Both Stevie *and* Christine definitely are going to make solo albums. I want to make one as well—in Africa. But if we can't do that without having to split the band up, then it's a bit of a pity."

Nicks is equally scathing, claiming not to know where such reports come from: "I don't talk about it. If someone's saying these things, they're not coming from me.

"But the legend of the birds of Rhiannon is something that's incredible. It's just about a lady who's a goddess of steeds and a maker of birds. And her birds are three—a gold one, a green one and a white one. Those birds are able to take away pain: there's a song that they sing and when the song happens and you're in trouble the birds come on in and you just go to sleep and when you wake up it's alright. They're like an incredible pain pill . . ."

Maybe Rhiannon's a brand name for morphine. But is that legend in something like *The Mabinogion?*

"That's *exactly* what it is," trills Stevie breathlessly, "it's an incredible thing, an incredible thing. I love it. And the 'Rhiannon' song is the song of Rhiannon. Without the words it's just the song of the birds of Rhiannon . . . And birds seem to surround me a lot now. It's very strange and very pretty and very wonderful. It's just *what it is now for* Rhiannon, And she's very good, so it's alright; she keeps us.

"She is as much mine as I want. There are many connections. The last woman that wrote about her is a lady whose name is Evangeline Walton who lives in Arizona and who must be about a hundred years old. Or at least 80 or 90. She started her work on Rhiannon in 1934 and finished in 1974. And I wrote 'Rhiannon' in October of 1974 when she'd finished.

"She's a tiny old lady with intense"—Stevie likes the word "intense"; she often uses it at inappropriate moments—"grey hair. She never married. She lives in a tiny little house in Arizona which is all pink satin. Very much like me. She's very intelligent."

Ah, if there were any of it around I'd suggest Stevie had been smoking too much dope. Talking of which, though, it is true that if all this were pouring out of the mouth of a Jamaican dread I'd be much more prepared to go along with it. As it is, though, Stevie's (un)enlightenment seems very much a product of the Guru Of The Month Club.

Anyway, I attempt to relate all this to possibilities of apocalypse and F Mac's living in Los Angeles. Before I can really formulate what I'm saying, though, Stevie's glugging the old brandy down and into a serious bit of communicating: "The most advanced city that can disappear the quickest . . . I just moved to the beach, to a place on the sand. I would never live there before, because I just thought, 'This is going to go so quick'. And then I thought, 'Well, maybe it'd be better to go quickly in the white sand and the clear water than to be up in Hollywood with all the people that were looting your house'.

"Maybe I'd rather just float out anyway. So I moved."

America, of course, I point out to Stevie, is a Gemini country—Which is why there are such extremes in it . . .

Stevie nods knowingly: "Very hardcore and very spiritual. And I do love the sunsets and the beautiful palm trees, but I also want to make millions of dollars.

"With all that's been going," she free-associates, "in the world of late I have to admit to myself that for the first time in my life I have felt a little bit of fear about the world. And *my* world has *always* been *wonderful* . . .

"I have a friend from England who walked in and said, 'Well, England has declared they're on your side if something happens over this Iran thing'. And I'm going to myself, 'Well, I suppose that's good as I have so many wonderful English friends'.

"But the fact is that I didn't really want to hear that anyway, and it scares me. It's very difficult for us because we've never been through anything like this—we just see it in movies. I've been watching it on TV noon and night. On all the news programmes they have these flashes: 'America Held Hostage—Day 42'. But change the subject, because I really don't know anything more about it, except that it makes me nervous."

Well, all I know is that the Shah is an evil figure . . .

"What is he doing here???? Especially what is he doing at a Marine airforce base. *Oh God!* Ship him out. Take him to Bora-Bora. Get him a great hotel. I have no death wish for anyone, but *get this person out of here!* He must have no honour, or else he'd go straight back there, take a poisoned pill five minutes before he got off the plane, say 'I hate all of you and death to you' and walk off the plane and die."

Real neat, Stevie.

"That's what I would do if I were him! I would say, okay, cue it, I'm taking my pill and going off on my little cloud. *But I'm not going to do this to America!*"

"Break out the Kool-Aid!"

"He's going to die anyway. He's old, The Ayatollah might as well paint on a little moustache. He could be the Ayatollah Hitler! This man is crazy. He's not thinking about those people. He's thinking about himself! He's on some high power-trip!"

But what if it's not really quite like we're being told it is, Stevie?

"He could start an *intense* religious war. If he says 'I will destroy you because you are impure', then that is a religious war. And we say 'We will destroy you in five minutes, Mr Shithead, with your beard and your robe and your stupid books on how we should live!'. A weirdo with a white beard looking like Rasputin who should've been born 50,000 years ago has no business being here now. He's a total space cadet. And we should send him to Mars. Tomorrow.

"I think we should kidnap the Ayatollah, cut off his beard, put him in a spacesuit, and send him to Mars."

I'm sure the CIA already have that planned . . .

"I think in America everyone is very *bummed*. I think it is drawing the country together in a way I've never seen before. I think everyone is much closer. But I am angry. I think those people are unfair and unkind to do this to anyone. I think it's *uncool* and not acceptable."

But in that light do you think that your fellow Americans are giving more serious scrutiny to such matters as the CIA having killed Allende in Chile?

"I don't know anything about that. I couldn't even comment. I should know something about it."

Phewwwwww . . . Oh dear.

"Anyway," Stevie fetches some more brandy for herself and me and resurrects the situation, "I had a wonderful time tonight. I think San Francisco is so special—the place from which both Lindsey and myself came. There's something very magic about this place—for me, anyway. I burst into tears at the beginning of 'Landslide'. I had a lot of trouble getting through that song, because the Coffee Plant where Lindsey and I recorded everything to get us our first deal is about five blocks from the Cow Palace.

"And when Lindsey dedicated 'Save Me A Place' to his mother I thought 'Well, somebody has to remember his father, because he was so strong behind us'. And when I walked out there and said 'This is for Lindsey's father who should be here; I just went '*BI-e-e-e-e-c-c-c-c-chhhhhhhh*'. You know how it is when you start to cry and there's nothing you can do to stop it. And I just couldn't do it. But at least I felt it was important for Buck that I remember he was a mainstay in the creativity and careers of Lindsey Buckingham and Stevie Nicks. Without him it wouldn't have happened."

AS Currie Grant, the F Mac lighting engineer, who I believe has been involved with both Christine and Stevie in the past, enters the room looking for a drink, Stevie starts to talk about the new F Mac 'Sara' single, her own composition: "The editing was cool. Any shorter than that and I'd have said, 'Forget it'. But they all know that this song is the pride and joy of my heart . . .

"I like 'Sister Of The Moon' very much, but that was written about three years ago and it was very much myself to myself when I thought that I was gonna die, because I didn't understand rock'n'roll or touring and I thought I might collapse. Now I know I'm not collapsing for anybody, because I'm much too strong for that. But at that point I wasn't sure."

Does touring do you in?

"Oh, the first tour we did did. We left on September 9 and came back on December 22. We were doing four gigs in a row, one day off. No limousines. We started the 'Fleetwood Mac' album in February of 1975. We joined the band on New Year's Eve, 1974. The album took three months. We went out for a few gigs in the summer which was no big deal. But then we went out on September 9th, which was going into winter. It started out cold and it finished cold. We just *never* stopped. But we played *everywhere*. We didn't exactly play teen clubs, but we might as well have."

Currie: "Almost three quarters of the way through that tour was when the album took off."

Stevie: "We *sold* that album. We kicked that album in the ass . . . But Fleetwood Mac knew what was going on. Christine slept on amps in the backs of trucks. I hadn't a clue! But I decided I was going to make it alright. There was no one going to say 'She can't cope. She should give it up'. But no one else can do that but yourself. No one else can say 'I don't want to go shopping. I don't want to go out to dinner. I don't want another drink'.

"Or at least if I stay up and rave all night I'm going to be in bed by six or seven, and, if I have to knock myself on the head so I can sleep all day and sing that night, then I will. In fact, I stay up all night every night. But I sleep in the day and don't do anything else. I haven't been shopping one time in 31 gigs. It's more important to me for people to say 'She's really holding up. She's good' than 'She has a terrific new wardrobe'."

Mitch the tour manager lumbers into the room. He is slightly drunk. He slumps down on the floor and begins talking to Stevie: "I've heard the tales of Nicks and Buckingham when they were playing their dues. He told me about the time he'd do supermarkets."

"Listen, I'll show," Stevie stands up and paces out a small area, "Here's our little sitting-room, right? Here's Lindsey and about eleven other degenerates on the ground smoking. And I am cleaning the house of our producer Keith Olsen for bread, right? This is 1971 in LA. I come walking in with my big Hoover vacuum-cleaner, my Ajax, my toilet-brush, my cleaning shoes on. And Lindsey has managed to have some idiot send him eleven ounces of opiated hash.

"Anyway, Lindsey and all his friends—Warren Zevon, right?—are in a circle. They smoked hash for a month, and I don't smoke because of my voice. And when you don't smoke there's something that makes you really dislike other people smoking. I'd come in every day and have to step over these bodies. Me, I've just been cleaning. I'm tired. And I'm pickin' up their legs and cleaning under them and emptying out the ashtrays.

"And a month later all these guys are going 'I don't know why I don't feel very good', and I'm going *You wanna know why you don't feel very good? I'll tell you why—because you've done nothing else for weeks but lie on the floor and smoke and take my money'.* I was making 50 dollars a week cleaning for the guy who did our albums."

Mitch: "I heard a story from Lindsey about you bunch doing bogus cheques in steak houses."

Stevie: "Lindsey and his friend Tom used to go into every coffee shop in Hollywood and write hot cheques and never go back again . . . The Copper Penny, Big Boy's . . ."

Mitch: "Boy, you two really fell into the American Dream, huh?"

Stevie: "Yeah, We actually fell into it out of nowhere. We were just nowhere."

The next night after the show I again find myself locked away in the middle dressing-room with the urinals and the toilet bowls and Lindsey Buckingham.

Brought up in Palo Alto, some 30 miles to the south of San Francisco, Buckingham was turned on to rock'n'roll in the shape of Elvis, Buddy Holly, Chuck Berry and Eddie Cochran by his elder brother. He started playing guitar when he was seven.

Pausing frequently for breath he's so shattered—obviously the oxygen tank doesn't work for him—he talks about the new, stronger role he has on 'Tusk': "It's scary. What I'm doing now is . . . a lot of the way my songs turned out was just due to the basic approach.

"When we started the album we had a meeting over at Mick's house and I said that I had to get some sort of machine into my house to have an alternative to the studio; the trappings and technology of the studio are so great that the blocks between the inception of an idea and the final thing you get on tape are so many that it just becomes very frustrating.

"That was why my songs turned out the way they did: because of the belief in a different approach. For me it wasn't really a question of changing tastes, but of following through on something I'd believed in a lot for a long time and hadn't had a means of manifesting. For a number of years it's been a process of having to sacrifice certain parts say, for example, to give to Stevie to contribute to her music. It's always been a process of being in the back without . . . I mean, making the choice of joining Fleetwood Mac was a very strange decision. It's been a very human sort of journey. I'm sure I'm not making a whole load of sense," he blusters very defensively and totally unnecessarily as he's making perfect sense, "it's pretty late in the evening to be talking about this."

Lindsey slumps back vacant-eyed into his chair. Thinking it may vibe him up, I suggest we smoke a joint. Goddamn! I should've remembered what Stevie told me about Lindsey being slumped out across their LA living-room floor . . .

A few tokes and he's nodded out! (So am I.) We're carried to the limo, and the in-depth profile of Lindsey Buckingham will just have to wait.

The appropriate sort of ending: A few days after I return to England I hear news of Peter Green. He's just been fined in court for curb-crawling in some Western London suburb like Osterley. Perhaps he was trying to pull women on their way back from Tupperware parties.

FLEETWOOD MAC'S LINDSEY BUCKINGHAM TURNS ANOTHER CORNER

Blair Jackson | January 30, 1981 | *BAM* (US)

The December 1980 release of *Live* occasioned this interview with Lindsey Buckingham. As well as discussion of the band's first in-concert album and whether Buckingham would ever record a solo LP, there is much talk about *Tusk*. The inquests were still ongoing as regards a very controversial album.

IT ONLY *SEEMS* LIKE Fleetwood Mac has been making hit records forever. In fact, it was just five years ago that the one-time English blues band, rejuvenated by the addition of Californians Lindsey Buckingham and Stevie Nicks, virtually took over American radio with the smash album *Fleetwood Mac,* which yielded the hit singles "Rhiannon," "Say You Love Me," "Over My Head" and "Monday Morning." And as astonishing as that album's success was, no one could have been prepared for what happened when the group's next LP, *Rumours,* came out in 1977. Behind the strength of hits like "Second Hand News," "Dreams," "Go Your Own Way" and "Don't Stop," *Rumours* became the top selling album in the history of pop music, eclipsing works by The Beatles and other legendary chartbusters. Fleetwood Mac was the most popular band in the world.

The secret was chemistry. The band offered a combination of five very distinctive individuals whose talents seemed to lock into place like the gears of a machine. The rhythm section, consisting of founding group members John McVie on bass and Mick Fleetwood on drums, could play with the power of a heavy metal band or the finesse of a light combo. Vocalist/keyboardist Christine McVie brought a dark melodicism still based a little in blues to her work with the band. Stevie Nicks, with her classic good looks, breathy voice and fairytale princess stage demeanor, added a deeply romantic feel to the group's sound. And finally, there was Lindsey Buckingham, the man who made the machine roll. Aside from writing many of the group's catchiest and most commercial songs—"Monday Morning," "Go Your Own Way," "Second Hand News," "Never Going Back Again"—he played all the guitars on the albums, mixing acoustic and electric axes in fingerpicking and conventional rock stylings; did most of the vocal arrangements, which became Fleetwood Mac's trademark; and had a heavy hand in the production of *Rumours*. And as his subsequent production work with John Stewart on *Bombs Away Dream Babies* and Walter Egan's *Fundamental Roll* showed, the Fleetwood Mac "sound" derived largely from Buckingham's ideas about mixing and instrumental layering.

But Buckingham's genius really came to the fore with the release of *Tusk* in late '79. A double record set of incredible depth and scope, it was anything but the predictable follow-up to *Rumours,* and that was mainly because of Buckingham's eccentric, sometimes downright bizarre compositions. The tone of the entire album was set by Buckingham's title tune, which, much to everyone's surprise, was a *bona fide* hit single like its predecessors on *Rumours* and *Fleetwood Mac.* On top of a truly strange drum beat, an almost incantatory vocal emerged from a cacophony of odd noises. The song built to a fever pitch as the USC marching band punctuated the song's second half, and Mick Fleetwood unleashed a maniacal, out-of-control drum break. Peculiar stuff, to be sure.

Other Buckingham songs were equally unusual, from the rowdy, insistent "What Makes You Think You're the One" to the quirky "Not That Funny," to the mad rockabilly drive of "The Ledge" and "That's Enough For Me," to the ethereal, quiet beauty of "Walk a Thin Line" and "That's All For Everyone." Buckingham was not only challenging our preconceptions of Fleetwood Mac, but of pop music itself, by throwing established "rules" about song structure and mixing out the window.

It was a brilliantly conceived and executed experiment, though not surprisingly, *Tusk* did not fare nearly as well as *Fleetwood Mac* and *Rumours* in terms of sales. Buckingham took a lot of heat for the album's relative "failure" (though four million copies of an expensive—some say "overpriced"—double album is really the equivalent of eight million records sold, not bad by any standards), but he will undoubtedly have the last laugh. *Tusk* is not going to sound dated in five or ten years, and I would be willing to bet that a lot more people will slowly be convinced of the album's greatness than will forget all about it.

IN EARLY DECEMBER, Fleetwood Mac released its first live album since Buckingham and Nicks joined the group. And though its pre-Christmas sales were not up to Warner Bros.' expectations for the two-disc set, it has been selling briskly since the new year began and is getting more airplay than *Tusk* ever got. The reason? The "hits" are all there—"Rhiannon," "Dreams," "Say You Love Me," "Go Your Own Way," "Don't Stop," and the list goes on. But the record isn't just note-for-note copies of the album versions. Far from it. This band rocks, propelled by the always dynamic rhythm section and Buckingham's searing guitar leads. Once again, it is Buckingham who takes the record into the stratosphere as he rocks Nicks' "Rhiannon" into high gear with a blistering lead at the song's conclusion, turns "I'm So Afraid" into a blues *tour de force* with a screeching lead reminiscent of Neil Young's "Like A Hurricane," and transforms "Not That Funny" into a bopping, shaking, and, ultimately, *exploding* rocker. "Monday Morning" is the perfect album opener, all kineticism and great hooks, and "Don't Let Me Down Again," an incendiary rock and roll song with definite rockabilly leanings (originally on the album Buckingham made with Stevie Nicks before the pair joined Fleetwood Mac), demonstrates the exceptional songwriting tools he brought to the band. His version of "Never Going Back Again," performed solo, backing himself up with acoustic guitar, is both sensitive and charming, and "Go Your Own Way" comes across as the show-stopper it was throughout the 1980 tour.

There are also three new songs on the album, which were performed live without an audience at the Santa Monica Civic. All three sound like potential hit songs—Nicks' "Fireflies," which is as good as any of her better-known compositions; McVie's lovely "One More Night"; and Buckingham's new contribution, Brian Wilson's "The Farmer's Daughter," which originally appeared on the Beach Boys' second album, *Surfin' USA*. "The Farmer's Daughter" showcases the band's harmonies at their very best; it is an inspired choice for the record. It is also a disarming way to end the album. Most live albums save the final spot for some intense rock rave-up, but "The Farmer's Daughter" rolls along like a small alpine brook, purposeful but beautifully peaceful. And instead of a sonic wash of cheers at its conclusion, a single person clapping is the last sound heard.

Anyone who attended one of the tour dates from which these performances were culled knows that Buckingham has emerged as the clear onstage leader of the band. During his frequent guitar solos, he would often position himself at the lip of the stage, hunched over in intense concentration, and just *wail* on his Turner electric. I recall thinking that Buckingham *must* be a crazy man, not just because his solos were sometimes so furious that he always appeared to be on the verge of hurtling into the audience, but because after each song, after the stage lights had dimmed for an instant, I could see his eyes still rolling wildly, as if controlled by a puppeteer's hand. With the possible exception of Graham Parker and Bruce Springsteen, I have never seen a performer so wrapped up in every second of a show as Buckingham was during Fleetwood Mac's two-hour-plus show.

BUCKINGHAM HAS been involved with music for most of his life, taking up guitar at a fairly early age and always loving rock and roll and folk music. Growing up in Palo Alto, Lindsey had an older brother (later an Olympic swimmer) who turned him on to Sun Records rockabilly and the folk music of the Kingston Trio and others in the late '50s. Lindsey remembers loving Buddy Holly's music; to this day he thinks of Holly as one of his primary influences. Northern Californians may remember Fritz, a band Lindsey and his friend Stephanie (later Stevie) Nicks were members of for several years in the late '60s and early '70s, and which became quite popular on the South Bay steak & lobster circuit.

Buckingham and Nicks put out their lone solo album (*Buckingham/Nicks,* on Polydor) in the early '70s—and became stars in Birmingham, Alabama, of all places, as a result of the record's regional popularity. The album's producer, Keith Olsen, used tapes he made with the duo to pitch his own talents to Mick Fleetwood, and the drummer was impressed with both Olsen *and* Buckingham/Nicks. So much so, in fact, that when Bob Welch left Fleetwood Mac to start his own band, the Californians were enlisted to join the group and Olsen tagged to produce the first album by the new line-up. The rest, as the cliché goes, is history.

ON A SUNNY DAY IN early December, I had the opportunity to interview Buckingham in his ninth-floor room at the Santa Clara Marriott, where Buckingham and his girlfriend were staying for the Thanksgiving holidays. (Buckingham is still close to his family, who live in the South Bay area.) Though he was still battling the flu, Buckingham definitely had his wits about him as we talked for close to three hours. Intelligent, witty, and obviously perceptive, Buckingham in casual conversation struck me as a slightly mellowed version of the dynamo I had enjoyed onstage a few months earlier. Our talk began with a discussion of the new live album, which was scheduled to be released in just three days.

What sorts of feelings go through you the week before an album of yours comes out?
Not surprisingly, the feeling I have when a live album is coming out is a little different than when I've spent a year in the studio working on albums like *Rumours* or *Tusk.* You spend a lot of time with a record and it starts to feel like your baby. Though with a group, obviously, it's everyone's baby. With the live album, the feeling isn't quite as tangible because I really didn't spend much time in the studio. It was more a question of assembling things that we already had, rather than building an album up from scratch.

Also, I must say, I'm not really a big fan of live albums in general. How many have you heard that really turned you on? *Rock of Ages* [The Band's first live record], *Kingston Trio Live at the Hungry i, James Brown Live at the Apollo.* I don't know—there just haven't been many that grabbed me. A lot of groups have been putting out live albums recently and I would hate for someone to think that this is just another in the pack. I don't think it turned out that way. I'm really happy with it. I initially had some reservations about doing it, but now I'm glad we did.

What made this the right time to put it out, aside from the obvious sales potential of the Christmas buying season?
It sort of put a cap on the last five years of touring and recording, I think. On this tour we really came together as a band in ways that we hadn't before, and I feel that the versions of most of the songs we were playing were as good as any we'd done. I think Mick wanted us to go right into the studio to start work on the next studio record, but instead we're taking a break, probably until May, to relax a little, work on our own projects or whatever. It feels good to have a breather for a change. It'll allow us to be fresh when we start the next album.

So, in effect, the live album lets you buy a little time by keeping the group's name out there while you rest.
That's not the main reason we did it, certainly, but yeah, it does do that. We need the time off, because as great as it is to play live for people and to feel the band getting stronger on the road, it's not a situation that allows you to grow, because of the repetition in it. It's not the same as being in the studio and being confronted with new challenges all the time that allow you to expand your horizons.

I'll be interested to see how people react to the album. Things that we take for granted as performers—like the differences between the live versions and studio versions—are things that a lot of people appreciate most about the group. That's something I don't even think about, because I can see the changes we have to make to adapt a song to live performance, and I live with the changes that we make as a song evolves onstage. A song like "Not that Funny" is very different live than on *Tusk,* and that may surprise some people. I've been able to see the song grow. A lot of the songs are quite different live; others are fairly close [to] the studio versions.

The record has a much looser feel than recent live albums by other top bands like the Eagles and Supertramp.
Well, we play a lot looser than a lot of bands. That comes as a shock to some people who like our records because, in general, those are pretty well crafted. But playing onstage is completely different than playing in the studio. Also, the looseness is something that's developed as we've become more comfortable with each other as musicians over the years. Spreading out, giving each other more room has been sort of a natural progression for us. And that's something, because we're talking about a band of five individuals who have huge egos in one sense or another. It's not one of those groups where one person dominates the whole thing, so we have to all give a little, which is healthy.

By the end of the tour—by the Hollywood Bowl shows—I think we were playing like a really tight unit. The shows got more rock and roll as we went along. But then I felt that *Tusk* was very rock and roll, and that's the *opposite* of what some people thought, because in one respect it wasn't as intense performance-wise, but it was *more* intense attitude-wise.

Part of your craft in making records has been layering different guitar styles by using overdubs. Is it frustrating that you can't really re-create the subtleties of your arrangements live?
It changes the way I play, of course. It's been a lesson in adaptability. Being the only guitarist puts a lot of pressure on me because I feel like I can't leave any holes. But I've never really played with another guitarist, so I'm not really too sure of what I'm missing. I'd like to try it sometimes. It might help me relax a little bit.

Obviously you can't *reproduce* "Say You Love Me," which has a twelve-string and all those overdubs on it, so you try something *different* and hope for the best.

How did you happen to choose "Farmer's Daughter" for the album?
I've always been a Brian Wilson fan, and so much of what he's done has either gone over people's heads or been ignored for one reason or another. A lot of people stopped buying Beach Boys records when Brian stopped writing about surfing, and that's a shame. There are a lot of great Brian songs that were never hits. "Farmer's Daughter" probably *could've* been a successful single for them if they'd released it. I think "Surfin' USA" was the only real hit from that album. But I've loved "Farmer's Daughter." It's obscure enough and contemporary enough that I thought it would be good for us to cover. I think it would be a great single.

You've mentioned that Brian was one of your biggest inspirations. Is that mainly in terms of songwriting, production . . . ?
Not really in terms of production much, though I like what he did with the Beach Boys stuff. I admire him most as a melodic writer, an arranger, and a vocal orchestrator. When people think of Brian they think of "Little Deuce Coupe" and "I Get Around" which *are* great songs, but there's also "Wind Chimes" [a bizarre tune on the largely psychedelic *Smiley Smile*] and all those other obscure but beautiful pieces of work. "Wind Chimes" is a classic. No one has done anything like it since. Even a lot of his later work stands up real well. *Beach Boys Love You* had great songs on it—great tunes with great arrangements—but it just sailed over the heads of everyone and didn't sell as a result.

When Fleetwood Mac *and* Rumours *came out, almost every song got airplay on AM, FM or both. I imagine the live album will also do well in that respect because so many of the group's hits are on it. Yet when* Tusk *was released, much of the album was totally ignored by radio. How much of that do you think is due to changes in radio, and how much to changes in the music itself?*
It was probably a little of both. There was some obscure stuff on *Tusk,* though obviously I thought it was pretty good. But radio has tightened up. The industry as a whole has tightened up. Take someone like John Stewart, who had a very successful album [produced by Buckingham] with two hit singles on it. He put out a follow-up

album [*Dream Babies Go Hollywood*] that didn't do as well and suddenly RSO drops him. I don't think it would be like that at every label, but I think it's an indication of where the industry is right now. The same is true of radio. The stations attracting the broadest audiences are going to be able to charge the most for their advertising, which is the name of the game. To attract those broad audiences, the stations are going to play songs that are real noticeable, accessible stuff. There's no mystery about it.

Tusk required more attention and a slightly different orientation to get into some of it, particularly my songs. Critically, it did very well for the most part. When people didn't like it, the criticism usually seemed to be along the lines of "How *dare* they put out an album so different than *Rumours*?" I don't think people were expecting an album like *Tusk* from us at that point, and the shock probably disturbed a lot of people. Some people who loved *Rumours* didn't know what to make of it and ended up feeling disgusted about it. But on the other hand, some people who thought *Rumours* was a little too middle-of-the-road liked *Tusk* a lot because it was more adventurous. I'm still very proud of it.

Several critics compared the record to The Beatles' "White Album."
I was real happy about that. Any comparison to The Beatles is a compliment in my book.

Actually, though, I felt some of that comparison was negative, because it implied—just as similar criticism of the "White Album" implied—that on Tusk *we weren't hearing much of Fleetwood Mac, but rather Lindsey Buckingham fronting a band for his songs, Stevie Nicks fronting a band for hers, and so on.*
I think the "White Album" is one of the most exciting and divergent albums The Beatles ever made. By *far. Revolver is* probably one of their best albums in most people's opinions, but even then it was Paul doing Paul's music and John doing John's with support from the others. They'd been doing that since *Rubber Soul,* yet no one criticized those albums for that.

I'm not sure it's valid to criticize something because on one record the approach is individualistic and on another it's collective. The question is, "What is the music giving off? Is it any good?" To criticize *Tusk* for that is silly. I think there are valid criticisms of *Tusk,* but that's not one of them.

What are, then?
Well, in terms of songwriting, there are levels that *Rumours* succeeded on that *Tusk* didn't, and vice versa. In the case of *Tusk,* I think it's important to think about some of the things we *didn't* do. We didn't harmonize very much, which was one of *Rumours'* strong points. A lot of the songs didn't use full drums, and the arrangements as a whole were a lot airier—there was more space. There were some odd combinations of instruments and sounds.

If you look at a song as something that should be crafted in a certain way—the design of it, the way the elements are combined together in a fashion to make them accessible, to make them "hits"—then we did not succeed on that level on *Tusk,* and on *Rumours* we did. *Tusk* was more fragmentary, but I don't look at that as a negative thing. I think it's good because if you turn on the radio, everyone is using the same tired formulas for songwriting and recording.

It seemed to me that on Tusk *you were trying to shake up people's preconceptions about mixing, both in the way you presented vocals, like on "Last Call for Everyone" and "Walk A Thin Line," and the way you put instruments together. A song like "The Ledge" sounds like it's just a drum and two fuzzed basses. The instrumental balance isn't what you'd expect on a conventional pop song.*
That's right. On "The Ledge" it's not two basses, though. It's a bass and a guitar that has been tuned down half an octave. And that is just a snare. I did that song at my house. It sounds to me like it was put in a cement mixer and almost spat out. It's actually one of my favorites on the album because it goes by so quickly that it almost sounds rushed, but if you try to get inside it, there's a lot there. People are expecting to hear something else and it catches them off guard.

That's what I mean. By this stage in the game, there's an "accepted" way of mixing drums and bass and guitars so that the relationship between them—their relative value in a song's mix—is fairly regular from track to track, even group to group.

That sickens me! I hate turning on the radio and being able to guess what an entire song is going to sound like in the first five seconds. I don't mean there aren't good songs on the radio—there are—but don't you get tired of hearing that same approach over and over again?

So, yes, part of the idea of *Tusk* was to shake people up and make them *think*. What is so weird about wanting to do something slightly off to the right or to the left of what people expect? I think it makes a lot of sense.

It's interesting, too, because when we go back into the studio to make our next album people aren't going to know what to expect. I like that. We're now in the position where we can really make something we believe in instead of what the public expects us to make. You should have a respect for your audience and appreciate their appreciation of you, but you cannot dictate your own taste through them, see yourself through their eyes, and you shouldn't be boxed into a format simply out of fear of not selling records.

In an interview you did with New Musical Express, *you complained that some people viewed* Tusk *as a commercial failure, even though it sold more than four million copies worldwide.*

I remember someone saying, "God, you must be scared shitless!" before we even started doing *Tusk*. "How are you going to follow up *Rumours*?" Well, maybe *Tusk* was the best way to do it. We couldn't go in and make *Rumours II* to try to sell another 16 million records. I'm sure Warner Bros. was disappointed with the sales of *Tusk*. I remember reading that when *Tusk* came out and wasn't the big hit that everyone expected that the people at Warner Bros. could see their Christmas bonuses flying out the window. [Laughs] That's how they were thinking about it, and they were probably right. They hear this artsy-craftsy piece of work and they say [rolling his eyes], "Oh my God, here we go!" I'm sure they expected it would sell more. We all expected it to sell more. Not 16 million, certainly, but a couple of million more wouldn't have hurt. [Laughs]

How could you have expected it to sell much more if you knew all along that the LP was a great departure and not what people necessarily wanted to hear from the group?

I expected people to be more open-minded about it, I guess. But I'm looking at it from the artist's standpoint, where it's a lot easier to move ahead and *crave* different things. The listening audience as a whole is probably not like that. Some feel that desire to stretch, but others have such a light surface appreciation that they're ready for more *Rumours* and really aren't the least bit interested in anything new. Maybe some of them just like what they hear on the radio and don't even know who's in the group or what the names of the songs are. You and I are not typical music listeners. Most people don't look at music in terms of how it is innovative or how it builds upon or changes the tradition or whatever. Most people really don't care about any of that. They just want to hear a good song. But I felt that more people would be appreciative of something that, to me, sounded very fresh and unusual.

Even before Rumours *really clicked, I remember reading that the group was planning a double LP. How much of* Tusk *was mapped out at that point, and how much was, as you've sort of indicated, a reaction against doing the same old thing?*

It's hard to separate the two. We wanted to do the double album, but I'm not sure at that point we knew what it would sound like. Speaking just for myself, it was important for me to depart and express a certain amount of individualism both as a songwriter and someone who casts a certain amount of color on the others' songs. But we didn't sit down and say, "Hey, let's make a strange album." The evolution of the tone of the album presented itself gradually after we'd started making it.

What was the actual recording like? I get the feeling that it was done under all sorts of different circumstances.

It was. A few of the songs I just did at my house. But in general, it wasn't *that* different than *Rumours.* We cut tracks, overdubbed some parts, put on the vocals. The departure, I guess, is that we had a 24-track machine in my house that I was using to experiment with different sounds and ideas. That approach, if used properly, can be really valid, I think. It becomes much more intimate. It's more like a painter because you can respond to your intuitions, take an idea and just go with it. Sometimes it's hard to stop. It gets very, very exciting.

Because the way the studios are now, you get a couple of engineers who work a certain way and you end up working in a fairly set format. They say a chain is only as strong as its weakest link. Well, a lot of times you'll get an engineer who can't respond to what you do on all levels and it holds you back. There's a blockage of energy going from step A to step B.

It's fun working alone. I have about fourteen songs right now that I've done varying amounts of work on. I don't know—we may all do solo albums in the next six months. Mick signed something with Warner Bros. to go over to Africa and record African drums. He's real excited about that. Stevie's planning a record. It's good that we have some time to think about these things. That's new for us.

A lot of the material I was working on at the end of *Tusk* and what I've done recently is more commercial, probably, than most of *Tusk*, but it's still experimental in some ways. I've learned more about the mathematics of songwriting—how to fit pieces together, line length, timing chords and melodies. It gets pretty complex.

Are you finding, though, that people have theories on what is "correct" that don't jive with your own?

I don't talk to people about what is "correct." I think if you're taught music in a college or something, there is definitely a theory of what is correct that you can learn from. But I've known a lot of people who *lost* a lot by studying it too much. When Stevie and I were in this band Fritz years ago, the organist used to write most of the music. When he was a sophomore in high school he was writing some great tunes. Since the band broke up, he went to college and got a music degree. I was with him recently and his writing is worse now than it was then! For all his knowledge, his writing is very stiff. His training doesn't allow for any creativity. Ideally, music education should teach you about possibilities, rather than formulas.

Are there specific groups or sounds that have influenced you recently?
Your stuff on Tusk *and the live album seems slightly new wave in spirit.*
I really wasn't listening to new wave that much, but I think it did have an effect. All the new wave stuff has been real healthy, I think. So much of it accomplished what its makers set out to do—give people a kick in the ass. It was influential to me in that it made it more tangible for me to proceed with experimentation itself. It wasn't a question of hearing a good song and then trying to emulate it. It instilled a sense of courageousness in me and solidified a lot of the ideas I had about my music.

Has the band been totally sympathetic to your desire to explore new directions?
It seemed so while we were making *Tusk*. I would be in the studio and do something and they'd say they liked it, or I'd come in after working on a song for four or five days and they'd never heard it, and they'd react well. In retrospect, though, I wonder how they felt about some of my stuff. Maybe if the album had sold more they'd be happier. [Laughs] That kind of worries me a little bit.

Did you see that article in *Us* that quoted Stevie as saying that doing the album was like being held hostage in Iran with Lindsey as the Ayatollah? [Laughs] That wasn't the feeling there at all! I mean, she wasn't even there most of the time. She'd come in to do her song once a week and that would be it. Hostage? [Laughs]

Mick has said since then that maybe I was getting too carried away with some of my music. It's hard for me to look at it that way. It's weird because everyone was very supportive at the time.

Why is everyone dumping on you?
Because I was the one who departed from the previously established Fleetwood Mac format. There already seems to be a little pressure to return more to that sound. I imagine, without really knowing, that our next album will represent a healthy compromise between the two approaches. We turned a corner with *Tusk* and now we'll turn another corner using what we learned there. It's still too early to tell.

This is sort of trivial, I guess, but I've always wondered about the background cacophony on the song "Tusk." Is that a tape loop of some sort?

The drum track is a tape loop, about a 20-foot section of tape. The drum track originally was part of another song which was a lot slower. We sped the drum track up in a VSO, cut it at a certain point, and edited it into itself so we had this giant loop. Then, what we had to do was run it from one reel through the heads. But somebody had to go out across the room with something that would act like a spool to keep the loop moving steadily while we recorded it onto another machine. That was one track of "Tusk."

The section you're talking about was a live recording of the noise at Dodger Stadium when we recorded the USC Band for the horn part. If you listen closely, you can hear someone saying something like, "How are the tenors?" It's a combination of about twelve people all talking together way in the background, and then repeated over and over so it comes out as this weird noise.

That wasn't the first time you'd worked that way, was it? I thought "The Chain" was also assembled originally out of various bits and pieces.

I think anyone who creates will tell you it's very difficult to work completely linearly to get what you're after. Hitchcock, I gather, worked like that. He would totally preconceive every scene and then try to get it as close as he could to that. I do that, too, in some ways. You hear something in your head and you try to get as close as you can. At the same time, the more you work with music—or art, for that matter—the more you learn that you have to let the work lead you to a certain extent. It has to be give and take. You can't always be exerting your own will over a painting or a piece of music because you have to follow your own impulses and there are always going to be a certain number of unknowns that you'll have to deal with. I'm not against planning, by any means. I think you should go into a project with as many specific ideas as possible. I just don't like to close myself off to other possibilities.

How much have Mick and John affected your ideas about rhythm? For instance, do you think you would be working as much with irregular rhythms if you were in a different band?
John and Mick have affected me *a lot* in the past six years. Mick has an exquisite sense of rhythm. He has no idea what he's doing, technically. But he's been playing since he was ten and his drumming is totally instinctive by this point. He's unique. There's a famous story about the little cowbell break in "Oh Well." Mick did that real off the cuff and then when he tried to repeat it, he couldn't do it! [Laughs] It took him a week of rehearsals to *learn* what he'd done in an instant.

When Stevie and I joined the band our approach to music was much more classical in terms of parts fitting together and being preordained. That's not how Fleetwood Mac works. It's much more spontaneous. It's more like the Stones, in the sense that Charlie Watts is not really a technician, but he creates feelings and has an innate ability to find the right rhythm for a situation. Mick's like that.

But would it be your idea or Mick's for, say, the sort of counter-rhythm on a song like "Go Your Own Way"?
That was my idea, but the point is, Mick couldn't *do* the beat I wanted for the song, so he did it his way. He got the general idea. A lot of my contribution to the band collectively has been as an arranger and producer.

Rumours is *the largest selling pop album in history. Does that make you feel strange?*
Not really. I think we sort of took it for granted at the time. "Oh it's Number One again this week . . ." [Laughs]

How can you be blasé about it?
Because as exciting as it was, it was the music that was most important to me. The phenomenon of it selling 16 million copies far outweighed how strong the music was in my opinion, so you have to keep it all in perspective. It's not like *Rumours* was "the best album ever made" because it sold the most copies. It did well for a lot of different reasons, many, I'm sure, that had little or nothing to do with the music. If I'm going

to believe it sold so well because it was so great, how am I supposed to interpret *Tusk* selling so many fewer copies? I like *Tusk* better. I just can't take it too seriously. Sales are not necessarily indicative of quality.

Did you ever feel that your success was affecting you negatively? Did it give you a swelled head?
Not yet! [Laughs] No, I never even put up any of my gold records. If you're a good craftsman, a good actor, a good *anything,* you know you can be better and that there's always another goal to shoot for. It seems more natural for me to keep striving, to keep learning, than to bask in the sunshine of external success.

When I look at bands like the Doobie Brothers and the Beach Boys and some of the other top groups, I can almost picture the "Incorporated" tag next to their names. How has as big an entity as Fleetwood Mac managed to avoid the appearance of being another corporate monolith?
That's an interesting question. I'm too close to it to give you a good answer. Part of it might have to do with the whole aura surrounding the *Rumours* album, which was somewhat of an expose on all our personal lives. That might have added a human touch to the band that still remains. Showing some of ourselves in a very honest and succinct way might have affected the way people view the group as a whole.

Another reason might be that we've had our drummer as our manager and never had an Irving Azoff type doing it. That's caused problems, too, because it's hard to be a player and a manager at the same time, but it might have kept us all a little more down to earth.

You've always been portrayed as a fairly private and introspective sort. How did it feel to have your personal life and your relationships splashed across the pages of half the magazines in America when Rumours *became such a big hit?*
I don't feel as though it happened to me that much. The "sensationalists," if that's what you want to call them, were always more interested in Stevie and Christine. It's only fairly recently that writers have begun to pick up on my energy, and so far it's been great. There hasn't been

much discussion of things other than my music. I've always been in the background more in terms of publicity or image or whatever. That's good. I have all the anonymity I want. I can walk about and nobody really bothers me.

Stevie can't, I imagine.
Stevie wouldn't really want to. She would always dress up as flamboyantly as possible when she went out, so she'd be noticed. She's a different kind of person than I am. People are appreciating me for the reasons I want to be appreciated for, and not for my chiffon gown. [Laughs]

What will determine whether you make your own album or not?
It just depends on how the songs turn out. If, as a collective group of songs, it's not something I'm *totally* happy with, I'm not going to put it out. I'm not in any particular rush to get "my solo album" out. It has to be done right or I won't do it.

Can you imagine what it will feel like to put out a record that is totally your baby?
I think it will be pretty nerve-racking. [Laughs] Because you can't hide behind anyone at that point. You're taking total responsibility.

That's something a lot of people who have gone solo miss. When Eric Clapton hangs out with Mick or us he's always saying, "God, I wish I was in a band again." That's because the burden is all on him. It's just not the same when, as a leader, you're paying people a certain amount each week to play with you. The balance of power is not the same, and it drains you. Bob Welch had a couple of successful solo albums, but now I think he misses being in a group where people will give you honest feedback, tell you when you've got your head up your ass. You need that thing when other people in a band have as much at stake as you do.

We could certainly all do solo albums, but that wouldn't be the death of Fleetwood Mac. There are still good creative ties and I think we all still enjoy—and need—the feedback we get from the group situation. I can't imagine not feeling that way anytime soon.

STEVIE

Fleetwood Mac's Siren Soars with Her First Solo Album, *Bella Donna*

Blair Jackson | September 11, 1981 | *BAM* (US)

In July 1981 Stevie Nicks released her debut solo LP, *Bella Donna*. Perhaps she'd had a premonition of how unproductive Fleetwood Mac was set to become: between 1968 and 1979, the band released twelve studio albums, one a double (a count that doesn't even include their two Chicago jam albums); by 2015 they had issued only a further five. She would have plenty more after-the-fact justification for inaugurating her extracurricular activities: the album was a critical and commercial success.

As would always be the case with solo-album promotional interviews, talk in this feature strayed naturally back and forth between solo work and Fleetwood Mac history and future plans. Here, Nicks denies she is bitter about her previous relationship with Buckingham, but in more than one place she seems to be politely sitting on seething indignation.

THE VIEW FROM THE living room of Stevie Nicks' Marina del Rey condominium is spectacular. As far as the eye can see there is nothing but an endless expanse of sand, ocean and sky. It is probably as close to a truly peaceful place as can be found in the Los Angeles area. Inside, the golden rays of a late afternoon sun cast a glow on the warm pinks and beiges that dominate the room. Two rooms away is the bustling nerve center of the household, where workers have been handling phone calls and a stream of interviewers awaiting an audience with the hottest-selling artist in rock and roll.

Actually, the word "audience" is terribly unfair, because it implies pretension, and Stevie Nicks doesn't have a pretentious bone in her body. Though she has been a platinum-selling artist for six years as a member of Fleetwood Mac, and her face has been steadily gracing the covers of magazines as long, the Stevie Nicks I interviewed for two and one-half hours recently seemed remarkably unaffected by success and candid almost to a fault.

Her first solo album, *Bella Donna,* is already a smash hit—it is sitting at Number One on *Billboard*'s chart as this is being written, and it looks like it will only be a week or two before "Stop Draggin' My Heart Around," the gutsy, rock single that she sings as a duet with the song's author, Tom Petty, also hits Number One. A new Fleetwood Mac album is due this fall, too, so it looks as though the airwaves will belong to Stevie Nicks for the next several months.

Nicks' rise to fame was a relatively quick one. She and Lindsey Buckingham moved to Los Angeles in the early '70s after several years as members of the once-popular Bay Area band Fritz. They cut an album as a duo (still available on Polygram) and then were asked to join Fleetwood Mac, which was struggling following the departure of Bob Welch. The first album the new five-piece Mac made, *Fleetwood Mac,* was an enormous hit, thanks largely to the presence of Nicks and Buckingham, whose songwriting and singing totally dominated the LP. "Rhiannon," a swirling Nicks tune about a Welsh witch, immediately established Nicks as one of the top women singer-songwriters in rock.

The follow-up to that album, *Rumours,* remains the best-selling rock album of all time, as well as one of the best. With the front-line songwriting talents of Buckingham, Nicks and Christine McVie, and the always powerful and inventive rhythm section of bassist John McVie and Mick Fleetwood (who were founding members of the one-time British blues band) Fleetwood Mac was invincible on the record charts. They had one hit after another—Nicks' "Dreams," Buckingham's "Go Your Own Way" and "Second Hand News," McVie's "Don't Stop." They seemed to capture a spirit and joyful melodiousness that had been virtually absent in pop bands since The Beatles. And then, of course, there was the personal side of the band, which made Fleetwood Mac so fascinating to the media. During the sessions for *Rumours,* John and Christine McVie were breaking up, as were longtime lovers Nicks and Buckingham. The songs on the LP "tell all," as the *National Enquirer* would probably put it. America has always loved soap operas.

Two years later, the group emerged from thirteen months of recording with *Tusk,* a double LP that enjoyed relatively moderate success (about four million copies sold worldwide, a fourth of *Rumours'* sales) but which showed that the band was not going to be complacent and simply churn out same-sounding hits forever. It is a dark, moody album, filled with songs that are at once dense and accessible. The band followed the album with a year-long world tour that found them playing with more fire than ever before. A live record culled from the tour, *Fleetwood Mac Live,* was released at the beginning of this year.

When the tour ended last fall, the members of the band went their separate ways for the first time in several years. Mick Fleetwood went to Ghana and made his first solo LP, *The Visitor.* Christine McVie produced an album by Robbie Patton. John McVie sailed around the world. Lindsey Buckingham recorded a solo album which should be out in October. And Stevie Nicks made *Bella Donna,* using top studio players like Waddy Wachtel and Russ Kunkel, "Professor" Roy Bittan of Bruce Springsteen's band, and Tom Petty & the Heartbreakers.

Bella Donna covers broad territory stylistically. "Edge of Seventeen" is a driving rocker; "After the Glitter Fades" has a country feel; "Stop Draggin' My Heart Around" and "Outside the Rain," two tracks featuring the Heartbreakers, sound like songs from a Petty album with a different singer; "Leather and Lace" is a beautiful ballad duet featuring Don Henley of the Eagles, an old friend of Nicks'. The album shows more facets of Nicks' personality than anything she's been involved with before. Certainly it proves her to be more than just the spacey siren in gossamer that she sometimes appeared to be during Fleetwood Mac's tours.

AS WE SAT TOGETHER on a soft section couch in one corner of her massive living room (which is filled with stereo equipment, a piano, an organ and a large screen TV on which she watches cassettes of Greta Garbo movies, Roadrunner cartoons and *The Muppet Show*) the light of the afternoon sun cut through a glass of white wine she sipped from and cast a glow on her radiant face. Our discussion began with *Bella Donna* and covered various aspects of her career and songwriting craft. For the spacey side of Stevie Nicks—a side she makes no effort to hide, incidentally—I suggest you read *Rolling Stone's* recent cover story, "Out There With Stevie Nicks," by Timothy White. What follows is Stevie Nicks, singer and songwriter.

Did it scare you at all to finally take the plunge to record Bella Donna?
I'm always nervous about doing something new. I was particularly nervous about making this album because I knew I wouldn't have four other people to blame if it didn't do well. In Fleetwood Mac, if I fail I fail with four other people. Here, if I fail I fail alone. It's always scarier to be alone. Fortunately, I had great people to work with who encouraged me constantly. The vibe I got from everybody was so positive that it made me feel strong.

From what I can gather by the number of different players you used, it seems not too much was preplanned, that you recorded whenever you could get the players.
That's exactly right. It was very, very spontaneous. We did it in sort of a piecemeal way because we'd only get people in for a few days at a time. Tom Petty & the Heartbreakers don't exactly sit around waiting for the phone to ring for session work. Russ [Kunkel] and Waddy [Wachtel] have impossible schedules. So we did the album around them. We'd get them for a couple of days and work fast.

Who worked out the arrangements for the songs? I know that in Fleetwood Mac, Lindsey would do almost all the arranging for you, putting on layers of different guitars and, in a sense, orchestrating your tunes.
That's one of the reasons I wanted to see if I could do it myself. When you work with somebody who is that much in control, and who has

always been that much in control—from, like, 1970 on—you forget that you're even capable of doing something yourself. I'd write my song and then Lindsey would take it, fix it, change it around, chop it up and then put it back together. Doing that is second nature to Lindsey, especially on my songs. He does better work on my songs than on anybody's because he knows that I always give them to him freely. It's a matter of trust.

So it was interesting to work without him, because my songs pretty much stayed the same; the only difference was what happened after I'd written them. When I write a song I sit down at the piano and play it front to back. For *Bella Donna* I would do that, or have a demo like that, and the other musicians would just listen to it, getting their own ideas of how to fill in the rest. Usually, by a couple of times through the song they had a good idea of what they could do with it. My songs aren't complicated, to say the least. The sessions went very quickly, really.

You said you'd felt dependent on Lindsey in Fleetwood Mac. Was it difficult for you to think for yourself during the sessions for Bella Donna?
No, it was exhilarating! Instead of just sitting around hour after hour, I got to be a part of it. Working with Lindsey, it's so easy to just let him take it. On this album I didn't have to fight to do my songs the way I wanted to. The other players just did them the way I wrote them and they came out great. We didn't do a ton of overdubs. We didn't put on 50,000 guitars because we didn't have Waddy around long enough to do 50,000 guitar overdubs. We were lucky to get him to do *one* guitar part.

Stylistically the album seems very eclectic to me. There's a little country, some gospel feel, rock and roll . . .
Well, it represents ten years worth of songs. In Fleetwood Mac I usually get two or three songs on an album, but here I got to do *ten*. The album is sort of a chronology of my life. "After the Glitter Fades" was written in '72, making it the oldest song on the record. "Highway Man," "Leather & Lace" and "Think About It" were written in '75. The most recent is "Edge of Seventeen," which is also my favorite song on the record.

Did you change the lyrics to "After the Glitter Fades"? It seems moderately prophetic.

Moderately? It's *very* prophetic! [Laughs] No, the lyrics are the same. Believe me, I'd seen a lot of glitter fade by the time I wrote that song, which was two years before Lindsey and I joined Fleetwood Mac. That was a tough period for us professionally, because we were very serious about wanting to be professional musicians. And we'd done well in the Bay Area with Fritz, but moving to Los Angeles was a big step and it seemed that we were suddenly back at point "A" again. Also, our lives were so different from each other then. I didn't have any friends in LA and he made lots of musician friends—Warren Zevon, Waddy, Jorge Calderon. And while he was making friends and playing music, I had to work.

You sound a little bitter.

No, I'm not really. It was the only way we could do it. Lindsey couldn't be a waitress. He didn't know how to do anything but play the guitar and I did, so it was obvious I was going to be the one to do the work if we were going to live. And he didn't want us to play at places like Chuck's Steak House or Charlie Brown's. I would have gone for that in a big way, personally, because singing in horrible places like those four hours a night is a helluva lot better than being a cleaning lady. That was the only real rift we had then. He won. But I loved him. I loved our music, and I was willing to do anything I could to get us to point B from point A. It's hard to keep the sparkle going when you face so many closed doors. But somewhere in my heart I knew that it would work out and that if I kept making enough money to pay the rent, that Lindsey would hang in there and get better and better on guitar and keep learning about the business.

You mentioned that Bella Donna *is sort of a chronological portrait of your life. Do you have any sense of what sort of picture of you listeners will get from it?*

Not really. I'm too close to it to know. Things that I know are in a song some people might not see. And then I never know how others are going to interpret my songs based on things in their own lives. I just hope people like it and it makes them feel good. My songs talk about problems everyone in the world has. They're not unique to me.

My songs don't change much over the years. I write much the same way I did when I was 16. I'm no better on guitar or piano. I do exactly what I always did: I just write about what's happening to me at the moment. I didn't pick out the songs on *Bella Donna* because I wanted to document my life. I picked them because I liked them. It just sort of worked out that way. At the same time, though, I like the way "After the Glitter Fades" was premonitory. And "Edge of Seventeen" closes it—chronologically, anyway—with the loss of John Lennon and an uncle at the same time. That song is sort of about how no amount of money or power could save them. I was angry, helpless, hurt, sad.

I recorded sixteen songs for the album and I wanted *all* of them to get on. I agonized about it. If I had put them all on, though, there wouldn't have been room for a label. [Laughs]

Well, you managed to get "Blue Lamp" on the Heavy Metal *soundtrack.*
It was very important that it found a place for itself. I love that song. It was really the beginning of *Bella Donna* because it was the first thing I'd ever recorded with other musicians, and it was the first time I'd ever recorded by standing in a room singing at the same time that five guys were playing. Fleetwood Mac doesn't record that way. They record from a more technical standpoint. When I'm recording, I like to imagine that I'm at a concert singing in front of thousands of people. I record for *feeling*. I'm not good at the technical stuff. I don't like standing there in a room, after the tracks have been done, and singing the same song fifty times in a row. I hate it. I want to sing a song once, maybe twice, and if it isn't working, maybe go on to another song. Fleetwood Mac is the opposite. They labor over every detail. I care about the final feeling when you hear it on a car radio or at home on your stereo.

In fairness to Fleetwood Mac, Stevie, even though you know what a long process recording is, the group's records don't sound cold or detached. There's plenty of feeling on every record Fleetwood Mac has done.
That's true. Don't misunderstand me. I love the way Fleetwood Mac sounds. I wouldn't be in it if I didn't. I'm just saying that on *Bella Donna* we managed to make a really good record a different way. We went

in and we just *did it*. *Tusk* took us thirteen months to make, which is ridiculous. I was there in the studio every day—or almost every day—but I probably only *worked* for two months. The other eleven months I did nothing, and you start to lose it after a while if you're inactive. You see, Lindsey, Chris, John and Mick all play, and I don't. So most of the time I'd be looking at them through the window in the control room. After four or five hours, they'd forget I was even there, they'd be so wrapped up in little details. It was very frustrating.

There seems to be a bit of revisionism about Tusk *going around. When the record came out, all of you said you were delighted with it. When it didn't do as well commercially as it was expected to, the opinions within the band about the project seemed to turn more negative.*
I never felt any differently about it. I was always up-front about it. I loved the songs for the most part. I even liked almost all of Lindsey's tunes, which were the most heavily criticized. I did *not* love sitting around for thirteen months and I never said I did. If *Tusk* had been terribly successful I wouldn't have taken the credit for it because I was not that much a part of it. It was out of my hands. I didn't want it to be called *Tusk*. I didn't like the artwork. I'm being totally truthful—I had *very* little to do with that record.

How does it sound to you now?
I love individual songs. Of my songs, I like "Sara" and "Angel" the best. I like most of Chris' stuff. Of Lindsey's songs, I guess I like "Save Me A Place" and "Walk a Thin Line" the most. Those are beautiful songs.

I love Lindsey's work. I didn't hang around with him for seven years for nothing, listening to him play guitar every single night, watching him fall asleep with his electric guitar across his chest. There were nights I had to *pry* the guitar off of him so he could sleep in a normal position.

My main complaint with *Tusk* isn't musical. It just went on too long. I think it could have been done in half the time. But again, I'm not a player. I'm the dancer and singer. I just want to get up there and dance and twirl my baton.

According to nearly everyone I've talked to, you are an amazingly prolific writer. Do you have a regular writing regimen?

No, I just write when I feel like it, which is a lot of the time. Sometimes I write every day, sometimes a few days will go by when I don't write anything. I get nervous that I'm drying up if I don't write often.

I have entire filing cabinets filled with stuff I've written. It's songs plus I've been keeping a journal for the past six or seven years, so I've got the history of Fleetwood Mac completely written. It could be an incredible book, but it would be a massive project to pull it all together. There are books within books within books—the making of all the albums, the tours, the relationships: John and Chris trying to work together, Lindsey and Stevie trying to work together. It's all there . . .

"Soon to be a five-part mini-series on ABC starring Morgan Fairchild as Stevie Nicks. . . ."

[Laughs] It really could be, and they wouldn't have to sensationalize a thing! You have no idea of all the stuff that's gone on. It's been fascinating.

Getting back to songwriting, though, *anytime* I think a part of a song might be coming out, I'll try to write it. Like I wrote a song in the middle of the night last night, which makes me very happy because whenever I write a new song I feel great for a few days. This new tune's about how the house shakes when the waves hit the beach. I've got a whole cassette of me sitting at the organ singing lines over and over again. Writing is fun for me. I've got a wealth of things to write about.

I've always thought your songs presented an interesting view of womanhood. It's not quite a "sisterhood is powerful" feeling, but some of your compositions seem to emphasize the bond you feel with other women in an almost spiritual way.

I think that's probably true. I'm surrounded by men in this business so I need a little feminine comfort, and one way to find that is to write about how I exist in this world of men, how I deal with them and how they deal with me. And I tend to talk about it as "we" instead of "I." I'm no great women's liberationist, though. I found out a long time ago that that doesn't work, so—

That's rather cynical.

It's true. I get a lot further with the men in this business by being feminine and sweet and not aggressive and quiet. They let me *in*. They *don't* let in aggressive, pushy women. Say one word too much and you're out. Well, I didn't want to be out. I wanted to be friends with them. They're my peers and contemporaries. They're people I have to work with and I damn well am going to be part of them. It took me a long time to be anything to them besides just a "girl."

How do you make the jump in men's minds from being just another "chick singer," as it is degradingly put so often, to being respected for your songwriting, which is obviously what you would like?

I just keep writing, playing and telling people how important writing is. I tell writers that it's not important to me to be a sex symbol. I tell them it's not important to me what people think of me dancing around in gossamer clothing onstage. I happen to *like* wearing clothing like that. It's fine for Gelsey Kirkland [a top ballerina] but it's not fine for me. If I was a ballerina, nobody would say one word about what I wore, and they wouldn't talk about my sex life—which writers don't know anything about anyway. But put on a pair of platform boots and walk out on a rock and roll stage and—WOW! All people see is an image.

I'm not going to change because I get criticized for what I wear or because, as you said, some people see only a "chick singer." I keep persevering and doing what I do with the hope that someday people won't care about any of that and instead they'll look up and say, "You know, she really *is* a pretty good writer." It's starting to happen, actually. It's taken six or seven years, but it is happening. You can't give up for a second.

I can't spot many specific influences in your songwriting. Who were you listening to when you started writing a lot?

Well, I've written for years and been influenced by lots of people, but I guess the stuff that really got me was Joni Mitchell's early songs. I learned so much from listening to her. In fact, I probably wouldn't be doing this if it hadn't been for her. It was her music that showed me I could say everything I wanted to and push it into one sentence and sing it well. *Ladies of the Canyon* taught me a lot. I remember lying on the floor, listening to Joni's records, studying every single word. When she came out with a new album I'd go crazy—"Don't bother me this week. I'm listening to Joni Mitchell."

The inspiration was more attitudinal than actual?
Right. I didn't want to play music like her. I couldn't if I'd wanted to—I can't play the guitar worth shit, and Joni's a great player. I just loved the way she was a very personal writer yet easy to relate to. She was doing what I wanted to do. I also loved all of Jackson Browne's records. Again, he could make the most intimate, personal things universal. This might surprise you, but I loved Jimi Hendrix as a writer—he put words together in really amazing ways. I loved Janis Joplin—the way she sang, the way she performed. I saw her one time and was completely riveted. I never forgot it. I have so many influences, but I can't really tell where they come in.

My writing style is very, very simple. I play so simply that I have to kill with my voice, especially in the beginning of a song or nobody gets it. The instrumental parts of my songs are not going to sell them. And because the structure and chords and all are so simple, it forces me—and the players—to really experiment with phrasings and ways of bringing out the melody.

Some people believe that writers—artists in general—work best when they have inner turmoil; that happiness isn't inspiring, but pain is. Do you agree with that?
I think a little turmoil probably helps. I don't go looking for it so I can write [laughs], but then I never sit down and write a *happy* song. I think there is something to that theory, because the person who is searching and never quite finding what he wants, who is constantly challenged, is going to write better songs than somebody who is blissfully happy. If you're blissfully happy, what else is there to say? And how many people are blissfully happy enough that they can relate to what you're writing?

As close as I get to writing happy songs are ones that aren't *un*happy. I've written my share of miserable songs, but I haven't recorded many of them.

There definitely is an overriding optimism in most of your songs.
People don't mind a little misery, but they also like happy endings. It's nice to leave some hope at the end that things will work out. See, Lindsey won't do that. He'll say, "Go your own way." I wouldn't, most likely.

Lindsey hates to write lyrics, though. Maybe that's why some of his songs are so negative. [Laughs] He'll have all these beautiful songs that are instrumentals for months. They have gorgeous melodies, layer upon layer of guitars. I exercise to his tapes, practice ballet to them. Then he'll write the lyrics for this beautiful song and it'll have a different feeling than the music.

I'm surprised the two of you haven't collaborated on songs since you've been in Fleetwood Mac. You love to write words and he's a nut for melodies.
I'm surprised, too. I always wanted to. It's strange. You would think he would ask me, but I think he really doesn't like my lyrics very much. They're too spacev for him. We think differently, I guess.

You and Petty obviously have a good rapport. Can you see yourself writing with him?
I think we will write together eventually. You see, Tom and I aren't going out. Tom and I aren't in love with each other, or haven't been in love and out of love. We're really just good friends so we probably could write together. Lindsey and I have *so much* behind us that it would be difficult to sit down and intensely get into lyrics. As it is he asks me, "Who's that one about? What are you talking about in that line? What does that mean?" [Laughs]

What did you contribute to the next Fleetwood Mac album?
I have three songs as it stands now, but I think we may replace one of them with another song. I wrote one of the songs a long, long time ago, even before Lindsey and I moved to LA. It's called "It's Alright." It's very simple; Lindsey just plays some really nice guitar behind me. There's another song called "If You Were My Love" that I wrote about a year ago after I'd recorded "Outside the Rain" with Tom Petty & the Heartbreakers. I spent a week recording with them and I had so much

fun that I was really bummed out when it was over. That's when I wrote that song.

There was also a song called "Smile at You" that I don't think we'll put on. I think Lindsey wants me to record another one and so do I. It's kind of a bitter song and that's really not where any of us are at right now, even though it's a wonderful song. My songs don't take long to record, so it shouldn't be a problem.

Did the sessions for this album have a different tone than past Fleetwood Mac sessions?
It went smoothly. It didn't take us as long. I think right now everyone is into making a good album that doesn't take a long time to make.

Is there any danger of Fleetwood Mac staying together beyond its natural lifespan? You wouldn't stay together for business reasons, would you?
Fleetwood Mac couldn't stay together if we didn't want to, because we're *all* far too volatile and passionate that it would be unbearable if we didn't want to be together. Fleetwood Mac is never boring. If it ever becomes boring we would stop it.

It's not like any of you would starve if Fleetwood Mac didn't exist.
That's right. We keep it going because we want to, because we obviously feel there's more good music to come out of us as a group. If that changes we'll be the first ones to recognize it.

It must be an awfully good feeling for you, though, to know you've done so well on your first project outside of Fleetwood Mac.
It feels wonderful. Now the trick is to keep my life going in a way where I can continue to do things outside of the group. I'd like to make more albums on my own. I'd love to do a record of songs aimed at children. I'd like to record songs by my grandfather, A.J. Nicks, who was a country singer. There's so much to do. *Bella Donna* is just the first step, but it was an important first step.

I just decided when I came off the year-long *Tusk* tour that I wasn't going to give up my life and die a lonely, overdone, overused rock star.

That has no glamour. I didn't want to be written up in 50 years as a miserable old woman who never got to do anything but tour and be famous for ten years and then everything was *over*.

I'm far too intelligent to not know that there will be time when I won't be 33 anymore, when I won't be that pretty anymore, I won't be sparkly anymore, and I'll be *tired*. I want to be able to know that I can still have fun and be part of the world, and that I didn't give it all away for Fleetwood Mac. That's what *Bella Donna* is all about. It's the beginning of *my* life.

BELLA STEVIE

Sylvie Simmons | November 1981 | *Kerrang!* (UK)

Another Stevie Nicks interview to promote *Bella Donna*. What strikes one most about this feature (apart from the incongruity of such a fey figure as Nicks being featured in a "metal mayhem monthly") is the revelation of the dramatic change in Nicks's status in Fleetwood Mac. With a number one solo album to her name, she had gone from the "baggage" Buckingham brought with him to being the group's most famous constituent part.

Notes: The *Crossroads* referred to was a notoriously cheesy British soap opera of the period.

For "Sarah" read "Sara."

HEAD PAST Marina del Rey towards the pacific. Step past the male models on rollerskates, the tanned girls in jogging shorts, the bicycles and Porsches and macrame plant hangers. And when you're as far as you can go without getting wet you're at Stevie Nicks' apartment.

Overlooking the sea. Not on a cliff (where the salt-kissed waves are thrust and caressed by the wayward wind as She stares, entranced, by the storm's dark passion, etc, etc, etc), but it *is* on the second floor, which affords a lovely view of the boats through Stevie's binoculars, or of the lifeguards outside without them.

This is where the Fleetwood Mac frontwoman lives, surrounded by pianos, plants, velvet, satin, women friends, stuffed animals and (probably unstuffed) poodles. If you could write interviews in 'Scratch 'n' sniff', this one's incense, roses and brine.

I'm watching a maid iron those chiffon Halloween party dresses Stevie always wears, while she's getting preened for the photographer. She emerges in archaic suede platform boots, flowing lace and corn-coloured (romantic heroines are never mere blonde) hair like some airbrushed cosmic cake decoration. She's beautiful; more natural and bright-looking than those pix where she succumbs to that blankest of blank looks, and stronger; not the wisp of a thing that needs propping up at the merest hint of a sea breeze that you'd expect.

Her first words simultaneously apologise, in that deep breathy voice, for the delay, offer us wine and encourage us out of the plush cushions on a grand tour of her musical gadgets, the latest being a rhythm machine that, she chortles, might yet have Mick Fleetwood out on the streets. Then she lounges on a large sofa. The place is most definitely set up for lounging, staring at the sea and songwriting.

"It comes incredibly easy, it's not work to me. I love writing songs more than anything in the world. I love sitting at my piano with a glass of wine and the lights kind of low and some incense and an idea. There's nothing I'd rather do. It's *what* I do." To the extent that 'Bella Donna', the solo album, could have been the first Mac soloist boxed set and there would still be plenty over.

"There's only one album every two or three years and, as a writer, two or three songs every two or three years is not much. It means you've got about 392 days a year to do nothing. And I write a lot all the time—sometimes three or four a month—so I have such an incredible backlog of material that there's no reason for me to ever have to write another song. Unless I can do records where I can put out 10 or 12 of my songs here and there—I have that many.

"I could start recording my next solo album *tomorrow*. That's how quickly I write. It's very frustrating when somebody walks past you when you're working and says: 'Ooh, you're writing another song? Why? We don't need another Stevie Nicks song, you've got too many already.' It rains on your parade and you start asking things like: 'Is this stupid? Should I really just sit around and watch television and not bother doing this?'"

The solo deal was signed over two years back; even a Mac member can't take that long on overdubs.

"My part was done in 2½ months," she says indignantly; it usually takes most megastar groups that long to find the studio. "But I had to wait until everyone else in the band did their outside projects. The album actually took no time at all. It was begun and finished in such a flash, so easy, and it's like—you know when you really don't want a good book to end and you'd rather read it slower than finish it? With 'Bella Donna' I felt that from the beginning.

"In 2½ months we had 16 songs recorded that were perfect, no problems, because I had it all worked out from learning it all right here in this room, and all the craziness that went on here meant there was no craziness in the studio. In fact, it all went so perfect that we got bummed out because we wanted to sing them again and he (producer and current boyfriend Jimmy Iovine) said: 'You don't have to' and we're going: 'Oh shit, it's finished, we're out?'"

Of the songs cut out, one's definitely going on the next record, one went on the 'Heavy Metal' soundtrack (the connection is manager Irving Azoff who's behind the 'HM' film project; Stevie's radio is tuned into an easy-listening station and the albums lying around are no heavier than Tom Petty).

'Outside The Rain', one of the Tom Petty collaborations, was added at the last minute because "it was the only link between Fleetwood Mac and me. It was the song they would have done if they were involved in this record. It was the 'Dreams' or the 'Sarah'. And it was important to me that there be that link in the chain there, because the rest of it was very much me and very much *not* Fleetwood Mac, and because it's important to me that Fleetwood Mac is still a part of my life and that they understand what I'm doing."

Why wouldn't they? They're all off working on their solo stuff, aren't they?

"Yeah, but I'm the baby of Fleetwood Mac. Ha, I'm 33 years old, a very old baby, but it's hard for them to watch me walk away and do anything. Because everybody in Fleetwood Mac, including me, is possessive, jealous. It causes us a lot of grief, but at the same time it's never boring. I research Fleetwood Mac all the time in my head and try to figure us out. But I can't. It's a strange grouping of people.

"JOHN'S ALWAYS going to the beach.

Mick's always going to the Renaissance Faire, Lindsey's always going to visit his tailor, I'm always going to a Halloween party, and Christine is like Christine always looks in her kind of cool clothes," Stevie giggles at the absurdity of this multi-platinum unit.

"It's funny to see us before we go onstage, standing in a circle. We look ridiculous! John's got his crew socks and his cut-offs and his T-shirt and baseball hat. Mick's got his velvet knickers and the same tights and shoes he's worn for a hundred years—you wouldn't want to be within 50 feet of him in that outfit, especially the next night when he's put it back on after it's been in the bus all day and never dried. Lindsey wears the same two Armani suits, one white and one grey every night."

And Stevie wears those tablecloths. Even around the house. Then again she did spend her formative years in San Francisco and when she joined Fleetwood Mac she decided "if I wanted to stay I was going to really have to figure out a gimmick, like toe-dancing or something that nobody else could do.

"At first they really didn't need another girl singer, why should they? They needed a guitarist, not a girl singer who couldn't really play piano or guitar or anything. It's human nature—they're not going to say; 'You stand out there now and be The Star and we'll just play', right? I know for a fact that I was simply being hired as extra baggage. They couldn't get Lindsey without me."

The Buckingham-Nicks package deal went back a long way, singing one song together in San Francisco, 1966—"I met him in college; I was a senior, he was a junior. I never saw or heard from him again for two years, when he called and asked me to join his rock and roll band out of the blue."

The only band she'd been in before was Changing Times, one of those California Mamas And Papas-type things. Now she was alone with her acoustic guitar and a bunch of self-penned songs.

She'd been singing since her grandfather (the late Aaron Jess Nicks, failed country singer, eccentric harmonica player, who lived in a trailer in Arizona when he wasn't bar-hopping and crooning) got her a "little outfit with guns and boots—I was a happening cowgirl" at the age of four and took her and her ubiquitous tambourine on the gin-house circuit.

Until her father (one time brewery president, now a concert promoter) put a stop to her going on the road and uprooted the family to Texas, Utah, Mexico, Los Angeles and finally San Francisco. All she remembers of her hometown, Phoenix Arizona, is cacti and meeting Tex Ritter.

"I was still singing all the time—to the radio, to the Ronettes, the Beach Boys, Janis Joplin, anybody I listened to, until I moved up to San Francisco and then I basically did my own music."

Didn't everybody. But Mum and Dad Nicks decided this was no career for their Stephanie, so she went to college.

"I wanted to go to hairdressing school"—you should know that this woman trims her poodles' hair herself, not to mention giving crew-cuts to the F. Mac roadies—"but they didn't go for that idea at all, so I did five years at college. I should have gone to hairdressing school because that would really have benefited me more. I was singing with Lindsey the whole time and found it real difficult to study."

Eventually Lindsey left his band Fritz, Stevie left her homemade candles and they moved to L.A. where they eventually got a Polydor record contract, preceded by "two years of solid depression. It was hard, you know, when you practice that hard and you sound that good and everyone tells you that you should be doing something else. You want to say: 'Well obviously we're not from the same planet, because I didn't sit down with this guy for five years and sing like this for you to tell me that nothing we do is commercial. You're crazy!'

"It was a terrible time, because Lindsey and I just couldn't understand how we could sing a beautiful song to you and nobody liked it and it was so pretty it made me cry. It was like: we don't belong here. Nobody understands us."

Except Fleetwood Mac, who discovered the matinée idol and the fairy princess and: "We were plucked straight out of obscurity—heavy obscurity. I was a member of Fleetwood Mac and still working in a restaurant (in Beverly Hills, a promotion at least from being the princess of Burger King) and it would have taken me weeks to make as a waitress what I was making in one week in Fleetwood Mac. But I wanted to give notice and leave on a good note because I liked my job and I didn't want to walk in there and go: 'Well now I'm going to be a famous rock and roll star', so I quit!

"Three weeks later we were recording. We finished the album in three and a half months. Four months later we went straight on the road and boy was it a big shock."

Considering they didn't want her in the first place, "They made me feel wonderful," she sighs, "and I fell madly in love with all of them, immediately, even though I knew in my heart they didn't really need me. So I'd try to be really good and maybe I'd find a way to be needed there. I didn't know what else to do. I liked them so much that I was willing to realise that logically I was lucky to get asked to join the band at all, so I would have to be so helpful in everything, right, or at least I could be a secretary or something, *anything*, because I wanted to be a part of it.

"And they knew it. They understood I felt this way. And they were real careful and never made me feel unwanted. Christine very willingly gave me the stage, which I thought was very cool for a woman to say: 'Oh, she's five years younger than me and I've worked for ten years on the road, killed myself, and here she is, our new frontwoman.' It was incredibly big of Christine to just move out of the way, because I do tend to kind of animate around and I drive Chris nuts. *Crazy.*

"Chris will tell you that there were times in the last six or seven years when she was a little jealous. And I swear to God I never knew. Never one comment to the effect of 'I could really have done without you'. And I'm sure there were times when I'm flying around the stage in my gossamer chiffon where she had to think to herself: 'Wow, what's this? Fairy school?' and never once did she make me feel that. She knew from the beginning that I was real sensitive and that I love her so much that anything she'd say to me would cut like a knife. So she was always very careful."

MOST PEOPLE are careful around Stevie. You know that scene in Nashville where they wheel Ronnee Blakely on in white lace, hovering over her? Just change the hair colour. This woman gets phone calls from her record company in which the word 'unit' never even comes up. The record company president calls "and he doesn't say: 'Do you know how successful this album is?' He says: 'Are you enjoying this? Are you working too hard? This is the best moment of your life, Stevie, and I want you to be happy.'

"They all know that I'm real vulnerable and real sensitive and that I can break real easy if I don't get back a little bit of the love that I try to put out, if I feel that I'm alone somewhere on an island by myself—then I start to die a little. And for some reason the business people seem to understand this—which is real hard, their job is on the line.

"I've had 50 people call me today to say: 'If it's too tough Stevie, stop. It doesn't matter.' With most artistes they say: 'Look, we need these photos, this interview. Too bad if you're tired.' They just seem to know when I'm bummed and upset and they call me. This wouldn't be amazing if it was my Mum, but it is amazing when it's the president of Atlantic or of Modern Records or Irving (Azoff).

"Something in my voice worries them a little. But only because I haven't done this before. I've always had four other people to work with. I can't call up John McVie or Christine and beg out—it's my gig. And it's not singing and it's not dancing, which I love to do. It's hard to do all this and none of the other."

Stevie proved more fragile than the others on the last mammoth 'Tusk' tour. Her vocal chords got shot, leading to nightmares about never singing again and trips to specialists, who virtually handed her a wreath as they sent her onto the next stop.

"My voice is all right now. I worked a long time on it. But a year is too long. I could probably work for six months a year solid but not twelve. I'm not 18, you know, and I'm not as strong as I used to be physically. It gets harder and harder to be wonderful every night in front of all those kids that you're 15 years older than. I don't want a tired Stevie walking onstage trying to do 'Rhiannon' when I'm dead, I've killed my voice. It's not fair to the kids who paid their twelve bucks to see the concert.

"You can never call in sick. You can be on the side of the stage with terrible, terrible cramps and all of a sudden you've got 30 seconds to try and not even let that come into your head. I've seen a lot of shows that, because of extreme exhaustion, aren't special. For me there's nothing I'd rather do than go to a great rock concert. But there's nothing I'd rather not do than go to a rock concert by a great band that isn't good."

A solo tour isn't planned, but a few dates in major cities are, which will be filmed "Like a live stage production of 'Bella Donna' with a great rock and roll band, so it would be like the best of both worlds. We could really do it like the Othello of the 1981s."

TALKING OF films, we might as well take time to catch up on her other projects. A ballet of 'Rhiannon', possibly a movie "though whether or not there's ever going to be the time is another question. If 'Bella Donna' was difficult enough to get together, to pull 2½ months out of a hat, to make a movie is a lot longer and I can't see that kind of space coming up anywhere."

There's also a series of children's stories (her favourite books, wouldn't you know, are fairy tales like *Beauty And The Beast, The Little Mermaid,* or her own short story *The Golden Fox Of The Last Fox Hunt,* tales of gothic horror with the pain merely suggested) and letters and an autobiography filled with the "love affairs, the heartaches, the tragedies, the incredible happiness" in her life.

"It didn't start out to be anything but my journal—I've kept a diary for seven years now—but as I became a better typist it became more formal. It's real intense. It's a story that Taylor Caldwell (author of her favourite novel, *Ceremony Of The Innocent*) should sit down and write as I tell it to her, because it's that kind of thing. The story itself is as incredible as any story you've ever seen in a movie and you wouldn't have to make up a thing. It tells exactly what it is."

The songs come from the same source. After a show she'll write down her feelings—at the hotel, on the plane, turning the prose into poetry and getting a piano "sneaked into the hotel room" (not an easy task, but easier with Mac money "which is why we didn't make any money on that last tour—the luxuries") and there comes another one.

Her songs are "running commentaries on my life, exactly. Absolutely real. I don't lie and I never write down anything that isn't totally true. But I'm like your romantic fiction writer—I flower things. I toss a gardenia in here and a rose in there, so that a lot of the things that are real serious I say in a way that they're pretty enough that they don't turn people—like the dental assistant who's worked from 9 to 5 and comes home and is dead tired and puts it on—off. They have a little magic, but is not all airy-fairy.

"There's the wild side to me and there's the free side. As I get a little older, though, I get a little wiser. And though the wild side doesn't want any discipline whatsoever in her life, the part of me that knows that the only way I can get to people is to not be so terribly out of control balances the two."

Not so easy when being in a band that can't fail to encourage the spoilt brat in you?

"I've seen the tides change," Stevie protests. "I've seen the people turn away—like 'Tusk' or the live album. I've seen people get the wrong impression of five people I love, because it doesn't work every time, especially if you're so confident that it *will* work. It's truly better to stay at number two because there will always be the hope of doing something more creative and better. When you're number one, everything goes to the wind, and there's no place to go except down."

Fleetwood Mac have been working on their next effort at the famed Le Chateau studio. "It should be finished pretty quickly unless everybody decides to re-do everything." Or if it gets delayed by ghosts and things that go bump in the night. Stevie had some kind of brush with the spirit world in her bedroom there, something to do with a ghostly bird.

THE COVER of the 'Bella Donna' album came to her in a dream. The record company was on the verge of a nervous breakdown as she demanded a last-minute substitution with the new sleeve, white on misty blue, which is "completely opposite" to the 'Rumours' sleeve, stark black on white. On the back's the three roses on the silver tambourine (three girl friends singing, three sides of the pyramid, she explains—she'd like to live in a pyramid if the Welsh cliffs are all taken—all very symbolic) and it means "coming in out of the darkness. A decision I had to make—a question whether or not I could do something alone without my comrades to hold me up. Because I'd been in a group so long that had been all in control."

When Mac tells her to jump, she jumps apparently. Only Christine McVie has the power to tell lanky Mick to stuff himself. John and Stevie get hysterical, Lindsey just stomps off.

Symbolism and dreams and things mean a lot to her (though there's no dream analyst in the spare room, "I prefer a little mystery in things") and so do spirits.

"I feel there are good spirits everywhere when I'm writing my songs, helping me. I just get a good feeling from, I don't know, the air. If we're talking vibes we're talking vibes."

And she believes in reincarnation. In her last life she used to be a monk. Inspirational fellows.

Tom Petty's a bit like that. Fan Stevie got together with the Heartbreakers, that bastion of Southern chauvinism, through Petty's wife of eight years (I didn't know either! They've got a little girl who just recently saw Daddy play for the first time, with Stevie).

"Jane and I figured it out long before Tom had any idea that we were scheming. And we did scheme. I knew we would be good together—I'm not joining the Heartbreakers or anything: I'm just a friend. But every once in a while we can start singing and give everybody a little extra magic. Because it *kills* me, so it's got to have an effect on them.

"I was brought up with a whole lot of men, those type of old-fashioned men that a woman mustn't get too pushy with if they're going to accept her . . ."

A song on the album, 'Highwayman', is about as romanticised a picture of these new skinny machomen as you're going to get.

"Men were my first entrance into the rock and roll world, singing along with them on the radio. And all I ever wanted from them when I met them—like the Eagles—was to feel they actually liked me and even think I'm not a bad songwriter. I never needed flowers. Rock and roll men are like the highwaymen of old, sometimes giving to the poor, sometimes keeping it, always on the road."

At a rock and roll party last year Ann Wilson of Heart caught Stevie's eye across the room and felt a kindred spirit. "Misfit," she called them, women rock and rollers.

"Absolutely true," Stevie nods. "Ann and Nancy are really the only other two I can relate to. Outsiders. Heart can't go onstage without Ann or Nancy, and Fleetwood Mac can't go onstage without me or Chris. We've fought hard to be anything but background singers—I think we'd all rather quit and do something else than be background singers.

"I go back a long way, to Janis Joplin. There aren't many in the rock and roll business who are women that I feel any kind of respect at all for. Not that I don't give credit to Pat Benatar, I do. She's wonderful—but she's new. There's nothing I'd rather see than a great woman singer coming along, one that I could listen to—because I like listening to other people—but there's not too many."

There's another kindredship with Heart. For a while they took over as the *Crossroads* of rock in the soap opera world of gossip mags. Lindsey and Stevie, John and Christine, biting the dust.

"Yes, it was like 'here we go again'. It's hard to be in a band with someone and love them and not get angry with them and go home and not remember they screamed at you onstage. But at least Fleetwood Mac stayed together completely. Heart kind of changed it. It's a rare group of people that could do that. But then we could never fire John. It would be like Fleetwood. You can't fire the Mac."

WHERE'S STEVIE?

David Gans | September 1982 | *Record* (US)

"Her success is making her feel that she can pull things that she wouldn't have felt comfortable pulling before." So caustically notes Lindsey Buckingham in a feature that reveals that Stevie Nicks's solo success was marvelous for her but intensely irritating for her colleagues.

The group was promoting that year's Fleetwood Mac album, *Mirage*, a move back to commercial soft rock following the experimentalism of *Tusk*. Another sign that the chemistry of the band was changing was the fact that *Mirage* was—in contrast to their usual globe-straddling promotional efforts—supported by only a short American tour.

Note: For "Larabie Sound" read "Larrabee Sound."

FANTASY ISLAND, Ca.—On the kitchen table in Mick Fleetwood's Malibu mansion sits a model of the stage design for Fleetwood Mac's upcoming American tour. In between the tiny amplifiers, drums and pianos stand cardboard cutouts representing the five members of the band. There's a Lindsey Buckingham doll, a John McVie doll, etcetera. Why does the Stevie Nicks doll have a cigarette burn where her heart is supposed to be? And why is a hand crumpling the flat, white expressionless thing into a little ball and tossing it into a trash can?

MALIBU, Ca.—This scenario is entirely fictitious. It is a product of a demented writer's imagination, fueled by observations of Stevie Nicks's apparent hostility towards the rest of Fleetwood Mac, encouraged by a sadistic editor, and starved by the brain-damaged illegals who run the hotel where I ordered a room-service burger that never came and attempted to write about what really happened at Mick Fleetwood's house that afternoon.

Certainly Mick Fleetwood, Lindsey Buckingham and Christine McVie, who were all present for the interview, did nothing to suggest the above fantasy; but all three did speak somewhat wearily of the constant speculation on the part of the press and public about the future of the band. They also acknowledged that there is more grist for the rumor mill than ever before: The roaring success of Nicks's solo album, *Bella Donna*, and her absence from recording sessions, interviews (at least those concerning Fleetwood Mac) and tour preparations seem ample evidence to support the notion that the singer has reached the point of self-sufficiency.

Whether the topic was songwriting, recording or personalities, the conversation kept drifting back to the subject of Stevie Nicks, while the equally-absent John McVie was discussed only briefly and in the most benign of terms. The bassist, a road animal and an acknowledged studiophobe, was sailing in the Virgin Islands at the time of the interview and was due to join the band a few days later to rehearse. Nicks, on the other hand, was scheduled to show up only for the last ten days of work prior to the start of the tour.

"She phones her part in," says McVie without a trace of irony. "She asks what songs we plan on doing and what songs we want her to do. The rest of it will be decided between Mick, Lindsey and me."

"I'm not that excited about touring myself," admits Buckingham, who frequently expresses his preference for working in the recording studio. "But it's something we should do, so I'm definitely going to do it. If you do an album, you might as well complete the cycle—otherwise, why do the album?"

Fleetwood notes that "for the better part of six years, we all had a huge commitment to Fleetwood Mac. All we did was tour, make albums, tour, make albums, and tour. I think that if after this much time there isn't some sort of base that can withstand a certain amount of pounding from the people who helped create it, then it's pretty useless.

"People have been waiting for us to break up for years, and the subject's coming up again. The most likely one to disappear is Stevie, but there's absolutely no way of telling whether she will or not. I'm sure at times she wants to go off and not be a part of the band, and at other times it's the opposite."

But there's more to it than that. In arranging this interview, it was apparent at nearly every turn that Stevie Nicks has set herself apart from the rest of Fleetwood Mac in a way which is not exactly in the spirit of commitment. She has a record company virtually all to herself—Modern Records has released no product other than *Bella Donna*—and she alone among the Mac is represented by the industry's most grudgingly-respected hardballer, Irving Azoff. Azoff, it should be noted, owns no piece of Fleetwood Mac's action; and though his interest in this matter is solely Stevie Nicks, there's no evidence to indicate that he's responsible for pushing her away from the band.

No one in the Fleetwood Mac organization seems to know for sure what Nicks's intentions are with respect to the band, and when asked if she would respond to specific issues raised in the interview with the others, a representative of Azoff's company said, "She just wants to work on her record."

It's not hard to understand why Nicks might be reluctant to return to the enforced democracy of a five-piece band after having established herself as a triple-platinum act with her own material and musicians—both in the studio and on the road—whose defined role is to play her music her way. But would Fleetwood Mac survive her departure?

"Why not?" asks Fleetwood from the vantage point of one who's seen some key personnel losses in his time: Fleetwood Mac numbers among its alumni Peter Green, Jeremy Spencer, Danny Kirwan and Bob Welch, all of whom were seen (by outsiders at least) as vital components of the Mac's music. "I don't think there'll be any reason to madly look for someone else. If someone disappears, then that's what happens. Who knows? The whole thing might blow up."

"I might leave," McVie chimes in. "How about that?"

Fleetwood then offers the ultimate scenario: "When it's all totally finished I'll probably still be standing there, totally deluded and thinking that everyone was still around me, waiting to go on stage." *Touché.*

Fleetwood seems less concerned with the prospect of another personnel change than with maintaining an emphasis on musical growth. "I respect the fact that we're still being creative and enjoying ourselves. The reason why we're still here is that there is an underlying commitment to respecting the band, no matter how many times you might get fed up with it."

"There is definitely a chemistry that transcends everything else that might happen before or after we're on stage," McVie elaborates. "We play well together and sing well together. That side of Fleetwood Mac I really enjoy. And I feel very comfortable working with Lindsey. Dare I say this with him present?" She casts an affectionate wink his way. "I have a lot of respect for this man; I don't really imagine anybody else being able to do what he does with my songs.

"There have been many rough times," she continues, "but we've always ended up on some high note, standing around and jamming, or whatever, just really getting a charge out of playing together. It's a joyous situation, and that takes over the bad points."

"That may have something to do with why Stevie is the way she is now," Buckingham suggests. "Because she is not a musician, she doesn't share in that thing with us. She can feel totally out of her depth—which she is, on some levels—and you can understand why she doesn't want to come down to the studio or be involved in certain things."

In spite of the overwhelming commercial success of her solo album, there is a certain, well, amateurish quality to Nicks's songs. The way she lays a lyric across a melody sometimes makes for awkward phrasing and contributes to the spaciness of her musical persona, as does her rather childish lyrical point of view regarding life and love.

Buckingham, Nicks's former lover and a bandmate of hers since the late '60s, when both were members of a Bay Area group called Fritz, admits to having always considered her songs "a little flaky." But, "there's obviously something about her material that people relate to. She's always been a little bit hard for me to take seriously, because I really appreciate a beat, having been weaned on Elvis and Little Richard and Chuck Berry.

"There's something emotional that gets through, though," he says, "and her voice is so recognizable. I've been listening to Stevie sing for years and years, and when you're that close to it, it's easy to overlook certain aspects of anything."

"Stevie's very prolific," McVie notes. "She writes constantly, and all her songs are like babies to her, even though some of them are rubbish. When I write, I sit down and work on an idea until it's finished, but Stevie cranks out songs all the time."

Between her songs and the way she appears to be conducting her life, Stevie Nicks comes off as a modern-day equivalent to the movie queens of the '30s, reaching inside herself for some ill-defined personal misery to fuel her creative machinery. Buckingham says that in all the time he's known her, "Stevie has never been very happy, and I don't think the success of her album has made her any happier. In fact, it may have made her less happy.

"She's flexing some kind of emotional muscles that she feels she can flex now that she's in a more powerful position. There's a certain amount of leeway in how you can interpret Stevie's behavior, I'd say, but at the same time there's no denying that her success is making her feel that she can pull things that she wouldn't have felt comfortable pulling before. And most of them aren't particularly worthwhile, but she's venting something—loneliness, unhappiness or something."

When a band member chooses not to participate fully in the process of making an album, it puts a certain kind of pressure on the people who do the work. Given the unique approach that Buckingham takes to record-making, it's easy to see how an artist as moody as Stevie Nicks could second-guess what he does to her material.

It's in discussing the musicians' studio relationship that the most complete picture of Fleetwood Mac emerges. Here, egos collide and coalesce for months on end; the pop magic that results has, ultimately, little to do with technology or technique, and everything to do with talented artists following the late sportswriter Red Smith's dictum on how to do your best work: "Open a vein and bleed."

"There's an exquisite sense of checks and balances in Fleetwood Mac, and that's one of the things that makes the band work," Buckingham observes. "Everybody's always checking each other out to a certain degree, not only in choosing the material but on every level of our creativity.

Maybe that contributes to the albums taking as long as they do—it's not the most efficient way to do things. But it does seem effective in the end."

While it's not unusual for a band member to walk into the studio, criticize the music and then walk out again, Buckingham is philosophical about it. "It's just something you expect to happen from time to time," he says. "It just goes with the territory."

Fleetwood agrees. "We definitely have a problem sometimes with Stevie and John, but if they hate being in the studio then they certainly have less right to complain about what's done. That's just a matter of fairness—and that's why I hate being *away* from the studio. There are usually two or three poignant moments during the making of an album where there are hurt feelings walking around—'What have you done to my songs?' or that sort of thing. But there's also a lot of stuff which is appreciated by the others."

"Having a producer's kind of mind, I might take something too far," concedes Buckingham, "but it's better to have too much on a track and prune it back than to not have enough."

"Lindsey's never that adamant about keeping a track a certain way," comments McVie. "If everyone says that they think it's caca, then obviously he's not going to feel happy about it being on there anyway."

Buckingham has been referring to *Mirage* as a "a reconciliation of opposites" from the time of the first sessions. "There are some aspects of *Tusk* and some aspects of *Rumours*," he explains, "but *Mirage* is much more of a band album than *Tusk* was. After *Rumours* sold 16 or 17 million copies, we had the freedom—and the courage—to try some other things.

"I got a lot of support from the band during the making of *Tusk*, but when it became apparent that it wasn't going to sell 15 million albums, the attitudes started to change. That was sad for me in a way, because it makes me wonder where everyone's priorities are. To me, the point of making records is to shake people's preconceptions about pop."

Fleetwood says that making *Tusk* was crucial from a strategic standpoint. "It was no big master plan, really, but *Tusk* may be the most important album this band will *ever* do—strategically, apart from the music.

"If we hadn't done *Tusk*, Lindsey would have a problem expressing himself within Fleetwood Mac," he continues, pointing out also that

Buckingham extended his *Tusk* experimentation on his solo album, *Law and Order*, and brought the fruits of his labors to bear more subtly on *Mirage*.

"One of the reasons *Tusk* happened the way it did was because I wasn't doing any solo work," Buckingham says. "On *Tusk* I was doing a lot of things at my house, playing a lot of instruments myself, just like I did on *Law and Order*. That's a valid approach to making records. But this time I wanted all my songs to be *band* songs, and the result of that is an album that is a little less bizarre. *Tusk* had things that were good artistically, but it wasn't good for the whole band, and I thought that I should limit that to my solo albums. If I want to be in a band, we should play as a band—and maybe the result of that is that *Mirage* is a little more traditional in some senses."

Traditional in every respect, one might say, except that 14 months passed between the first sessions (at Le Chateau in Herouville, France, later switching to Larabie Sound and the Record Plant in L.A.) and the album's release. Buckingham quips that "Fleetwood Mac albums take about five years off your life," but is stumped when asked to explain why.

McVie jumps in. "Well, this particular one wouldn't have taken quite so long had it not been for all the other albums (meaning Lindsey's, Stevie's and Mick's solo LPs) that were being made as well."

It's fitting that McVie came to Buckingham's aid when he was at a loss for words: although it's not generally recognized, the two share a mutual respect for each other as musicians that pulls the band together in a special way. "I'm a musical stylist," Buckingham states. "I'm not really a writer. That's not my strong point, lyrical or melodywise. 'Trouble' (on *Law and Order*) is a good melody, 'Go Your Own Way.' I've had my moments, but I don't consider that to be my strong point at all. It's the style involved."

Says McVie: "I don't tell Lindsey, for example, 'I want you to play such-and-such kind of guitar, that lick.' That's why Lindsey has got the (additional production) credit on the album—he's been largely responsible for helping to bring across on the record the atmosphere that I want to come over on a song that I write."

"She and I have a real valid kind of rapport between us," Buckingham continues, "something that was there before we even met. It's like she can play the piano and I can play the guitar just wonderfully along with her. It's almost like parallel lines during our formative years of music until we met, and it gave us a lot of common ground."

For McVie, the bottom line is that "we play well together, we sing well together," referring to the entire band. "A lot of parts of Fleetwood Mac are really fun and rewarding. Of course, there are other people that we all play with and work with that are just as much fun, but not quite in the same way, I dare say, just because of the amount of years we've had together."

"When you play with other people, of course, it's a lot of fun," Fleetwood states, "but I would say it's very unlikely—certainly, for myself—that this situation will ever happen again in the reference of a musical combination. That commitment's really the reason why the band is still here."

With the mention of the word "commitment," the talk again turns to Stevie Nicks. The disinterested observer can't help but question her contribution at this point, but the musicians who work with her are a bit more charitable in their analyses and deductions.

"There've been many times when she might come out in the studio and try and sing along, and we'd tend to say, 'Don't do that right now, let us work this out first,'" says McVie. "Now she'll just go to the studio and go, 'There's no need for me to be here.' She does feel left out."

Fleetwood's take on the whole situation is that the process Fleetwood Mac goes through from day one in the studio through to the finished product is a highly-disciplined one, and that "Stevie doesn't have that appreciation. She just emotes and goes into something, which is exactly her forte. But she does that all the time rather than being able to control and place where she does it—which is not a fault, it's just the way it is."

But the key to understanding Fleetwood Mac in 1982 is not in wondering so much about its future without Stevie Nicks, but in understanding that the point is, was and always has been to make good music, and have fun doing it. Maybe that's why Fleetwood himself can seem so unconcerned when discussing Nicks—the band plays on, regardless: "That notion is *the* most important thing: appreciating in a non-belabored way that the key element with all the people in Fleetwood Mac is that you're not involved in making an album which is a bloody bore! A lot of people make the mistake of being very boring, and realizing all too late that they are fucking boring. Then the magic's gone; whatever's there has long since passed you by.

"I consider myself very lucky to have been involved in a situation which had a lot of groundwork that led you to being able to make very objective, humorous analogies to what you're doing, and having no puffed-up illusions about how important you are."

And at that point, the question of whether or not *Mirage* is the end of Fleetwood Mac as we now know it is moot. In fact, McVie says "it definitely isn't.

"This band has lived from day-to-day for seven years or so," she points out, "and there's always been some kind of turmoil from within—that's common knowledge. I'm quite sure we'll go on for another seven years doing the same thing."

FLEETWOOD MAC

Return Without Leaving

J. Kordosh | September 1987 | *Creem* (US)

By April 1987 and the release of *Tango in the Night*—the fifth studio outing by the *Rumours* Five—more things had changed in Mac-land. Not only had the band's productivity entered a steep decline (*Tango in the Night* was the first Fleetwood Mac studio album since 1982's *Mirage*), but *Rumours* had lost to Michael Jackson's *Thriller* its crown as history's biggest-selling noncompilation album.

A decade on from *Rumours*, *Tango in the Night* sought to take the Mac formula into a new era, bolting it to eighties production techniques. The result was highly successful, commercially and artistically. Extraordinarily, it would in later years be revealed as a piece of smoke-and-mirrors production genius by Buckingham designed to disguise the fact that Stevie Nicks and Mick Fleetwood were either largely absent or not fully functioning.

In light of Buckingham's comment herein, "I feel that this is going to be the last Fleetwood Mac thing," it doesn't seem surprising that the album's apparent triumphant reassertion of the band's relevance was in fact a harbinger of rupture.

The interview, incidentally, puts to rest rumors that the breathy, erotic female vocals heard on "Big Love" were supplied by Madonna.

Note: For the song "Christine" read "Caroline."

Up in the hills of Bel Air is Lindsey Buckingham's house, Lindsey Buckingham's croquet-perfect lawn, Lindsey Buckingham's pool, Lindsey Buckingham's radio-controlled toy submarine that's busted, but could be fun in the pool, Lindsey Buckingham's home studio, The Slope—where the final work on Fleetwood Mac's *Tango In The Night* was done—and, indeed, Lindsey Buckingham himself.

Lindsey, like everyone in Fleetwood Mac, will tell us something of this latest record—and something of this immensely popular band. Their times and their troubles, stuff like that.

Fleetwood Mac's saga has been a strange one: since Lindsey and Stevie Nicks joined up in 1975, the band's made five studio albums, including *Tango*. The first four have sold something like 33 million copies—about 20 million of those courtesy of 1977's monstrous *Rumours*. You can perceive that, despite their relatively sluggish output, this band has a lot of fans. As I write this, *Tango* is safely ensconced in the Top 10, where it may well remain for eternity or the next Fleetwood Mac album, whichever comes first. But, coming almost five years after *Mirage,* we can correctly assume that there's a story behind the story, so let's start here . . .

WHY WOULD LINDSEY BUCKINGHAM WANT TO MAKE ANOTHER FLEETWOOD MAC RECORD?

"Well, I don't know," he says. "OK, I have a very good answer for that, and I think it's not just a pat answer. You may get something else from John and Mick, or from Christine: I feel that this is going to be the last Fleetwood Mac thing. Stevie and I have been in the group for 12 years and the group has been together since, when?—'68, or something very long. We're closing in on 20 years and there's a time to put everything to rest and get on with other things, and I would like to do that.

"I think the *Mirage* album was not a very positive way to leave Fleetwood Mac. We did the tour, but it was an ambiguous album—it was not an album of vision, it left a lot of things dangling. And, for me, this album took a lot of the emotions or the finances or whatever realm you want to get into, and tied it all up in a nice, strong package.

"I wouldn't have wanted to leave the Fleetwood Mac situation—none of us would—with the *Mirage* album. And I may be wrong; I may be talking up my 'arse' here. But right now, you're right—I don't know why anyone would want to keep going with just one thing the rest of their lives when there's other things to delve into and to try."

Lindsey is certainly the pivotal member of the group right now—he and Richard Dashut produced the new album, and Lindsey not only stopped working on his own solo LP to get into the Mac project, he brought some of *Tango*'s best songs—"Family Man," "Big Love," "Christine"—along with him when he did so.

WHERE WAS STEVIE NICKS?

Although not quite missing from *Tango In The Night,* Stevie Nicks isn't exactly all over the thing. To be precise, she contributed two songs of her own ("Welcome To The Room . . . Sara" and "When I See You Again") and a third song by her friend and collaborator, Sandy Stewart ("Seven Wonders").

"In the beginning part (of making *Tango*) she was touring," Lindsey explains. "She was having her own problems. Without being judgemental about her reasons, she made herself very hard to get ahold of. When her own tour was done she went off to Australia for some reason—felt she had to do that. So it was hard to pin her down.

"Once she settled down"—a small laugh here—"she was fine. She came in towards the end—it really was towards the end of the project that she made herself available, constructively. And so we had to work with a limited amount from her."

Christine McVie, who contributed quite a bit to the album ("My favorite group of her songs on any album," says Lindsey), offers this: "The studio junkies, if you like, are pretty much me and Lindsey and Mick. John spends a lesser amount of time in the studio; he doesn't like to hang around doing nothing. Neither does Stevie, because she doesn't actually play any instruments in the band—that drives her crazy when there's nothing for her to actually do."

STEVIE NICKS SPEAKING

"I was there at the very beginning," she says, "but you plan an album on a cycle kind of thing. What happened is everything took a little longer, so I ended up being on the second single from my album and getting ready to go on the road when Fleetwood Mac really got started on it.

"Lindsey was doing another solo album, too. If he hadn't been Lindsey—if he'd have been *me*—then he could've gone ahead and done his at the same time Fleetwood Mac was doing theirs. But Lindsey, having to be the boss—and pretty much the head of this particular tribe at this particular moment—he couldn't do both. I could, because there wasn't all that much for me to do, in the technical sense, at the beginning of the record. I didn't feel weird about it because I didn't have any choice."

Later on, when asked if she doesn't feel a bit short-changed by the way *Tango* turned out, she adds: "I could feel short-changed if I wanted to look at it that way. I would prefer to look at it that I had my own thing going, and if I had been there more I would be on it more.

"If I want to blame everyone else for it, I suffer. If I want to blame myself, then I can deal with it."

SOME RETROSPECTIVES

After *Rumours* came a crucial period for Fleetwood Mac. Their next record was the rhythmically crushing *Tusk,* a double album that cost at least $1 million to make and a work that puzzled many. It was an album that saluted Lindsey's role in the band, at the same time nearly undoing the band.

"I remember Lindsey came up to my house," says Mick Fleetwood, "and he was very preoccupied at that point, compared to me: I would never think as intensely about certain things as I know Lindsey does. Too intensely, where you feel it'd be better for him if he relaxed, but he's like that by nature.

"Therefore, in regard to coming out of the *Rumours* album, Lindsey—as a player and an artist—had obviously done a lot of pre-thought before ever talking to any of us about what on earth we were gonna do. He had paid a lot more attention to that subject than myself, certainly, and more power to him.

"The most obvious thing that came out of that album was the expressed wants of Stevie and Lindsey, more so than Christine, of wanting to do something more than just live and breathe Fleetwood Mac, which—to me—sounded like 'My God, if that happens, it will be the end of Fleetwood Mac.' I was completely wrong."

"It was like a necessary valve," adds John McVie.

"And it turned out to be an extremely healthy thing," Mick continues. "Without that album, I don't think the band would be together today, quite honestly. I think it was a very necessary exercise—and to some extent, it *was* an exercise."

Christine McVie repeats the same story independently, as if by magic: "I think if we hadn't done that album, then Lindsey might've left. We 'allowed' him to experiment within the confines of Fleetwood Mac instead of saying, 'We don't want you doing stuff at your studio and putting it on the Fleetwood Mac album'—he might've said, 'I'm gonna leave, then.' We didn't want him to leave, for obvious reasons. Because of that, I believe the band is what it is today. It's possible that we'd not have been a band."

And what does Lindsey Buckingham say about the whole thing? "A little bit later, Mick said we really went too far with that, or *I* went too far. You know, there was a lot of that type of thing at the time. There's been a lot of reappraisal of that album within the group since then, but—at the time—I was the one who was getting the flak for that.

"There's this great story, which—I doubt if it's true—we finished the *Tusk* album about Christmastime, or a little before Christmastime, and someone said that when they played *Tusk* over at Warner's all the people saw their Christmas bonuses flying out the window. I've always loved that connection," he adds, laughing.

THE ORIGINS OF TANGO

For a group that sees as little of each other as Fleetwood Mac (and a group that takes as much time between records as Fleetwood Mac), one might wonder just what it took to get these people in the studio for *Tango*.

"I'd been asked to record an Elvis Presley song for a movie Blake Edwards produced," says Christine. The movie was *A Fine Mess*—we won't get into the implications of that—and the song was "Can't Help Falling In Love."

"It's a wonderful song," she continues, "and, if I do say so, my version was fabulous. But anyway, Lindsey's a huge Elvis fan"—'strue, I saw three Presley posters in a relatively brief walk through The Slope—"and they gave me total freedom as to who I wanted to use. So I called up Lindsey and we got John and Mick to play bass and drums . . . and the atmosphere in the studio was so instant we jammed for hours and played some of the old songs. At that point we sat down and said let's get serious about the studio again."

John McVie notes that "we dribbled into it," and Mick Fleetwood says that, "Speaking for myself, I'd been thinking of making an album two years before we did. But we all learned that the only way for this band to continue was to not force anything."

"Richard Dashut and I were about halfway through my solo album and the needs of the many started to outweigh the needs of the few," says Lindsey, quoting Mr. Spock. "And, at this time, it had been so long since we had interacted that lawyers and people like that were sort of getting into it. Their idea of how to get Fleetwood Mac back together to make an album was to bring in a young, hot producer. So Richard and I were going to just sort of waltz through and get my tunes done and go back to work on my solo album, and this guy would finish up Fleetwood Mac. But it just didn't work out that way: he didn't know how to handle us salty old guys—and I realized, too, that if we were going to do it all, it just wasn't our style to go in half-assed and be a part of something that was piecemealed together. So this guy went back to New York and Richard and I sort of took over and went from there."

The rest, of course, being history.

TANGO TRIVIA

Lindsey: "Everyone's been asking about 'Big Love' and who the woman going 'ahhhh' is—that's me. *People* magazine said it's my girlfriend, which she wasn't too happy about (*laughter*). I don't know where they get that stuff." Likewise, the low voice on "Family Man" is a sped-up/slowed-down Lindsey.

Stevie: "'Welcome To The Room . . . Sara' is very much a secret kind of song. Sara is from *Tusk,* that's the same Sara we're talking about—and she just has some experiences that she's talking about. I don't really want anyone to know whether I'm going into her room or she's coming into mine, or what's in the room. This room is an ominous room. I'm not Bob Dylan, but every once in awhile I've gotta say something."

Lindsey: "Most of my solo stuff just went over onto the Fleetwood Mac album, the theory being you're just indicting your own capabilities if you say this has to be for one thing—if you've got it and you need it, you should use it. There's always something better coming along, ultimately."

Stevie: "How do you like my slow song with Lindsey singing at the end ('When I See You Again')? That's one of my favorite things . . . I *made* him sing with me; I said, 'Lindsey, you're gonna sing on all my songs whether you like it or not—you *have* to sing this with me.' So we went out and sang 'If I see you again, will it be over?'—we sang it in unison, then I snuck in and took my voice off. Otherwise, I'd have never gotten him to do it—see, Lindsey's pretty shy and he's singing differently there than he is on anything else on the record. He wouldn't think to do that: to sing on my song at the end. He would think to sing with me, but he wouldn't want to end it. But that's what I wanted, to leave people feeling they are really talking to each other."

WHERE'S THAT TOUR?

The last Mac tour was back in '82. Given their present circumstances—since each member has their own manager, "there's basically 10 people in the band," as Christine McVie so neatly puts it—a tour might not be the easiest thing in the world to put together, especially for a band that "dribbled" into their album. Like so much of Macdom, it would seem to revolve around Lindsey.

"Inherently, Lindsey's—I wouldn't say adverse to playing, because he enjoys that function—but, given the choice, he would be happier sitting in the studio," says Mick. "I have a sneaking suspicion that we will tour . . . it's just a question of when."

"I think it's important that we do," says Christine. "This is my, and only my, opinion: we've never released an album without backing it up with a tour, and I think this album should be no exception."

Let's hear from Stevie: "I love to go on tour, whether it's Fleetwood Mac or me or anything. Tom Petty, Heart, anybody'd who'll ask me to go, I'm duffle bag packed and on the bus the next day. But it's up to Lindsey."

When it's put to him, here's what Lindsey has to say: "Ooooh. Ooooh (*laughter*). I don't know, probably—I know they're going to start talking about it real soon. It would be lucrative. I . . . I . . . don't know.

"I've never toured myself," he continues. "That's something I'd like to try doing. I'd like to put something somewhere between Laurie Anderson and Frank Sinatra together, as far as a stage show. Get some Sam Shepard plays in there onstage.

"In that light, that's the kind of touring that interests me now. There are certain aspects of a Fleetwood Mac show that would have to be inherently nostalgic, and going up there and playing 'Rhiannon,' quite honestly, doesn't really appeal to me now. But, hey—if it's playing ball again, if it's finishing out what needs to be done for this album—well, then, I'll do whatever needs to be done."

IS FLEETWOOD MAC A VIABLE GROUP
OR A COLLECTION OF PEOPLE WHO GET TOGETHER
AND MAKE A RECORD EVERY FIVE YEARS?

"Well, that's a good—I don't know what you call it."—Lindsey Buckingham.

THINGS THAT WILL FOLLOW

Tour or not—heck, *band* or not—the various members of F. Mac have numerous projects to occupy their time. Mick Fleetwood plays with his side group, the Zoo, really unable to keep from performing while the Mac machine moves in its necessarily sluggish fashion. Christine McVie will get to work on her next solo album next year and has already asked Lindsey and Richard Dashut to produce some tracks. John McVie is a sailor, the owner of a 60-some-odd-foot boat that cruises the world. And Stevie is Stevie, so she'll always have something to do, one supposes.

As for Lindsey, he says this: "I've worked a long time to get to the point where a lot of things seem as intact as they are now. As much as I love this album—and I think it's done well for my, and everyone's, morale—I feel like I'm really on the threshold of a lot of other things that are going to be even more exciting for me. And that's a nice feeling to feel."

Although not interested in becoming a "production factory," there are people he'd like to work with. Brian Wilson is one.

"He's been one of my main guys," Lindsey says with enthusiasm. "I like his real experimental period, too. But he seems to want to do a teen/pop album and—to me—if he were to pick up on where 'Wind Chimes' left off, think of himself as more a pop Philip Glass . . ." the thought trails off.

"I gave him a tape of Laurie Anderson, Peter Gabriel and some of his old stuff—'Wind Chimes' and some really experimental stuff—I don't think he ever listened to it. He didn't seem to get it. He brought this song over and he said, 'Do this thing like this (*begins chunking out a 12-bar rhythm*),' so I tried to take something out of that and make it something other than a 12-bar, which it was. And finally, after about three different tries, I came up with something. It's not 'Wind Chimes,' but it could be more atmospheric, like Phil Spector's 'Walking In The Rain,' which would certainly be a step in the right direction. But I have yet to call him."

Lindsey says he'd also like to work with Laurie Anderson, and mentions that Stevie was recently asking him on the phone if he'd like to do another Buckingham/Nicks album.

His voice becomes more pensive than usual, which is getting pretty pensive. "You just don't usually have to do that sort of thing—to break up with someone and then see them for the next 12 years. That's just not normal . . . it's not even very well. It's sort of an ill thing to have to do, but what the hell.

"I've gotta tell you, the last 12 years, I think I've probably blocked out some of the more painful aspects. It seems like a big, long dream from which I'm just now awakening. I feel younger now than I have in years. I feel more *new* than I have in years. It's a surreal thing, on that mega level.

"It's gonna be a good year."

DIRTY DANCING

Fleetwood Mac Swap Partners for Tango Tour

Dave Zimmer | October 23, 1987 | *BAM* (US)

This interview feature could have been titled "Where's Lindsey?"

In almost the bookend to David Gans's 1982 feature "Where's Stevie?," it is Lindsey Buckingham's turn to feel the wrath of colleagues who feel he has deserted them. Earlier in the year, he had departed from Fleetwood Mac in an ugly incident that will be touched on in several other places in this book. Although the band members are circumspect about the events, a coldly furious Nicks doesn't hold back on what she considers to be Buckingham's character flaws.

Buckingham's departure ostensibly sunk the opportunity for the group to promote *Tango in the Night* with live work. Yet despite the members admitting in this interview that *Tango* was essentially Buckingham's album, they elected to tour regardless. After all, replacing personnel had been an integral part of the Fleetwood Mac story since way back when. Perhaps significantly, though, it took two people—guitarists Billy Burnette and Rick Vito—to fill the space Buckingham had vacated.

When Lindsey Buckingham announced his departure from Fleetwood Mac in mid-August, he threw the band's future into doubt. "A lot of people probably expected us to do the ol' roll over on your back trick," recalls Mike Fleetwood. "What were we supposed to do?" asks Stevie

Nicks. "Lindsey left. So did that mean we were done? No. Why should the rest of us quit just because of him?" Mick adds, "Rather than shut down, we decided to press on and get out on the road."

Tango in the Night, their first album in five years, was selling briskly; it recently passed the one million mark. There was every indication, then, that a Fleetwood Mac audience still existed. But who was going to fill Buckingham's shoes on stage? "We didn't hold auditions or anything," answers Fleetwood. "I'd been working with Billy [Burnette]—he played guitar with my [solo] group Zoo and had done some writing with Christine [McVie]. But he's not a lead guitar player, he's a great rhythm player and singer and writer, but he's not a lead man. So I also rung up Rick [Vito, who had previously played lead guitar with John McVie and John Mayall, as well as Jackson Browne and Bob Seger]."

Vito remembers, "I devoted a couple of days to learning the material. After I played with the band for a few hours, I think it was obvious it was jelling. I realized this could be fun and pretty great. But this chance . . . it wasn't something I would have sat down and thought about as being in my future."

But both Vito and Burnette, introduced as "permanent members" at an August 18 press conference, are very much a part of Fleetwood Mac's future. "The group will be my first priority," says Burnette, who released an engaging solo album last year and is the son of '50s rocker Dorsey Burnette. "I'll continue to write on my own, but how much will depend on what they want to do." After a brief pause he corrects himself: "I mean what *we* want to do."

"Good answer," snickers Stevie Nicks, seated next to him at a large conference table. The other members of Fleetwood Mac are there too. Seeing them all together in one room—an extremely rare occurrence away from the studio or concert halls—it's hard to ignore the magical aura they still project. They *look* like stars. There's Stevie's charming, impish smile, Mick's rolling, Marty Feldman-eyes, Christine's glimmering sapphire eyes, and John's distinguished-looking salt and pepper stubble. Even Burnette and Vito could pass for daytime soap opera actors. Yet it's easy to understand how the guitarists, having only rehearsed with the band for a couple of weeks, could still feel like outsiders. But Nicks stresses, "They aren't just fill-in guys. They're in the group. And everybody is playing as one unit now. Neither Billy nor Rick are freaking out on stage trying to get all their licks in."

While it might seem odd that Buckingham was replaced by two guitarists, this move actually brings Fleetwood Mac closer to its original instrumental format. When the group was formed in England back in 1967, guitarists Peter Green and Jeremy Spencer worked in tandem with the enduring Fleetwood (drums) and John McVie (bass) rhythm section. A year later, Danny Kirwan was brought on board as a *third* guitarist.

"This process shaped the bluesy sound of Fleetwood Mac," says singer/keyboardist Christine McVie, who officially joined the group in 1971. When Californians Bob Welch, Bob Weston, then Buckingham eventually filled the guitarist's spot, the group's sound, not surprisingly, shifted into more of a pop direction. Christine believes, "I can now see us getting back to more of a blues thing. Rick . . . I don't want to say he's like Peter Green, but he plays wonderful blues *a la* Peter. And Billy's got this great hard, driving voice. So we've definitely got a whole new can of beans here."

This represents the first personnel change in Fleetwood Mac since 1975 when Buckingham and Nicks (formerly a duo act) joined up and helped catapult the band into American superstar territory. The albums *Fleetwood Mac* and *Rumours,* featuring such songs as "Rhiannon," "Say You Love Me" and "Dreams" (the group's first number one single), topped *Billboard*'s charts. And *Rumours,* which has now sold over 20 million copies worldwide, held the number one spot for 31 weeks (a record surpassed only by Michael Jackson's *Thriller*) in 1977. Mick reflects, "We'd already been a highly successful band in England. In 1969, you couldn't get any bigger than we were over there. We didn't reach that level in America until eight years later. But we could see it coming. It's not like we were a bunch of 18-year-old kids that had just put a band together and boom! and we have an album go through the ceiling. We were prepared and could deal with the inevitable comments like, 'Ah, look at you now, you've gone commercial on us.'"

"When Lindsey and Stevie joined up," says Christine, "we didn't consciously alter our sound, but at the same time, I thought, 'Hmmm. I think this is something special we've got here.'"

Stevie says, "The very first big concert I played with Fleetwood Mac, at the Oakland Coliseum with Peter Frampton [in 1976], I couldn't believe all those *people* were out there. We weren't famous. The record [*Fleetwood Mac*] had just come out. We hit the road. Then, within three months, we were all famous and on our way with the hits."

Rather than follow up this commercial well-spring with similar material, the band unveiled an ambitious double-record set called *Tusk* in 1979. Filled with both conventional pop and adventurous percussion-dominated tracks, it cemented Lindsey Buckingham's role as the group's arranger/producer/musical director. He continued in this capacity for *Fleetwood Mac Live* (released in December, 1980), *Mirage* (June, 1982) and *Tango in the Night* (April, 1987). Christine admits, "Lindsey and [co-producer] Richard [Dashut] were at the fore, without question, when it came to the ideas and the sound and the production. And they were very good at it. Of course, one has to say, *nothing* went on the albums that the rest of us didn't like. If anything got a bit too left wing, which it might have in certain cases, I definitely would have put my foot down and said, 'Wait a minute lads.'"

Stevie Nicks, whose stormy relationship with Buckingham has been well-documented, offers a different viewpoint: "In the studio, if Lindsey said the wall was gray, I'd be absolutely sure it was pink. In order to get one of my songs on a record, I'd have to say, 'OK, the wall's gray, Lindsey.' Otherwise, it was the back of the bus. Now this has nothing to do with the other members of Fleetwood Mac, who, from the beginning, have always been lovely to me, have always known how important my songs are to me, whereas, with Lindsey, he would rather I just stayed at home doing laundry. We're talking about a man who was in love with a woman and would just as soon she had faded out and just been his old lady or wife. Period."

"Whooo," sighs Christine after a full five seconds of silence.

Mick interjects, "That situation changed somewhat, in my opinion."

Stevie narrows her eyes and says, "Not when it came down to the real thing. Uh uh. Never changed."

When she launched her solo career in 1981 with the release of *Bella Donna*, Stevie admits, "There was a part of me that was saying, 'See, I can do it myself. I don't need you every second to do everything for me.'"

On her first solo tour, however, she remembers, "In Houston, in front of 12,000 people, when they said, 'Welcome, Stevie Nicks,' I turned around and looked for Mick and Chris and John and couldn't believe I was walking out there by myself. I'd do a song, then instead of being able to saunter off, have a touch-up done on my make-up, have my hair fluffed, and put on a different jacket, then saunter back on, I'd hear, 'Hey, this ship is gonna sink if you go in there for five minutes!' So I ran around on stage in circles for a couple of weeks." Stevie adds, "I would just as soon not be the captain. I never liked being responsible for everything. Too much time is wasted handling problems that have nothing to do with music. Basically, I don't like being a businesswoman, which is what I *have* to be when I'm on my own. Again, the only reason I started a solo career is because I wanted to do more of my songs. I'd much rather work within Fleetwood Mac."

Christine McVie echoes this sentiment. "I was never too keen on the idea of a solo thing," she says. "I don't enjoy the pressure of being the only one up there who everybody looks to for leadership. I like being part of a group. But the time was trickling on by and [in 1983] I could see Fleetwood Mac wasn't going to be happening for awhile, so I did an album [*Christine McVie*] and a tour [in '84]. That was hard work. I had to do my own make-up and the whole bit. My make-up used to run down my face and by the end of the night it was horrific. So no, I wouldn't want to tour [solo] again. My life, musically speaking, has always been Fleetwood Mac—at least for the last 20 years—and I've enjoyed it thoroughly."

It's doubtful anyone could have been happier to return to the Mac family than Mick Fleetwood. While he kept busy working with his side band, Zoo, and gave acting a shot, Fleetwood also ran into financial difficulties and had to file for bankruptcy. But the even-tempered drummer managed to keep his life together. Says Christine: "Mick is like the daddy for us all and he always sort of has been." John McVie adds, "Musically,

Mick is my first lock in." "John and Mick," Christine concludes, "they're the ol' backbone of the group."

By his own admission, John needed a little support himself earlier this decade. Before the *Tango in the Night* sessions began in 1985, John's life was dominated by a drinking problem—which he has since recovered from. Christine says, "He's really doing wonderfully now." But he's not the type of person who enjoys talking about himself. Like a great many rock bass players, he prefers to remain in the background. "By nature," says Christine, "John's a very quiet, private person. He likes to read and keep to himself. On stage and in the studio, he's always so steady, he never loses the groove. On the last record, he played amazingly."

Listening to *Tango,* the entire band appeared to be reaching frequent musical peaks. Stevie has never sounded better (During "When I See You Again," she sings the word "baby" about ten different ways). Christine's "Little Lies," the current Top 20 single, is poetic whimsy at its best. As for Lindsey Buckingham, he not only arranged and produced the record, but had a hand in writing seven of its 12 tracks. He sings so forcefully (particularly throughout "Tango in the Night"), plays guitar with such vigor and assurance, and seems to bring out the strengths of everyone around him, it's tough to figure how he could just walk away.

"During the sessions," recalls Christine, "we sensed this was probably the last thing Lindsey would do with us. It was sort of said, but not said, you know? He admitted his solo career was becoming his priority. But by the end of the album, he did sort of agree to tour, then at the eleventh hour, he just pulled out, saying that he simply couldn't cope with it."

Here's Lindsey's statement, issued through his manager. "In 1985, I was working on my third solo album when the band came to me and asked me to produce the next Fleetwood Mac project. At that point, I put aside my solo work, which was half-finished, and committed myself for the next 17 months to produce *Tango in the Night*. It was always our understanding that upon completion of the *Tango* album I would return to my solo work. Of course I wish them all the success in the world on the road."

Christine reveals, "Whenever we played live, Lindsey always did it sort of under sufferance. He simply doesn't like touring. He would just as soon stay in the studio. And that just isn't the case with the rest of us."

Buckingham chose not to respond further on his departure from Fleetwood Mac, and is now in the process of finishing up a solo project. He's also been in the studio as a producer for the Dream Academy and Brian Wilson.

"I have nothing but respect for Lindsey and what he's doing," says Christine. "He was never less than honest with us. And after 12 years in the band, it must have been something of a wrench for him [to leave]. But if someone's not happy, then *nobody's* happy. I think his decision was best for everyone's concern."

During rehearsals for the current "Shake The Cage Tour," Mick says, "It felt good to be playing again and the songs came together rather fast. Before our last tour [the three-month "Mirage Tour" in '82] a lot of time was spent cogitating, then we'd creep up onstage and play a bit. Now we seem to be much more focused, there are no distractions and the onus is on the band vs. the individual. I'm all for solo projects, but when they create these long time lapses, everyone gets jittery. I mean, Fleetwood Mac used to be road *dogs*. So when we have a gap like this last one . . . over five years . . ."

"It makes you feel like you don't have a job," says Stevie.

With Fleetwood Mac's touring schedule set to cover America this fall and include dates in Australia and Europe next year, she shouldn't have to worry about checking the classifieds for awhile. And she can put her solo career on hold indefinitely. "That's no problem," Stevie says. "I can't think of nicer, more talented people to work with. I look forward to seeing them. I really do. For me, this is a pleasure thing. It makes everything else all right."

1987 marks Fleetwood Mac's 20th Anniversary, so it's surprising that the band (or their record company, Warner Bros.) hasn't made a bigger deal over the milestone. But as Mick points out, "Besides me and John, there've been so many different players."

Stevie admits, "I've never met half the people who used to be in the band."

But the odds of seeing a grand anniversary celebration on stage is highly unlikely, says Mick. "It might be fairly bizarre, though. I guess we could have then called this 'The Rolex Tour.' But we've got enough going on without taking time out to look back. We're touring to establish the band as it is now."

In the wake of Fleetwood Mac's personnel shuffle, one has to wonder how it affected the balance of power within the band. "What power?" asks Christine. "No one is coming out as a kind of boss. I guess you could say Lindsey used to fill that role in the studio, and at some point I'm sure someone else will emerge. Right now, I seem to be the one who's taking care of the primary business, and Mick, like I said, is the group's daddy. But we really don't have one person who acts as boss. We all just sit around and mutually agree on things. It's hard to say what will happen in the studio. We'll just have to wait and see."

THE SUPERNATURAL

Harry Shapiro | May 1994 | *Mojo* (UK)

By 1994 the fact that it had once been "Peter Green's Fleetwood Mac" was fading from public memory, and even unknown to many of the millions who owned *Rumours*. This article reminded people of the onetime Mac lynchpin. By talking to musicians who worked with him before and after Fleetwood Mac, it explores nonchronologically how Green's extraordinary talent evolved, then crashed and burned.

Pete Moody
Former bass player with The Grebbels
"We were support band to The Yardbirds at the Crawdaddy and Peter used to come along and watch Eric [Clapton], and also our guitarist Roger Pearce who was quite well thought of at the time. When The Grebbels broke up early in 1965, Peter came round to Roger's house and asked him whether he wanted to form a band. That band was The Muskrats which had Dave Bidwell on drums [later of Chicken Shack] and which eventually became the first incarnation of the John Dummer Blues Band. I first saw Peter play guitar when he was rehearsing with The Muskrats in Sheen. It was a very, very explosive style, the way he was heard with John Mayall and Peter Bardens . . . magic."

Snowy White
Guitarist
New album Highway To The Sun out soon in the US and Japan, featuring Chris Rea and Dave Gilmour

"I first met Pete in 1970. I phoned him up and said, like, You're my favourite guitar player, can we have a jam together? I thought he'd just say Piss off, but he said, Right, come down tomorrow. He was still living with his mum and dad and the parrot. We both had Les Pauls and played all afternoon without even plugging them in. He wasn't really doing anything at that time—he'd just left Fleetwood Mac, although he went back for a while after Jeremy Spencer disappeared. After that we knocked around together; he'd come and borrow my car or sleep on the settee as he gradually became more reclusive.

"At one point he gave me his guitar to keep and then he wanted to sell it to me for what he'd paid for it. I was flat broke at the time and it would have meant me selling my Les Paul to afford it. I thought about it for ages, but in the end I told Pete, Look, don't sell it. If you don't feel like playing it, just keep it in the attic. But he took the guitar back and the next thing I heard, he'd sold it to Gary Moore.

"That special Peter Green sound came about partly by accident, when the pick-ups were changed and put back out of phase. When that happens you lose certain frequencies and you get this middling flutey sound that Peter made his own. With Peter's guitar, the pick-ups were switched out of phase, so you couldn't go back to normal sound, which was why I didn't want it.

"His magic lies in the strength of his confidence in what he's doing plus a lack of confidence that makes you more sensitive, plus he left all these spaces in the music, didn't have to prove how fast he was."

Roger Pearce
Former guitarist with The Muskrats

"Even though Peter was playing bass at the time, he could already play Eric's lead break from The Yardbirds' I Ain't Got You. Nobody except Peter had worked out what Eric was doing. When The Muskrats did the song live, we did the solo twice, I'd take the first one and cock it up and then Peter would do it faultlessly on bass. He was a very, very good bass player, but he obviously came to the realisation that he could play guitar just as well as anybody else.

"We did this one gig at a posh rowing club near Staines and we had to play outside doing R&B standards with all these people walking around in blazers and boaters. We were playing near the water at full volume and of course, sound travels across water like anything. We were well into the first set when this guy in a blazer comes up red in the face, looking like Captain Mainwaring from Dad's Army, and demanded that we stop playing. We carried on and Peter was just doubled up pissing himself laughing. Eventually we stopped and they threw us out.

"Even after he started with Peter Bardens, he'd still come around, tell me what he was up to and he'd want to know what I thought of his playing and he'd show me things on guitar and ask me what I thought. Well, what can you say when somebody is standing in front of you being so flash without meaning to be and so obviously in control of what he was doing? He once said to me that he wanted to express as much as he could using as few notes as possible, and I think he succeeded in that. Need Your Love So Bad says it all."

Jeff Whittacker
Leader of Peter's last band, Kolors
Currently planning to open the Flowerpot Club in Stamford Hill as a rock venue

"Peter and I had a mutual friend in Godfrey McLean who was the drummer on The End Of The Game and it was really because of Godfrey that Peter and I came together. I was asked to fix [get the musicians together] for In The Skies and What'cha Gonna Do? which were the two albums for PVK after Little Dreamer. But I was also working in Germany, and when I came back Peter didn't seem too happy and said he wanted me to be more involved in the next album, which was White Sky (1982). It was really then we realised that we worked very well together.

"Eventually we got a band together that was a good cover for Peter because he was not well by this time. But we got gigs all over Europe; we were on tour for over three years at six weeks at a time. Eventually it was what was happening on the business side that broke the band up. We had dates in various countries; Peter wasn't allowed to go and was freaking out about money because of all the problems he had in Fleetwood Mac. He was sitting in his house refusing to move and that was that.

"There are too many people, fans, who seem to look to Peter for answers and if you are like that with Peter, you scare the hell out of him because he knows he ain't got no answers. Once we had a gig in Finland and we were just coming back to do the gig after the sound check and there's a queue and a couple of fans recognised him. Oh, Peter Green, you're my hero, you're my hero. And Peter turned round and said, Yes and you're my hero too. And the guy got really upset and was shouting. Peter turned to me and was laughing and said, See, see what I have to deal with.

"I still believe that Peter is the best feel guitarist in Europe even today. He can still do it because he is a strong man and he loves music, and when he's in the right frame of mind and not scared by any elements, and not hearing all the voices in his head, he can play. I've been with him in his front room only 18 months ago, he played the hell out of that guitar."

Maggie Bell

"I met Peter Green in 1972 through Steve Thompson who'd been with John Mayall and who played bass in my band, Stone The Crows. Steve said that Pete had been out of the limelight for somewhile and would be good to get as a replacement for Les Harvey [who died on stage in May 1971]. We picked him up at the station and he had this rucksack and his hair cut really short and looking very healthy. We were supposed to do this festival and we spent six weeks rehearsing at keyboard player Ronnie Leahy's house. He was playing so well right through rehearsals, and then two days before the festival we got a phone call to say that he couldn't make it. It just wasn't to be.

"Peter was a very quiet and shy person; he seemed to think that people were looking at him or taking the piss. Fame can be a terrible thing . . . Peter wasn't into all that; he'd just as easily sleep on your sofa, he despised money. As long as he had enough to get along, enough for a packet of cigarettes and a couple of beers, he was quite happy."

Ed Spevock
Drummer
Formerly with Babe Ruth and Chicken Shack
"I first got to know Peter at school when I was about 14; we were in the same year at the Elliot Comprehensive School. I'd got interested in drums and Pete said he played bass. I met up with him about three or four

months after we'd left school and he said he'd joined a pro band called Errol Dixon & The Honeydrippers. When Peter was in Peter Bardens's band and then John Mayall's we used to keep meeting on the train going into town, when I was still working during the day, and by then he had changed a bit. He used to be a very quiet fellow, but now he came across as a much stronger personality and it made me think: I really want to be a pro musician, that's what it does to you. Peter knew what he liked and didn't like and was authoritative when it came to music.

"Once Fleetwood Mac got big, we sort of lost contact, but around 1976 just as Babe Ruth was coming to the end, he phoned up one day and we saw each other quite regularly after that. He seemed very tired at that point, as if the spark had gone out of him. He told me that when Fleetwood Mac went to America, it all got too much for him because everybody was looking to him for guidance and leadership. I think most of the fun in a band is looking forward to something you haven't got—once you've got it, maybe you realise that the best part was wishing for it."

Ronnie Johnson
Guitarist
Played on the sessions for Peter Green's solo albums Little Dreamer (1980) and What'cha Gonna Do? (1981); currently with Van Morrison
"I got involved with Peter through Peter Vernon Kell who ran PVK records. PVK had already done one album with Peter and I think they wanted to change the musicians a bit to try and get him to play a bit more. Also I came from a different area of music, more jazz influenced.

"The sessions were interesting and a lot of fun. Peter arrived at the studio for the early sessions with these incredibly long nails and the producer was frantically trying to cut them so Peter could play. Another time, we were really going well and suddenly Peter stops and looks across at John and says, No, no, no, you're taking me to Brighton and I want to go to Shepherd's Bush. We just all collapsed laughing. That might sound a bit bizarre, but in terms of the music, there was an element of truth in what he said.

"Peter grew in confidence as time went on. The last sessions I did with him were for an album called White Sky (1982). He bought himself a Marshall amp with a Leslie hooked up to it and was trying out different sounds. On the days when he was alright, he was very together and playing extremely well."

Zoot Money

"I knew Peter back in the Flamingo Club days with John Mayall, but we didn't get to play together until he phoned me about his solo album, The End Of The Game, which he owed Warners. He said he hadn't prepared anything, but would I like to come and play? Which is exactly what we did; we just played away and took the tapes and put it all in some sort of order. It started around 10 in the evening and it was heads down until around four then it was like, Right, ta-ta, hope that was enough.

"He stayed with me for a brief spell, one of his 'spare' periods about 1975-1976 when he wasn't playing at all. I brought a guitar down and left it around and found him playing it one day and next thing I knew he was in the studio recording. At the time, I didn't ask for anything because I just wanted to play. But when Peter was staying with me, he was going through some kind of redemption, restitution phase, you know, What can I do with my life? And I said jokingly, Well yer bugger, you can start by paying me that session money. And about two weeks later after he'd gone, I got a cheque in the post!"

Mike Vernon
Producer of John Mayall and Fleetwood Mac

"The first thing I ever knew about Peter Green was when he turned up at Decca in West Hampstead. Me and Gus Dudgeon were looking across at him and thinking, Who the hell is this? Where's Eric? John Mayall just said, Oh, he's Eric's replacement. I hadn't even heard that Eric had left the Bluesbreakers. John said Peter was as good as Eric, which was a bit hard to believe at first until he actually plugged in and then we thought, Ummm, he can play a bit!

"To start with, everyone was making comparisons with Eric, but once we got into recording Hard Road, Peter was obviously trying to carve out something that was his own. The Supernatural was a major departure in sound and feel from anything we'd done with Eric.

"Peter was able to really put good melodies together within his playing, probably more so than Clapton who had a much more rhythmical approach, he never got out of the groove. Whereas Eric had energy in his playing, Peter had a deftness, a touch and a more melodic style, and actually at that time he probably had a deeper blues than Eric.

"In my own personal estimation, Peter Green was just the very best blues guitarist this country has ever produced, and if anybody wants any proof of that all they have to do is listen to the Otis Spann album I did with Fleetwood Mac, The Biggest Thing Since Colossus [shortly to be re-released on CD]. Some of the guitar playing on that is absolutely stunning and it's all from the heart. B.B. King has said about Peter that here was a real bluesman and it was a privilege to work with him."

Dave Ambrose
Former bass player with Peter Bardens

"Peter and I were in all Peter Bardens' bands at that time and Shotgun Express with Mick Fleetwood. We came across Peter Green who was actually a bass player then, but he wanted to play blues guitar. So he joined and we played an awful lot on the Ricky Tick club circuit with John Mayall, The Who and so on. We were doing afternoon sessions, all-nighters—we were working very hard and it just taught us how to play.

"We were doing instrumentals, Booker T, Mose Allison stuff. It took us a while to realise just how good Peter was. Rod Stewart and Beryl Marsden came in as singers and the band changed to the Shotgun Express, doing mainly soul and Tamla Motown songs. We did a single which was a minor hit, but shortly after a lot of soul searching on his part, he left the band.

"He was a straightforward person, no nonsense, never said much—me and Mick and Pete Bardens were much more kind of wild and debonair. It was a good mix. In those days everything was just healthy, naïve, good fun, like hiding from each other in cupboards. Peter would always turn up wearing these baggy dungarees which I think was all part of trying to be a blues man."

SHALL I TELL YOU ABOUT MY LIFE?

A Rare Encounter with Peter Green

Mark Ellen | May 1994 | *Mojo* (UK)

In the pre-Internet age, artists who stopped giving interviews acquired a mystique unknown today, when fans are at least able to pick up fragments of information from the web and even "sightings" captured on smartphones. Peter Green's gradual disappearance from public life from the mid-seventies onward engendered all sorts of gossip about the fragile nature of his mental condition. This, his first published interview for nearly two decades, shockingly seemed to confirm those rumors.

At the time of this disturbing, sad Q&A, Green was still only forty-seven years old. Not only is he spiritually old before his time, he is unrecognizable from the vibrant, intense young man seen in the first two chapters of this book. Like Pink Floyd's Syd Barrett, Green's talent and very personality had been hollowed out by using LSD. It all makes clear why it had been impossible for him to remain in the band he founded.

I LAST SAW PETER GREEN AT THE GOLDEN LION IN THE Fulham Road in about 1982. A dispiriting night, even for someone prepared for the worst. Like anyone who'd religiously supported the original Fleetwood Mac till Green's departure, I'd heard the stories about his subsequent decline, but the sad, shivery, disembodied figure at the side of the stage—seemingly unaware that he was there or what was required of him—was simply heartbreaking.

His band shuffled into a series of slow blues patterns and then just stood around watching him, willing him to play something, anything at all. Another guitarist stood behind him and knocked out the sort of efficient solos Green might have conjured up on an off-day, while the old boy stared awkwardly at his fretboard, his scuffed fingers fiddling at the controls, as if even the most basic elements of his craft had forsaken him.

Since then, I'd heard very little. We ran a piece about Fleetwood Mac in Q in the late '80s and mentioned what various tabloids had rather gleefully discovered, that the great man had been sleeping rough in Richmond and had apparently hit rock bottom. So I was astonished when Mick Fleetwood gave me his lawyer's phone number and suggested we try and contact him. (Up to this point we hadn't imagined that Peter would be remotely interested in being interviewed—he hasn't given one since 1976.) She said she'd ask him and, if he felt like it, he'd call me at home.

What follows is virtually all of our 45-minute conversation. I haven't left much out—just some stuff about how he felt victimised by the noises outside his house, about relationships, and about the day centre he now attends, all of which was pretty upsetting, to be honest.

But for the most part he seemed thrilled to be finding new things to engage him—films, discovering Björk, going for walks. He can't (or won't) analyse anything and distrusts opinions, as if they are the indicators of sinister conspiracy. But, apart from those who put him in jail or treated him in hospitals, he seems utterly forgiving about everyone, stoically resigned about the past 20 years and, just occasionally, optimistic about the future.

———————————

Is this MOJO magazine?

It is. Thanks for ringing, Peter. I talked to Mick Fleetwood last night who said he listens to your old records all the time. I said, Does Peter? And he said, You ought to ask him.
No I don't. I'm going through a stage where I don't. I haven't got a record player set up, for the first thing. But it took me so long to record

those things that I really know them quite well, you know. But I do like listening when other people are listening. If I go somewhere and there's a jukebox on and it has one of my records on, I enjoy listening when other people are listening, seeing what they think of it.

Which records do you like hearing the most?
Um. Green Manalishi. Need Your Love So Bad. Albatross. Albatross I like. The mixing. I did most of it. Took over. I shouldn't have done that. I'm not happy with that. We should have had a separate producer instead of the group producing the records. It gets to be a bit too much for them. If I ever do music again I'll have a separate producer. Sometimes we had Mike Vernon, Blue Horizon Records, which was quite good. Not taxing the musicians too much.

Do you listen to any music?
We've got a record player. It's my brother's. But we don't often use it. It's got lots of books piled on top of it and things. I watch the MTV a lot, on Sky Television. I like Björk, is that her name? I'm a fan of hers. I enjoy watching her ever so much. She really brings me alive. I tried to buy her video, Human Behaviour, but it wasn't the same one as on television. It was a horrible one. Big noisy thing, it was. Like a disco thing. The kind of music that would ruin a disco! Pounding away. She's singing the same words but there's this boom-boom-boom drowning her singing.

What do you like about her?
I don't know how to answer that question, actually. I don't know how to answer it.

What else do you like on MTV?
I like that one, Circles, You Were Making Circles Around Me. I don't know who it's by. A folk group. I watch MTV at least once a day, but sometimes my brother and his wife think I should have a rest from sitting there glued to the telly. But Björk was on tonight. I Play Dead.

Did you see her on the BRIT Awards with Polly Harvey? They were fantastic.

Yeah I did! I was pleased with it. Satisfaction. I liked her having a go at it, yeah. Quite good. That's the first time I've seen her [Polly].

What else do you do?

Nothing much. I don't do much with my life at all. Just survive. I got into trouble, a hell of a lot of trouble. I ended up in prison. For threatening behaviour. A long time ago. But I haven't been doing much since I went to prison, 'cos they change your metabolism. It all changes into a kind of very plain ordinary thing, you know.

When was that?

I'm not sure if I can keep track of the dates. I threatened to shoot Clifford Davis, the group's manager. I wanted some money from him 'cos I was living in people's houses or hotels and things, sleeping around. He said he hasn't got any of my money, David Simmonds has got it, our accountant. I said, Look I'll shoot you. I recently bought a gun from Canada. It was like a fairground rifle, pump-action thing, made of nickel. It looked really nice. It was only like a toy but it did fire bullets. The police picked up on me and said, We hear you've got a gun. I said, Yeah, are you going to confiscate it? 'cos where I bought it you don't need a licence but in this country you do. They confiscated it and took me down to Marylebone Station where I spent the night and from there on I went to various prisons.

How long were you in prison for?

A couple of months, I'm not sure. I'd forgotten what I did. Also I got married, but we split up almost immediately. A girl called Jane. I met her at Steve Thompson's house, a friend of mine who plays bass . . .

He played with John Mayall. He was on Turning Point.

Yeah, that's him. I used to go round to his house a lot at nights and listen to records. Listen to Aretha Franklin, King Curtis, black music, old blues, all kinds of things. I met her round there! I proposed to her from a hospital where I was. I'm not sure why I was there. I think it was because I was giving my money away and they put it down to drugs, too much LSD. Giving me tranquillisers was the only thing they could think of doing. Any money that I didn't need I wanted to give it to buy food for starvation round the world. I asked the rest of the group if they wanted to do it, but they didn't want to do it, not really. Mick Fleetwood didn't want to do it, the rest of them said they would.

I talked to Mick and John about this very incident last night.
You talked to John, did you? Where did you contact John?

In Los Angeles.
I thought John was living in Hawaii on a boat. I saw a picture of it.

Well he was in Los Angeles last night. We talked about lots of things, about the way you made the records. Mick said you "already had the big picture" in your mind, that you knew how you wanted everything to sound.
Nah. It was nothing like that. There's such a lot of stuff . . . I was with a guy who wanted to do my autobiography. I didn't want to do it at first. Then I asked myself, Why don't I want to do it? Perhaps I should do it. So he came down to see me and all he had was quotes from other people who know me who I met up in the business. And the quotes about me were just wrong. They were wrong. Completely wrong.

You mean the information was wrong or you didn't agree with their opinions?
Wrong information. Not their opinions. It was just incorrect information. It just kept feeding through. It kept on coming. You're doing that as well now. You're giving me wrong information.

Well, I'm just telling you what they told to me.
Yeah, well they must be having a joke with you.

What do you remember about Fleetwood Mac? Are they happy memories?
I remember all of it. I was the founder member. It was down to me they existed. Mike Vernon or someone—Johnny Gunnel of Gunnel's Agency who had John Mayall—said you can make records with Blue Horizon, they're just starting out, they're looking for blues groups. So I did. Mike Vernon sent me up to see Jeremy Spencer. I went and saw him. I could see he was a little villain, you know. I thought I'd give it a try. Mick on drums. He said, all right. I couldn't get John McVie 'cos he was with John Mayall. So I got Bob Brunning, I thought he might develop nicely. Making Green Manalishi was one of the best memories. The mixing down of it in the studio. And listening to it back. I thought it would make Number 1. Lots of drums. Bass guitars. All kinds of things. Doubled-up on bass guitars. Six string basses. Tracking on it. Danny Kirwan and me playing those shrieking guitars together.

I was listening to Oh Well just last week. It still sounds wonderful.
I like the B-side of Oh Well. The Spanish guitar bit was the first bit I had of Oh Well. Didn't have the rest of it. I had the Spanish guitar bit come to me. I bought a Flamenco guitar to play it with. It was on Side Two. You like it? I heard people like it. The group carried on doing it, didn't they? Lindsey Buckingham carried on doing it.

Have you heard it recently? You should listen to it again!
No. A little bit of it comes on to Sky Television on an advert for jeans, a little bit of me singing about Oh Well.

I bloody well hope you're getting some royalties for it.
Woooah. I don't know. I can't tell. My lawyer is collecting for me. She said I should collect my money. I wouldn't know how to chase up about it, but my lawyer, she would know how to do it.

How did you get the others to play the music the way you wanted it?
I taught them it. I taught them their lines. I said, It goes like this. Which is hard for John 'cos he was a pretty hard customer to please, 'cos he'd played with Eric Clapton.

When did you last pick up a guitar?

I don't know. Long time ago. Hell of a long time ago.

I saw you in the Golden Lion in Fulham Road in about 1982.

The Golden Lion? Was I? Don't remember that. You sure it was me 'cos there's someone going around imitating me?

Oh it was definitely you. I get the impression that you're a lot happier than you appeared to be back then.

No, I'm not really happy. I'm very plain. When you've been stuck in prison and you're in London and you haven't done very much. I feel very plain. Life is very plain. Very truthful, like. When you're in prison for something you didn't really do . . .

But that was a long time ago, wasn't it?

Yeah, that was a fair while ago. I can't remember the date. I'm not good on dates.

But it still upsets you.

Nah, I didn't get upset . . . I quite enjoyed it! You got up early. Never know when night falls. They'd turn the lights on for a while and then they'd turn them off.

What happened after you got out of prison?

Nah, I'm sorry. I don't keep track of every moment 'cos you don't need to. You don't think it's going to come in use for anybody.

Well I'd love to hear about the early days in London, the blues clubs.

I saw Jimi Hendrix. I quite liked him. I used to idolise Eric Clapton at first. I thought his playing was absolutely thrilling, yeah.

A hard act to follow in John Mayall's group.

Oh, I couldn't hardly play anything at all. I was very novice.

How did you get the job then?

John said I could play a little bit and he said, You've got the feeling, or something like this. Anyway, he let me on the train. I did well for myself. I was only there for a week, then I got in with Peter B's Looners. I was with his band for about a year, then Eric Clapton was forming The Cream and I bumped into John Mayall on the road and John Mayall said Eric Clapton's going to form The Cream, with Ginger and Jack, do you want to come with me and get some experience? And be a blues band again instead of Booker T & The MGs and soul sections? I said, Yes I would very much like it. But I was only just starting. I wasn't a blues guitarist. I could play Hank Marvin stuff, Teen Scene by The Hunters, those old instrumentals. I could play all those fine. Semi-pro I was. But I chucked in my job . . . I've done a lot of jobs, you know.

What jobs have you had?

I worked in a graveyard once. Grave maintenance. Just cutting grass.

I remember that. Why did you do it?

I don't know. I just think I had to go to work. I don't know why. To make someone laugh, in the end, probably. But anyway, it didn't make me laugh. It was hard work sometimes.

Was it a deliberate attempt to get as far away from being a rock star as possible?

No, no. No deliberate attempt, no. I just use to take LSD and I took it one time too many. I only took it about eight times in all.

John said there was a terrible incident in Munich . . .

Yeah, they said they had a mansion, a house in the country, great big place it was. And I went back with one of the road managers and he gave me some LSD, so I ate it and I'd got my guitar so we played around with some music for a while. And then I just sat around and thought about everything. I was thinking so fast! I couldn't believe how fast I was thinking! And I kinda run out of thoughts. I must have been thinking solid for about an hour. Just sitting down on my mattress.

Have you got any regrets about the things that have happened to you?
Nah, not really. No. No, I haven't.

You wouldn't have lived your life any other way?
What would I leave out? What would I change? I wouldn't know where to begin changing.

John and Mick send their love to you. Is there anything I can tell them from you?
Tell them I'm sorry I let them down. I couldn't carry on doing it, for whatever reason. I think it was too much drugs. They [the management] tried to put someone onto me—a tough guy, a sparring partner—and he tried to punch me back to life but it didn't work.

Who was he?
Some bloke. Some tough guy. I don't really think I should talk about it. 'Cos he could get done for assault and battery. 'Cos we started off walking along together and . . . he was trying to show me that I wasn't prepared for everything that could happen to people.

Who sent him?
Clifford Davis, I imagine.

The manager?
Put him onto me. Gave me a bit of a bashing.

I can't believe how optimistic you sound now. You've had so many terrible experiences.
Yeah. I feel I'm coming through now. I'm hopeful nowadays.

Why?
I wouldn't know the answer to that question. Tell John and Mick if you see them that I'm sorry I couldn't be more help to them. I took one too many LSD trips. And that one puts me in the Care & Attention category.

You give me the impression you're getting better, though.
No, not really.

Do you keep in touch with the outside world?
No, I just zombie around. That's what I do. I'm taking tablets of some kind. I don't know what they're supposed to do for me. They make me sleepy. I fall asleep in the daytime. I never used to do that.

Do you read the papers or watch the news?
I don't read the newspapers. I didn't use to watch the news when I was a musician. I watch whatever's on, whatever my mother and my brother are watching. We watch a lot of films on Sky Television—all kinds, Westerns, you name it, swashbucklers.

What was the last concert you saw?
Eric Clapton, I suppose, at The Rainbow. Oh no, I went to see my brother's son. He plays saxophone in a Canvey Island group. Friday People they're called. They done the Rock Garden a few weeks back. They were good. Little bit loud.

Do you ever meet people who recognise you?
Yeah. Someone recognised me at the day centre the other day. Great long ginger hair he had. He said to me, You're not *the* Peter Green are you? And I said, yeah I suppose I would be. He kept asking me questions. Just like you!

SOUND YOUR FUNKY HORN

Mick Fleetwood

Johnny Black | December 1995 | *Mojo* (UK)

Mick Fleetwood's musical abilities are often overlooked in the rush to pay homage to the song-writing and musical abilities of the people who down the years he has recruited to Fleetwood Mac. When *Mojo* invited him to choose his favorites from his own catalog for the magazine's regular Sound Your Funky Horn feature, the resultant article provided an uncommon opportunity to dwell on some of Fleetwood's finest moments behind his drum kit. Meanwhile, Fleetwood's often joyous memories of what it was like in the early days to play with Peter Green serve as a counterbalance to the melancholy Green articles by which this feature is preceded in this book.

Note: For "Lindsay" read "Lindsey."

Shake Your Moneymaker
From Fleetwood Mac LP 1968 (Blue Horizon)

My ineptness to do separate things at speed became my style of drumming. When it got to a certain speed in the early days, the only way I could hang in there was if all my hands and feet were doing the same thing on the same beat. Shake Your Moneymaker is one where everything is going flat out and doing the same thing, so it kind of defines my style, the ultimate blues shuffle. Onstage it often ended up three times faster than the album version, and that's already fast enough.

As a song, it's what the original Fleetwood Mac was all about. Elmore James was top of the list. Dust My Broom and so forth, endless funky chunky shuffles and, in retrospect, I must say we were darn good at doing them. At that time, though, we didn't actually know what we were doing, we were just doing it.

Red Hot Jam
From Blues Jam At Chess LP 1969 (Blue Horizon)
This was just a riff we used to jam around on live a lot. I have a curious problem, partly, I think, because I'm dyslexic. I keep perfect time but I can lose track of where the off-beat or the on-beat is. Now if you're halfway through a song and the drummer changes from the on-beat to the off-beat, it's like a train wreck. It happened once at The Marquee. In full audience glare, I lost it. Pete was laughing at me, but you have to keep going, and Pete came back, physically grabbed my wrist and put me back in time. I nearly died of embarrassment.

When we went to Chess Studios in Chicago, we had the absolute thrill of jamming on the same thing with Buddy Guy, Willie Dixon, Otis Spann. When we walked in, these old guys were going, like, "OK, we'll do this, but we really don't know what these little punks think they're playing at." They were friendly, but they had no idea what to expect. When we actually started playing, they suddenly realised that Peter was for real. They didn't understand it. Why this should be coming out of England blew anyone's logic.

Oh Well
Single 1969 (Reprise)
In the Peter Green era, a lot of stuff we did was harder than it sounded. Guitarists still ask me how Peter played that Oh Well riff. What it is, is that there's a couple of notes in there where he bent the chord so that certain notes sounded like other notes. That song drove me crazy because it's a very structured song. I was used to counting in, starting and then steaming ahead and then finishing, but Oh Well is so tightly structured that you have to pay attention all the time. The famous little cowbell signature was a mistake, but Peter liked it and decided to keep it in. So I had to re-learn my mistake, which was not easy.

I did it OK on the recording but the hardest thing was miming it for Top Of The Pops because it happens when nothing else is going on. It had to look perfect. So for 10 days I took a little portable tape recorder everywhere with me to get it right. In the end I greased it off really well.

Man Of The World

From Live At The BBC LP 1995 (Castle Communications)

This is the song that breaks my heart. It has some great sections, a totally composed song. You cannot substitute technique for feeling, because feeling will always win out. Man Of The World is somebody, it's Peter Green, crying out at an early stage, and I now wish I'd realised it at the time, because as a friend I might have been able to help when he went into his darkness of depression. This is everything about Peter, certainly prophetic, in the sense of what later happened to him and the journey he took. I lost the person I knew for a while, but I'm happy to say he's back in my life and doing pretty damn good in terms of coming back into the everyday bustle and hustle of life.

Hypnotized

From Mystery To Me LP 1973 (Reprise)

In England our Bob Welch period meant very little but in America we were doing OK on the underground college circuit. Hypnotized is classic Bob Welch from a relatively unknown era of Fleetwood Mac that gets overlooked. It was one of Bob's first songs for us, and lyrically interesting because it deals with UFOs, which he was fascinated by. I started a groove in the session, we added the band when we rehearsed it. It's so damn simple. Ba-ba-ba-bom, ba-ba-babom, ba-ba-ba-bom, ba-ba-ba-bom. No drum fills, nothing. It's so simple, but drummers used to ask me how to do it. It's nothing but a snare drum and the rest of the beats are on a bass drum, fairly briskly played, yet they never cop it.

This is also the beginning of the vocal harmonies which later became our trade mark.

Go Your Own Way

Single 1977 (Warner Bros)

I don't write songs in Fleetwood Mac, but I have to say I have a lot to do with how they end up. Most of my best ideas are glorious accidents, but there's a great knack in learning to be objective about your accidents.

Go Your Own Way's rhythm was a tom tom structure that Lindsay [Buckingham] demoed by hitting Kleenex boxes or something to indicate what was going on. I never quite got to grips with what he wanted, so the end result was a mutated interpretation of what he was trying to get at. It's completely back to front, and I've seen really brilliant drummers totally stumped by it. When Lindsay went out on his own, he took three drummers onstage and they did Go Your Own Way, but they couldn't get it right. It's a major part of that song, a back to front approach that came, I'm ashamed to say, from capitalising on my ineptness.

Tusk
Single 1979 (Warner Bros)
This came from a riff we used to jam on in soundchecks. When we started the album we worked on it but everybody lost interest in it. It went in the dustbin for about a year until I pulled it out again. I took it with me to Normandy as a rough track and had the idea of using a brass band and about 45 drummers.

When I said I wanted to record the USC Marching Band at Dodger Stadium they were sure I'd gone round the twist, so I paid for it myself. We even filmed it, and they really thought I'd blown it, way off the deep end. Despite having virtually no lyric, it became one of our biggest hits. It really worked and it's a glorious noise, something I'm very proud of. I still find it on juke-boxes. And later, we got to play live with the marching band which was marvellous.

Rattlesnake Shake
From Mick Fleetwood solo album The Visitor 1981 (RCA)
I did this just for me. A lot of what I do is for Fleetwood Mac, so I suppose I indulged myself. Rattlesnake Shake is an old Peter Green song about my ample habits as a young masturbatory male. I'd leap out of the van, they'd turn the lights on me and I'd mimic the art of wanking.

I redid it in Ghana with a fantastic drum ensemble. I took a mobile studio to Ghana at great expense, because I knew I'd find great drummers there. The eldest guy was just 14 and the master drummer was seven years old, and it absolutely blew my mind.

I took it back to England, put the London Philharmonic on at the end, and I even got Peter to add a little bit of guitar at the very end. It's that same old magic, one note reverb sound just put in the right place, and of course he sang it.

Shakin' The Cage
From Shakin' The Cage LP by Mick Fleetwood's Zoo 1992 (Capricorn)
The title track epitomises what we were doing musically. There's a fun drum break in the middle, almost the same approach as that wild thing in the middle of Tusk. Totally off the wall, a combination of conventional kit playing and other percussion.

I formed Zoo with an Australian singer, Billy Thorpe, who was a great influence on AC/DC and people like that. It turned out to be almost a training ground for young Bekka Bramlett, who is now in Fleetwood Mac. Billy Burnette, also now in Fleetwood Mac, wrote Shakin' The Cage with Billy Thorpe, so, atmospherically, those sessions brought energy back to Fleetwood Mac.

I liked that band a lot. We nearly had a shot at making it, but then probably if we had, Bekka Bramlett wouldn't be in Fleetwood Mac, and it would be my side-band.

These Strange Times
From Time LP 1995 (Warner Bros)
This is almost new age meets Burundi. It's a spoken word piece of mine, using a lot of drums I got in Ghana. I mean, I haven't opened my gob in nearly 30 years, but I had this little philosophical, anecdotal thing I just had to get off my chest.

It means a lot to me. The subject matter is inspired by Peter Green, but it's also about me. I nearly destroyed myself with drugs and alcohol and crazy behaviour, and this is a positive thought mode that you can get out of the dark, into the light. I was a functioning addict for a long time. It wasn't as bad as it sounds, because as long as I had my stuff, I functioned perfectly normally and looked just like anybody else, but I was dependent on drugs to maintain that state. So this song is about getting out of that mire.

MICK FLEETWOOD, 1997

Steven Rosen

Following his traumatic exit from the band, Lindsey Buckingham could be posited as having had the last laugh: the public did not warm to Fleetwood Mac without him.

The Billy Burnette/Rick Vito configuration recorded *Behind the Mask* (1990). By the recording of *Time* (1995), Vito and Nicks had left and vocalist Bekka Bramlett and ex-Traffic guitarist Dave Mason had come aboard. The former album was greeted with lukewarm sales, the latter with abysmal ones. In 1995 the band astounded the world by announcing that Fleetwood Mac was no more, an implicit acknowledgment that, for the very first time, personnel changes had not effected regeneration.

The split didn't last long. It soon emerged that the *Rumours* Five—who had briefly coalesced in 1993 to play at Bill Clinton's presidential inauguration—were working together again. In 1997 they issued *The Dance*, a live album recorded for an *MTV Unplugged* performance. It took Fleetwood Mac back to the top of the US charts for the first time since *Mirage*.

This Mick Fleetwood interview was conducted to promote *The Dance*. Originally published in Japan, this is its first appearance in English. As well as discussing the new record, Fleetwood gives an insight into how the first line up of Fleetwood Mac came together.

Ten years ago, could you have imagined that you'd ever be playing with these musicians again?

In the back of my mind, and the only mind it would be in the back of, my fanciful mind would have said, "I would love for that to be a possibility." And therefore I would be dreaming that it could happen. The reality was a lot less likely, but if you have a dream, they often come true.

Were those last days of Fleetwood Mac pretty ugly?

Ugly? Yeah, we were angry. Lindsey was at the end of his tether in terms of his emotional stay with Fleetwood Mac. He wanted to move on; he wanted to go other places. He couldn't envisage taking that journey being a part of Fleetwood Mac. And he figured twelve years was a lot of time to give and it is; and he attempted to do the right thing. He said he'd go on the road and at the last minute, he just realized he could not do it. And therefore we were all very disappointed and angry and "How could you do this?" And he said, "I have to," and that was your ugly bit. Looking back on it, I'm glad he did leave because we would have all been miserable and he probably would have had a nervous breakdown. And Fleetwood Mac would have done way more damage than it had already done. So, what can you say? Lindsey very specifically went off on his journey (and ended up recording three solo albums) and having come through that journey, he's able to do what he's doing now with a lot of strength and not feel threatened.

The first Fleetwood Mac album came out about thirty years ago. How much has changed between the release of *Fleetwood Mac* and *The Dance*?

People say, "What's your favorite Fleetwood Mac album?" and I'm bound to say there are two of them. The first one set the precedent; the law of the jungle was laid down in my mind by Peter Green and the sensibilities he had and also the band that was Fleetwood Mac. Because we functioned purely on basic emotions, we identified with a form of music that was very specifically Peter and something he had welded himself into and associated himself in a very uncanny way. We lived and breathed that and it was very profound and sometimes I listen to stuff from that era and it's as if the whole bunch of us, even though we were only nineteen and twenty years old, I wonder where did that come from? We were just a bunch of young English chaps and I say that very unabashedly because that band played blues like no other English band had done before or since. In my opinion, it was extraordinary.

So you move on through the history of Fleetwood Mac and the next major time that happened was with this band that we're talking about now. A very different musical sensibility but the feel and the depth and the emotional play that was part of, and still is a part of, these people. There are not too many nights when I'm standing by the side of the stage and listening to Stevie and Lindsey doing "Landslide" together—and I spend that time listening, unless I have to desperately go to the toilet or something—that I'm not extremely moved by it.

If I'm not emotionally involved as a player, I don't play well. My whole dynamic and John's [McVie] whole dynamic is that thing and it's very real. It's what I crave and what I was taught, whether it was taught or playing with Peter Green. Again, my standards were very high and it taught me to be a supporter and that's what I am. I get as much pleasure connecting with Lindsey as I did in those old days.

Lindsey has that same fire Peter Green possessed?
Lindsey is a very emotive person; he's always about to explode and to be honest, he's too intense. I'll have to say, "Hey, hey, hey, relax!" But when he's onstage, he's like a damn animal and it's all feel and his guitar stylings are very different from Peter Green. But his whole function within this band is amazingly similar to Peter's. Musically always alive, musically always thinking of how things can be done. That's why quite often he's responsible for arranging and layering. In years gone by, I think quite honestly, it's driven him nearly to distraction. I'd say, "Lindsey, you've got to stop; it sounds fucking great; don't redo that part, you're out of your mind."

Peter was like that when we started overdubbing. Like on, "Oh Well, Part 2," Peter had all those parts in his head. On *Then Play On*, Peter was stretching out and the reality is, had he not taken that left turn, it's unimaginable what that chap would have created. He was starting to use cellos and timpanis, and this was a blues band. You know what I'm talking about? He was an alchemist and for all intents and purposes, he stopped. He made some music outside of Fleetwood Mac, uninspired solo albums, but I never thought it was very focused. He was already on that road that led him down a very dark and tragic period of his life.

Can you remember the first time you heard Peter Green play?
I never saw him with [John] Mayall; I saw him when he turned up to audition for a young band I was in called Peter B's Looners. It was me

and a chap called Dave Ambrose [bass] and we said, "Well, he's OK, but he plays the same thing. He's only got a few notes." What a fuckup that was! Peter Bardens [keyboards] said, "You're wrong." Peter had just changed from bass to guitar and Peter [Bardens] gave him the gig and within a very short period my mouth was hanging open. We'd play stuff like "Green Onions" and Steve Cropper licks and Peter had his own thing, this rhythm thing. Ever since then I'd like to think, on a humorous level, that I was so wrong about that call that ever since then I've made some fairly good calls as to who played in Fleetwood Mac. Tell me I'm right?

Your first performance with Peter was at the Windsor Jazz and Blues Festival, which also included Cream, Jeff Beck, and John Mayall. What was that like?

That first gig we played was in August 1967. Chicken Shack also played and I think [Pink] Floyd were in there somewhere. We went on before John Mayall, and you have to remember we wanted John [McVie] to be in Fleetwood Mac; hence the name. But John stayed with Mayall for whatever reasons; maybe he had a good pay packet coming and he just wasn't sure. We were called Fleetwood Mac then, a few weeks before he joined. A few weeks later, he phoned up and said, "I've had enough; John Mayall is doing these jazz excursions with sax players. I can't handle this."

When me and John and Peter were with John Mayall for a very short time, Mayall very graciously gave Peter some studio [time] with Gus Dudgeon [producer] at Decca Records. And we recorded a song called "Fleetwood Mac," an instrumental. There were a couple of other songs we did, but that's where the name came from. And Peter said, "This is Mick and John. Let's call it Fleetwood Mac." My tenure with Mayall was short and brief and I went my merry way and not too long after that Peter phoned me and said he'd left.

We had no intention of plotting and meeting to form a band, and a few weeks after that he was sort of persuaded by the agent. He had a great following. Peter Green had another Eric Clapton vibe happening. He said, "Everyone's telling me to form a band; do you want to play drums?" and I said, "I'm right there with you, Pete." And then Mike Vernon [producer] got very much involved and told Peter about Jeremy

[Spencer, guitarist] up in Birmingham and Jeremy came down and Peter saw him play and said he was great. We had to get a bass player and that was Fleetwood Mac.

It's interesting that all the early material was based on two guitars and yet Lindsey now covers all the guitar parts himself.
You have to understand that Lindsey is like having three guitar players; he's got all these fingers and countermelodies and bass lines going on. It's wild.

You saw that Peter Green had that Eric Clapton type of vibe. Were you influenced at all by your drumming contemporaries, players like Ginger Baker or Mitch Mitchell?
No, I was not that type of player; I was into the blues guys. I remember the chap who used to play with B. B. King, Sonny Freeman; he was the guy who did *Live at the Regal*. I prided myself on playing a pretty decent shuffle and that came from listening to Jimmy Reed and sometimes the stuff without drums on it. And I'm a great fan of Charlie Watts. I think he's right up my alley. He comes from behind, so far behind you think he's falling off a log.

Do you think the more recent incarnations of Fleetwood Mac have been treated with a bit of indifference?
I think the last band John and I put together with Dave Mason and Billy Burnette and Bekka Bramlett was in true Fleetwood Mac tradition. It was a long shot and it was totally reliant on whether the music would be accepted. It wasn't. And quite honestly, I don't think the record company heard the music either. We may as well not have made that album. It took its course, or didn't take its course, and it was nonexistent. This Fleetwood Mac had made its mark to such an extent that when Stevie left, in retrospect, it should have stopped. But in fairness to me and John, we've always continued. The reason Stevie and Lindsey were in Fleetwood Mac was because we didn't jack it in. We just said, "Next." I don't mean that flippantly, but the turnover had happened so many times before and we'd survived and quite honestly we were doing quite well. We always survived.

Was *Rumours* then the pinnacle of that period with Stevie and Lindsey?
I think *Tusk* was. I think that told a major story. If we hadn't of made that album, Lindsey would have left a lot sooner, and Stevie was getting creatively frustrated because she is very prolific. And having three frontline artists within a band means that they don't have a lot of song content, or not nearly as much as if they were on their own. So we made a double album against all advice, but we stuck to our guns and it was actually very successful. It was a great album. Everyone has their purpose. John does his parts and leaves. He can't stand being in the studio. And me and Chris and Lindsey are always there.

You obviously have a very strong vision of where you wanted to take Fleetwood Mac. What contribution do you think you've made to the music world?
Me? I don't know. I think I would seriously like, with all the hogwash of, "He's the granddaddy of the band," is that [they'd say], "He was really a pretty damn good drummer." When I first started playing with Peter, I had no confidence at all. You can't measure feeling sometimes. There are drummers who have certain chops, but when it's just a person who happens to play drums and you play, for better or for worse, in a certain way, it's hard to measure that sometimes. Peter taught me how to feel good about who I was. When people say, "You have great time," that's all I want to hear.

JOHN McVIE, 1997

Steven Rosen

John McVie is the archetypal bass-playing "quiet one": he has probably granted fewer interviews about Fleetwood Mac than even some of the Fleetwood Mac members with the briefest tenures.

This 1997 McVie interview, intended to promote *The Dance*, has never previously been published.

Ten years ago did you ever think Fleetwood Mac would get back together?

That long ago? No, I wouldn't have thought so. Everyone was pretty much set on their own course. Mainly Stevie and Mick, and I don't know if Lindsey had his band together then.

The band broke up in 1995 and now are back together in '97. How did that happen?

As Lindsey said, it was him doing an album and Mick got involved. They needed a bass player, so I got involved. They needed some vocals and keyboards and Stevie and Chris got involved. It's like that old Andy Hardy movie with Mickey Rooney, like, "Hey gang. Let's rent a barn and put on a dance." It was pretty much like that.

What was happening with Fleetwood Mac at the time it broke up?

We had [Dave] Mason, Bekka Bramlett, and Billy Burnett and it was a very good, tight band. But it was a losing proposition. We'd go out and just lose money, which no one can afford to do. So New Year's Eve two years ago we said, "Well, that's it." Knock it on the head and see where we go from there.

Previous to that, Lindsey wanted to go out and do his own thing?
Yeah. I think everyone had just reached the end of their years of touring. Lindsey could see himself writing in a different vein, as it were. Which sort of was covered by *Tusk* so he could sort of stretch for that. I don't know. It became just a little bit too much I think. After all those years of people going, "Shit, I need a break," we took a break, and then during that break other things came up with other people. Not so much myself.

What did you do?
I did a little project but mainly I was going on the boats.

You didn't have much desire to play music?
Not really. No, I was quite happy playing with these people. Basically Mick because we worked very well together.

You've played with Mick Fleetwood for virtually your whole career.
There were a few other drummers. There was Hughie Flint and Micky Waller—Micky was in [John] Mayall['s Bluesbreakers] for a very short period—Aynsley [Dunbar] and a guy called Peter [Barnes], who was the first drummer. He was an accountant at the time, so we'd kinda do weekends. He lived in Manchester, which was about 120 miles north of London. Who else was there? Keef Hartley. He was in Mayall also.

When you sit down and play with Mick Fleetwood, it's second nature?
Pretty much. I mean he can still throw a few surprises.

Do you remember the first time you met Mick?
Yeah, it was a club called the Flamingo in Lower Wardour or Gerard Street. We were doing all-nighters. You'd play up north in Sheffield or Manchester and finish that gig and drive down the M1 and get in about one or two o'clock and then play till like four, five, or six o'clock. He

was in the Cheynes I think it was. I just saw him walking down the aisle when the lights dropped at the club with his sister, and I couldn't decide who was who. They both had long, very straight hair. I looked at him and said, "All right? Hello." And then we bumped into each other over the years, and then he joined Mayall after Aynsley briefly.

But Mick never recorded with Mayall?
No. He was there for a couple of weeks.

Who was playing guitar at that time in John Mayall's band?
It might have been Peter [Green]. It might have been towards the end of Peter's tenure. Yeah, then soon after Peter left, but Mick left before Peter. It's a while back. Then I think Peter roped Mick in and Fleetwood Mac started. I still played with Mayall and eventually joined after about a month.

The band ultimately got back together by working on Lindsey Buckingham's project?
Yes, and it grew from that. Then the MTV thing came up [*The Dance*] and basically he shelved his album, and then we comfortably rehearsed for the MTV show. There were three new songs in there and there's an album out soon. It's not too bad. I heard it when my daughter was playing it this morning. She's an eight-year-old fan. But she's a Pat Benatar fan. We did a tour with them in Europe and my daughter was out for a little bit. Pat had her up onstage with someone else's kid and she was doing "Hit Me with Your Best Shot."

The first time you started playing with the band again, how did it feel?
I was nervous. The first day I was really nervous. But then it was just like riding a bike.

There was no excess baggage there?
Emotionally you mean? Uh, relationship-wise, no. I think that's all gone. I hope.

If Lindsey hadn't called Mick to come play on his project, do you think the band would be together now?

I would tend to doubt it, unless it would have come from the managerial side like the way it happened with MTV. "Why don't you ask the guys to do this?" But it just evolved. I'm still playing it a day at a time.

Really?

Oh, yeah. We're supposed to be rehearsing in August to go out on the road in September. I just had a messenger up at the house yesterday with the contracts. I don't see Stevie's signature down there and Mick. And I'm like, "Well, all right. We'll see."

Do you think about other bands that are sort of contemporaries of Fleetwood Mac like Steely Dan getting back together for reunion tours?

As in *Hell Freezes Over* [Eagles reunion tour]?

Right. Does that mean anything to you?

Only in terms of, "Well, they did it." I'm intrigued to see who's gonna show up. I mean I hope someone shows up because it's gonna be a generational thing. But how many of them? It could be a shock. It could be great-grandchildren. But the band is very tight. I was well pleased. It's slightly quieter. We don't have the massive power we used to. A lot more is being done through the front board and we're miking a lot of stuff offstage and a lot of direct stuff. You don't have to be that loud. That is well-pleasing. You actually hear people playing. Plus you've got two players: one's a keyboard and guitar and one's a guitarist. Brett Tuggle and Neale Heywood. English guy. I played golf with him. There are a couple of backup singers, which we've had for a while [Sharon Celani and Mindy Stein] and a percussion player [Taku Hirano].

What kind of gear will you be taking out?

SWR stuff. Henry the [8×8] and SWR tops and Ampeg bottoms. Fifteens underneath them and four-by-twelves next to that so it's compact. A couple of slave Carvin and SVT slave amps. Tobias basses, one Turner, and one [Fender] Precision.

You started out playing Fenders?
Yeah, and it got ripped off in Redondo Beach. Serial number L12304. Yeah, it was all stripped down. Chris [McVie] had drawn a dragon on it and I carved it out. Yeah, it's a shame. It was a nice bass. It used to be pink but it was a bit much. Eric [Clapton] had a stripped-down Strat. I stayed at John Mayall's house one night and a bunch of newspapers and a scraper and a bunch of paint stripper. All night. It just took years. Have you ever tried stripping anything? Those Fenders are covered. They make them bulletproof. But yes, it got ripped off.

How would you describe the sound you're looking for on a bass?
I'm trying to tighten it up a lot. It seems to have got tighter over the years. When I listen to the old Fleetwood Mac stuff and we were trying to emulate what was coming out of Chicago, which was pretty full, round, and almost sloppy. But I don't think we really got close to that. But I'm trying to just tighten it up a bit. We used a compressor and a limiter just to put a spread over it. Almost but not quite a McCartney thing. He's got that deep thing but still tight. Like a loaf of crusty bread. It just has a nice edge and there's kind of a doughy thing.

How does a Fleetwood Mac track happen?
Ninety-nine point nine times with the advent of home-recording things, which goes way back to Peter and Jeremy. When the band got a little bit successful [and] there was a bit of money, they bought a Revox A77 to bounce tracks in. So instead of sitting around and playing, the tape player would be brought in, and then he'd play against that and see what works and see what doesn't and then just cut it. Usually Mick, myself, and recently with Lindsey and before with Christine, we'd figure it out and whatever mistakes were made we'd go back and drop in.

Are the tracks pretty much first take?
No, unless the feel is right. If it feels good, then blunders and glitches will be accepted and fixed later as long as the actual track feels good. So Mick's got a constant thing going through it; you can always patch it up later.

Are you critical of your own performance?
Yeah, it's got to be on.

It's been written that Lindsey wasn't used to the way you played bass.
Oh, yeah. We had a couple of run-ins. I wasn't used to taking direction, but there's not that much of it. Obviously major changes you go with, but I never had direction before. We butted heads a couple of times but it wasn't as bad as it could have been.

Did you listen to much American music?
Oh, yeah. That's what I grew up with after the Shadows. I was handed a stack of records by Mayall and he said, "Listen to this stuff." Steve Miller we used to listen to a lot. I love Steve Miller. That was almost like mandatory. We used to live in a big house with Mick, Chris, and me and Jeremy [Spencer] and I think at one time Danny [Kirwan] did too. And Steve Miller was always going. We opened for him and we were like, "Oh, shit."

Were you aware of other bass players around London at the time?
[Jack] Bruce. But mainly the players I listened to were Willie Dixon, [Charles] Mingus, and a lot of McCartney.

Did you ever see the Beatles?
No. I met George once. That's my claim to Beatledom. Oh, and I saw Ringo get carried out at a party. Bless his heart.

Was there any anxiety about putting the band back together in terms of all the prior success you'd had and what kind of music would you write?
It was the usual "What on earth do we do for a set?" Even more so now because it's X years later and everyone's got a whole nother slew of songs. It wasn't that much of a problem, because we had to balance it out between what Stevie's doing, what Lindsey's doing, what Chris is doing, and what the band is doing. Do we do drum solos? Does Mick

get up and pound his chest again? Do we drop that? Do we bring in the USC band?

But you knew there were some songs you had to play from the back catalog?
Yeah. It's pretty obligatory. The live show is gonna be twice as long [as *The Dance*]. So there'll be a lot more newer stuff I would think, especially from Lindsey. We rehearsed more songs of Lindsey's than we needed. We dropped a couple, but we felt these deserved to be in.

What are your feelings about new songs like "Temporary One" and "My Little Demon"?
Those are Fleetwood Mac. It's just what we do. Whether it's right for the times? I don't know. We just write for people's ears. We've never felt like, "Everyone is using synthesizers like Stevie Wonder, so you guys write something in that vein." Or, "The album after *Rumours*—make sure it sounds like *Rumours*." So it's never been that, which is why it's been up and down all the time.

Has there been one period that stands out for you?
It's been up and down. There's been the Peter [Green] period; there was the *Rumours* period; and the Bob Welch moments. Some great stuff with Bekka [Bramlett], Billy [Burnette], and [Dave] Mason. You know there's some very sort of duff stuff too. [*Laughs.*] Like, "What the hell are you doing?"

The period with Rick Vito?
Rick Vito, exactly. He was a good player.

That early period of Fleetwood Mac with Peter Green was pretty special.
Yeah. If we knew then what we know now in terms of recording, I think it could be a little punchier. He [Mike Vernon, producer] was trying to make it sound like an upright and doing this. It all got too muddy, but you can still hear it.

When Lindsey and Stevie first came into the band, could you hear that it was going to work?

Yeah, within ten minutes. The main thing that leapt out was the vocals between Lindsey, Chris, and Stevie. Just the blend was right and we were going "Whoa," and obviously Lindsey's playing.

One of the few guitar players using his fingers rather than a pick.

At that time there weren't many guitarists that could pitch. I mean the note's there but it'd be up and down and the vibrato would be unuununun [*simulates strange vibrato*]. But he just had it right there à la Peter and Danny. Very much straight on the money. His style has changed a little bit. It's gotten a little more attacky, if you like.

Do you remember the first song you worked on?

No. It might have been "Go Your Own Way" or something. I just thought it was something with harmonies, and me and Mick thought it was pretty damn good.

Do you sing at all?

I sing on this album. Well, it's not really singing. We were in rehearsals and we said, "Let's pick one of the oldies and do something different with it." It was "Say You Love Me" and Mick's up there with his stand-up drum and it's pretty much acoustics about playing the Turner bass. And as a joke I sort of walked up to the mic and started doing the bass line by doubling it. Chris goes, "Why don't you do that?" and I said, "You must be joking. I can't sing." But as it turns out, if it's mixed right, which it is and it's not deedodeedo [*mimics corny bass line*], it's a bass line doubled up. So it gives it a little sound. And I'm out front for that little bit and Christine seems to take great pleasure in saying, "My ex-husband's going to sing for you." It's like, "You can say the *ex* bit, but *husband*?" Yeah, I wish she'd knock that off.

You and Christine did make an interesting musical couple.

When she puts her mind to it, she's a great pianist. In the recent years, she hasn't had any call to do that. But when Chicken Shack were backing up Freddie King, before he came over he'd make sure Christine's in there. That's how I met her. In fact she was playing in the next tent at a festival. Mayall was headlining. It was Fleetwood Mac's first gig and I wasn't playing bass. I was still with Mayall. It might have been Reading or Windsor. But I went over and I heard this young lady playing and we kept bumping into each other around the circuit.

Was Eric Clapton in Mayall's band at that time?
It's when we had the horns. I think it was probably [Mick] Taylor. Yeah, that's when we had Rip Kant. I think Eric had long gone by then.

Do you remember recording the *Blues Breakers* album?
Oh, yeah.

Did it feel special?
It was a day in the life. It was right next door to a gig. I think that was done at Decca in West Hempstead. There's Decca and on the corner there's a pub called the Railway Arms, which was on the pub circuit. We used to play there like every third week. Then we had another place down in Windsor and another place on the road to Southampton on the A3. That's when we were backing Sonny Boy [Williamson]. I remember seeing Elton John—who was Reg in those days—and he used to play up there. Brian Auger was also part of it and [Long John] Baldry and Rod [Stewart]. We'd work all week, and then Friday, Saturday, Sunday, you'd double up. Do an early show and come back and play the all-nighters.

These were the rooms they'd use for wedding receptions attached to a pub. I think the Nag's Head was not much bigger than this room [referring to the conference room in which this interview is taking place]. I mean it was miniscule. You get ninety people in there and it would be like the Black Hole or something. Other places were slightly larger. The one at Windsor—the Ricky Tick—was a big old mansion, which they converted and painted black. We backed Sonny Boy down there, T-Bone [Walker], and John Lee [Hooker], Eddie Boyd.

John Mayall was the support band for all these visiting American blues players?
Yeah, he was almost like the house band. Whereas I think before that it had been Cyril Davies, who unfortunately died, and then Alexis [Korner] became the backing band, and then Mayall.

Did you have any sense where your career would go all these years later?
No, it was always one day at a time and it still is.

There have been some pretty great days in there, though.
Yeah, and hopefully it will [continue]. It still is. No, I never could have seen it. It was just a lot of fun.

When people look back at your career, what do you hope they see?
Me? I was honest. [*Laughs.*] I never tried to be anything more than I was. Support the front line.

Any plans to do a new record?
Not that I know of. It makes sense to do that, but I think Lindsey has to finish his album first and get that out. I don't know if he's going to go out and support that. I know Chris wants to do something, so we'll just play it by ear. I'd like, if I had my druthers, that we should take this on and do some stuff outside the country, maybe in Europe and Australia. But I think Chris is in a holding pattern for that. She just wants to wait and see how this is gonna go as far as personalities and acceptance. But that would be nice. I'd like to do that again. My bags are packed.

MAC IN THE SADDLE

Alan di Perna | September 1997 | *Guitar World* (US)

This feature offers Lindsey Buckingham's take on the reassembling of the *Rumours* Five, then—as with the other members' contemporaneous interviews—digresses into band history.

Buckingham's reminiscences also act as a useful counterbalance to Nicks's previous withering criticisms of him, particularly his revelation that it was his loyalty to her that secured Nicks the life-changing Fleetwood Mac gig, and his admission that, after their breakup, he had to overcome his disinclination to help optimize the quality of her contributions to *Rumours*.

ADULT ROCK. THOSE two words might never have been used together had it not been for Fleetwood Mac. Or at least they wouldn't have sounded as convincing together as they did in the mid to late Seventies, when Fleetwood Mac were piling up the platinum with hits like "Over My Head," "Rhiannon," "Say You Love Me," "Dreams," "Don't Stop," "Go Your Own Way," "The Chain" and "You Make Loving Fun."

Adult rock was a historical inevitability as baby boomers moved beyond college and into the slower-moving but potentially more treacherous waters of marriage and career. Fleetwood Mac were wired into that passage in an uncanny way. Their 1977 album *Rumours* (25 times Platinum and counting) is a landmark, not only for its well-crafted songs but for the way it reflected the very public break-ups of the band's two couples that took place during recording sessions for the album.

Bassist John McVie and keyboardist Christine McVie divorced, and guitarist Lindsey Buckingham split up with singer Stevie Nicks. The creative processes of the album got all mixed up with the disintegration of the musicians' romantic relationships. With *Rumours,* Fleetwood Mac blurred the distinction between art and life—not only their own lives, but also the lives of countless listeners embroiled in those dysfunctional Seventies relationships that would go on to give birth to rootless, disgruntled Generation X.

"That was part of the appeal of the album for the audience at the time," says Lindsey Buckingham, relaxing over coffee at a Beverly Hills hotel between mixdown sessions for Fleetwood Mac's televised reunion on MTV. "It was clear that there was something going on beyond the music: the theater of interaction between these people making the record. Probably nine out of the 11 songs on that album were written specifically about other members of the band. It was a musical soap opera, if you will."

Fleetwood Mac's close link with the aging Sixties generation was reinforced at the start of this decade when Bill Clinton used the band's hit "Don't Stop" to cinch the boomer vote. But shake the songs free of all that cultural baggage and you just might find that they stand on their own merits as elegantly spare, pop rock gems.

Other Seventies artists tried to make rock for adults by defecting to more "grownup" genres. Steely Dan went for overcooked jazz chords. The Eagles forged a self-conscious style of country rock. But Fleetwood Mac remained faithful to the pop idiom that they and their audience had grown up on. Their streamlined song structures and effortless vocal harmonies flowed from the same timeless pop sources that had nurtured everyone from the Shirelles to the Beatles to Todd Rundgren.

Lyrically, Fleetwood Mac's straightforward approach connected with audiences on a more immediate level than the abstruse verbal self-indulgences of Donald Fagen or Don Henley. Much of the Mac's knack for classic pop understatement is attributable to Buckingham, who was not only the group's guitarist, but also a key songwriting voice and a major production force within the band.

"I grew up listening to pop in general," he says simply. "And pop always tries to economize. I've always loved that about it."

BEFORE LINDSEY BUCKINGHAM and Stevie Nicks came along, Fleetwood Mac were pretty much a rhythm section in search of an identity. They'd started off as a blues rock band in 1967 when John McVie, drummer Mick Fleetwood and guitar legend Peter Green broke off from John Mayall's Bluesbreakers. By the Seventies, McVie and Fleetwood were the only original members left, and the band had undergone numerous personnel changes, eventually morphing into a mildly successful soft-rock outfit with Christine McVie on keyboards and vocals and guitarist/singer Bob Welch as front man.

But things didn't really crystallize for the band until Buckingham and Nicks were drafted to replace the departing Welch in 1974. A Northern California duo who'd only just begun their recording career, the couple brought fresh young blood and new life to Fleetwood Mac.

As a guitarist, Buckingham's craftsmanship served to support and subtly enhance Fleetwood Mac's songs. His compact, ethereal acoustic tones added shimmer to the group's trademark vocal trio harmonies, and his electric playing injected a shot of grit into a sonic recipe that might otherwise have amounted to mere ABBAesque candyfloss. Buckingham has never been a showoff on guitar, but six-string aficionados have come to value the seeming effortlessness with which he can move from intricate fingerstyle playing to incandescent flashes of rock solo brilliance.

Complementing Buckingham's guitar, vocal, songwriting and production skills, Stevie Nicks swelled the ranks of Fleetwood Mac with still another distinctive songwriting and singing voice. She also brought Fleetwood Mac something it had always lacked: a captivating frontperson.

Nicks' hippie/gypsy/sorceress style and Lady of Shalott ringlets bewitched pop culture bigtime. She was the first siren of adult rock. Throughout the Eighties, her image telegraphed the message that a mature woman could be just as hot as some sweet young thing bursting out of a halter top. Visit any shopping mall today and you'll see that the "Stevie Nicks look" never really died out.

Fleetwood Mac had that ability to be all things to all people. They struck an ideal balance: comprised of three English rockers (Fleetwood and the McVies) and two Yanks (Buckingham and Nicks), they were also a "mixed gender" band that had blues roots *and* pop savvy. It was a magic combination that held together for 12 years and four studio albums, despite internal conflicts, drug excesses and all the other pressures that go with life at the top of rock's game. These problems eventually led Buckingham, and later Nicks, to tender their resignations.

Two Fleetwood Mac albums were released after Buckingham's 1987 departure: 1990's *Behind the Mask* (with Nicks on vocals) and 1995's *Time* (with Bekka Bramlett on vocals). Both met with fairly indifferent responses from public and press. Meanwhile, Buckingham consolidated a solid critical reputation with his 1991 solo album *Out of the Cradle* and his two Mac-era solo discs, *Law and Order* and *Go Insane*. It was actually work on Buckingham's forthcoming new solo album that led to this year's Fleetwood Mac reunion.

"I happened to cross paths with Mick, who had gone through a lot of changes since the last time I'd seen him," Buckingham reports. "We got together and had breakfast, and we were getting along so well that I said, 'Mick, would you like to come in and play drums on some tracks on my solo album?' He did, and we got some great tracks.

"From there, since I still didn't have a bass player, we thought, 'Let's get John in.' We did that, and I found my take on John was totally different than it had been when I was in Fleetwood Mac, because I had learned a lot in those 10 years away from the band. I was able to appreciate John a little more. Then we said, 'Well, now we need some keyboards,' and we obviously thought of Christine.

"So suddenly, there were the four of us sitting in the control room one day, going 'hmmmm.' It felt really good to be together. And that sort of switched the light bulb on in our heads."

Stevie Nicks, who'd been pretty much out of the public eye since her 1994 solo album, *Street Angel,* also assented to a Fleetwood Mac reunion. So the group went into rehearsal and did two days of taping for MTV. The performances will also be released on a live album, all coinciding with the 20th anniversary of *Rumours'* release. The reunited quintet also plans to play 40 live dates in the States and possibly some shows in Europe. Besides revisiting their old hits, the band tried out four new numbers for the MTV show and live album.

"Stevie wrote a sort of country ballad called 'Sweet Girl,'" says Buckingham. "Christine brought in an uptempo song with a pop feel called 'Temporary One.' Mine is a real barn burner called 'My Little Demon.' We also did a song from my new solo album, but I'm not sure if it'll make it onto this live album or not. It's called 'Bleed to Love Her.' There's some imagery for you."

In all, Buckingham seems pleased with the way things have turned out: "When I left Fleetwood in '87, it really was as a physical and emotional survival move. The situation then was not a very kind one for creativity, not a very nurturing one. But during the 10 years since then, I've been able to re-focus my energy and idealism. To bring that back into the chemistry of the group now, and to have the support of the other four people, has just been tremendous."

GUITAR WORLD: When did you first meet Stevie Nicks?

LINDSEY BUCKINGHAM: In high school. She's a year older than me—I graduated in '67 and she was in the class of '66. She first arrived at my school when I was a junior, and she just kind of flew in somewhat flamboyantly and became popular at school. I think she was working on being a bohemian type even then, with the poetry and all of that.

I had met her briefly at some social occasions. She was aware that I played guitar, and I was aware that she played guitar and sang. We had some rapport, but that was about it. Then she went on to junior college, I stayed on in high school, and we didn't really hook up again until the next year. We got together in a band called Fritz; I played bass and she sang.

But it wasn't until that band broke up in 1971 that Stevie and I became romantically involved. That's also when we began doing music as a duo. We moved down to L.A. in '72. We got a record deal and put out an album the following year [Buckingham Nicks, *Polydor, 1973*]. We were trying to make a second record when the offer to join Fleetwood Mac came along.

GW: The story goes that Mick Fleetwood "discovered" you and Stevie at Sound City [recording studio] in Van Nuys, California.

LB: Yeah. Mick was looking for a place to record the next Fleetwood Mac album, and heard good things about Sound City from a friend. The studio was owned by an engineer named Keith Olsen, who demonstrated the sound of the facility by playing Mick "Frozen Love" from *Buckingham Nicks,* which had been recorded there.

My guitar playing must have made an impression on him, because when Bob Welch quit Fleetwood Mac in late 1974, Mick called Sound City and told them he wanted the guitar player he'd heard.

But I said, "Well, Stevie and I are a package deal." He took that information back to Christine, who, I'm sure, had to think about that a bit.

GW: Had you been a Fleetwood Mac fan prior to being asked to join the band in 1975?

LB: There were so many incarnations of Fleetwood Mac. I was not aware of many of them. When I was still living up in Northern California, I was aware of *Then Play On [1969, Reprise]* because the album's single, "Oh Well," was maybe the only thing by Fleetwood Mac that had made it onto the radio back then. So I'd heard that whole album and obviously loved it, but that was it, really. So when Stevie and I were asked to join Fleetwood Mac in 1975, we actually had to go out and buy all the Fleetwood Mac albums to get a sense of how the band had evolved since the '69 lineup with Peter Green.

GW: Was that whole blues guitar idiom that Fleetwood Mac came out of an important part of your development as a guitarist?

LB: Not at all, really. Which was one of the reasons why, at first, I wasn't sure if I was going to fit in. I was more interested in songs. A 12-bar gets boring for me after the first couple of choruses. I can appreciate that there's a lot going on within that structure, but that wasn't my thing. I grew up listening to Elvis and the way Scotty Moore played, who used a pick but also used his fingers. Then I got into a lot of folk things after that and picked up the bluegrass banjo. So there's a finger style that runs through all of what I've done. I've always appreciated people who were able to incorporate the guitar into good record making. Like Chet Atkins' playing on the Everly Brothers' records. You don't really notice what he's doing, but if his guitar wasn't there, it wouldn't be a record. It's just an understated thing that comes in and goes out: a lyrical, rhythmic way of filling a hole and then receding into the background. That's something that I have always aspired to. And the blues, to me, was not that kind of craft, not that kind of mentality.

GW: Was that trademark Fleetwood Mac vocal harmony blend there right from the start?

LB: Yeah, right from the start. I mean Stevie and I had this great two-part thing going—kind of an Ian and Sylvia tension *[Ian and Sylvia Tyson were a husband-and-wife folk duo who recorded in the Sixties—GW Ed.]* As singers, Stevie and I both are on the nasal side, which works really well in a two-part Appalachian kind of harmony style. And Christine has this very round, flutey voice that warmed up the whole thing. It's probably even a voicing that you could put down to some theory. It was just apparent right away that it was something that really worked.

A lot of things were apparent early on. Going into the rehearsals, Stevie and I had a backlog of material, so there was enough quantity for the rest of the band to be able to look at what we had to offer them, songwise, and feel comfortable in choosing what would work with what Christine had to offer. There were no problems going in. That itself was almost a little unsettling.

GW: Did any songs from the Buckingham Nicks-era make it onto the *Fleetwood Mac [Reprise, 1975]* album?

LB: Yes, a song of Stevie's called "Crystal"; that was the only thing. But on the *Fleetwood Mac Live* album in the early Eighties, we did a Buckingham Nicks song called "Don't Let Me Down Again."

GW: What were the politics of songwriting like in Fleetwood Mac, as far as whose songs got used? Was it strictly a "one of mine, one of yours and one of yours" type of arrangement?

LB: To some degree. We tried to make it as democratic as possible. You want to have the band as a whole giving thumbs up or thumbs down to any particular offering. That's always a good filtering system. Because I tend to write more uptempo material, there would usually be a song or two more of mine in the live set, just for the momentum of the show. But on record we tried to make it as even as possible. Although sometimes that didn't work.

GW: How did playing with the legendary Fleetwood and McVie rhythm section affect your guitar style?

LB: I don't think it affected my playing in too many ways, except that I had to leave more holes and there was less for me to do sometimes. John is an aggressive bass player. It took me a long time to appreciate that. When he and I first were in the studio, I was always saying, "make it simpler, make it simpler." Sometimes there was a "this town ain't big enough for both of us" kind of vibe. But somehow we made it work. I had to back off. And sometimes he backed off if I hounded him. It's not so much of a problem now—I appreciate his artistry a lot more. He's a very sophisticated bass player, somewhere between McCartney and Mingus.

GW: What are your memories of making *Rumours [1977]*?

LB: Christine and John were breaking up. Stevie and I were breaking up, although in a more drawn-out, ambiguous way than Christine and John. With Christine and John it was over really quick. Whereas Stevie and I were more like, "Well I don't know . . ." There were times when we were sleeping together and times when we were officially something else. But there was definitely a moving apart.

GW: And all of this was happening while you were in the studio, working on the album?

LB: Yeah. So then you start writing songs about what's happening to you. You've got these dialogues that are directed at other members of the band and that are about what's going on while you are recording the songs. It was just such a crazy time. We started up in Sausalito *[at what was then the Northern California Record Plant—GW Ed.]*. I don't know why Mick wanted to do it there, but Sausalito was filled with freaks back then and is probably still pretty crazy. And there was a lot of pressure. "Over My Head," off the *Fleetwood Mac* album, had become a hit. And then when "Rhiannon" kicked in, it really raised the stakes for us. But we didn't want to repeat the previous album's formulas. We wanted to break away and find the unexpected through chaos a little more. And clearly there was chaos. That's the way the album felt. After Sausalito, we worked in Florida for a while because we were still touring and working on the album between legs of the tour. Then we came back and worked at Wally Heider's in Los Angeles. It was a long haul. And I don't think we necessarily realized how close to the bone the music was until we started assembling it. The whole process had been a challenge. Like with Stevie's music. I'd always been this kind of soulmate who always somehow knew what to do with her music—how to complement it and bring out its best. But there were times when I really had the urge not to do that, you know? So I had to keep checking myself—keep challenging myself to be a better person than I felt like being at times.

GW: Guitarwise, what do you remember about making *Rumours?*

LB: I think we were interested in getting a little closer to the approach that we had on stage. The first album was a little lighter. Some of that was Keith Olsen's approach to getting guitar sounds. On *Rumours* we got a little bit of a ballsier thing going on guitars.

GW: Is the song "Gold Dust Woman" an early comment on drug excess in Fleetwood Mac?

LB: I believe so. You'd have to ask Stevie *[who wrote the song—GW Ed.]*. I think it's a song about keeping going and trying to maintain [yourself] under bad circumstances. But it is a drug song, though. No doubt about it.

GW: Had that situation reached critical mass as early as *Rumours?*

LB: No, not with *Rumours.* As far as I'm concerned, it reached critical mass sometime in the mid Eighties. It was a factor in why I left the band after *Tango in the Night* in 1987. But not the only factor. I felt as if I'd been treading creative water ever since *Tusk.*

GW: *Tusk [1979]* was, for you, an album made very much in the shadow of punk rock.

LB: Not "in the shadow of." It was more that punk rock was a motivator. It encouraged me to see that there were other things going on that resonated with ideas that I'd been having.

GW: You were one of the few established rockers back then who really acknowledged punk's existence. For the most part, the attitude was, "That doesn't exist."

LB: Right. That was the feeling within the rest of the band. I'd bring in a record by the Clash, or even something like Talking Heads, and the others were just turned off by it. I guess because it was young and enthusiastic, and maybe not at as high a level of musicianship. It wasn't as mature as the rest of the band saw themselves. But that music was so open to new ideas, and that's what got me.

GW: There's a real sense on *Tusk* that you're in one place, and everyone else in the band is somewhere else entirely.

LB: Yeah. I always felt it was my first solo record. It's too bad it couldn't have been more of a synthesis between what the band felt comfortable with on *Rumours* and some of the new places where I wanted to go. It's said that when Warner Brothers, sitting in the board room, heard *Tusk* for the first time, they "all saw their Christmas bonuses flying out the window." There was a lot of political backlash when *Tusk* ended up selling only five million, or whatever it sold, rather than the 16 million that *Rumours* sold at the time.

GW: Is *Tusk* the first album in the Fleetwood Mac canon that you started to record at home?

LB: Yes. And that was not an easy thing to pull off. I remember going up to Mick's and having a band meeting. I said, "Look, there's some areas I want to grow into, and maybe initially to do that I need to futz around at my house and experiment—have some psychic space to myself." That was not a good meeting. I understand: in everybody else's eyes, I was being a troublemaker. I wasn't playing ball. It was just one of those things that was nobody's fault. There was no one right point of view. In retrospect, I've heard everyone in the band say, "Gee, *Tusk* was a really cool album. But it took a long time."

GW: A lot of the guitar tones on *Tusk* are dry, strange and wonderfully peculiar.

LB: Yes, they were. A lot of that was because I was working at home and didn't have any outboard gear at all. I had a 24-track tape machine, a small microphone preamp and a tiny little monitoring console.
And I had a great-sounding bathroom right across the hall. I used that for ambience. So it was all very much "on the natch."

GW: How did the others in the band react to ideas like using the USC marching band on the record?

LB: Well, that was Mick's idea. It was a stroke of genius. I had the song "Tusk," and we had it all done. I don't know how he came up with the idea of adding a marching band to it, but it was brilliant. The challenge of that was getting the marching band on the existing track, in sync with the other instruments. Mick had this whole idea where he wanted to film it. We went to Dodger Stadium and got the band out on the infield. They had a remote truck there. Needless to say, it took a while.

GW: What was life on the road with Fleetwood Mac like?

LB: Some people lived life to the hilt more than others. I was never a big party guy. I had an eight-track recorder in a case that I'd take into my hotel room. And on days off, I'd try to work on stuff.
But we all had our moments. The craziest times for me personally—as far as fun times with women and that kind of stuff—were during the early days, right after Stevie and I had broken up. By the time we got into touring, after *Rumours* and after *Mirage,* I was living with someone, so that kind of thing didn't really come into play. And, you know, drugs were more a part of life for some than for others. That's all I can say. I was never a big druggie. I mean I'll smoke pot and do . . . I never bought cocaine, really. Too expensive.

GW: Were Fleetwood Mac part of the much-vaunted decadent, L.A.-in-the-Seventies, hot-tub, Steely-Dan kind of lifestyle?

LB: You mean the social scene? It's possible. I wasn't. I never went anywhere, really. Mick had a scene going up at his house in Malibu. Richard Dashut *[Fleetwood Mac/Lindsey Buckingham co-producer and co-writer]* was right down the street. You know, Malibu is and was a magnet for all sorts of strange types. But I hardly ever went out there. They were there, and I was in Bel Air just trying to work and carry on a relationship. I border on being . . . not antisocial, but I'm just not a party person. A lot of times I'll say, "Yeah, I'll be there!" And at the 11th hour I'll chicken out and stay home.

GW: *Mirage [1982]* has such a classic American pop sensibility to it: Brill Building, Brian Wilson . . .

LB: It does, yeah. I think that happened almost by default. Those pop aspects were always there, even on *Tusk* and certainly on *Rumours* and *Fleetwood Mac*. But there were other things going on to maybe mask those elements a little more. This is just a theory of mine, but I think that whatever was missing by the time of *Mirage*—in terms of unity within the band—made the constructions underlying the songs a little more apparent. The spontaneity had gone out of our playing, so the artifice began to show through a little more. In the beginning, we'd had this great sixth sense of interlocking as four musicians. But by that point the musicianship had gone down a couple of notches. It was almost more of an overdubby kind of thing. And to some degree, even the writing had become less tied to the spontaneity of a process or an idea which was in that moment. With those elements missing by the time we got to *Mirage,* what was left was sort of a classic American . . . I don't want to say cliché, but a thing that's more identifiable with something you've heard before.

GW: The other thing is that *Mirage* marks the advent of compositional collaboration in Fleetwood Mac. You started writing with Richard Dashut, and Christine began working with a few different co-writers.

LB: That's right. And again—not taking away from Richard, who has a lot of great raw ideas—I think that came about through the absence of my own resolve. I'd been feeling a little weak and was looking for a shepherd of sorts. But having said all that, I do think there are some really good things on *Mirage*. I think "Gypsy" was one of my best collaborations ever with Stevie. Not that I co-wrote it with her, but in terms of what I do for Stevie as far as arrangement and things go. I think that was one of the most effective pieces we've ever done.

GW: Her country rock songwriting direction on that album brought out a high, lonesome kind of guitar style in you.

LB: *[reluctantly]* Yeah . . . we bring out the corn in each other.

GW: Your production role grew steadily within Fleetwood Mac, to the point where you get the "lead" production credits on *Mirage* and *Tango in the Night [1987]*.

LB: Actually, no. My production role didn't grow steadily. The style of production just became more visible. I mean, if you were to ask Richard or any of those guys, "Who produced *Rumours?*", they'd all say, "Lindsey was the guy with the vision." I didn't ask for a production credit on *Rumours* and I didn't get it. Richard feels bad about that. There were band politics involved in that. Even on *Tusk*, you may notice, it says like "special thanks for . . ." Come on! I don't think I had any less of a hand in what you'd could call production on *Rumours* than I did on *Tango*. It was just a different thing. By the time we got to *Tango*, the constructions are more obvious than they are on *Mirage*. Because there was less of a band presence to work with. So it became more adorned. You had to make up for a natural interplay of musicians that wasn't really there.

GW: Now, you worked on that one at your house in Bel Air.

LB: Yeah, everyone was up at the house. We had a Winnebago parked in the driveway. It was a major scene up there.

GW: You've said that *Tango* is the album where the drugs really took their toll.

LB: That album took close to a year to make, and I think we saw Stevie for about three weeks out of that time. And these weeks weren't the greatest three weeks. Nobody was in a good place, really.

GW: That's also the album where you began using the Fairlight [*an early digital keyboard workstation—GW Ed.*].

LB: A little bit. We just did whatever we could, really. We had to take little bits of Stevie just singing off the cuff and make a whole vocal track out of that, because that's all we'd get out of her. I played a lot of the bass parts on that.

GW: Did your flirtation with the Fairlight affect your approach to guitar in any way?

LB: Only in that it made me play guitar less. For a while, I'd turn to that rather than pick up a guitar when I had an idea in my head.
So it took me away from my center—my guitar playing. There are two songs in this new live show, "Big Love" and "Go Insane," where I'm just playing guitar and singing by myself. And that's when I feel I'm really at my best.

GW: How did it feel to get together with Fleetwood Mac and play all those old songs?

LB: It was a little weird the first couple of days, I have to say. I was sitting there going, "Now, what was it I used to do on this song?"

GW: Can you remember the first one you tried?

LB: I think it was "You Make Loving Fun," and "The Chain." A lot of it was like getting back on a bicycle after you haven't ridden for years. You never really forget. Maybe 80 percent of it was like that. It's the other 20 percent where you feel the pressure, like being on a putting green. There was a week or two of panic; we'd only given ourselves six or seven weeks for rehearsal. I think we were lucky that it was for TV. Because if you blow a part, you can start over again and the audience digs being involved in the process. In the end, though, I think we managed to pull it off.

GW: Are there plans to do other projects as Fleetwood Mac, beyond this?

LB: That depends on whom you ask. If you ask Mick, he'll say, "Oh, we'll probably go in and do a studio album." If you ask me, my first priority really is finishing this solo album that I'm working on. I think it's the best thing I've ever done. Hopefully, it will come out in the spring. Beyond that, I can't really say. I'm not discounting the possibility of going in the studio with Fleetwood Mac again. We're all having a good time. It is a nice family feeling, to have all these people you care about around you and not have all the emotional baggage that used to be there. So we'll see what happens.

THE WAY WE WERE

Dave DiMartino | September 1997 | *Mojo* (UK)

An in-the-moment look at the *MTV Unplugged/Dance* project. Despite the tone of rap-prochement underpinning this and all the other Fleetwood Mac interviews of the time, the "to be continued" status optimistically suggested by Dave DiMartino about what he calls "rock's greatest soap opera" took a long time to be fulfilled.

IT IS *DEJA VU* OF THE VERY STRANGEST SORT ON this May night in Burbank, California. Thrilled to be at this invitation-only event, each and every one of us crane our necks at the five, well, *geezers* on the stage who have chosen to open their first full-length concert together in 15 years with a song called The Chain. Yes, Fleetwood Mac: ex-British blues sensations, former middling rock 'n' roll band with an ever-shifting line-up, and one-time makers of *Rumours*, the extraordinary pop record which, since its 1977 release, has shifted more units than nearly any other album in the history of popular music.

It is a glorious rock 'n' roll event. It is an unbelievable reunion. It is the sort of thing big bands do when the aroma of money is in the air. And this cavernous structure on the Warner Brothers lot is reeking of the stuff tonight. Sniffing the scent are record company label executives looking for an early answer to that annual question regarding the probability of a Christmas bonus. Then there are radio contest winners who've been shipped in to see history in the making. All of us are the sort of people who really don't feel the need to go to concerts any more, frankly, but what the hell—this beats seeing U2 as four pinpoints on the horizon any day. And our number includes lanky journalists scratching heads and wondering what Don Henley and his overstuffed wallet spawned when this reunion business started three years ago.

We are witnessing an MTV Event, one of two consecutively filmed reunion shows featuring the five members of the most popular Fleetwood Mac ever—Lindsey Buckingham, Stevie Nicks, Christine McVie, John McVie, and Mick Fleetwood—with not one, but five intended purposes. An MTV special. A VH-1 special. A new live album. A teaser for the upcoming 40-date North American concert tour. And a commercial home video release? Would you bet against it? So a lot is riding on the performance Fleetwood Mac are giving tonight. MTV know it, Reprise Records know it, the audience know it, and the band—oh yes, the band—they know it too. And what is strangest of all at this most artificial of events is how good Fleetwood Mac sound and look.

When The Chain is finished and the audience whoop, a familiar opening riff begins, and all eyes turn to Stevie Nicks, dressed in her trademark black chiffon. For one who has in recent years waxed matronly, she looks oddly like, well, Stevie Nicks. And then it happens. Stevie sings the opening line to Dreams . . . and forgets the words. It is the only Number 1 single in her life—maybe her most important song ever—and she flubs it. She stops—this is TV, remember—and starts over. And then she flubs it again.

It is a tense moment. Some in the audience giggle, nervously. Others silently speculate on whether a refresher visit to the Betty Ford Clinic might be in order. But the moment passes. Stevie finally nails it, and Fleetwood Mac, as the saying goes, Then Play On.

"YOU KNOW WHAT?" STEVIE NICKS asks me later. "I wasn't pissed off at myself, I was scared—the words went out of my head. The first time it was like, OK, this is all right. The second time I started to get a sick feeling. And then the third time I thought, Somebody, *Lindsey*, come over here and tell me these words, because we're not gonna get *through* this thing."

We are sitting in a small waiting room at Conway Studios in Hollywood, and Nicks is addressing the press. She is charming, reassuringly chiffon-clad, and surprisingly lucid for someone who has spent thousands collecting stuffed animals, you know.

"But," she adds, "also I'm thinking, the audience is gonna really *enjoy* this—they're gonna see that I *too* am stupid and an airhead, and things go wrong for me too, and everything isn't perfect. And they're gonna not have a problem with it."

That, ultimately, is what caps the concept of a Fleetwood Mac 'reunion' in 1997: no-one is really going to have a problem with it. Not the pop audience, who bought this quintet's six albums from 1975's *Fleetwood Mac* to 1987's *Tango in the Night* by the squillion and heard their music blaring on their radios for more than a decade. And not even most critics, who have for the most part come to regard the Lindsey Buckingham 'version' of Fleetwood Mac especially highly. And certainly not the executives at Warner Brothers and Reprise Records (their current label), who saw Fleetwood Mac's enormous multi-platinum sales figures plummet with the group's first post-Buckingham album, 1990's *Behind The Mask*. US sales statistics alone: *Fleetwood Mac* (1975), five times platinum (over five million albums sold); *Rumours* (1977), 17 times platinum; the two-disc *Tusk* (1979), double platinum; *Fleetwood Mac Live* (1980), platinum; *Mirage* (1982), double platinum; *Tango in the Night* (1987), double platinum; and *Greatest Hits* (1988), four times platinum.

No. As always, the only party likely to have a problem with a Fleetwood Mac reunion in 1997 would be Fleetwood Mac themselves. Fleetwood Mac: the band, the often prone-to-excess individuals within it, the money-making entity they were and perhaps still are, and, of course, the soap opera.

" . . . *SUDDENLY DENNIS DUNSTAN AND STEVIE'S MANAGER TONY Dimitriades pulled Lindsey off her and told him that was enough. Lindsey then came back into my house, very distraught. He shouted, 'Get that woman out of my life—that schizophrenic bitch!'*

"*Christine was furious. 'Lindsey, look at yourself, screaming like a madman.' There was a silence. And John McVie quietly said to Lindsey Buckingham, 'I think you'd better leave now.' 'You're a bunch of selfish bastards,' Lindsey said, and walked out. He sat in his car in the driveway*

for 15 minutes, obviously distraught, but nobody wanted to go to him. Eventually, we heard him start his motor and leave."
(From Fleetwood: My Life And Adventures In Fleetwood Mac by Mick Fleetwood with Stephen Davis, William Morrow & Company, 1990)

MICK FLEETWOOD'S MEMORABLE account of Lindsey Buckingham's departure from Fleetwood Mac often inclines toward the melodrama of TV soaps like Dynasty and Dallas—also icons of '80s pop culture in their day—but in 1997 is a damn fun read. "We decided to be comfortable and lost control," Fleetwood confides in its pages. "If Stevie wanted a hotel suite painted pink with a white piano in it, what are you gonna do? Say no?"

Indeed, the tales of conspicuous excess, hyperinflated egos—and humungous quantities of Peruvian flake—are what you'd expect from a phenomenally successful band comprising ex-lovers at the very height of their fame. For it was during the making of *Rumours* when Christine and John McVie, married in 1968, effectively split, when Fleetwood divorced his wife Jenny Boyd (sister of Patti), and when newcomers Buckingham and Nicks ended their tumultuous four-year romance. That Fleetwood Mac lasted as long as they did thereafter is a fitting testimonial to the power of music, money, or both.

When Lindsey Buckingham left Fleetwood Mac in 1987, his two replacements—guitarist Rick Vito and singer/guitarist Billy Burnette, initially hired for touring purposes—joined the four remaining Macs for 1990's *Behind The Mask*. Disappointingly, the album peaked at Number 18 on the Billboard charts, though it did manage gold status (over 500,000 copies sold) before completing its run. Nicks and Christine McVie both quit touring with the band at the end of that year, guitarist Vito split the next year, and by '93 Nicks and Burnette officially opted out. When their replacements were announced by the year's end, it was something of a head-scratcher: Bekka Bramlett, daughter of Delaney & Bonnie Bramlett and singer in Fleetwood's side-project The Zoo, and the man who wrote Hole In My Shoe, Mr Dave Mason of Traffic fame. Suffice it to say, their sole LP, 1995's *Time*, failed even to *enter* the American charts.

"It was fine," says drummer Mick Fleetwood. The beanpole who once seriously considered giving his coke dealer a sleeve credit on *Rumours* ("Unfortunately, he got snuffed—executed! Before the thing came out," his book wryly recalls) is talking about the last days of the Bramlett/Mason Mac. "It was an experiment in true Fleetwood Mac tradition, that me and John have always kept going. The reason Stevie and Lindsey were in Fleetwood Mac is because we kept going and didn't say, Oh, it's over now that Bob Welch has left the band. What'll we do? We haven't got a lead guitar player and a songwriter . . .

"It's what I've done for 30 years, so it was very normal behaviour. And we made a really good album that didn't do diddleyshit. We went out on the road, and we did OK. But without a hit album, and a reaffirmation with new members on radio, we didn't stand a chance. It was a good band, with the wrong damn name."

"I was sad to see it go," agrees grizzled penguin-lover John McVie. "But it was necessary. It started getting financially tough to run. You couldn't support yourself on the gigs; basically you were going out and playing for nothing." And when it ended? "I said, OK, I'll sit on a boat for a while. Which I did."

Also appearing on *Time* was one Christine McVie, who politely notes that her appearance, "was something that I had not volunteered to do; it was contractual. I don't like to harp on it very much, but I thought the music was starting to get a little strange, the choices a little funny. I wasn't really enjoying that particular incarnation of the band, and I left." At that point, the former Miss Perfect's plans included moving back to England—she's had a home in Kent for five years—and pursuing the hobbies one would expect of a former member of Chicken Shack: "Painting, illustration, I'd like to write a book, I'd like to go to cooking school. I know it sounds utterly absurd, but I really love cooking and I take it very seriously." Plus a solo album "sometime before the next millennium".

MEANWHILE, *OUT OF THE CRADLE*, LINDSEY Buckingham's first album as a fully-fledged solo artist soared all the way to Number 128 on the Billboard charts in 1992: an undeservedly poor showing for a fine album. The brand name, it seemed, was everything.

And Stevie Nicks, by far the most saleable solo Mac artist, seemed to be stumbling badly too. Most troubling were the two new tracks featured upon her otherwise solid 1991 greatest hits collection, *Timespace*: Sometimes It's A Bitch, penned by Jon Bon Jovi and Billy Falcon, and Love's A Hard Game To Play, co-written with Bret Michaels of poodle-metal band Poison. Two words: clowns all. With 1994's *Street Angel*, which peaked at Number 45 and became her poorest-selling solo album ever, failing even to go gold, her stint with longtime label Modern Records ended. She is now signed to Reprise, as are both Buckingham and Fleetwood Mac proper.

Which brings us back to Lindsey Buckingham, who, like everyone else today, is at Conway Studios dealing with the mix of select live tracks and determining which will make the final cut for the album. We are talking about the bands that played under the name Fleetwood Mac following his departure. "I did sit in once when Stevie was touring with Rick and Billy, at the end of the show," notes Buckingham, his Eraserhead hairdo mercifully long-gone, and the words "that schizophrenic bitch" likewise conspicuous by their absence. Though he maintains a house in plush Bel Air, it is currently being renovated; the man who gets royalty cheques larger than those of Sebadoh and Savoy Brown combined is now slumming it in the Beverly Hills—adjacent (as we say in the real estate business) to the Four Seasons hotel. Surprisingly chipper, he chooses his words carefully. "The shows that they did with Rick and Billy when Stevie was still in the band were fine. But I think when you cut to Fleetwood Mac being middle-billed in a nostalgia package with Pat Benatar and REO Speedwagon—that hurt me a little bit.

"But in Mick's defence—Mick and John own the name—the very thing that Mick did after Peter Green, this constant process of opening up the band to various incarnations, a lot of which were kind of *non sequiturs*, that was the very process which led him to us. And I think in his mind he was just doing the same thing he always did. And maybe the difference is that after a big success, that idea doesn't work so well."

Oddly, it turns out, Buckingham himself is most responsible—albeit indirectly—for the current Mac reunion. While recording the follow-up to *Out of the Cradle* last year, he began using drummer Fleetwood, and before long, both John and Christine McVie came on board for the sessions as well. Additionally, the Buckingham/Nicks team was reunited for Twisted, a cut on the Twister soundtrack, a track also featuring Fleetwood. "Basically the whole band had made music during the course of that year," the drummer notes. "And at that point there was no mention from within the ranks that it was all leading to something."

"When I left in '87, it really *was* a survival move," recalls Lindsey Buckingham from his studio chair. "Emotionally and physically. The atmosphere was not very conducive to being creative. A lot of the people had personal problems. It was just in order to regroup and get back on a track where I felt I was really grounded in the process again. And was sort of, in theory, doing it for the right reasons again.

"So, cut to nine years later—last year—and I run into Mick and we go out and have breakfast, and he's a totally different person. He's changed a few things about his life, and I realise that we have an awful lot to talk about. And the chemistry was just very present—as it had always been, but without the baggage. I'd done some healing and some refocusing and hopefully some growing, and so had he."

As the former members of Fleetwood Mac gathered together, whether in Buckingham's studio or at dinner, "suddenly there was this implication," Buckingham remembers. "And at some point I'm sure a light bulb went off over in Burbank at Warner Brothers—and I think probably for Mick, too. Because as much as he loved working on my stuff, Fleetwood Mac is a priority for him." There stood Buckingham, with a new solo album "nine-tenths done", and suddenly Russ Thyret, the chairman of Warner Brothers Records, was calling, asking *Do you want to do this?*"

Buckingham laughs.

"I had cut loose of all of the things that were baggage in my life. I had new lawyers, a new girlfriend, a shrink for the first time, and these lawyers were saying, 'Look, this could be a good thing to roll over into the visibility of your solo album.' But is it the type of visibility you *want*? At the time you just don't know. Fleetwood Mac had come off that last incarnation of Dave Mason and Bekka Bramlett—there was some damage control to be done, right? I thought, OK, I know these people care—it's not just a money thing for them, although of course bottom line is always that. I asked Russ Thyret on the phone, I know you haven't heard my album yet—if you had it in your hands, and were just totally convinced it was a smash, would you still be telling me to do this? Would you be giving me the advice? And he said, 'Absolutely.'

"So I said OK."

THERE IS, OF COURSE, THE MATTER OF MONEY. WORD HAS it that concert promoters will be guaranteeing the band $400,000 per show, and it estimates Fleetwood Mac's potential gross via ticket, album and merchandising sales could reach half that of The Eagles' 1994-96 world trek—which some contend exceeded $500 million.

"I hope people turn up," smiles an affable John McVie sheepishly. "They might think it's just a bunch of old farts out to make a buck."

Really?

"It'll be surprising if someone *doesn't* think that. There have been a lot of people who shall remain nameless who did that. I don't think any of us are that financially strapped that you have to go and sell your soul to do this." "Once we get on the road we'll take a few hits," Buckingham notes. "But in the same way, maybe people *can* sense Don [Henley] and Glenn [Frey] maybe aren't that crazy about being up on-stage with each other, they can sense that we *are* really digging it. Even more, I think that we are actually playing better than ever." These bothersome Eagles comparisons keep arising. Among the biggest-selling recording groups ever, both acts opted to reunite on an MTV stage set up within precisely the same building on the Warner Brothers studio lot. Indeed, it is difficult to pretend that reunions of this sort are about anything— anything at all—other than power, prestige and money. But there is indeed an important difference here, and it isn't only musical. Stevie Nicks—whose 1981 solo hit Leather And Lace featured a duet vocal by Eagle Don Henley—puts her bejewelled finger precisely on it. "You're never going to take away the fact that there's two ex-couples on that stage, you know. And you're never gonna take back the fact that a lot of those songs were written about each other. So no matter how cool anybody is, when you get up and *sing them* to each other . . . We can't *ever* look at each other as if we hadn't been totally involved. *Especially* when you get up there on the stage, and you're all wearing black, and I'm in black chiffon, and there's beautiful lights, and . . . you know, it's rock 'n' roll and everybody's in love again."

Rock's greatest soap opera: to be continued.

NEVER BREAK THE CHAIN

Amy Hanson | November 21, 1997 | *Goldmine* (US)

This sprawling Mick Fleetwood interview from America's premier record collector magazine was one of the most comprehensive examinations of Fleetwood Mac's family tree up to that point. Although much has happened in the band's career since, it remains a thoroughly absorbing piece of work that explores biographical avenues that standard article limits usually prohibit.

They are the biggest band in the world, midway through the fastest selling tour of the year, playing selections from one of the best selling albums of the decade. Yet talking to drummer and founder member Mick Fleetwood, you cannot escape from the feeling that if his phone had just rung a few months earlier, he would currently be powering a very different reincarnation of Fleetwood Mac indeed.

"Peter Green phoned me up like two weeks before we set out on this tour and said, 'I'm doing a tour in Europe and I want you to come over and play drums . . . ' and I went 'oh, fuck!' It was mis-timed . . . I'm doing what I'm doing. But one day, even if it is literally a day, the blessing is that I know I'll get to play with Peter again. And I couldn't have said that three years ago."

Peter Green. His name echoes through the corridors of time, across oceans, across generations, across too many songs to count. Thirty years ago, almost to the month, Peter Green's Fleetwood Mac took their first tentative steps onto the live stage, at Britain's annual National Jazz And Blues festival, and proceeded to blow the world away. And through a multitude of lineup changes, through the lean years of the early-mid Seventies, and even amidst the magic of the *Rumours*-mongering quintet which made the original band's achievements seem small, still Green's spirit hangs silently in the shadows, as if to say, "yes, that's it exactly. Keep going."

Which is precisely what Fleetwood Mac has done, and still do. Reunited for an MTV special which in turn spawned both a new album, *The Dance*, and a massive American tour, Christine McVie, Stevie Nicks, Lindsey Buckingham, John McVie and Mick Fleetwood are as familiar to their fans as a lover's touch, musical icons for an adoring public. But there are other names, too: Danny Kirwan, Jeremy Spencer, Bob Weston, Bob Welch, Dave Walker . . . this is a haunted band, one in which the past walks hand-in-hand with the present and future alike. And it is the culminated vision that these people collected which has allowed Fleetwood Mac to survive and grow.

In strictly historical terms, there is but one Fleetwood Mac. Musically, though, there are three: the Blues band which birthed them; the Modern superstars created when Nicks and Buckingham first arrived, and the five year drifter which divided the two. Three very different bands, three very different audiences, and three very different sets of expectations.

But these three seemingly disparate eras really are indelibly linked. Each is vitally, magically, important to the band as a whole, and they are connected by that magic. That, and the ghosts.

Fleetwood Mac was always Peter Green's band; it was modesty alone which demanded he name it after the drummer he had, and the bassist he wanted. John McVie was still gainfully employed with John Mayall's Bluesbreakers when Green and Fleetwood debuted their dream, but even their original bassist, Bob Brunning, knew it was only a matter of weeks before he was ousted. McVie finally moved over in September, 1967, and today, he and Fleetwood remain the linchpins around which the band has continued to function.

"Without John McVie playing with me, this band would not exist," Mick Fleetwood states unequivocally. "The music and the musicality of Fleetwood Mac would be a totally different character. The character which John and I create by playing together is a major, major part of what Fleetwood Mac is."

And an intrinsic part of that character, though he left the field long ago, is Green, the brilliant young guitarist who recognized Mick Fleetwood as an equally brilliant young drummer. "He saw what I had a long time ago, and it was not what people normally see, because I'm not horribly technical. It's just all emotive. I'm an emotional player, and he read that and made me really strong. But that's what it all about, bands. . . . It's feeling. I don't want to play with some guys just sitting there, being clever. On the premise that I'm a good drummer, I have a lot of musical smarts that I directed entirely to emotions, and that's how I play. When people say 'you look like you're really enjoying it,' I am! My heart, my smile, my everything, is in those moments when you're playing with someone."

With guitarist Jeremy Spencer filling in the gaps between Green's so-expressive liquidity, and the mighty Fleetwood/McVie rhythm section, the original Mac line-up would survive unscathed for the next three years; indeed, following the addition of a third guitarist, the teenaged Danny Kirwan in August, 1968, Fleetwood Mac was outselling every band in Britain, the Beatles included. So, when Green quit in May, 1970, few people gave them any chance of survival whatsoever.

With just a hint of reluctance, Fleetwood agrees.

"When Peter was there, no matter what happened, he was the head honcho. Just because he was that incredible. And so powerful."

His departure left the remaining frontline, Spencer and Kirwan, at a complete loss: "they felt so stripped of the security that Peter had given to them, and to the band. For what ever reason, they especially felt very naked. The band was in so much need of help. So we asked Chris to join."

"Chris," of course, was Christine McVie, bassist John's wife and, in 1970, the proud holder of Melody Maker's prestigious "Female Vocalist Of The Year" award. Following a stint in Stan Webb's Chicken Shack, the erstwhile Christine Perfect's recently launched solo career had already spawned a massive hit, with a beautiful rendering of Etta James' "I'd Rather Go Blind," but within a year, she'd had enough.

"I quit," she later explained, "and returned to life as a housewife."

Three months later, Fleetwood Mac asked her to join.

"When we asked Chris to join the band, we really needed help," Fleetwood recollects. "And she really helped that situation, and made us into a whole band again, by bringing in her own very specific talent. This band didn't start with five people, but if you look at the history of Fleetwood Mac, the good, powerful parts where we really, I think, have shone, are often, if not exclusively, when we've had three singer/ songwriters in the band. With Jeremy, Danny and Chris, we were then back to that. We had three people functioning in our front line on an equal standing."

Despite Ms. McVie's reassuring presence, the band now lurched into almost half a decade of uncertainty, hosting a revolving door of musicians around what was the core trio of Fleetwood and the Macs. Kirwan and Spencer were both gone within two years, and only American guitarist Bob Welch brought any additional stability to the band. He joined in 1971, following Spencer's departure, remaining a solid fixture until 1974—when he left, and the title of the group's latest, ninth, album suddenly seemed frighteningly appropriate: *Heroes Are Hard To Find*. Particularly guitar heroes.

Reduced to a three piece, once again Fleetwood Mac were left holding the ball on shaky ground, Even with the McVie/Fleetwood bond still firmly in place, it was either push on or quit, although Fleetwood insists, "we weren't thinking that at the time."

He explains, "I think there are so many eras in Fleetwood Mac, and they all sort of blended. When Bob Welch left, we were basically thinking 'what do we do next to enable us to carry on?' Which is really a part of the history in total. One of the umbilicals that goes through the whole history of this band is that that's been the work ethic. It's never been 'oh we're breaking up' it's always been, 'well, who's next?'"

Whoever it was would certainly have their work cut out for them.

An unannounced group hiatus the previous year had seen their erstwhile manager piece together an utterly spurious Fleetwood Mac line up, purportedly to fulfill obligations which the real band had left outstanding. The ploy failed, commercially and critically; now it was winding its way through the law courts, but U.S. promoters burned by the bogus band were now unwilling to re-book the real one, and while Fleetwood Mac's label, Warners, had renewed contracts, it was with considerable trepidation.

Commercially, meanwhile, the group was all but stagnant: album after album, sales bottomed out at around 250,000 copies; single after single flopped; airplay was confined to a clutch of "safe" neighborhoods. Fleetwood Mac was going nowhere, and the only real question was, how much longer could they keep doing so?

In the end, of course, these questions would never require an answer. Welch quit, and in his place came the duo who would help take Fleetwood Mac into an entirely new era, cultivate a new type of fan, and catapult the band to the top of the charts, and the middle of hearts across the globe.

Lindsey Buckingham and Stevie Nicks were busy with their own agendas when their path first crossed with Fleetwood Mac's in 1974. The two had met at Menlo-Atherton High School in San Francisco in 1967, where Nicks was a senior; Buckingham a junior. With fellow classmates Javier Pacheco and Calvin Roper, Buckingham and Nicks formed The Fritz Rabyne Memorial Band, and even after Nicks moved on to San Jose State, the band continued, with Nicks driving down from school to gig with the others.

Buckingham graduated, and the band—now better known under the abbreviated name of Fritz—went professional, sliding neatly into the non-stop San Francisco scene which was flourishing at the time. They apparently opened for most of the big names, local and national, but according to Nicks, the most important was Janis Joplin.

"We opened for her in Santa Clara. She walked on stage, and for an hour and a half my chin was on the floor. You couldn't have pried me away with a million dollar check. I was absolutely glued to her, and that is where I learned a lot of what I do on stage. It wasn't that I wanted to be like her, because I didn't. But I said, 'if ever I am a performer of any value, I want to be able to create the same kind of feeling that's going on between her and the audience.'"

Fritz would break up in 1971 but the Nicks-Buckingham team was going strong, and the two continued to write songs. The early culmination of this partnership was the formation of Buckingham-Nicks.

Still a sonic product of the San Francisco scene, Buckingham and Nicks secured a one record deal with Anthem (a local label handled by Polydor), and the services of producer Keith Olsen, at Sound City in Los Angeles. Work began on their self-titled debut album in early 1973.

More acoustic than rock, and with raw enthusiasm taking the place of studio polish, the songs which Buckingham and Nicks took into the studio already had that special something that is a precursor to greatness.

Certainly Buckingham was in full command of his craft, while Nicks was already feeling her way into that powerfully fragile and frighteningly sexy style she would hone with Fleetwood Mac. From the opening "Don't Let Me Down Again" and the aching "Crystal" (which would be reprised on *Fleetwood Mac*), to the stellar seven minute "Frozen Love," which closes the album, the two together sparked utter beauty on vinyl, and though it sold next to nothing, their eponymous debut album was a major triumph.

Still sorely overlooked, *Buckingham Nicks* nevertheless remains a collectors' favorite today, and while it is surprisingly easy to find, the prices this record fetches are oddly erratic. The original American gate-fold issue can bring as much as $30, with the German pressing worth less, and the 1977 American reissue averaging $10. But while die-hard fans and the impecunious curious alike have been screaming for *Buckingham Nicks* to reappear on CD, only the Goldtone bootleg label has thus far obliged—with a copy which was clearly lifted from the vinyl.

Mick Fleetwood, of course, knew none of this when, in early 1974, he set out scouting studios, searching for a suitable base for his own band's next album. Even with such a depleted line-up, life would go on. Sound City Recording was just one of many studios which he planned checking out, and when Keith Olsen slapped on a tape of the Buckingham Nicks album, he intended simply to demonstrate the production and sound of his studio's work. But that was all Fleetwood needed to hear. In every way, he knew immediately that Fleetwood Mac had found exactly what they had been looking for.

Looking back, he explains, "it was a very right feeling, and their music spoke in a way that obviously, initially, I noticed. Then I took that information to John and Chris, as to what I thought would be our next move to continue the band."

Fleetwood Mac were looking only for a guitarist, "but realizing that Lindsey and Stevie came as a songwriting team was all I needed to know, because I liked what I was hearing, and they created that, as opposed to having it produced around them. It was a great feeling."

Buckingham's guitar style struck a particular chord with Fleetwood. While he is the first to admit that he adores the band's past, as a musician, he was constantly looking to move forward, searching only for whatever would click with the band, and add to the existing talent, with little regard for precedent. That is why, when Peter Green left, they never replaced him with an imitator; it was far more exciting to go somewhere else instead, and that is the doctrine which sustains Fleetwood Mac to this day.

The Buckingham Nicks team certainly fit this bill. Always working from his initial gut instinct, Fleetwood says, "it was just lucky, certainly, that they had a product they had made. The *Buckingham Nicks* album spoke for itself and it was very apparent, certainly to my ears, that these people were really talented and Lindsey was truly a great, very different guitar player to what I had been used to in terms of his background."

What was especially interesting, he continues, was "Lindsey's sense of melody and economy. Although he's a very proficient player, he enjoys the one note approach very often, not always, but he has a real sense of that and that's something that struck home with me."

"Mick called us right after Bob Welch left," Stevie Nicks affirms. "He never said 'do you want to audition,' or 'do you want to come over and we'll get to know each other,' or anything. Right from the beginning, it was 'do you want to join?'"

A couple of days later, the five musicians got together for the first time, meeting for a Mexican meal, "and it was 'rehearsals start next week. See you there.'" The next thing she knew, "we were rehearsing, and two weeks later, recording."

Lindsey and Stevie were flabbergasted by Fleetwood's invitation to join the band. Even more astonishingly, although they knew that the band had an illustrious history, they hadn't actually heard anything Fleetwood Mac had recorded. Nicks remembers catching them on TV one evening, and seeing Christine perform "Show Me A Smile" (from 1971's *Future Games*), but aside from that, they were completely in the dark.

Nicks continues, "this friend of ours was really into Fleetwood Mac, and he told us about seeing them at Winterland, and how they'd driven away in big black Cadillac limousines. So there I was in my waitresses' outfit and white nurses' shoes, going 'oh my God!' and imagining those limos. I think that was the only time I've ever been really awestruck about this whole thing, seeing that picture in my head."

Immediately after the meal, the duo headed out and bought up every Fleetwood Mac album they could find, then sat down and listened to all of them straight through: *English Rose*, the blues-drenched compilation of the band's first U.K. albums; *Then Play On*, Peter Green's mystical, but so aptly named swansong; *Kiln House*, the almost folk inflected sound of the newly shorn band getting it together in the country; *Future Games* and *Bare Trees*, with Bob Welch's signature "Sentimental Lady" positively aching for recognition; *Penguin* and *Mystery To Me*, with another Welch classic, "Hypnotized," and *Heroes Are Hard To Find*.

It was a matter, Nicks insists, of the two of them discovering not only what they could bring to the band, but also what Fleetwood Mac could do for their own style and direction.

Obviously they liked what they heard.

Fleetwood continues, "we went into a brief rehearsal. We hadn't played a note together, yet we had full commitment that they were in the band. We rehearsed for about two weeks. We rehearsed in ICM's basement, which was our agency, and went straight from there to make our next album, *Fleetwood Mac*."

With those brief rehearsals gelling the band, of course, it was a very natural progression to the studio. *Fleetwood Mac* would be the beginning of a compositional style that would endure throughout the next two decades.

Every Fleetwood Mac album is driven by distinctive styles that the band has blended together. Songs belong inherently to Nicks, Buckingham, Christine McVie or to the band as an ensemble but over them all, there is the pervasive sound of the band itself.

Even so, it swiftly became apparent that all three principle writers had very different methods of working. According to Fleetwood, "Christine's songs were usually more formed than some of Stevie's, but Stevie and Lindsey had always had a work situation where Lindsey would musically put her songs together, take what she had done and rearrange it. And yet my sense of it is that the survivability of the essence of Stevie's songs is usually so strong that Lindsey has the smarts to realize what that essence is, and often stays with that essence.

"He has an incredible knack, which is part of their magic and what they brought to the band. He just knows how to interpret her, without taking something that's precious to her away. And her songs are extremely precious, sometimes almost to the point of she can't let go of them. Especially her words.

"But that's how this band is. Everyone's got an opinion. Certainly Stevie had an onward going relationship with Lindsey, where she respected and trusted what Lindsey would do. That was their partnership. Lindsey and Christine had a different relationship, because theirs' was much more of a musical one, because she's a player."

Where, then, does Fleetwood himself come into this mix?

"I came in like a big lump of glue. I was, and am, one hellishly healthy sounding board; one that has very strong opinions, and feels very often flattered with always being consulted. I usually get 'what do you think, Mick?' and I'll come in with the old vibemaster and I'll say, 'you know what? That's the take for me,' or 'that's the way that vocal sounds great.' Or, 'I love that guitar part.' It's somewhat vicarious, but sometimes, it's even more specific than I realize. So that's where I come in. Right from the beginning. Right to the end. I will always be there to let people know. And it's all done from the gut. Totally from the feeling. I will always react to what my feelings are. That's my relationship with my fellow players. Always was and always will be. It's a real thing."

The band were fresh and feeding on the excitement of new beginnings. Stevie and Lindsey's San Francisco sound was punched up immeasurably by the driving perfection of the Fleetwood/McVie rhythm section, and Christine McVie's masterful piano arrangements and vocal harmonies. Conversely, the three core Macs were surrounded by Buckingham's rocking-to-achingly soothing guitar, and that one-of-a-kind voice from Nicks.

From the soaring punch in "Monday Morning," through to the haunting "Landslide" and the reprise of "Crystal", *Fleetwood Mac* set a pace which would not be eclipsed until they themselves deigned to do it themselves, with the release of *Rumours*. Yet though it remains a wonderful album all the way through, there is one song that struck especially hard, and left a world begging for more.

Quite simply, Nicks' "Rhiannon" defined an entire generation of listeners. It was the song of the year, and perhaps somewhat bittersweetly, it shot Nicks to the very forefront of the band. That swirling, whirling gypsy child with scarves trailing was the image that stuck in 1975, and one which Christine McVie would marvel over for years to come.

"'Rhiannon' created a huge impact on stage, with little Stevie floating around in her black chiffon and top hat—people got really excited about it."

And yet, although "Rhiannon" exists, for many fans, as the redefining moment in Fleetwood Mac's history, the song itself only made it to #11 on the U.S. charts and never even cracked the charts in the U.K.

While many cite the song as the beginning of mystic, magical compositions for the band, Nicks was only stamping her name upon a supernatural element which had long been current within Fleetwood Mac's musical make-up, as far back as "Black Magic Woman" and "Green Manalishi," from the Peter Green era. More recently still, the phenomenal "Hypnotized" had opened even further the door which Nicks burst through in 1975.

At the same time, however, the true power of "Rhiannon" has never been unleashed upon the record buying public. Caught live on the group's 1975 tour, it expands to eight or nine minutes, gains an entirely new lyrical hook, and ends with Nicks' vocal and Buckingham's guitar literally dueling for supremacy. Simply listening to it is an emotional drain, and one can only regret that by the time Fleetwood Mac came to release an official live album, in 1979, sheer familiarity had dulled the naive exuberance of Nicks' earliest performances.

Making *Fleetwood Mac* was an immensely wonderful experience for the band, although Fleetwood and Nicks both vividly recall the awful moment when they suddenly realized that they had lost the finished masters! All that work, all that effort—the group tore the studio apart, finally coming across the tapes amidst a pile of tapes which had been put aside to be destroyed!

In all, *Fleetwood Mac* would spawn three hit singles, while the album itself reached #1 on the U.S. chart. Christine McVie's "Over My Head" was first, jumping in on December 13, 1975, and coming in to rest at #7. It was Fleetwood Mac's first ever U.S. Top 40 hit.

The song's success surprised everybody, its composer in particular.

"It was the last track we kept [while we were recording], and we really didn't know what we were going to do with it. All it had was a vocal, a dobro guitar and a drum track."

Later, she added a Vox continental, while Buckingham came up with a guitar motif, but still, "it was the last track we ever thought would be a single."

Of course, this song, too, carries the sweet spirits of earlier Mac days. Its chorus slides perfectly into the melody of "Albatross," a 1968 Peter Green composition that McVie herself greatly admired.

"Rhiannon" followed in April, 1976, and "Say You Love Me" slid into the charts at #11 in July as radios across the county ate the band up, slamming songs into heavy rotation and never letting them go. A quick perusal of the radio dial today reveals that not much has changed since then.

Speaking at the time, Christine McVie summed it up best.

"We have a situation now that's a little bit different . . . we have run across a very unique formula, that happens to be commercial, while retaining the quality of the [different] Fleetwood Macs. And it happened without our doing anything that was sacrilegious to our tastes."

Armed with what they knew was a good album, the band set out on a tour to reintroduce themselves to the world, aware that this time out, they appealed to both the old school die hards and to new fans. The divide which would later become apparent in the band's audience had yet to manifest itself; instead, there would be something for everyone on this first tour.

Nicks remembers, "one of the big things was that we went right out on the road. We played constantly, and everywhere, places like Casper, Wyoming and Normal, Illinois. And people were so wonderful and gave us such good vibes."

Indeed, the audiences were astonishingly receptive, no mean feat for a band who really had changed their core sound. And although the group cared not one whit what others thought of them, the positive response could only have boosted the great wave which they suddenly found themselves riding.

In part because the band had only the eleven songs from their album to play, they pulled some old Fleetwood Mac and Buckingham Nicks favorites to add to the set. Bob Welch's "Hypnotized," Danny Kirwan's "Station Man," "Spare Me A Little" (from *Bare Trees*) and "Why" (from *Mystery To Me*) were all retained in the group's hour long show, while both "Don't Let Me Down Again" (from *Buckingham Nicks*) and "Oh Well" (from *Then Play On*) would survive as live staples until as late as the *Tusk* tour, with Buckingham keeping the spirit of the songs alive even as he added his own unique flair to the proceedings. In fact, live versions of both "Oh Well" and "Green Manalishi" really do emphasize Buckingham's ability to retain the spirit of that old blues band, while powering the new pop group to its peak.

But it was the new songs that garnered the loudest applause. Night after night, Nicks' poignant "Landslide" would bring a caterwauling crowd to its knees, enveloping the venue in such complete silence that, listening to live recordings of the song, one could almost believe she was performing to an empty room.

And if there was any resistance from the diehard blues fans, Fleetwood insists he never heard it.

"You always get, 'oh it's not like the old days of playing the blues'. We had a fair amount from people I talked to. Suddenly there were two girls in the band . . . real different. But I think that the new audience that we attained was such a whole wave of new audience that any negativity that might have been, we just really weren't aware of."

As the new year dawned, coming in off a balls-out tour, and a string of successful singles, Fleetwood Mac returned to the writing board to prepare a follow up. Unfortunately, things would never move as smoothly as they had in the past.

The recipe which would end with *Rumours* is almost depressingly familiar today: Stevie was breaking up with Lindsey, Christine and John were divorcing, Mick and his first wife were separating, and it all went haywire from there, helped along by liberal doses of libations and cocaine. It was the stuff of tattle tale tabloid dreams, and of course the media would make the most of it. But there was actually a hell of a lot of good stuff going on beyond, as Fleetwood himself puts it, "the smut."

Recording was tough. Compared to the three months it took to lay down *Fleetwood Mac*, this new album would end up taking a year, as the songs laid bare their composers' almost painfully autobiographical emotions. The band members' private life inevitably carried over into the studio, too; clipped voices and facetiously civil tones looming over the actual creative process. And if this weren't enough, the recording studio was home to a temperamental tape recorder which threatened to eat the takes, rather than record them!

Everyone was shaken, frustrated, and half insane with the effort, although Fleetwood remembers Nicks struggling harder than anyone to prevail in light of the circumstances.

"She did her first take of 'Gold Dust Woman' in a fully lit studio, and as take followed take, she began withdrawing into herself. So we dimmed the lights, brought her a chair, a supply of tissues, a Vicks inhaler, a box of lozenges for her sore throat, and a bottle of mineral water. And on the eighth take, at four in the morning, she sang the lyric straight through to perfection."

Perhaps that is why *Rumours* was so damned good. But could it have gone the other way? No-one seems to remember the chronology of events, which songs were written in answer to others, or even whether or not malice aforethought played a part in the process. Nevertheless, *Rumours* can be read as the unfolding diary of a string of acrimonious break-ups, all taking place just as the band was poised to really take off.

It could have been so easy for the disintegrating personal side to undermine the music, but Fleetwood is quick to deny that ever seemed likely.

"No. But were we fragile! I was pretty clued in to what was happening, and the driving energy that we were all involved in was so strong that I have no recollection of ever sitting down with any one member of this band [to discuss breaking up], and I think I would have known about it if that had been in the air. I was somewhat the dad of the band, and would know what was going on. It was crucifyingly difficult at certain points, but there was such a bond musically, and we were so engrossed in what we were doing, realizing that we had been given an opportunity, as individuals and as a band, that may only come once in a lifetime. And to throw it away would have been a sin. And that's how we looked at it. And we got round all the other stuff . . . the bedroom stuff."

Which must have been difficult during the recording, with all these people in the studio and nowhere to go. One can only imagine the horror. Indeed, "Go Your Own Way," "I Don't Want To Know" and "Songbird" virtually breathe on their own, with the little demons circling round like vultures.

And then, in the midst of the madness, "The Chain" crashes through like a self-repairing, and ultimately, self-fulfilling, mantra. With lyrics by Nicks, and an opening riff which recalls the beginning of *Buckingham Nicks'* "Lola, My Love", "The Chain" is credited to the whole band, and would itself become the intangible thread that wove itself into the very fabric of Fleetwood Mac, allowing them to group and regroup over the next twenty years.

Released in the spring of 1977, *Rumours* would remain on the U.S. charts for 134 weeks, 31 of those at the golden #1. Britain, too, was now back in love with Fleetwood Mac, having all but ignored the band since the golden age of the blues, almost a decade before. Fleetwood and the McVies' homeland would make up for lost time with a vengeance, keeping *Rumours* on the U.K. charts for a staggering 443 weeks, a total which only Meatloaf's *Bat Out Of Hell* has eclipsed. To put this feat into even weirder perspective, *Rumours* alone has spent longer on the U.K. chart than the rest of Fleetwood Mac's catalog put together!

Back in the U.S., while *Rumours* went platinum within a month of release, all four singles culled from the album would go on to break the top ten: "Go Your Own Way" (#10), "Dreams" (#1), "Don't Stop" (#3) and "You Make Loving Fun" (#9). Simultaneously, Fleetwood Mac and Buckingham Nicks' entire back catalog was given a major overhaul, with both their older albums and selected singles being reissued to capitalize on the success of *Rumours*. Early material was repackaged onto greatest hits collections; Mick Fleetwood's pre-Mac stint with Shotgun Express was reissued; Christine McVie's 1969 solo album returned to the chart; the entire music industry, it seemed, had embarked upon a feeding frenzy, all powered by the mighty Mac.

In March 1977, the band commenced a grueling seven month tour, beginning with a month in the United States. Breaks in between legs were scattered and often used to complete the various and sundry side projects which were always in action behind the scenes—Nicks and Buckingham guested on new albums by California songwriter John Stewart and Warren Zevon; Fleetwood, Buckingham and Christine McVie appeared on Bob Welch's *French Kiss* solo debut. In light of all the recent upheavals and the paces the band were putting themselves through, only a superhuman could keep it together, although Fleetwood is quick to point out, "there were good times."

"It was just the experience of having such a profound awareness that people were digging what we were doing, and giving us so much feedback that it was so undeniable. Every day. Everywhere we went. It was all people reaching out and feeding us this huge amount of energy, that we feasted off. How could you not go on?"

The changes on the road were quite significant. Fleetwood Mac had gone from playing, as Fleetwood puts it, "colleges and small 1500 seaters," as well as "some festivals, second on the bill, or third or fourth or whatever on the bill," to a full-on large venue and stadium assault.

They scoured the United States, and then it was back to England for their first tour with the new line up, an outing which was surely a gratifying experience for the McVies and Fleetwood. They had left England without much fanfare, and were returning just under four years later, as giants.

Fleetwood remembers, "It was just part of the gigsters' life, you know. We weren't playing tiny places, but we were playing Hammersmith Odeon type places, 2,000 seaters. I think, really, it was such a celebration of us coming home and we were certainly lucky.

"The celebration was, especially for the English contingent, that we were going back, having left England, having had the original Fleetwood Mac be such a success in the '60s. A phenomenal success, not in the States, but all over Europe and especially in England. To come home and sort of say, 'well, we're back and we're different. But it's still Fleetwood Mac'.

"*Rumours* was a huge album in Europe, just as big as it was [in the U.S.] all over the world. It certainly wasn't like going back and thinking 'whoops, we're going back to tiny venues.' They were all fairly substantial places. But it was a very schizophrenic experience, because so many people remembered the Peter Green days, and for good reason. And now, whatever amount of time had lapsed, and they were confronted with 'it's Fleetwood Mac, but it's not Fleetwood Mac.'"

Indeed, "it's not Fleetwood Mac" were Fleetwood Mac, and they were the biggest band in the world in 1976-1977. As the tour ground on, over continents and time zones, the rush of on-stage adrenaline was both complemented and complicated as friendships and working relationships were defined, then undermined by the upheavals that were occurring regularly. But it was never the truly gruesome bloodbath that outsiders like to recreate.

Fleetwood himself reflects on the tour as an intense time of bonding.

"I was probably, certainly not oblivious, but I was spared because I wasn't working with someone that I had had a serious relationship with. I think maybe some other lads and lasses might react slightly differently in terms of other members of the band. It seemed to me that I was really in there with everyone, and I have to say that there were good times, and there was bonding during those days.

"Stevie and Christine sort of drifted off into different worlds there. Nothing bad, it was just that their lifestyles were so different. But what they had, especially during those days, they bonded as ladies. Just to get them through these not good times.

"I remember John and I spent a lot of time together as we generally feel comfortable doing anyhow. And I think socially, Lindsey, mainly because he's such a private person anyhow, probably tended to be a little bit on his own. Looking back on it, if I'd been more aware, I would have done more reaching out than I did to him. It was a strange situation."

The tour over, the band would only break temporarily before commencing, in May 1978, on their next album, the double whopper, *Tusk*, a set which Fleetwood credits with keeping the band together. The group had already been through the mill; its massive success notwithstanding, beginning work on *Rumours* so soon after coming off the *Fleetwood Mac* tour had been a dreadful mistake, and yet here they were doing it all over again.

But just as the common goal of completing *Rumours* had ensured Fleetwood Mac remained together at a time when each member of the band had some very real, powerful reasons for not wanting to meet with another, so this new project—which swiftly developed into the absolute antithesis of its predecessor—would serve an even greater purpose. It would prove that Fleetwood Mac didn't have to remain stagnant to retain credibility.

Today, it is very fashionable to describe *Tusk* as Lindsey Buckingham's pet project, and indeed, it may have started out that way. By the time it was over, however, it was very much a Fleetwood Mac album, and—perhaps surprisingly—very much in keeping with the end of the Peter Green era recordings, a point which Mick Fleetwood in particular relishes. Just like *Then Play On*, it was to be, as Fleetwood sums up, "a statement of what Fleetwood Mac was all about, a sense of grandeur with intimacy. That was the vision that came together in the aural collage called *Tusk*."

Fleetwood recalls, "there was some, initially, some reaching out in terms of Lindsey having very specific desires. To me they were never problematic. But I think Lindsey almost felt they were more problematic than they really were, in terms of 'Can I try to play some drums . . . ' I had done very similar things. I've had this with John and Peter [Green], where whatever it takes is okay, as long as you're not suggesting that you make a solo album, and pretend it's Fleetwood Mac.

"I think that was the only shaky area, which was not shaky for very long. And musically and aesthetically, in terms of what command it had, in terms of signposting, *Tusk* was a very prophetic album. It sort of hinted at what was going to happen. That everyone was eventually going to go and make their own albums. And we allowed ourselves to make a double package album that was unheard of, especially in those days when the whole record industry was about to die."

As far as Warners were concerned, indeed, 1978 certainly wasn't the year to try out a "progressive" double album named for a whopping great phallus—for that, Fleetwood laughs, is the meaning of the "tusk" of the title. What Warners wanted was another *Rumours*. But of course, the band, with Fleetwood (the band's manager since 1975) firmly in control, refused to give in to any industry pressure. Fleetwood admits that Warners reaction was "not good." But the band didn't care.

"Warners tried to persuade us not to do it, and we told them 'forget it.' And in the long run, I'm sure they were very glad we did. Because that album, the fact we did make a double album, and the fact that the band came to terms with Lindsey reaching out into areas that were very cool, was very important.

"And in retrospect, [Buckingham's avenues] were way cooler than we realized at the moment. It was fantastic! That was the essence of how Peter Green ended up. He started out playing blues, and then made albums like *Then Play On* with really progressive things for those days. There was a lot of happenstance in terms of it being very similar, looking back on it, between Peter and Lindsey; creative nuts and bolts . . . the way they approached things."

And despite the band's initial reservations, they all realized how important it was not just to Buckingham, but to Fleetwood Mac, to make this record. Even Nicks came around, and that despite spending the actual sessions convinced she was trapped within a "big rumpled up ball of Tusk-ness"—although she did threaten to quit when she found out what the title meant!

Instead, she turned in a clutch of her most powerful songs yet, with "Storms," "Sara" and "Beautiful Child." Across all three, her voice resonated with emotion, following on the path she had started in *Fleetwood*

Mac, but more confident now, and stronger. In the old days, she admits, she almost wrecked her untrained voice, trying to keep things going onstage every night. Now she knew precisely what she was doing, and how she would do it, and while she would, of course, lose some of the natural beauty of her natural tones, replacing it perhaps with a more studied approximation, the alternative would have been disastrous.

"Sara," in particular, was a masterpiece, and when *Tusk* was first released on CD, several years later, it seemed (and still seems) incredible that, with so many songs to choose from, it was "Sara" that Warners chose to "edit," so as to fit the two record set onto a single CD. Indeed, the outcry from fans was so great that when a Fleetwood Mac *Greatest Hits* album was mooted for release later in the decade, an unabridged "Sara" was among the first tracks shortlisted for inclusion. At least, that was the official story. A few conspiracy theorists, on the other hand, reckon they planned it that way all along.

At the time of *Tusk*'s original release, of course, the most attention (good and bad) was lavished upon the album's title track, particularly after it was released as a fall, 1979, single, shortly ahead of the album. In terms of a major band's release schedule, there had never been anything like it before, a three minute percussion loop shot through with disconnected voices and chants, no discernible tune and absolutely no common ground with the hits of the recent past. And the song still stands today as one of the very, very few truly unique compositions ever to have been recorded.

"Tusk" started life as nothing more than a few bars which Buckingham and Fleetwood played as a sort of sound check before gigs; first, it was transformed (by longtime engineer and producer Richard Dashut) into a twenty second tape loop, which was then recorded from one track to another, before some overdubs were added. The resulting mass would become the bones of the song.

After some thought, the brainstorm hit—use a marching band to play "the riff," over which the rest of the song would be recorded. This was duly done live (except for John McVie, who had laid down his bass parts earlier) at Dodger Stadium, with the University of Southern California's marching band. And that, as the old saying goes, was that.

Nothing on the album could ever hope to compete with "Tusk"'s utterly alien landscaping, although Buckingham's blend of power pop mantras and proto-New Wave guitar picking certainly tried. Through "The Ledge", "That's All For Everyone" and the almost manic "Not That Funny Is It?" came a glimmer of what would become standard musical stylings just a few short years hence.

Not to be outdone by her bandmates, Christine McVie also came out on top, with two beautiful compositions, "Never Make Me Cry" and "Brown Eyes." Even more importantly, however, the haunting latter also brought Peter Green back into the fold, as an uncredited guest guitarist.

Green and Fleetwood had kept in touch through the years (indeed, Green also appears on *Penguin*, contributing a brief, but readily recognizable, guitar to "Night Watch"), their bond rattled, but not broken by the many waters which had passed under the bridge since the guitarist first walked out on the band.

Fleetwood explains, "I love Peter, and he is really the reason why I'm here in terms of the musician. But it was strange, because Peter was no longer the Peter I remembered, really, because of his illness. Peter had an onward going struggle with paranoid schizophrenia, and it was a real illness. So he was sometimes there, and sometimes not."

Recent years had seen Green emerge from the private hell which had enveloped him, to relaunch a career which all but the most devoted fans had completely given up dreaming about. Under Fleetwood's own management aegis, the guitarist traveled to L.A., and the drummer continues, "I saw Pete socially. He got married at my house. But I was in a very different sort of world and quite honestly, it wasn't like the old days. I was, at that point, living in hope that he would snap out of it, but he never did until quite recently."

But Fleetwood got Green into the studio to lay down some guitar nonetheless.

"It was so brief, and it was bittersweet. It worried John, because he really didn't want to see him like that."

But Green was, at the time, well enough to contribute, and Fleetwood takes a moment to reminisce about his feelings at this undoubtedly trying time.

"You know, I've cried myself to sleep many a night listening to early Fleetwood Mac and going, 'what happened to this guy?' Not that he wasn't in Fleetwood Mac, but why isn't he playing, what happened? This is a fucking tragedy.' And could I have done something, could I have done this . . . especially when I was drinking.

"I'd always get people in the hotel room [on tour] and say 'now I want you to hear Peter Green. This is where it all came from.' I'd put on a record and I would always end up in tears, listening. Because he was a great player.

"And those sorts of standards set a precedent through the years, where I certainly tried with the likes of my sensibilities, and Lindsey's guitar playing, again very different to Peter, but he had something. He was making a statement. His style was very unique and that whole thing came from me having someone with such a profound effect that Peter had on me musically and personally. I never forgot that. I tried to keep that standard of flag flying. The right sort of flag should be in flight and that's what I did through the years."

So Green was still moving through Fleetwood Mac some ten years on, in the guise of Lindsey Buckingham. And there are striking similarities between the visions of Green and Buckingham. In essence, *Tusk* is a logical progression along a skewed path from *Then Play On*. Play the two albums side by side, and the path becomes crystal clear.

A massive tour had been planned around *Tusk*, a year long, round-the-world-and-back-again extravaganza which not only saw even more splintering of relationships within the band, it also provoked the departure of Richard Dashut, after five years working with the band. Tired and burned out, he just couldn't do it anymore, and as it turned out, neither could the rest of the group. Nerves were frayed, and constant contact had taken their toll.

The tour was the biggest the band had ever undertaken, in terms of length and individual venues. Even in Britain, a country not then renowned for vast indoor gatherings, ticket demand was such that Fleetwood Mac found themselves playing what Fleetwood remembers as "funny factory sheds and things. I remember playing Birmingham

[Christine McVie's hometown], in some dreadful sounding place, covered in tin, and you know, it had 12,000, 15,000 people in there."

Amid all this, ever wilder rumors circulated that the band were breaking up. Every gig in every city saw some journalist ask that loaded question. The answer was always "no," but behind the scenes, matters were coming to a head.

Warners were still seething over the band's decision to issue a weird double album, instead of simply rewriting *Rumours*, and the sales figures backed them to the hilt: *Rumours* was still outselling its successor by five or six to one. The tour, too, had failed to turn the expected profit, and at a band meeting shortly after the tour ended, Mick Fleetwood was removed by the rest of the band (via their own individual representatives) as the group's overall manager.

It was this which toppled an already precarious situation. Fleetwood Mac were so huge that it was becoming more about managers, middle-men and go-betweens, and less about five people sitting down and getting on. It was clearly time for a break.

The band didn't break up, however. Rather, they chose to take a nine month hiatus, going their separate ways while each band member (John McVie excepted) launched their own solo projects. That nine month break, however, would turn into three long years.

Early into the interim, in time for Christmas, 1980, Warners released *Live*, hoping to recoup some money from the four-million-copy-selling "failure" that was *Tusk*, by releasing another double record set. Obviously the band had proved their point well, when they insisted that a double album would sell just fine!

Live contained performances culled from shows around the world during the *Tusk* tour. All the standard favorites were there, and this album has become, for many, the quintessential Mac album, showcasing as it does the unbelievable vibrancy and pure power of the band's live sets. To sweeten the deal, several "new" songs were etched into the vinyl grooves. "Fireflies" from Nicks, Christine McVie's pristine "One More Night," and "Don't Let Me Down Again" that familiar blast from the *Buckingham Nicks* past. The last, and a surprising addition, was a cover of Brain Wilson's "The Farmer's Daughter," credited with many thanks to the old Beach Boy.

Meanwhile, the individual members began enjoying what would swiftly prove a very productive break. Fleetwood, for example, turned his full attention onto his interest in African rhythms (an African "talking drum" has long been part of his stage set up), by relocating to Ghana to record his *The Visitor* solo album—again with help from a passing Peter Green.

Nicks launched her own solo career, taking "Rhiannon" to the logical next level with *Bella Donna*, and a clutch of songs she had written—but been unable to fit into Fleetwood Mac—over the past four or five years: According to Nicks herself, that album's biggest hit, "Leather And Lace," dates back to the *Rumours* period, and was originally demoed as a duet with Don Henley.

Lindsey, too, had been noodling down his own avenues, working on what would become *Law and Order*, and of course there is nothing like a few solo albums to set the hounds sniffing. Once again headlines screamed that Fleetwood Mac was dead during the early months of 1981. The band, however, were having none of it. They reconvened in France in May, to begin work on *Mirage*.

Whereas *Tusk* reached back to the end of the Green era, *Mirage* was a step back to recreate *Rumours*, perhaps to give the fans (and of course, the label accountants) what they thought they wanted.

"Yes, *Mirage*, in retrospect, was a little bit of backtracking, where Lindsey came back into the ranks of Fleetwood Mac creatively, rather than leading the rest of us on his own tangent. And was that album a mistake? No, because I don't think any album is a mistake. But I think, had we stuck to our guns, and Lindsey's guns a little bit more, we would have maybe taken it in a bit of a different route."

But there was more than a little pressure being exerted on the band members, an attempt to get them back to the sweet spot, and *Mirage* would fill that gap well.

Although each member brought songs to the studio, as usual, Fleetwood insisted that unlike *Tusk*, this time they work collectively, doing what they do best, with all five playing on every track. And the immediate response was good: *Mirage* went to #1 and all three singles—"Gypsy", "Hold Me", and "Love In Store"—would chart in the U.S., while the U.K. would put "Oh, Diane" in at a peak position of #15.

Again in the short term, the album sold better than its predecessor. But it failed to hit the same chords that *Rumours* twanged, and at the end of the day, *Mirage* just didn't feel right at all.

Fleetwood admits, "after *Rumours*, *Mirage* was not by any means a failure . . . but it wasn't *Rumours* in terms of the dreaded ratio of success.

"We allowed, and probably Lindsey, if he were talking to you, would regretfully let on that he, against his better judgment, decided to really get into finding out what the band would do without any one person saying 'this is the root.' And that's what came out. There are some good things on that album, [Nicks'] 'Gypsy' is a great song. But there was a very slight element of saying, 'well, I wonder what we'd do if we were doing these songs in the same sort of musical frame of mind as *Rumours*?' Just playing, that's how it was when we made *Rumours*. It was just a bunch of people playing. Whereas on *Tusk*, there were some real inroads creatively made and spearheaded by Lindsey, *Mirage* was back to business as usual."

But it wouldn't be back to business as usual for the band after the record was released. The cracks were widening and for the first time, Fleetwood Mac would not tour in support of the record. Instead they undertook a paltry eighteen show stint in the United States, culminating in the monstrous U.S. Festival in California. After that, the wind scattered everyone back to their own lives, and solo careers. It was an ill wind which rattled Fleetwood to the quick.

"I felt sick when we stopped touring. I wanted to be on the move, touring until the cows came home. But the others were less enthusiastic. Christine had sessions for her own solo album scheduled, and we'd have been lucky to get Stevie at all."

Again, the doomsayers were swift to pen the band's obituary, a task which was only made easier as the next three years placed the individual members [of] Mac very firmly inside their respective solo careers. But the spirit that held them together was ever present, and to insiders, it was inevitable that Fleetwood Mac would reform. Fleetwood himself credits Christine McVie with finally drawing the band back together.

Fifteen years had passed since McVie's last solo venture, the so-called *Legendary Christine Perfect Album* which was originally released before she joined Fleetwood Mac—and had finally charted in 1976. Now, *Christine McVie* had taken her into the Top 30, spawned a couple of hits, and placed her in a position of considerable power. She had even been asked to record Elvis Presley's "Can't Help Falling In Love" for the film *A Fine Mess*, and as the session beckoned, she called in Richard Dashut to produce her.

Dashut, meanwhile, had been working with Buckingham on his solo material, and one day, he casually mentioned that Buckingham might want to be involved, as Elvis was a performer near and dear to his heart.

As always seems to happen with this band, the jungle drums rumbled on, and soon, both Fleetwood and John McVie found themselves in the studio, working on the song. And with four out of the five finding themselves having fun, the obvious choice was to call in the fifth, and make a new record.

But it would prove to be far from easy. Five members whose relationships are strained, plus five managers who only have their client's purse strings at heart, do not an easy reformation make.

Workwise, too, the situation was far from ideal. Buckingham was heavily ensconced in his own album, and Fleetwood remembers had to threaten to bring in a new guitarist before he would commit to a new Fleetwood Mac project. Nicks, meanwhile, was touring heavily to support her own latest album, *The Wild Heart*, at the same time as undergoing enormous difficulty with drugs and alcohol. John McVie, too, was battling a drinking problem.

But the deal was finally cemented, and the band returned to Dashut and Buckingham for production.

Buckingham brought songs from his solo project to the recording studio, and wrote "Mystified" and "You And I" with Christine McVie. Nicks literally flew in for a few days at a time to add her parts, including the moving "Welcome To The Room, Sara" written about her recent stay at the Betty Ford Center. Slowly, and with much gnashing and pushing and pulling, *Tango In The Night* finally came together, and was released in the spring of 1987.

The album saw a string of singles, with "Big Love" and "Little Lies" coming into the top ten in the charts, simultaneously pulling the group into the MTV vortex. The music video moguls held record companies firmly in hand by the mid '80s, impressing upon everyone that if an album was cut, there had better be some videos to back it up. Sales were driven less by radio and more by video, so Fleetwood Mac were duly dispatched to the front of the cameras. Bizarre images though they were, "Little Lies" and "Seven Wonders" went straight into heavy rotation at MTV, giving a plastic public what they wanted.

Fleetwood Mac had never been shy about releasing singles, and this album was no different. What was bizarre was the proliferation of strange, and strangely contemporary, remixes with which they saddled both "Little Lies" and "Big Love," none of which really seemed to fit the band's ideals. The marketplace, however, seemed to be lapping it all, up . . . and then the real blow came.

Tango was proving to be a highly successful album after such a long hiatus, and the inevitable topic of touring came up. Buckingham firmly refused to go on the road this time. He had pretty much affirmed that he was through with the band, going so far as to tell *Creem* magazine that he simply couldn't do what he wanted to do with Fleetwood Mac. It was a hurtful blow to the others, who may or may have not felt the same way, but didn't need to say it publicly.

Buckingham continued to waver on the subject of touring, and after a major band blowout, he walked out and essentially left the band. For good.

Looking back today, Fleetwood can understand his emotions.

"Lindsey is always looking to the future. I do, and I see vision, and God knows, I've been party to it. But I'm also an Irishman and I'm sentimental. I'm proud of the work I've been involved with in my duty with Fleetwood Mac. I don't have a problem in going, 'well, it'd be sort of cool to do this and maybe we could put this back together and do this and do that.' But then you get Lindsey going, 'but, why?'."

And this time, nobody could answer him.

Reeling, the others decided to tour regardless, and promptly recruited singer/songwriter Billy Burnette (who had worked with both Fleetwood and Nicks in the past). But Fleetwood Mac still needed to fill Buckingham's lead guitar strings. Rick Vito bridged the gap perfectly. Well respected, Vito is a great blues fan and had cut his teeth on the old Fleetwood Mac blues albums in the '60s. He was a perfect fit.

Despite its obvious potential, this newest incarnation of Fleetwood Mac would be brief. Having contributed a couple of new songs to the forthcoming *Greatest Hits* album, a steady seller through 1988, the Burnette/Vito line-up made its long playing debut on 1990's *Behind The Mask*—which in turn proved a frustratingly slow seller. Even more damagingly this new album spawned but one top-40 single, Christine McVie's "Save Me" limping to #33, before falling into the same obscurity as the rest of the album. Yet at least one track from *Behind The Mask*, the epic "In The Back Of My Mind," ranks alongside any of the band's most adventurous (and successfully so) songs, and the album itself remains something of an overlooked gem.

Its failure, however, could not sustain the band. In September, 1990, both Nicks and Christine McVie announced they would be leaving the band at the end of the current tour, a sold out show at the Great Western Forum in Inglewood, CA. The appearance that same night of Lindsey Buckingham, on stage for an encore of "Landslide" and "Go Your Own Way," only added to the sense of finality. Reunited for one last time, the "classic" Fleetwood Mac was no more.

Fleetwood and McVie announced their intention to continue. By fall, 1991, however, Vito, too, had quit, and both Fleetwood and McVie were embroiled in their own solo projects: McVie's wryly named Gotta Band, and Fleetwood's Zoo. Both would appear, to muted applause, in 1992, and even a brief one off reunion at the request of President Clinton at his January, 1993 inaugural ball couldn't bring Fleetwood Mac back together. Once again, the Buckingham-Nicks-Fleetwood-McVies team reunited onstage, to perform the President's adopted anthem "Don't Stop," but it was only because when the president asks, one doesn't really say no.

Meanwhile, Fleetwood was also performing what many observers believed was essentially the last rites, compiling the four CD Fleetwood Mac retrospective, *The Chain*.

He explains, "I think one of the things I like is when . . . the Rolling Stones are a band that really reconfigures a lot of their old work. In all sorts of different packages, and different running orders of albums and songs, things from *Between The Buttons* put with *Aftermath* and whatever. Quite frankly, it's good marketing. They remarket their wears and tears, and I love all that. I'll always go and buy *The Best Of The Byrds* or Marvin Gaye's *Greatest Hits*. I'm a sucker for that, and I actually like it and think there is a real demand for that. That's just part of my onward going thing where I see that type of thing as a bigger picture."

Fleetwood Mac, however, have never been adequately repackaged. True, their early blues albums have been mixed and matched ad nauseam, with the original lineup's first three records now available in so many permutations that it is sometimes hard to remember how they originally flowed. And of course, there was 1988s *Greatest Hits* album, concentrating on the post-1975 lineup's most successful confections.

But never had anybody sat down and seriously attempted to establish an historical perspective on the band's entire career. That was the task which Fleetwood set himself, and in many ways, he succeeded. *The Chain* was a very interesting set, loaded with rarities and unreleased material, but it had its downside as well, as Fleetwood himself acknowledges. It was slanted far too heavily in favor of the post-1975 line-up, at the expense of all that had gone before.

"That box set was about the history of Fleetwood Mac," he agrees, "and to a certain extent, weights and balances sway a little too much attention to the band that I'm on the road with now. I like that box set more now than when I put it together. I put it more or less together with Ken Callait and Richard [Dashut], and the rest of the band really weren't that involved." Indeed, Stevie Nicks' only involvement appears to have been when she called up asking that Fleetwood drop her "Silver Springs" from the running order, so that she might include it on her own, forthcoming, solo best of.

He refused: Since the *Rumours* out-take first appeared on the b-side of "Go Your Own Way" back in 1977, demand for it to be included on album had grown immeasurably. For it to be omitted from this latest

Fleetwood Mac project would, in Fleetwood's eyes, be tantamount to treason.

Rumors that a second box was imminent, bringing together the best of the band's post-Green/pre-*Fleetwood Mac* period, proved premature; and while the band's blues era has remained well cataloged (in Britain, Castle/Essential brought most of it together in the three CD *The Blues Years* box), the only "official" archive release of note since *The Chain* has been *Live At The BBC*, a two disc collection of Green era radio broadcasts.

Fleetwood continues, "I would have liked to have some more obscure stuff on *The Chain*. I would have liked to have had some Buckingham Nicks stuff in there. I'd have liked to have had some more of the early blues stuff. But I sort of was a little bit restricted and I think, unfortunately so. There was a precedent and a framework that I knew I had to work with, which was a little bit restrictive."

But not, perhaps, as restrictive as the band's own legacy. In July, 1994, Fleetwood and McVie unveiled yet another new Fleetwood Mac line-up, taking the stage at Fleetwood's own, eponymous restaurant in Alexandria, VA, with ex-Zoo vocalist Bekka Bramlett and former Traffic stalwart Dave Mason now in tow. This quartet, augmented by Billy Burnette, and the return of both Christine McVie and producer Richard Dashut, would record and release one album in 1995, but *Time* flopped disastrously.

Although Fleetwood Mac had always been about the moment and the musicians, it seemed that the public could not and would not accept a line-up without Nicks or (although he did make one backing vocal appearance) Buckingham. And as *Time* quickly and quietly faded from view, it seemed, even to its stubborn founder, that Fleetwood Mac was finally over. Fleetwood was finally ready to let it all go.

"At the end, it was starting to be too much hard work. We'd made an album that was a total failure, and I just couldn't see myself starting all over. So we stopped."

And stopping was possibly the best thing that could have happened to Fleetwood and, in turn, the rest of the band. In ending an era and killing the beast, the past struggles ceased to matter, didn't exist anymore.

It was finally a time when letting go of everything quietly set the stage for yet another rebirth.

Oddly enough, it would be Buckingham who would be instrumental in bringing the supergroup back together. Despite the appalling nature of Buckingham's departure from the band, he and Fleetwood had remained in touch. The two had, as friends do, always planned to work on something or other over the years, but had never gotten anything together.

Eventually though, Fleetwood found himself in the studio working on some of Buckingham's solo material for what he figured would "take a couple of weeks. I ended up staying for a year." John McVie came in to lay down some bass parts, and then Christine McVie turned up, just like old times.

Buckingham and Nicks, meanwhile, had collaborated on the title song for the *Twister* soundtrack, and before long, all five were playing together. But unlike the *Mirage* reformation, there was neither emotional, or business baggage to contend with. It was a free and easy period, akin to the magic they had all experienced in 1974, just a bunch of friends sitting around and playing music together.

Nicks reflects, "up until about a year ago, I thought this might happen one day. But then, for some reason, I changed my mind. I didn't think it would be any fun to be in Fleetwood Mac again, and I didn't want all that conflict back in my life."

But even she overcame her reservations, and all it took was walking in the room to see just how much things had changed.

Fleetwood puts it all in perspective.

"Lindsey was very much the focus of how it all got back together. I've gotten real close to Lindsey over the last year, to a place we've never been before. He's saying, 'well, that's what you do.' I'm a player. I have thirty years of playing my instrument, as it were, and that encompasses my lifestyle, my emotions. A great deal of that is in what I do playing-wise, versus someone who's a studied, technical crony. And Lindsey's really reminded me of this.

"I know what I do and it's nice to be reminded of this. Lindsey, as of late, has really given me a lot of major confidences in those sorts of areas. Where it's just nice to be told that 'oh my God, I wouldn't like you not to be there.'"

So it's true then, that time heals all wounds, and all Fleetwood Macs. Coming together again, with the wisdom of twenty years and the friendship and musicianship that never died, had created a stronger bond than ever before. After the joking turned to seriousness, Fleetwood Mac discussed recording one more album, no strings, no management involved. Just them. Just the way it used to be.

And that's how *The Dance* was born. The band worked on some new songs, but wanted to keep things simple and spirited. New songs for the album came from jamming in the studio, and playing what felt right to play. Old songs fell into place in the same relaxed manner. Then they put together a handful of live shows, with invited audiences and the MTV cameras to capture it all, and ran through a set which conveys a love and an energy that had been missing since *Rumours*. And when asked about the first show of the 1997 tour, in Hartford, CT, the joy and enthusiasm in Fleetwood's voice is a testament to the whole experience.

"It went incredibly well! It was somewhat of an historic moment, I should say, in the onward going saga of this band. The audience were incredible. It started off as a small gig . . . basically, it was the first show, and there were some production things we were making sure of, although we were ready. Any beginning of the tour, you're always changing the set list or doing something, tweaking up which is unavoidable no matter how prepared you are.

"From what I gathered the venue wasn't anticipating a large gig. So we'll keep it quiet and do a small show for five or six thousand people. The reality was that they went ballistic. There were so many people! They weren't expecting that. They opened this lawn section out, so instead of 5,000, we had 19,000 people there. It went from a very understated thing to a real major gig. Which was good, because it put us in a whole . . . whatever frame of mind you get, when you go 'oh my god, we'd better be fucking great.'

"We were all a little nervous here and there. But the audience were so great. We got that feeling that you just can't explain, when all those people are standing there and they are just digging you."

But maybe you can explain that feeling. It is the sense of liberation and excitement which comes from knowing that there is no pressure this time out. People are digging Fleetwood Mac as they have been for the last twenty two years, and more, but for the first time in almost as long, Fleetwood Mac are digging Fleetwood Mac as well.

Again, Fleetwood credits Buckingham with catalyzing the reunion. "Lindsey as a person, and as a musician, is always moving on. His sensibilities are all wound up in that, and that's why this crazy bunch of people, when it does convene, and it's all in tune and in sync, really works. We turn around and say, 'why would this work?' and at one stage we're going 'don't even ask . . . just do it.' There have been moments when it has been public knowledge, and our knowledge, that the last thing you want to see is that person. And you think, 'never again.' The Stones have had that. They're at odds. But look at the magic. Those guys get on the stage and boom!"

So do Fleetwood Mac. *The Dance*, the album drawn from the MTV filmings, went straight into the charts at number one; a single of "Silver Springs" has all but made daytime radio its own, and so Mick Fleetwood leaves us with this final thought.

"I'm all present and correct. . . . it's fantastic. We've grown, and we don't want to press buttons and go places unless it's in good humor. Basically everyone in this band has been lovers, you know. It's funny. I've watched Stevie and Lindsey every night, and when John turns around and we all give each other a hug before and after shows, certainly before, it's the real thing. I look over at John, and it's like 'wow'. And he leans over and gives Chris a peck and says, 'I love you' and he means that: "I love you." So that's where we're at. Right now it's a love thing and I hope it stays that way."

MICK FLEETWOOD, 2001

Sean Egan

This interview with Mick Fleetwood has not previously been published in this form. It was conducted at a point when the drummer was filling in time between musical projects: he was promoting the music memorabilia company Fleetwood-Owen.

Rock band manager, club manager, restauranteur, music publishing company owner—just some of the jobs known to speckle the CV of . . . er, Mick Fleetwood.

That's right. The man familiar to the public as the drummer and founder member of Fleetwood Mac has in fact a lesser-known hinterland as a businessman. He brings up those previous jobs for the benefit of people who might be surprised by his latest venture: Fleetwood-Owen, an entertainment memorabilia auction business run in conjunction with business partner Ted Owen.

"It's my nature," shrugs Fleetwood. "Business ventures are a very normal part of my life. I personally managed Fleetwood Mac for many, many years, so this whole concept of 'How could you suddenly be doing this?' is not a correct concept. I've been doing business, all of which for the most part I have really enjoyed. I do a lot of things. My input on this is not a slap-my-name-on-it-and-disappear type of [thing]."

Fleetwood Mac as a studio outfit has effectively been on hiatus since 1995's ill-received *Time*, so perhaps it's only reasonable that Fleetwood should seek to fill in the interregnum prior to the upcoming reunion with his Fleetwood Mac colleagues.

Fleetwood apparently effortlessly taking center stage dates back to 1967 when Peter Green—a hot young guitarist forming his own band—decided to name his new ensemble after Fleetwood and bassist John "Mac" McVie. "It came about when all three of us were in John Mayall's Bluesbreakers," explains Fleetwood. "John Mayall gave Peter Green a birthday present, and that was some studio time at Decca Records up in Hampstead. Peter played an instrumental. Me and John were playing on it as we were part of that session, and [producer] Gus Dudgeon said, 'What's this one called?' Peter said, 'Well, 'Fleetwood Mac.''

"We had no idea we were forming a band and, when that happened a few months after that session, Peter called the band Fleetwood Mac. Me and Pete started the band and then John joined after the fact. We always knew that we could get him in the band. We wanted John to play bass and he knew it. He was a security-minded type of guy, so he waited for us to show him that it was a real gig and, when it was, he jumped boat."

Peter Green's Fleetwood Mac—as they were originally billed—were in many senses a throwback: several years after people like the Rolling Stones and the Animals had moved on from rhythm and blues, Mac was absolute in its blues purism. Did it not worry them that in the ferociously fashion-conscious sixties the band would be perceived as a bit dated? "We weren't that type of a band," Fleetwood responds. "We weren't looking to do anything other than play the music we loved. That wasn't even a thought. The reality is, that had no credence at all because we became very popular playing fundamentally straight-on blues music.

"We were a blues band more than anything—Elmore James and early B. B. King–type shuffles. In fact, it was fairly extraordinary to see the first Fleetwood Mac album—the greater portion of that album was Elmore James songs—up there with the Marmalade and bands like that. It's hilarious. We were doing what we wanted to do and luckily having it be very successful."

Said eponymous first album was the biggest-selling LP of 1968. Did that surprise him? "Are you kidding? I couldn't believe it. Especially because we didn't pay any heed to commercialism at all. We didn't even know what that was. Which is very much like early Rolling Stones: it translated into a whole underground thing that became very un-underground, so it was a weird transition. One that, I might add, some of our fans had a hard time with 'cause they felt that they owned us, 'cause no one knew about us. When they see you on *Top of the Pops*, they're going, like, 'You've sold out!' But it was the same music that they came to listen to in the pubs, so it didn't make much sense."

The band made the jump from emulating their heroes to playing with them around this point when they recorded *Fleetwood Mac in Chicago* vols. 1 and 2 with blues luminaries like Willie Dixon and Otis Span. "It was fantastic," Fleetwood recalls. "Great sessions and, happily, all those recordings are still available. It does hold up. We were totally blown away and the nice thing was that, I have to say without blowing the horn too loud, we were a darn good band. I don't quite know where it all came from, because the reality was that we were playing black man's music really well.

"So much so that when we went to Chicago, Peter Green especially was totally taken under the wing of Willie Dixon. [The rest of the band] had their minds blown because to them it was the real thing. They were going, 'How did it happen?' Well it happened by a bunch of English lads having a dream about playing those guys' music. There's no doubt that it was a real blessed bunch of musicians. But there was also a real energy, especially from our lead people, who at that point were Peter Green and Jeremy Spencer. They were truly phenomenal exponents at reproducing, very genuinely, the blues."

While the group's hit singles were informed by the soul and grit of blues, they were of a more commercial bent. Among them numbered the slinky "Black Magic Woman." Not only was it a 1968 UK top forty but three years later it lucratively entered the US top five courtesy of a version by Santana. "Pete was stoked," says Fleetwood, who adjudges Santana's version "good." "We knew that it was gonna happen. Carlos is a major, major, major fan of Peter Green. When he came to England, he purposefully sought out Fleetwood Mac and thus Peter Green. It was after that that he cut that track. It's done very well for Pete."

Perhaps not quite as well as "Albatross," a tranquil instrumental that was a UK number one for Fleetwood Mac in '68, then a number two fully five years later, and has remained the first choice of TV documentary makers who require background music for pictures of birds in flight. Although its commercial potential is now indisputable, a gentle track with no vocals must then have been the last thing considered to be hit-single material. "It's somewhat groundbreaking," says Fleetwood. "'Albatross' is probably the only instrumental that really meant a shit from the gap from the Shadows until 'Albatross' hit the charts. Again, it was slightly strange for a lot of people who followed Fleetwood Mac, but that was the natural progression the band and the writing took and we put it out as a single. We had no idea that it was gonna be a number one single and almost an anthem."

Even musical gods were impressed. The Beatles' 1969 album *Abbey Road* contained a track called "Sun King" whose dreamy arpeggios seemed to take inspiration from "Albatross," something Fleetwood thinks a "major compliment." He recalls, "We were in between coming from somewhere and the whole band was in the van and we actually heard John Lennon very graciously admit to that on the BBC. They were going track by track and he said, 'Oh yeah, this is where we do our Fleetwood Mac thing.'"

Even better than "Albatross" for many veteran Mac fans is the following year's "Oh Well," a single with an unforgettable snaking riff and a lyric of merciless self-examination ("I can't sing, I ain't pretty and my legs are thin") that sat oddly with the sort of breast-beating fare to which the charts usually played host. Fleetwood declines to state whether he thinks it's the original Fleetwood Mac's finest moment, asserting that it's up to others to judge stuff like that, although he does go so far as to say, "I certainly think 'Oh Well' would be up there in the top three of Peter's songs." He also offers, "That set a template for a lot of people. The way that that song was constructed influenced a lot of people in bands. The use of melodic riffs and the acoustic[-electric] blend became quite apropos in certainly lots of things Led Zeppelin did."

Tragically, by the following year Peter Green's mental state was such that he was lost forever to the band he formed, and even, in any meaningful sense, to music per se. Fleetwood says he didn't notice many warnings but adds, "Looking back, you can see the danger signs. If you just listen to the words of 'Green Manalishi,' you would feel devastated if you knew that he basically was crying out. The line 'I wish I'd never been born' is slightly devastating, but the reality was we truly didn't know that Pete was in the beginnings of having a lot of trouble with himself." However, he adds a comment that challenges the consensus about the reasons for Green's departure from the ranks. "Peter left Fleetwood Mac not because he had emotional problems. They were part of it, but musically he would have left anyhow. He wanted out. He wanted to play different, weird music and thought that we couldn't do it."

Kiln House (1970), the first Mac album released after Green's departure, was a respectable effort, but Fleetwood admits that the magic wasn't quite there without his old mate. "At the time we were very nervous, not having Pete in the band," he says. "It was the best we could do." Guitarist Jeremy Spencer assumed Green's front man position with mixed success. "When Jeremy was put in that position, the reflection musically was more retro: the Buddy Holly–, Fabian-type songs that were on that album. I think it's a really charming album, but we were quietly aware we had a challenge ahead of us without Peter."

It was a challenge they initially tried to meet via lateral means. John McVie's wife Christine came aboard as vocalist and keyboardist. Fleetwood: "We were about to go on a tour in the United States. She'd heard us rehearse. We all lived in this house together. We were starting to go, 'Hmm, the band sounds a bit empty.' Literally a few days before we left, we said, 'Chris, you gotta join the band. We need that extra voice and we want the piano.'"

Guitarist Bob Welch joined around the same time. The sequence of five albums on which he appeared constitutes the least remarked-on stage of Fleetwood Mac's career, but Fleetwood insists, "Bob Welch was a major part of Fleetwood Mac. Not really well known here, but in the States we did really well with Bob pretty much in the lead position. This was not something that just was a flash in the pan. This was a major part of Fleetwood Mac's history that had all the respect and credibility that it should have. We weren't huge, but as an underground band we were really well respected."

Fleetood Mac's Welch period was, of course, largely washed from history because of the spectacular success of the lineup that came into being when he left at the end of 1974 and was replaced by a pair of unknowns named Lindsey Buckingham and Stevie Nicks.

For Fleetwood, their recruitment created a magical combination of musicians. "It was the second one. The first one was when the band was formed with Peter. Certainly not to degrade anything in between. When Steve and Lindsey joined, it reminded me of the power and chemistry we had when we first started. Not musically, but just the feeling with the people and knowing something was looking really strong and good."

This lineup's second album, *Rumours* (1977), was a triumph for a reason a lot more profound than this now American-market-oriented group successfully insisting on the British spelling of the title word. *Rumours* became one of the biggest-selling albums of all time. The ultimate vindication in the face of criticisms of Fleetwood's decision to continue with the Fleetwood Mac name throughout the personnel changes? "It's never been an issue," he says with apparent surprise. "I've never heard that once in my life."

Following up a phenomenon like *Rumours* is always difficult. Fleetwood Mac's next album was *Tusk* (1979), a double set that veered between their now familiar MOR and something approaching punk. The public did not take to it like they had its predecessor. "That's probably my favorite Fleetwood Mac album of all time," Fleetwood reveals. "I think musically that album has influenced anyone from the Corrs to Aerosmith to a whole load of people. We were pushing some rather strange envelopes. When you get a magical formula that works, it's very tempting just to repeat it. And we didn't. Lindsey was a big influence to really push and do something different and take the risk of it not being a huge success."

Lindsey Buckingham was still on board for 1982's *Mirage* (like *Rumours*, but not as good) and 1987's *Tango in the Night* (unlike *Rumours*, and arguably even better), but bailed not long after the latter album's release. Was this a shock? "No, he was unhappy. He'd had enough. He'd done fourteen years in Fleetwood Mac and he wanted to move on and do different things and we had grown apart as people. He had a vision for his own creative journey and, much like Peter Green, didn't see it as part of Fleetwood Mac."

When, three years later, Stevie Nicks followed Buckingham through the exit door, an undaunted Fleetwood, together with his perennial partner John McVie, put together a new lineup of Fleetwood Mac and released the album *Time* (1995). For the first time, though, replacing the departed personnel didn't sustain the success. "It didn't work," admits Fleetwood. "Quite simply, it was a really good band but the one major misjudgment in terms of carrying on. At that point, we didn't have either Christine or Stevie on the road. Christine made the album but she elected not to go out on the road, which made it very awkward. The reality is, it was too much to expect our audience to accept a new lead female singer." Moreover, "The album was not in retrospect as strong as it should be."

The classic Fleetwood Mac *Rumours* lineup got together a few years back for the live album *The Dance*. The $64,000 question is, are they planning any more projects? "We're going back in," Fleetwood confirms. "Stevie's doing a solo project this summer and me and Lindsey are going to go out and do some road work with a solo project of his that I worked on with him. Hopefully by September, Fleetwood Mac will be in the studio."

Meantime, Fleetwood is keeping himself occupied by dealing in autographs, musical instruments, clothing, and other paraphernalia that has been within touching distance of celebrities. Allegedly. He doesn't deny there are a lot of forgeries in rock memorabilia, but says, "The reality is, one takes a lot of care. I don't think it necessarily is as bad as I'm feeling you're thinking it is. You have to be real careful, but Ted has a vast experience and, where he doesn't feel he covers bases, he has experts in many fields, such as autographs. That's all part of this line of business and we pay a lot of attention to it."

Fleetwood-Owen secured an early coup by selling John Lennon's famous white "Imagine" piano. The buyer was George Michael, at a price of $1 million. "It's an instrument that came out of John's apartment at the Dakota building," explains Fleetwood. "The whole length and breadth of the story behind the piano was very much personalized for me when I was sitting talking with the family member, Mr. Steinway, and he said, 'Let me go upstairs to my office.' He comes down with the receipt, with the whole thing, with an appointment that Mr. Lennon was coming in to buy the piano. John personally went in and chose that piano—which is all really cool. When you're selling and representing a piece of merchandise such as that piano, those are the type of things that we like to seek out. The more personalized a piece of product is, the better."

Yet this line of work might not necessarily go down well with the sort of people with whom Fleetwood has been rubbing shoulders since he was a young man. For instance, witness recent newspaper articles about Paul McCartney taking legal action to retrieve examples of his handwritten lyrics that have found their way onto the market. Fleetwood offers, "All I can say is, for instance, Paul is a major, major fan and collector of Buddy Holly. Well, I think he's just having a problem that people look up to him in the same way that he does to Buddy Holly. He adores his work, he respects his work, he bought his whole publishing rights to his songs, etcetera. I'll be so bold as to say that if I walked in with Buddy Holly's guitar, he'd buy it."

And what happens the day someone approaches Fleetwood-Owen with, say, a memo written by Fleetwood to Lindsey Buckingham? "I've already gone through that experience so much," he reasons. "You gotta let that stuff go. It's almost like the Grateful Dead theory: everyone's welcome; bring your tape machine; bootleg the show. We signed so many things over the years. You sign things that quite frankly people are gonna go out and sell. I really don't mind. The only rule I have is when I see the same guy with the same stuff, I say, 'You know what? I signed about twenty of those the other day and I think that's enough.'"

He does add, "If I had a personal diary that meant a hell of a lot to me and suddenly it appeared, I would go, 'That is mine and I'd really like it back.' I would probably then find out that the person who had it bought it in good faith, and then I'd have to keep my mouth shut and say, 'Flog it back to me,' or something."

NICKS OF TIME

Brian Smith | November 29, 2001 | *Phoenix New Times* (US)

This pause-provoking interview, granted to a newspaper in her hometown, finds Stevie Nicks discussing comebacks for both her solo career and Fleetwood Mac, yet simultaneously lamenting the fact that she and her colleagues now feel in some ways out of place in an industry they once dominated.

When Stevie Nicks returned to her Phoenix home at the tail end of 1994, just a year after quitting what was once the biggest band in rock 'n' roll, she figured that her career was all but over.

There was lots of wreckage in her wake. Earlier that same year, she had released her fourth solo album, the dodgy, drug-addled *Street Angel*, a flop of a disc that didn't go anywhere near platinum. The then-46-year-old rock star had spent the previous six months in an L.A. rehab clinic kicking a gnarly Klonopin habit (a drug prescribed to supplant a heady coke addiction).

Nicks spent months lodged in her desert house doing little else but nursing a depression that was larger than most of the arenas she had played over the years. Here was a woman responsible for some of the most enduring and celebrated pop ever recorded: a woman who had sold more than 50 million records.

Nicks contemplated calling it quits. She had guessed that nobody cared about her anymore. She figured herself too old to be relevant in an industry that was, after all, becoming increasingly dependent on the dreaded youth buck.

"I fired people and wasn't really nice to people and just lived in my 'oh, whatever' world," she says when asked about the years leading up to 1994. She's on the telephone in her rented Santa Monica home. "So when I went back to Phoenix, I was really freaked out. I thought, you know, I can't do it again." She pauses. Then she adds, with a hearty laugh, "I can't make that many apologies across the world again."

The easy, fish-in-the-barrel reference to insert here would be to Norma Desmond, the forgotten movie star in *Sunset Boulevard*. However, that would be far too easy, and lazy. Nicks wasn't about to be put to pasture, not against her will, anyway.

Enter ex-Gin Blossoms guitarist Jesse Valenzuela and, later, Tom Petty, the two people Nicks credits for helping lift her out of the depths of career despair. They got her off her ass.

Valenzuela and Nicks began recording songs at Vintage Recorders in Phoenix, one of which (an acoustic cover of Ricky Nelson's "It's Late") wound up on Nicks' 1998 boxed set, *Enchanted*.

"When I first started doing songs for *Trouble in Shangri-la*, I met Jesse through a local studio owner, and Jesse was so cool," Nicks explains. "I was coming out of rehab, and I was sad and I was trying to figure how to get my voice back and if that was even possible. That's where Jesse came in. He really was a strong force in talking me out of that. Jesse had just said, 'Don't be stupid. This is good. Let's get your singing chops back and get the excitement back.'

"Jesse really was an important factor in that. He was so wonderful to me, and supportive of me, that it was amazing. It really helped me to get back into the flow. I think Jesse is awesome. Later, I got a lecture from Tom Petty at the Ritz-Carlton, and I was able to say, 'You know, I can really do this again. . . .' I can, because what in the hell else am I going to do?"

Turns out Nicks was a big Gin Blossoms fan and thought it stupid that the Tempe-based band called it quits. She even goes so far as to suggest that, had the Blossoms not broken up, they might have attained a success on a par with Fleetwood Mac. If anybody could write the book on sustaining and overcoming inner-band fucked-upedness, it is Nicks. Fleetwood Mac taught us this.

"I was very sad that the Gin Blossoms broke up because I felt that they really had a shot at being a big band," Nicks says. "That decision that Robin [Wilson]—is that his name?—made was really a bad one. Because they could have all gone off and done solo things and not broken up that band. Because the Gin Blossoms could've been one of those bands, you know, a Fleetwood Mac type of band, a band that hung around for a long, long time and sold a lot of records. It was a unique sound, very different and very much unto themselves."

When Nicks speaks, the words shoot out quickly and offer little in the way of melodic variation. A wordy monotone implies a certain serious-ness and masks self-deprecation. There is, however, a self-deprecating side to her. She pokes fun at herself surprisingly often ("I know four chords on the guitar and I don't play piano very well. . . . I throw in a bass note wherever I can figure it out.").

Since completing a North American tour that started in mid-summer, Nicks has been off the road for a week. She says she spends all her non-working time at her Phoenix home. Her voice is gruff, hoarse from spending long hours the night before doing vocals for a new Fleetwood Mac album.

"I'm so exhausted and I didn't get home until way late last night," she says, laughing. "When I woke up today, I went, 'Whoa, now I remem-ber what recording is like.' It's over and over and over, you forget how tedious it is."

When talking Stevie Nicks 2001, all *Sunset Boulevard* bets are off. Of late, Nicks is a woman saddled with a few decidedly simple and un-rock-starry habits. The blow and pills are long gone. In their place, she's developed a soap opera habit and has taken to jogging.

Nicks' new album—four years after the surprisingly triumphant Fleet-wood Mac reunion tour—*Trouble in Shangri-la*, is actually good. Really good. *Shangri-la* finds Nicks sounding almost animated, energized, with very few lapses into self-parody. She's not the diamond-studded-coke-spoon-wielding mystical chanteuse of yore, nor is she the aging star sitting atop a pedestal of vain self-fulfillment. At worst, the songs that are cringingly navel-gazy and touchy-feely still resonate as if shot up straight from the gut.

Much of *Shangri-la* was written by Nicks and produced by pal/fan Sheryl Crow (who brought along her sideman/writer, the brilliant ex-Wire Train guitarist Jeffrey Trott). What's weird is that Nicks' patented hiccupy croon sounds ageless. The record sounds youthful.

Nicks says the Peter Pan thing reveals itself in her writing. "I really write the same way now as I did when I was 16. My songs pretty much come from poems that pretty much come from what's happening to me in my life. So that allows me to write, I think, with a more kind of youthful feeling. Because, at 53 years old, I'm not much different from the person I was when I was 20, when I was wondering about that world of romantic possibility."

This from a rock star whose career saw a grand exit on the heels of sour record sales figures and coke-binge rumors, only to return after a sobering hiatus to find revisionist historians lauding her as a grand pop matriarch.

She's learned that in this life, timing is everything. Moreover, it is now cool to dig Stevie. Courtney Love, of all people, sings her praises. As does Macy Gray. Destiny's Child samples her and invites her to be in a video. Even Patti Smith has come clean. Sheryl Crow hails Nicks to the heavens. Nicks sounds genuinely confounded by so much slobbering reverence from those she influenced. "I didn't expect it at all," she says.

In the 1970s, songwriters did what they did and could become famous simply because other people dug it. It was a time when you could sell tons of records, become a huge pop star, all on your own terms. Hence, Fleetwood Mac. When all that started to change late in the decade (again, in part, because of Fleetwood Mac), when the process became fodder for corporate schemes, the artist took a seat at the back of the bus. The record biz became little more than a glorified drive-through.

Nicks agrees that pop music in the '70s, and that which she grew up on, was at the very least allowed to breathe. The songs weren't squeezed of their soul simply to fit formats. But she won't take blame for the latter.

These days, a pop star has one, maybe two hits and she's out. All this after having to nearly disrobe for the privilege. For Nicks, this new pretty-in-pink, here-today-gone-today nature of the record industry took a bit of getting used to.

"The companies are very different now," she says, with an audible shrug. "For Fleetwood Mac, in the beginning, for the first, say, 10 years between '75 and '85, we had such a close relationship with Warner Bros. We would go over to the label and we knew everybody by name. There seemed to be a true artistic relationship between the industry and the artists. That's very hard to find now. You know what's in those Top 10 spaces and it's a lot about rap and it's a lot about Britney Spears and it's a lot about that total teen thing."

In theory, an audience could grow old with an artist. It's an idea that seems wholly antiquated now. Picture Britney and her fans at Nicks' age. Grace is hard to imagine.

"The only bummer about that whole thing is what about all the people that are my age," Nicks continues, laughing. "All the people that were Fleetwood Mac fans in 1980, what happened to all of them? So I kind of said, especially with *Shangri-la*, all these songs could fit into a 17-year-old's life. Because it's all about angst and searching and life."

Nicks echoes Peter Pan pathos. She simply refuses to buy into the dead-at-30-buried-at-60 pop mythos. "You have to be philosophical in this day and age. Because if you are not, you will just get depressed and stop playing music and become an old person. This is even true for young people. Even young people who just stop listening to music and become old. People my age are searching for that song that comes on that just knocks them out like when we were 25. I know I am. I am always waiting for that song by somebody else that just kills me. But, again, I don't let what is going on affect me too much. Because I know when it all comes down to push and shove that the really good song is gonna win. Doesn't matter if I'm singing it or Britney is singing it or Backstreet Boys are singing it or 'N SYNC is singing it. It doesn't matter who is singing it."

Nicks levels her career perseverance on the fact she's eschewed the wife-and-kids routine. Career and longevity are two ostensibly mutually exclusive terms when Rock Star is your job description. If only to sustain the idea that there is a possibility of being adored at an advancing age, the hit tunes have got to keep coming. Nicks claims no worries when it comes to dwindling sales success, even after *Shangri-la* stalled in the lower reaches of the *Billboard* charts: "As soon as somebody says to you, 'Okay, write a Top 10 single,' you run screaming from the room. What is a hit single? Really, what is that? As soon as you start thinking about music in those terms, you're messed up. It will taint everything that you do."

Nicks, in fact, considers herself no different from "all those little 16-year-old girls who are searching for the love of their lives. We are all searching. So that's how I write my music. Really, my songs aren't so very different than the very first song I wrote when I was 16. I think that when you get married and have children and divorce your husband and have to pay child support and blah, blah, blah, you don't write the same anymore. That's how I feel with this record."

What did former beau and bandmate Lindsey Buckingham think of *Trouble in Shangri-la*?

"He thinks that it is a very good record. Lindsey does not ever and has never thrown out compliments to me about anything outside of Fleetwood Mac. And on this record he said, 'I think that is the best thing that you have ever done.' That meant a lot."

"I was in Aspen a week ago for three days," she continues. "I wrote 'Landslide' there in, like, 1974. So I was walking around the streets of Aspen going, 'You know what? Aspen has served you well for "Land-slide," and that song has served me well my whole life. So I thought I'd better write another song, so I wrote about what happened in New York. I just gave it to Lindsey last night—just the raw cassette and a set of words—and I'll see when I return in two weeks what he has done with this song."

THE RUMOUR MILL

James Halbert | June 2003 | *Classic Rock* (UK)

In 2003 finally came the proper reunification of Fleetwood Mac that had been in the offing since *The Dance*. Only *Say You Will* wasn't quite the long-awaited new studio album by that classic *Rumours*-era lineup: in the interim, the group had once again lost Christine McVie. Moreover, as this feature makes clear, tension between Buckingham and Nicks was perennial. Their bickering about song inclusion hardly seems logical in light of the increased running times enabled by a CD age that was now a decade-and-a-half old: *Say You Will*'s seventy-six minutes actually makes it longer than *Tusk*.

IT'S ANOTHER sunny California morning, and there's a genuine sense of occasion in the warm, dry air. It's some weeks now since Fleetwood Mac invited *Classic Rock* to visit them at Culver City Studios in Los Angeles, and now we're pulling up to the main security gate. The colonial mansion that forms the exterior facade of the studio building was featured in the 30s classic movie *Gone With The Wind*, and it was also here, in 1933, that RKO Radio Pictures filmed *King Kong*. With its grandeur and its A-list showbiz credentials, Culver City Studios is an auspicious setting—and one wholly in keeping with the legend that is Fleetwood Mac.

The band are here to rehearse for an upcoming US tour in support of their new album 'Say You Will' (reviewed in issue 52). The record is their first studio work since 1987's 'Tango In The Night' to feature guitarist Lindsey Buckingham; thus it's the Mac's first studio record since 1987 that really matters. But what God has given with one hand, he seems to have taken away with the other, for keyboardist and valued songwriter Christine McVie is now no longer in the band.

Bassist John McVie has decided he doesn't want to take part in today's interviews with *Classic Rock* and other sections of the international media, but genial drummer and Mac founder member and linchpin Mick Fleetwood is game for a chat, as are the American contingent of Stevie Nicks and Lindsey Buckingham. We've been told by the band's record company WEA that the latter two won't be doing their interviews together, but that we shouldn't read anything into that. Being journalists, however, we read plenty into it—mainly that rock's greatest soap opera seems to still have plenty of episodes left.

That soap was undoubtedly at its most lathery around the time of the band's 1977 album 'Rumours'. But the events surrounding that record's recording have been well-documented elsewhere, so let's nail that essential piece of back-story quickly and succinctly.

Here we go: 'Rumours' was a certified AOR masterpiece. It sold zillions and topped charts around the world for months at a time. Fuelled by a veritable snowdrift of cocaine, the making of it saw Stevie Nicks break up with Lindsey Buckingham, Christine McVie part from her bass-playing husband John, and Mick Fleetwood begin divorce proceedings with his then wife Jenny Boyd.

Songs like 'Go Your Own Way', 'Dreams' and 'Second Hand News' channelled the heartache directly. And then things got more incestuous still: Christine McVie started dating the band's lighting director, Curry Grant (sic); Nicks and Fleetwood had a brief fling of their own. That, in a nutshell, was the script.

"You couldn't make that story up," Fleetwood said years later in 1997. "You'd say: 'How could they possibly continue to play music together?'"

But continue they did. And as 'Say You Will' testifies, four of the five people who created 'Rumours' all those years ago are still creating great music together today as Fleetwood Mac.

I hear Stevie Nicks's distinctive drawl before I see her; she's recording 'drops' for Australian radio and I'm listening outside the door: "Hi! I'm Stevie Nicks of Fleetwood Mac, and this is our new single 'Peacekeeper'," she chirps with practised precision. I'm thinking: 'That voice belongs to a woman who is best mates with Tom Petty; to the gal who is now due another huge royalty cheque thanks to The Dixie Chicks' recent cover of her wonderful 1975 ballad 'Landslide'. She's also the woman, I'm thinking, who once did so much cocaine damage to her nose septum that she allegedly resorted to imbibing it up her a . . .

" . . . Okay, you can go in now," a PR person barks, interrupting my train of thought.

When Stevie and I meet, I'm pleased to note that her big hair is still intact and blonde. She's wearing a sweatshirt, not leather or lace, however, and her Yorkshire terrier Sulamith (named after Sulamith Wulfing, the German painter of fairies and elves) is perched on her lap. "I'm gonna put you on the floor, honey," she says to the pooch, doing so. But Sulamith jumps up again and continues to eye me suspiciously.

She tells me that she misses Christine McVie and her "crazy English humour" every day. "It used to be like that show *Charmed,* where they go: 'The power of three!', she laughs. "Chris and I had the power of two. But now some of that feminine energy has gone."

The good news, Nicks maintains, is that Lindsey, Mick and John have become a power trio again—although not one that has lost sight of what made the Fleetwood Mac of the 70s and 80s such a chart-storming colossus. "When I started working with the guys again last February," she recalls, "I thought the new album was going to sound way different than 'Rumours' or 'Tango In The Night'. But in fact I don't think it does."

Given that Nicks's last solo album, 'Trouble In Shangri La', did very nicely indeed, I put it to her that she might have had less reason than her bandmates to put her picture in the frame of the reconvened Mac.

"I could have toured my album for another year," she agrees, "but I love this band, and I felt it was important that we do one more record. Also, the ' . . . Shangri La' tour became very difficult for me to deal with around 9/11. I was in New York at the time, and my Rochester show was cancelled due to an act of war. At one point we had a military escort on our wing, which was scary but riveting. That whole period nearly drove me into a mental home."

Before beginning that tour, in July 2001, Nicks had left demos of five new-ish songs with Buckingham, Fleetwood and John McVie. But the origins of the 'Say You Will' album stretch back much further than that. You may recall that the Buckingham songs on 'Tango In The Night' were originally earmarked for a solo album. Intriguingly, the same is true of his songs on 'Say You Will'. Indeed, some of them were written more than six years ago, and thus predate Mac's 1997's MTV-led live album 'The Dance'.

UNSHAVEN, SOCK-LESS AND WEARING A BEATEN-UP leather jacket, Lindsey Buckingham still does the 'just out of bed' look rather handsomely. He's relaxed and attentive when we talk, and has a gentleness about him that is difficult to equate with the man who once slapped Stevie Nicks then bent her backwards over the bonnet of his car, before being restrained by two of the band's managers (see Mick Fleetwood and Stephen Davis's *Fleetwood: My Life And Adventures With Fleetwood Mac*).

Listening to 'Say You Will' tracks like 'Murrow Turning Over In His Grave' and 'Come', it's clear that Buckingham's voice and guitar playing have lost none of the feral passion that so was evident on the version of 'Big Love' on 'The Dance'. How has he retained that edge?

"Let's go back a bit to try and answer that," he says. "'Tusk', from my point of view, was an attempt to derail the machine that kicked in after 'Rumours'. 'Tusk' was an artistic success, but because it didn't sell 25 million the band and the record company were like: 'Oh, well we're not going to do that again.' Cut to the difficulties that we had making 'Tango In The Night' [for example, Nicks was undergoing treatment at the Betty Ford Clinic for her cocaine addiction, and attended few of the 'Tango . . . ' sessions], and there was no atmosphere whatsoever that was conducive to growth. I had to say: 'Sorry, I love you guys, but this isn't working for me.' Whatever edge and realness I have today is because I took myself off that treadmill and tried to keep in mind what was important."

Distanced by what he describes as the drummer's "drug madness" ("He didn't want me turning up at his house coked out of my head," Fleetwood tells me later), Buckingham didn't see Fleetwood for some eight years after leaving the Mac in 1987. But then they ran into each other again in 1995. Buckingham picks up the story: "Mick was evidently a changed man, and we had plenty to talk about. I was just about to go into the studio with [producer] Rob Cavallo, and I said: 'Why don't you come down, Mick? Let's cut some tracks.' So we started, and it was going great. And eventually we got John [McVie] down to play some bass.

"What happened next, though, was that somebody over at Warner Brothers—and maybe this was the agenda all along—said: 'Do you want to do a live Fleetwood Mac album?' I was like: 'No, but okay' [laughs]. It was great to get together again for 'The Dance', but from my point of view it wasn't that important. It was just a restatement of a body of work, and I'm much happier working on new stuff."

Unsurprising, then, that when 'The Dance' was finished Buckingham quickly resumed work on his solo album. But when he delivered it, Warners were nonplussed. Or at least that was what they said: "Russ Thyret, for whatever reason, said he just couldn't hear it," Buckingham says. "But I knew AOL were about to buy Time Warner, so rather than put the album out with a lame duck regime I decided to wait for the new one."

By the time the new regime did come into Warners, however, Buckingham, Fleetwood and co. had decided to use the guitarist's stockpile of songs on a new Fleetwood Mac album. And that, we can safely assume, made AOL Time Warner's accountants very happy indeed.

At this point, 'Say You Will' didn't have a title and was scheduled to be a double album. Christine McVie's absence meant that all the songs were either Buckingham or Nicks compositions, and his songs far outnumbered hers. However, a look at a finished copy of 'Say You Will' shows that the former sweethearts ended up with exactly nine songs apiece on it. But whether or not that was down to the bargaining power of Nicks's manager (the man Buckingham calls "big, bad Howard Kaufman") isn't that easy to determine.

Nicks: "What happened was that when I went home to Phoenix for Christmas I realised that I needed to say how I was feeling now; how I was feeling after that horrendous tour of mine. The way things stood, none of the songs on the new album were actually brand new, and as a writer that is not acceptable to me. So I went back to my journals and I wrote 'Destiny Rules', then 'Silver Girl', then 'Illume', then 'Say You Will'."

Buckingham: "Howard has his formulas, and he's very much in control of certain aspects of the business side. He's not really concerned with anything creative, he's concerned with getting this project up and running and making Stevie the money that he feels he wants to make her. There's a strength to that, but there's also a weakness to it. That approach was less of a problem with something like 'The Dance', but with an album like this, which I feel transcends all of that . . . well let's just say I sense there's something large looming up ahead. Whether that turns out to be the case, I don't know."

EVEN AT 55 YEARS OF AGE, MICK FLEETWOOD CAN'T HELP but make an entrance. Given that he's six-foot-six it's mostly a height thing, but he's also dressed impeccably and doused in a potent, expensive-smelling cologne. Around a year ago, his wife Lynn bore him twin daughters, Ruby and Tessa. "We're thrilled and it's a total trip," he says. "I also have two grown-up daughters, Amy and Lucy, so that makes four girls. This time around I'm much more aware of what's happening, though."

Fleetwood describes his band as "the most abused franchise in rock". But no one has worked harder than he has to stave off the demise of that franchise. The Buckingham song 'Peacekeeper' isn't about Fleetwood, but it might as well be. Indeed, you could reasonably argue that neither 'The Dance' nor 'Say You Will' could have happened had Fleetwood not put so much effort into repairing his friendship with Buckingham.

"Lindsey knows that I understand elements about him that others don't," he says simply. "And I really do. With a passion." But Fleetwood also understands and adores Stevie Nicks. And you sense that as he moves between she and Buckingham's worlds, his diplomacy skills are frequently called upon.

It was also Fleetwood, it seems, who put the most effort into trying to lure Christine McVie back for The Full Mac Monty: "I hear from Chris quite a lot," he says. "She would ring up and say: 'How are you doing? How's the album going?' For a while it was maybe she will, maybe she won't. She could still have come on board in the early stages of the recording, but as time went on that became more impractical. Eventually I said to Lindsey: 'My read on this—and I know Chris very well—is that this isn't going to happen.'

"After that, Lindsey really took the reins in lieu of the fact that Chris wasn't there as musical partner, and with John's and my support he got a very clear picture of where he wanted to take things. Chris is still there on one of the older tracks, though—she's singing and playing organ on 'Bleed To Love Her.'"

Sheryl Crow, meanwhile, sings back-up and plays keyboards on the title track of 'Say You Will'. Elsewhere on the album Nicks's 'Silver Girl' is about Crow, and seems to repay the compliment that Sheryl paid Stevie when the former wrote 'It's Only Love' for her around the time of 'Trouble In Shangri La.'

Asked if Crow might play live with the Mac, Fleetwood quashes any rumours about her replacing Christine McVie, yet leaves the door open slightly: "If you're asking me if she'd be welcome to come up on stage and sing a few songs with us, the answer is yes, of course. But we have nothing official planned."

In the words of Lenny Kravitz: it ain't over till it's over. And in the words of Jeff Buckley: *'It's* never *over/A kingdom for a kiss upon her shoulder'*. The point I'm trying to make is this: even though it's many, many years since any members of Fleetwood Mac were romantically involved with each other, the love triangle that once involved Buckingham, Nicks and Fleetwood still seems to exert an influence on the band's dynamic. In fact how could it not?

Certainly it's there in the new album's lyrics. Or at least it seems to be; and you suspect that we're supposed to think it is. Can it really be mere coincidence that Buckingham's 'Say Goodbye' (*'I let you slip away/There was nothing I could do/That was so long ago/Still I often think of you'*) closes the album in conjunction with Nicks's 'Goodbye Baby'? (*'Goodbye baby I hope your heart's not broken/Don't forget me/Yes, I was outspoken'*)? Extremely doubtful. Time to ask some more searching questions.

"'Thrown Down' is about Lindsey," Nicks says candidly. "But I wrote that around the time of 'The Dance' tour. Suffice to say that there are new songs about him, too. It's terrific that [he] continues to be a well of inspiration."

It would be easy to infer that her friendship with Lindsey is stronger than it's been for a while. As for whether she herself would say that:

"Um . . . Lindsey and I's relationship is sort of the same. We work together and write together. He quit in 1983 and was gone. Then he came back in 1987 for about half a year and we made 'Tango In The Night', which none of us were very much a part of [tell that to Buckingham or Christine McVie!]. He quit again right after that, and then I didn't see him until we played at President Clinton's inauguration, which was like two days.

"Then we did a song together for the movie *Twister* in 1996, and then I didn't see him until we went into rehearsal for 'The Dance' in 1997. We've been apart for gazillions of years now. And as I tell him: 'You have to understand that when I come in with a pretty-much finished demo, that's because you haven't been in my life. I had to go and learn how to make music without you.' And I did. And I learned it very well; I don't always need Lindsey to make my music come true."

Lindsey Buckingham is now 53 years of age. Although he once thought he'd never have children, he and his wife Kristen now have a four-year-old son, Will, and a two-year-old daughter, Lee Lee. Asked whether he thinks people still tend to assume that he and Nicks's lyrics are about each other, he responds thus: "I'm sure they do. And in Stevie's case at least some of them may be about me. Why do I say 'may'? Because it's not for me to say if they're about me. I suspect some of them are. Then again," he laughs, "there are songs that Stevie has written all throughout our relationship which I assumed were about me, then discovered that they weren't, or that they were hybrids. I can be as confused about that as the general listener, believe me."

And his friendship with Stevie—would he say it's stronger now than it's been for a while?

"In some ways it is. But right now it's a little tricky. Towards the end of the album we had some problems with the running order, and there were some issues with that that got Stevie and I into some over-the-phone conflicts. She was in Hawaii on location, and I was here in LA trying to master the album. It got difficult.

"You know, it's been hard for Stevie to feel good about what we've accomplished with this record. And I really hope she will at some point. She's yet to say: 'Good work on my songs, Lindsey', even though that was basically what we were working on for the last year. She wasn't that way at the start of the record, and she wasn't that way in the middle of it. But I don't really know what goes on with that. It's all off and on."

IT'S A FASCINATING BAND DYNAMIC, IT REALLY IS. And while you shouldn't underplay the value to the band of John McVie as one half of a fine rhythm section, it's the roles of Buckingham, Nicks and Fleetwood that continue to make Fleetwood Mac a potent and lucrative force.

First there's Fleetwood. He's the band's most fervent flag waver; a lanky emblem of the band's longevity, who, along with John McVie, has been its backbone since 1967 and Mac's years as the UK's premier blues band. Buckingham, meanwhile, is the band's wild card and life force; the art-for-art's sake guy. And in terms of man hours spent on it there can be no doubt that 'Say You Will' is predominately his baby. And then there's Stevie Nicks, the rock matriarch and would-be Welsh witch from whom we should take nothing away. Three of those songs that she wrote in Phoenix—seemingly at the drop of a black, pointy hat—are genius. Let's not forget, either, that there are reasons why Nicks's solo albums have always been much more successful than Buckingham's. And even art-for-art's sake kinda guys want the biggest possible audience for their work, right? Which explains why another Buckingham solo record has effectively been incorporated into a Fleetwood Mac one.

Mick Fleetwood is obviously thrilled with 'Say You Will.' Asked to single out a couple of favourite tracks, he opts for 'Come' and 'Illume.' The former is a deliciously barbed, Buckingham-written rocker which goes: *'Think of me sweet darling/Every time you don't come'*; the latter was written by Nicks as a personal response to the events of 9/11. Given that some commentators have alleged that 'Come' is about Buckingham's former girlfriend Anne Heche (after they split, she went on to have a lesbian relationship with fellow actress Ellen Degeneres), it's not surprising when Fleetwood says he shouldn't speak about the song's lyrics.

He has plenty to say, however, about Nicks's 'Illume': "Stevie wasn't that sure about it. She was like: 'Is this any good? Is it doing enough?' I said: 'My opinion, Stevie'—because she ended up singing what I think is a truly great vocal—'is that this is all about you.' I said: 'This is classic

Stevie Nicks; this is your modern-day 'Gold Dust Woman'. It's that Edith Piaf element of Stevie coming through on a lyric that's incredibly personal to her.

"You know, everything that's happening around this record is almost frightening for me," Fleetwood continues, broadening the horizon. "I've seen this kind of thing before with this bunch, and I think something rather good and grand is probably about to happen. The truth is I don't even know how we get stuff done, because we're a semi-dysfunctional family with about five different managers. It's a fucking nightmare, really."

But his relationship with Stevie is obviously still good?

"Oh, yeah," he says. "Absolutely. Stevie and I were, of course, an item for some time. And that was part of the ongoing saga of what makes this band rather . . . unique. Unique even to this day, let me tell you [laughs]. I went to Hawaii fairly recently, where I have a home, and Stevie rented a house just two minutes down the road. I was there with Lynn and the kids, and Stevie was with us all the time. She and Lynn have become great friends. Lynn is my soul mate, but Stevie's a soul mate, too. And my wife knows that. There's so much you can enjoy within that dynamic."

STEVIE NICKS IS STILL SINGLE. "LINDSEY AND I WERE AS close to married as I'll probably ever be," she told MTV in 1998. "I adored him. I took care of him. I embroidered stars and moons on his jeans." These days Nicks seems content with the love of family and friends.

And her friendship with Mick Fleetwood—how is that now?

"Mick and I really do have a great love and respect for each other," she says. "That relationship we had all those years ago was so short that it didn't have time to build up animosities and jealousies. It began, it was, and it was over. Mick will tell you—and I will tell you—that a lot of the reason our relationship didn't continue was because we knew it would be the end of Fleetwood Mac. I certainly didn't want to break up the band, and Fleetwood Mac is everything to Mick, and I didn't want him to resent me for the rest of his life.

"So we were smart about that," she continues, "and we were grown-up and we made good decisions. We didn't throw all that shit at each other, didn't say horrible things to each other, didn't go through that terrible,

terrible break-up thing over many years. Mick and I's affair was like a little dream. And now his wife is my new best friend."

It's been a fascinating time at Culver City Studios. But although I've just witnessed another instalment of rock's greatest and most gripping soap opera, it's not quite a wrap. The closing, six-million-dollar question goes to Lindsey Buckingham. And, to his credit, he actually tries to answer it honestly. The question I put to him is this: which would he rather have saved—Fleetwood Mac, or his relationship with Stevie?

"Oh, boy. What an interesting question. What a tough question," he says, seemingly not quite sure how best to answer it. And then eventually: "I'm 53, with a beautiful wife and two beautiful children, so I can't say that my life has gone any other way than the way it was supposed to."

So destiny rules? I ask, name-checking one of those Stevie Nicks songs that sounds like it could be about him.

Buckingham laughs. "Yes."

WAR AND PEACE
AND FLEETWOOD MAC

Bill DeMain | May 2003 | *Performing Songwriter* (US)

This feature on Buckingham and Nicks focuses on songwriting and recording. The pair—interviewed separately—seem to agree to differ on how much Buckingham's arranging work brings to Nicks's creations.

Stevie Nicks calls it "the chaos." For Lindsey Buckingham, it's "the soap opera." Over the last 30 years, it has taken many forms, from shouting matches and onstage feuding at its worst to silent standoffs and uneasy truces during more peaceful times. It drove Buckingham to quit the group in 1987 and Nicks to depart in 1991. It's a landslide of jealousy, resentment, willfulness and personal problems, tempered by a big love, deep and enduring. It's at the core of what makes Fleetwood Mac such a compelling band, and it gives depth and emotional weight to their most enduring songs.

As Nicks says, "It's not easy for us. It never will be. It hasn't ever been. Whenever we get back into a room together and start working, we don't agree on a lot of stuff. Especially now, because we're really settled in our ways. It's no different than it was in 1975 when we went into rehearsal for *Fleetwood Mac*. We were fighting then, and we have fought all through every single record we have ever made. So I think if it wasn't like that, we'd probably all be walking around going, 'What's the matter with us?'"

Buckingham adds simply, "Our real lives have been laid bare in vinyl."

A little history: When Stevie and Lindsey joined in 1974, Fleetwood Mac was a rickety blues-rock band. Though drummer Mick Fleetwood and bassist John McVie were one of the tightest rhythm sections around, they'd been plagued by years of personnel changes and were struggling to find a new direction. Fleetwood heard something special in the *Buckingham Nicks* record that his new recruits had made (in his autobiography, Mick says, "Nobody ever auditioned for Fleetwood Mac . . . people were *meant* to be in this group"). Keyboardist/singer Christine McVie felt a similar sense of harmonic convergence upon meeting Stevie and Lindsey. In 1990, she recalled, "The first time I started playing 'Say You Love Me' and I reached the chorus, they started singing with me and fell right into it. I heard this incredible sound—our three voices . . . and my skin turned to gooseflesh."

By 1977's landmark *Rumours,* that incredible sound—a swirl of pop, blues and folk filtered through Southern California cool—made the Mac the biggest band on the planet. Buckingham, Nicks and McVie were each writing hits—"Go Your Own Way," "Dreams," "Don't Stop." The future looked bright. But there was always that volatile core threatening to implode and take the whole beautiful dream down with it.

The turning point in many ways came with *Tusk.* It was a bold step forward, experimental and defiant in its production and style. Though it sold over four million copies, it was perceived as a failure in the wake of *Rumours.* As Buckingham says, "I had been through quite a battle just to get that album made in a post-*Rumours* environment. It was exciting for me, a feeling like I had gotten to something that was more challenging and that was going to confound expectations. But the politics after *Tusk* dictated that we weren't going to do that as a group anymore. So we kind of backtracked into some sort of vague no man's land a little bit."

The classic Mac lineup released two more albums, *Mirage* and *Tango in the Night,* before things fell apart. By then, Nicks had a strong solo career going and Buckingham was close behind. Mick Fleetwood and the McVies soldiered on into the early '90s with new members. Then in 1996, the classic lineup patched up their differences for a tour and a live album, *The Dance.* A handful of new songs pointed the way to what is, almost seven years later, surely one of the unexpected events of spring 2003—a new studio album from Fleetwood Mac.

When groups of a certain vintage release new music, there's always worry and trepidation. As a rule, it rarely measures up to their best work. That's what makes *Say You Will* such a triumph. Though Christine McVie has retired from the band, the record boasts all the Mac signatures—Gibraltar-like grooves from Fleetwood and McVie, inspired guitar wizardry from Buckingham, inventive production flourishes, sweet vocal harmonies and, of course, songwriting that draws from the ever present tripwire emotions between Stevie and Lindsey—the chaos and the soap opera. Led by tracks such as "Peacekeeper," "Say You Will," "Thrown Down," "Silver Girl" and "Say Goodbye," this is a Fleetwood Mac that sounds as passionate and vital as they did in 1977. They're keeping their promise to—as they sang back then—"never break the chain."

LINDSEY BUCKINGHAM

I met Buckingham at Culver Studios in Los Angeles, where the group was getting ready to rehearse for an upcoming world tour. Dressed in jeans, a V-neck white T-shirt and a black leather jacket, he looked lean and healthy. In conversation he's very earnest and likable, with a producer's keen sense of diplomacy.

What kinds of feelings do you go through in the weeks before a new Fleetwood Mac record is released?
With this record, I'm actually euphoric. This project, for me, has been kind of an epic effort, more than anything I've ever done in terms of length of time involved to keep the eye on the ball, the ways in which it could have come out as a solo album, and finally what it ended up being, and somehow still maintaining its integrity, in terms of my songs and Stevie's songs. In many ways, I feel like I've been working for the last 25 years of my life for this, not just the last six years that it's been literally worked on. A level of maturity, a level of creativity and a vision that I've been trying to get to have now infused into the whole thing,

with a great rhythm section, and Stevie, who I've known since I was 16. It's just a very exciting and profound thing.

What impressed me right away about the record is that you sound like you mean it. There's a commitment that you don't often hear with bands who've been around for over 30 years.
I think the sense of a band who is all 50-something coming up with something like this is a little bit profound. I think it breaks a lot of the clichés about rock 'n' roll. A lot of artists in other forms, whether they're novelists or moviemakers or composers or painters, a lot of them maybe hit their stride at 50. It's only this rock 'n' roll cliché that you burn out by the time you're a relatively young age, and it is just that—a cliché. So all of that informs the way I feel about not just the release of the album, but this whole year. Hopefully, if things go the way we pray they will, next year we can do another album. It feels like a whole open-ended thing that's happening here.

Did you have to work to change the vocal arrangements now that Christine wasn't in the mix?
No, not really. Stevie and I realized that even though it's just the two of us now, we weren't particularly interested in trying to go back to a literal two-part harmony presentation. We didn't want to make a complete vocal left turn and not have it feel like Fleetwood Mac. We were sort of mindful of trying to find a middle ground, and I think we did pretty well. There are things where she and I are singing on our own, but there's still an orchestral element there. And that was a function of not wanting to be too bold in terms of redefining the sound, but it was also what the songs needed in her case, and what they already were in my case.

Listening to your songs on the record, one theme I picked up on was the idea of taking responsibility. Has your songwriting changed since you've had children?
It has certainly affected the way I feel. I think I've calmed down quite a bit (laughs). I think that these are the best lyrics that I've ever written, without getting specific. There's a sense of safeness that now is part of

my life, as part of a larger picture. Things that are more important than writing a song have made it easier to write better lyrics. And I think also that it's a skill that gets better the more you work on it, and I've tried to work on it. In terms of the theme you're talking about—taking responsibility—I think you're right. There is a kind of subconscious element that has kind of worked its way in, that makes it less about the neurosis of me and my needs, and more about an overview. It's still about me or us, though maybe a small group of us. More concern for trying to do the right thing, and not just a neurotic, selfish point of view, which was a lot of what Fleetwood Mac's dialogues to each other were always about (laughs).

What are the most mysterious parts of the songwriting process to you?
It's an interesting thing. In many ways, I still don't think of myself as a songwriter. I know I've written a lot of songs. I tend to think of myself as a stylist. I think that the way a lot of people do it is they come up with a tangible thing that you can call a lyric and a melody. Then they take it into a situation where it might evolve as a record. I might go in with fragments or ideas that are not particularly well-fleshed out, or they're as well-fleshed out as I'm able to make them. And then I start to work the painting.

What do you mean by that?
I make that analogy because I can sit with a tape machine and use that as a canvas. You commit to a certain melody, then you commit to a certain guitar part, and one affects the other and maybe the melody begins to change. It's kind of an abstract expressionist way of doing it. At some point that starts to lead you, as a painting would. Then when you get to a certain point, suddenly you're on automatic. It's hard for me to divorce the process of the songwriting, because I'm not Burt Bacharach, unfortunately, who can sit down and have a complete overview and understanding of so many things that he's been taught, so many European principles and all that. I have to find a different way to do it. So the actual record-making side of it affects to a great degree the writing and vice versa. And I suppose that is the mystery

right there, is that it comes in little fits and starts, and it's maybe like making sculpture. You have to really pat it around quite a bit and change it and lop off the nose and start over again, and there's a kind of abstractness about it.

I've always admired your guitar playing, especially your right hand, which is so fluid and precise. Can you talk a little about your technique?
I never really used a pick very much. When I was seven I was listening to Scotty Moore, who had a fingerstyle in which he used a pick along with his fingers. When rock sort of took a dive for a while there, I started listening to folk music and bluegrass. I never really got any serious chops on banjo, but it helped my speed. But the Travis picking is the basic template for everything I do. It's just something that evolved. I think a real breakthrough for me in terms of translating this thing that you're talking about to the studio and record-making beyond the level of, say, "Never Going Back Again" was when I started playing "Big Love" live. That was before *The Dance,* when I did a tour after *Out of the Cradle.* I started doing "Big Love" very fast, in a Leo Kottke-meets-classical on acid (laughs), whatever you want to call it. It got such a strong response, and it got me back to reminding myself that whatever I can do as a producer, this is the center of what I do, and it's not something to be taken lightly. This is somewhere I want to go now, to take that element, the energy of that, and the singularity of that, and build on it in a much more sublime way.

I read an interview with Christine where she said how much she admired your abilities as a producer. She mentioned how you took Stevie's "Gold Dust Woman," which has a repetitive chord sequence, and made each section distinct. Since Stevie isn't really an instrumentalist, how do you approach an arrangement for one of her songs?
You are in some ways adding to the writing process on the set, so to speak. "Okay, this doesn't work, let's try this." It's very much like that. If I am able to do that for Stevie, it doesn't mean I'd be able to do that for everyone. Maybe that's part of what makes Fleetwood Mac what it is. We just happen to have a set of cross references where I have what

she needs. I don't know how it would work if I were to try to do it with another group or artist. In many ways, you might say that was more of the profound gift that I had for Fleetwood Mac, more than as a guitarist or a writer or a singer. I was someone who could make all that stuff into a record.

Is there a certain thing about Stevie's songwriting that you like best?
I understand the primitive aspects that she has going. I understand what she's trying to get at. She may not even articulate it herself, but I see what it is. I can understand the potential. What I like about her songwriting is her sense of rhythm. It's superb. Obviously you have to like her lyrics and her voice, but she does a lot with a very little. Sometimes if you examine her melodies, they are not particularly elaborate. She can do repetitive phrases, but it's just how she does it and where she stops doing it, and where she makes a little change-up and how I seem to be able to move sections across that—change what's going on beneath it.

Can you think of an example?
"Gypsy" is a great example. If you were to just pull the melody out from that without any of what's going on beneath, it wouldn't hang together. Without having the instrumental parts (hums counter line in chorus) that allow the potential of what she's doing to come out, it wouldn't make it. So she needed that. Maybe that's my favorite example of it [Stevie's writing and Lindsey's production] coming together. If you sing "You see your gypsy, you see your gypsy, yeah," it doesn't really depart anywhere at the point it needs to. It just sounds like someone kind of jamming with their voice, but it allows the openness for me to do things of my own. It's a real collaboration, even though I'm not writing the song.

There's always a very personal element in Fleetwood Mac where listeners are tempted to interpret the lyrics as a dialogue between the members.
I think we always were doing that, and probably still are in quite a few of the songs (laughs). We are in a more peaceful place than we were in terms of a functional working band, not just a band who's

doing a restatement of their body of work as in *The Dance,* but a band who's in the trenches doing something new and vital to what's going on with them now. We are much more at peace, but it's tenuous still. And then how that relates to the world-view of things enters into some of the songs. Who knows how much of that element was responsible for the phenomenon that was *Rumours?* At what point did the music itself, which was very good music, sort of give over to the musical soap opera element? If you want to look at it in a cynical way, that's part of the gimmick of the band and always has been. It's a hook. There's nothing wrong with that, because it's not a pretense. It's not something where we sat with a PR person and said, "Well, this would be a good thing to try (laughs)." Our real lives laid bare, not just in terms of the media, but in terms of the vinyl. There was a great appeal to that, not just in terms of the voyeurism of it. It was a very touching thing—the fact that we would go through all forms of denial in order to push forward as musicians and really allow ourselves to become quite dysfunctional as people. Not that the whole rock genre doesn't make you that way eventually anyway (laughs), living in the subculture of drugs and all that at that time, but I think with us it was bitter and it was sweet and it was tender and it was brutal all at once.

And now it's going to be a Broadway musical.
(Laughter) I've heard that. We haven't given anybody our blessing yet, but I wouldn't doubt it at all. If not this year, then next year. We'll see.

LINDSEY'S GEAR
Rick Turner Guitars
Gibson Chet Atkins model
Taylor acoustics
Ampeg amps
Mesa-Boogie amps
SWR Acoustic "California Blonde" amps
Trace Acoustic amps
Roland GR-50 Guitar Synth
Boss Digital Sampler

Boss Super Overdrive
Alesis Midiverb
Ernie Ball strings

LINDSEY'S ESSENTIAL LISTENING
The Beach Boys—*Today*
John Lennon—*Plastic Ono Band*
I think it had a lot to do with me thinking it was okay to be that rude in my own songs (laughs).
Any collection of Elvis Presley stuff.
I wouldn't be here at all without Elvis Presley and without my older brother who bought the record of "Heartbreak Hotel." Before that it was Patti Page (laughs).
Any number of Beatles albums, maybe *Revolver* or *Rubber Soul*.
Laurie Anderson—*Big Science*

LINDSEY TALKS ABOUT HIS SONGS
GO YOUR OWN WAY
That came very quickly. I remember sitting down and putting that together when we were taking a break in Florida. We rented a house to start rehearsing before *Rumours*, and it was an immediate song. It was a very present thing in terms of the response it got from the band. The drumbeat that Mick did in the verse was actually his version of trying to do something that I asked him to do that he couldn't do. What he did was better. I'd been listening to "Street Fighting Man," and Charlie Watts does this kind of offbeat rhythm. Mick, either he didn't want to do that or he couldn't get it, so he came up with his own version.

NEVER GOING BACK AGAIN
A very naive song. Never going back again? Sure (laughs). I think the guitar work was inspired by something I heard by Ry Cooder. The lyric as I recall was very much a miniature perception of things. I had broken up with Stevie and maybe met someone. It could have been someone who really didn't mean a thing. Maybe someone who had kind of resisted getting to know me and then finally broke down and let me in. I don't

remember who it was now. In the days after Stevie and I broke up, before we started recording *Rumours,* there were a lot of women who would just come and go in a very short time. So in that sense, it was one of those people. The lyric seems not very deep. "Been down one time, been down two time, never going back again." There really is nothing particularly definitive about it. You think about how naive that was and very much in the context of not particularly being about something that was even important. And maybe that's why it's sweet—it was just a frivolous little thing. Of course, it seems to take on more sweetness and a deeper feeling when it's placed on the album with all the other songs (laughs).

PEACEKEEPER

I wrote the song about two and a half years ago. It was, in a very ironic way, looking at the kind of thinking that is matter-of-fact and desensitized towards certain actions that go on in the world, and the kind of blankness and conformity that goes along with that. And then trying to look at what does that do for a married couple trying to work out their problems. How does it affect them? What is peace, really? The whole idea that there can be any static condition is obviously an illusion. So can there ever really be peace? There can be moments of peace or long periods of peace, possibly, whether it's in the world or in a relationship. But it seems to me what peace really means is valuing the ideal of that and just being mindful of it—working towards the maintenance of it, even though you understand it will not always exist. But the irony of being matter-of-fact about not thinking that way is really what the song is doing.

MURROW

It was inspired by watching TV and seeing what it's become, how horrendous it's become as a tool to do exactly what Edward R. Murrow warned against when he gave his famous speech. He said if TV is allowed to distract and delude people, then there will be a large, large price to pay down the line. And we're seeing that coming true on so many levels. Especially in the world today, where all the media is basically owned and controlled and edited to a certain point of view, in the name of objective news, by all the same people who are tied in with another company. A good example would be GE owning NBC. Murrow would be turning over in his grave if he were to see all of this. Not just the propaganda that passes for news, but the trivialization of so many things, and the intent to distract and delude that he was talking about.

STEVIE NICKS

Stevie Nicks lives in a beautiful Spanish-style house, high on a hill in Santa Monica, overlooking the Pacific Ocean, and it was there where we met. The decor is a mix of the fanciful and practical—antique velour chairs and paintings of dragons and gypsies share space with a Precor treadmill and exercycle. Stevie looks terrific, her long wavy hair spilling over a black shawl. She carries her 50-something years with grace and confidence and is still quite alluring. During our interview, she is very open, sharing everything from her private journals to her thoughts on why she has remained single.

In Fleetwood Mac, there's always an added layer of intrigue with your songs and Lindsey's in that listeners wonder if you're singing about each other. Are you still dealing with unfinished emotional business?
Of course. It's not a lot of fun, but it certainly does lend itself to great writing. If everybody's happy and everything's going along, then you have nothing to write about. So Lindsey and I write about the chaos of our relationship, which is ongoing. We're both really selfish, and it's like, "No, I want it to be this way!" It's like you have two serious bulls in a pen, and we argue all the time. There's continual trauma. But does it make for incredible works of music? Yeah, it does.

At the same time, you have to put a lot of trust in Lindsey because he's the producer and arranger on your songs.
Well, he doesn't do a whole lot of things with arranging, because my demos are pretty much there. That doesn't mean that they're not 100 percent more terrific after Lindsey works on them. I'm very territorial about the way my songs are arranged. What he does is take the skeleton and

then he goes in for hours that we never see him and he plays parts and parts and more parts. He arranges right underneath my little skeleton. It's like I laughingly said to him when we first started this new record, because his songs were pretty much done, I said, "Your songs are like beautiful, handcrafted Russian boxes with enamel and cloisonné and sound like you've worked on them for seven years, and my little songs are like pine boxes (laughs)." I said, "You've got your work cut out for you, because you have to somehow make my songs compare a little bit to yours." He said, "Don't worry."

How has it been without Christine in the band?
Taking away the piano made the whole music tend to focus more on a guitar-oriented thing, which is great. Not that we didn't miss having somebody to play the piano, because we did. But in fact, it forced us to go much more towards a power trio sound. Lindsey and John and Mick, they became like Cream (laughs).

"Thrown Down," "Say You Will," "Running Through the Garden"—I think these new songs are some of the best you've ever written.
Thank you. I agree with you. How conceited am I to say that (laughs)? But they say you are supposed to get better as you get older, and they say if you keep practicing your craft you have to get better. So I'm not one of those people who is ever going to accept the fact that I can't write a song that will appeal to somebody who's 20 because I'm in my early 50s. And I'm never going to accept that when I'm like 70, I can't still write something that is current. To me, we just have to get better. That's how we all looked at this record. This wasn't going to be just a dumb, stupid album. It's not going to be because we just felt like doing a record. This is because we needed to do this, and this musical entity needed to come through all of us, and we are serious as a heart attack about this.

I've read that you're very dedicated to keeping journals. How does journal writing relate to songwriting for you?
Sometimes I pull my lyrics right straight out of my journals. I'll show you. [She goes in the next room to get journals.] See, I write prose on

the right hand side, then on the left, I'll write poetry and lyrics. This is from the anniversary of 9/11: (reads) *The murder of innocence cannot be explained, only endured. And I who went to sleep in tears woke up in tears. And I who never said goodbye, said goodbye again. I did go to sleep in tears last night, and I woke up in tears about an hour ago. I laid in my bed and that moment before you really wake up, the tears just started streaming down my face. Fleetwood Mac is mixing our first song from the record today. We start at 3:30. Today, half of me wants to call in sick, the other half of me knows that the people who died one year ago would want me to finish this music in their honor and not give into this feeling that makes me want to put the TV on the Design Channel and hide away.* This is "Illumé," the song, that's right where it came from. In another two years, I will go back through what I'm writing today and I will pull out stuff, and they will become poems on this side of the book. I'll go through and make the prose into poetry, and that's how I get my songs. I very seldom write just straight poetry or lyrics. It will usually come from me writing about what's going on in my life.

Do the songs you write for Fleetwood Mac feel different than what you do for a solo album?

My solo career is very precious to me, but it's nothing like Fleetwood Mac. It can *never* be like Fleetwood Mac. For each of the members of the band and everyone surrounding us, it's so much more heavy. When I'm working by myself, it is by myself. I'm very inward and very much a loner and I live here by myself, but Fleetwood Mac just overwhelms everything, takes everything. Everything you do is completely built around Fleetwood Mac. So I don't know what else to say about that. It makes my whole face turn red. I get a fever.

In the liner notes on Trouble in Shangri-La, *you thank Tom Petty for an inspirational lecture he gave you. Can you share what he said?*

That was in Phoenix in about 1996. I had been in and out of rehab for the Klonopin that I'd been taking for eight years. I went back to Phoenix and I was really down. It was like, 'I obviously didn't create anything worth talking about in the last eight years, so am I going to be able to create now?' And Tom was playing in town, and I went down to dinner with him the night before, and I asked him if he would help me write a song. And he just flat out, in the Tom Petty swamp dog way, said, "I'm not going to help you write a song, because you are, in my opinion, Stevie, one of the premier songwriters of our time. I don't need to help you write a song. You just need to go back to your house and sit in front of your piano and start writing." And something about the conversation really hit me. I walked out of the Ritz-Carlton with a new lease on life. If Tom Petty thinks I can do it, then I guess I can. I went home and I started writing, that night. Sometimes a really good friend is the only one who can say to you, "I know you may not want to hear this, but I need to tell you . . ." Whether it's something bad or something good, they get through to you finally.

Sheryl Crow is also your close friend. Do you guys talk shop a lot?
Very much. I think Sheryl and I are a real mutual admiration society. She did a lot of shows with me on the *Trouble in Shangri-La* tour. When you're on the road together, you really do bond. It's like an encounter group. The people that you travel with are all you have, so Sheryl and I became really good friends, not to mention that she produced half of my last record. We've spent hours, here in this room, working on songs. Sheryl and I will absolutely do a record at some point—it may be the next thing I do. We said seven or eight years ago that we're going to become a valid musical entity, just the two of us. So that if we want to go on the road by ourselves, we're going to be able to do it. Because we have now built up a repertoire between the two of us—we've got 10 or 12 songs we could already do. Isn't that wonderful that that's out there for me, and for her? It's one more really creative thing.

How do you feel about The Dixie Chicks covering "Landslide?"
It's a great honor. I am very good friends with them, and hope very much to do a record with Natalie at some point in my life. I have to show you what they sent me [brings out a lovely ceramic bowl engraved with the lyrics of "Landslide" in a spiral]. It's all perfect. The neatest part of the song is all inside the bowl. So beautiful and so special. When I'm 101,

walking around the house, that will be an inspiration to me—to see that somebody cared enough to do this. These girls are very precious to me. I think if I'd ever had a daughter, I would want her to be Natalie. I love her and I care about her in a way that's very motherly. I think she's about the best singer out there. I thought that the first time I heard her sing. I was in Phoenix, and it was the middle of the night, and I heard "There's Your Trouble" on the radio. I wrote it down and went straight to the record store the next day. So I made the decision then, years before I ever met them, that I wanted to work with her someday. So it was very karma-inspired that they would pick up "Landslide" and want to do it. I think that Sheryl Crow is the one who suggested it to them.

These are all like your daughters.
They *are* my daughters, and I love that, because since I didn't have any daughters, I feel like I have them now. And I have Norah Jones. I love her. Can you believe, eight Grammys? Norah, this is your *Rumours.* Your life will never be the same again. And I love Michelle Branch. And I adore Gwen Stefani. They are all a delight to me. They are all multi-talented, and I feel very grateful that these women care about me and care about my music. They make it all so very worth it for me. To know that I have reached out and gotten to each one of them and maybe made them be a little better, be a little bit more profound, work on their songwriting a little bit more, work on their stage performance a little bit more. I see little bits of myself in all of them, and it makes me cry.

It's almost like your songs, as they reach new generations, are helping to keep you young.
Whenever I do a record, I'm able to go back and pull some really interesting songs out that were written when I was really young, and then mix them in with what I'm doing now. I feel very lucky that I don't listen to all these songs and go, 'Oh, that's from 1976, that's from 2003.' That's why I say that I will be 90 years old some day, and I will still be writing things that are relevant. I think if you keep that innocence, if you try to hang on to that innocence and believe that there is love and there is God and there is beauty, then you will be able to be relevant. I think when you start to

become really jaded, that's when you can't write relevant stuff anymore. People who are in their teens, 20s and 30s don't want to hear you write about stuff that is so miserable that they can't even deal with it.

I think, for me—because I haven't been in a horrible marriage and I don't have delinquent children that I'm trying to get through college—I haven't had a lot of those bad experiences that really twist people's minds. That's when you stop writing about love and you stop writing about the possibility of love, and when you stop writing about the possibility of love, you are no longer relevant. I don't really care if I get married at this point, I'm quite happy by myself, but I do live in the realm of romantic possibility. Mr. Right. It's possible that he's around the corner—that he could just be driving up the street, and I could have a flat tire and there he is (laughs). That allows me to write with hope.

STEVIE TALKS ABOUT HER SONGS
LANDSLIDE

It was written in 1973 at a point where Lindsey and I had driven to Aspen for him to rehearse for two weeks with Don Everly. Lindsey was going to take Phil's place. So they rehearsed and left, and I made a choice to stay in Aspen. I figured I'd stay there and one of my girlfriends was there. We stayed there for almost three months while Lindsey was on the road, and this is right after the *Buckingham Nicks* record had been dropped. And it was horrifying to Lindsey and I because we had a taste of the big time, we recorded in a big studio, we met famous people, we made what we consider to be a brilliant record and nobody liked it (laughs). I had been a waitress and a cleaning lady, and I didn't mind any of this. I was perfectly delighted to work and support us so that Lindsey could produce and work and fix our songs and make our music. But I had gotten to a point where it was like, "I'm not happy. I am tired. But I don't know if we can do any better than this. If nobody likes this, then what are we going to do?" So during that two months I made a decision to continue. "Landslide" was the decision. [Sings] "When you see my reflection in the snow-covered hills"—it's the only time in my life that I've lived in the snow. But looking up at those Rocky Mountains and going, "Okay, we can do it. I'm sure we can do it." In one of my journal entries, it says,

"I took Lindsey and said, 'We're going to the top!'" And that's what we did. Within a year, Mick Fleetwood called us, and we were in Fleetwood Mac making $800 a week apiece (laughs). Washing $100 bills through the laundry. It was hysterical. It was like we were rich overnight.

SILVER GIRL

That's written about Sheryl Crow. In the song where it says, "She would have preferred the last generation," Sheryl absolutely would've preferred to be my age and to have been in our generation and to have been in her own Fleetwood Mac, more than to be in this generation. We all love her and try to take her along with us because we know that. It was very fun when she came to record with Fleetwood Mac. Lindsey likes her a lot and Mick loves her and John loves her, and she's one of our little adoptees. So the song is like an ode to the girl rock star, an ode to the question, "Is it possible to find somebody to love?" When you're rich and famous, it's very hard to find somebody. That's not taking away the hope, but it is stating that it's difficult. When Sheryl asked me, "Am I ever going to find anybody?" I say, "Well, who knows? If you want to attain a certain amount of fame, then you have to work all the time, which is what you do. And you don't hang out very much, you are on the move. You're in New York, you're in L.A., you're in Switzerland, you're in Vietnam, you're never around for very long. You're like a willow wisp. So it kind of depends on what you want to do." I kind of made a choice when I was Sheryl's age, when I was 40, that I didn't really want to be tied down. There are many times during my life that I could've been married and I could've had children, and I made the decision to not do it. So I don't know, with her; the only advice I can say is that "You live in the same realm of romantic possibility that I do."

RHIANNON

I read a book called *Triad*. It was just a stupid little paperback that I found somewhere at somebody's house laying on the couch. It was all about this girl named Rhiannon. I was so taken with the name that I thought, "I've got to write something about this." And I sat down at the piano, and I started writing this song about a woman that was all involved with these birds and magic. Come to find out years after I've written the song that in fact Rhiannon was the goddess of steeds, maker of birds. Her three birds sang music, and when something was happening in war, you would see this horse come in and it was Rhiannon. This is all in the Welsh translation of *The Mabinogion,* their book of mythology. When she came, you'd kind of black out then wake up and the danger would be gone, and you'd see the three birds flying off, and you'd hear this little song. So there was, in fact, a song of Rhiannon. I had no idea about any of this. Then somebody sent me a set of four books written by a lady named Evangeline Walton, who is now dead. She spent her whole life translating *The Mabinogion* and the story of Rhiannon. She lived in Tuscon. I went there in 1977, after "Rhiannon" had been a big huge hit. Her house was totally Rhiannon. She spent her whole life on the story of Rhiannon. She never married—she in essence had almost become Rhiannon, and it was trippy. She had heard about the song. She told me about her life and how she had been entranced by the name, just like I had. It's so interesting, because her last book was 1974, and that's right when I wrote "Rhiannon." So it's like her work ended and my work began.

STEVIE'S ESSENTIAL LISTENING
Everly Brothers
The Ronettes
The Supremes and all the Motown records
The Beatles
Jimi Hendrix
Janis Joplin
I watched Janis one time—we opened for her [when Lindsey and Stevie were in their first band, Fritz]—and that's the only time I ever saw her. We opened for Jimi Hendrix, too. I got to stand on the side of the stage and watch him for two hours. He and Janis both died shortly thereafter. But I got the essence before they left. So that was the most amazing thing. That's when I really decided that I wanted to be a rock singer and not a country singer, and that I really wanted to concentrate on songwriting. I was not going to be a stupid girl singer. I was going to be way more than

that. Lindsey will laugh, but I was not going to carry equipment and not going to have my salary docked because I didn't. "You will pay me as much as you guys get, or I quit." That's when I gained my strength and my confidence. And that confidence never went away. It became part of me, and I have it still today, and I'm very grateful for that.

FIVE GO MAD

Nigel Williamson | May 2003 | *Uncut* (UK)

This feature was another article that coincided with the *Say You Will* album. As was now becoming the norm, it fleetingly mentions the new product before delving into the band's endlessly fascinating hinterland, particularly the trauma surrounding the recording of *Rumours*.

AUGUST 7, 1987. Fleetwood Mac are enjoying a third burst of success after the Peter Green/"Albatross" years and *Rumours* heyday. Their new album, *Tango In The Night,* has just topped the charts in Britain and America on its way to global sales that will eventually approach 10 million. But all is far from well in the camp. When the band meets at Christine McVie's Hollywood home to resolve their differences, the atmosphere is venomous.

A row breaks out over Lindsey Buckingham's refusal to tour, and when former lover Stevie Nicks tries to remonstrate with him, the highly-strung guitarist explodes. "Get this bitch out of my way. And fuck the lot of you!" he screams, as he pushes her over the hood of his car and delivers a slap. Vowing never to speak to the band again, he drives off into the sunset with the parting shot, "You're a bunch of selfish bastards!"

Flash back more than a decade. You could be forgiven for thinking that the pinnacle of Fleetwood Mac's convoluted, incestuous, drug-fuelled, trash-novel insanity had been reached in 1976 when they were recording *Rumours.* In fact, it was only the start of what was to become rock 'n' roll's longest running real-life soap opera.

The omens could not have been less propitious when the band went into the Record Plant studio in Sausalito, San Francisco. Their previous album, 1975's *Fleetwood Mac,* sat at the top of the US charts. But nobody knew if they could stay together long enough even to complete the follow-up.

The torrid six-year romance between Nicks and Buckingham has recently ended in bitterness and rancour and the two are only speaking to each other to hurl insults and recriminations. John McVie and Christine McVie, married for eight years, are not speaking at all, except through the expensive lawyers negotiating their messy divorce. Mick Fleetwood, too, is going through a divorce of his own and is about to complicate matters further by embarking on an affair with Nicks.

Outside of being trapped in the same band and writing songs to each other, detailing every jealousy and betrayal in the emotional maelstrom they have created, the only common currency is the huge, velvet bag of cocaine which engineer Ken Calliat keeps under the mixing desk and which the band demands at regular intervals to 'refresh' themselves.

Yet out of this traumatically troubled and tangled web comes the bestselling album of all time (at least until Michael Jackson cleans up with *Thriller*). Ultimately, *Rumours* will shift more than *25* million copies and set Fleetwood Mac up on millionaire's row for life, an amazing achievement for a band—one with an entire pre-history—born out of the British '60s blues boom.

The phenomenal success of *Rumours* keeps Fleetwood Mac together. But it's against all rational judgement, and at a price. In the intervening decade the dysfunction and trauma they turned to such positive and creative effect on *Rumours* has gone from bad to worse. Much worse. With lifestyles that would not have been out of place on the set of *Dallas* or *Dynasty* and the most outrageous touring circus this side of Led Zeppelin, the band descends into a collective drink and drugs hell.

Excess of every kind is the order of the day. Nicks has an affair with Don Henley of The Eagles, falls offstage and checks into the Betty Ford Clinic for cocaine addiction. Then, on her release, she sinks into an even deeper and more debilitating dependency on the tranquilliser Klonopin and nearly dies all over again. John McVie has an alcohol-induced seizure and is busted at his Hawaii home with four-and-a-half grammes of pure cocaine and a collection of illegal firearms. Christine McVie has an affair with the band's lighting director and then falls for doomed Beach Boys wild-man Dennis Wilson. By her own admission, it's taking a magnum of vintage Dom Perignon a day just for her to get by. Mick Fleetwood is busy blowing his millions on debauchery and is deep in his own brain-frying self-destruction, involving industrial quantities of cocaine washed down with bottles of brandy.

BY 1986, WHEN IT COMES to recording *Tango In The Night* after a four year lay-off, the task of ensuring the record is not a complete disaster has fallen overwhelmingly on the intense and nervy figure of Buckingham. Nicks, little more than a sedated zombie, barely attends the year-long sessions, and Buckingham is forced to doctor the tapes to kid the world into believing she is on songs that she has never even heard. A half-crazed Fleetwood spends much of the recording nodding out in a Winnebago parked outside Buckingham's home studio. Bass player John McVie only turns up when absolutely necessary to put down his basslines, while his ex-wife Christine, for whom he still carries a torch, views all the madness with increasing distaste.

Left almost single-handedly to fashion the album and having successfully delivered his less-industrious colleagues yet another bank-filling, career-saving, multi-platinum winner, a frustrated Buckingham decides he has finally had enough. His colleagues are appalled. However out of it they may be, they're not too far gone to realise that, without their main musical focus, they're in trouble.

Throughout the summer of 1987, the rest of the band has attempted to twist his arm to join them on their forthcoming world tour. At one point, Buckingham's agreement appears to have been secured and a celebratory dinner is arranged. By that evening, he has changed his mind again and fails to show up at the restaurant.

Tired of his vacillating, the rest of the band summon him to a final showdown at Christine McVie's house. When their pleading and cajoling continues to fall on deaf ears, the exchanges grow angrier. Finally, when Nicks intervenes, Buckingham snaps. Although the couple had broken up back in 1976, a decade's worth of pent-up emotion spews forth and Buckingham walks out on the band.

MORE THAN 15 YEARS LATER, Buckingham is back, rehearsing for a new stadium tour at Culver City Studios, Los Angeles, and with a new Fleetwood Mac studio album, *Say You Will.* Christine McVie has gone, having moved back to England to retire with her husband to a big house in Kent. Otherwise, it is the classic Fleetwood Mac line-up. Older and wiser and a little less volatile. But back with the same melodic and beguiling sound they perfected on albums such as *Fleetwood Mac, Rumours* and *Tusk.*

And after years of being regarded as the enemy, it seems that Fleetwood Mac are cool again. "I think the intriguing thing to a lot of people is that there's never been a period in rock as debauched as the period after *Rumours,*" said Courtney Love, who in the late '90s covered Stevie Nicks' cocaine-inspired "Gold Dust Woman". "Nobody's touched it."

Ex-Smashing Pumpkins leader Billy Corgan is another fan (in the mid-'90s he recorded a cover version of "Landslide" from 1975s *Fleetwood Mac*). And when *Uncut* recently visited Tricky at his home in Venice Beach, California, even the dark one was playing Fleetwood Mac, proclaiming them to be "fucking brilliant".

For Buckingham, *Say You Will* is the first Fleetwood Mac studio album he has been involved with since the fateful *Tango In The Night,* and although he disputes some of the details of the confrontation that resulted in his 1987 departure, he concedes euphemistically it was "not a happy day". Yet he regards the new album as a "vindication" of his walk-out. "If I hadn't left then, I wouldn't be in this place now," he reasons. "So it all makes sense in some way. That's part of the beauty of us being back together."

At 55, Buckingham seems far more relaxed and less intense than the character we met on Fleetwood Mac's 1997 reunion tour. Sitting cross-legged and relaxed on a couch at the Culver City Sound Stage rehearsal space in LA, he scratches his head and laughs lot. When the band's US publicist sticks her head around the door to say, "Five more minutes," he replies, "Hey 10, 15, whatever, it's cool."

"I'm now married and I have a four-and-a-half-year-old son and a two-and-a-half-year-old daughter," he explains. "I think all that calms you down in increments, without you even being aware of it. You get more balance and you feel like there's something greater than yourself in the scheme of things. I'm just happier. I spent quite a few years in emotional exile and that includes all my time in Fleetwood Mac, really."

There was never a time in the band when his relationship with Nicks wasn't characterised by "dysfunction" and "denial", he admits with total candour. "That sounds strange when we had split up so many years earlier. But most couples in that position don't carry on seeing each other all the time. Being in a band is like still living with someone. We weren't able to resolve things because I don't think we were focused enough even to know what needed to be resolved."

Even on the 1997 tour he feels there was still a "residue". Since then he's gained a family of his own for the first time and has finally been able to move on. "And this time when we started again I found I really liked the chemistry of the band without the baggage we carried around for so long. We can acknowledge what happened. But we are different people."

Talking to Mick Fleetwood at the rehearsal studio where the band are preparing for their forthcoming tour, the drummer agrees. But he also says that the unique chemistry that created *Rumours* has not entirely dissipated. "There's an incredible amount of emotional investment outside of the music within this band. The vibration of what happened is still alive. It's not theatre, it's real," he adds, stretching his long frame across a couch, still the elegant English dandy.

"Christine has gone, but Stevie is surrounded by three men, two of whom she's had relationships with. This still makes for interesting copy. My friendship and absolute love for Stevie is still able to exist. She's my wife's best friend and we've all just come back from a vacation in Hawaii together. It's not corporate. It's still a powerful thing emotionally. There are areas for Stevie and Lindsey that are still sticky for them. But we've found a road map where this can happen."

TALKING TO NICKS, who seems animated and incredibly open, the Fleetwood Mac story is not so much soap opera as gothic romance.

Either way, it's a tale in which she believed the final chapter had been written with the band's 1997 reunion tour and subsequent departure of Christine McVie. *"Not all the king's horses and all the king's men could put it back together,"* she sang on "Fall From Grace", from her 2001 solo album, *Trouble In Shangri-La.*

"Yes, that was totally about the band," she admits now. Yet she had no hesitation in signing on again when approached. "It's like the restless spirit of Fleetwood Mac still needs to find peace," she says. "That sounds a bit *Wuthering Heights.* But in a way it is. I don't think any of us could be in any other band."

Say You Will features 18 tracks, nine written by Nicks and nine by Buckingham, who also produced (with assistance on some tracks from Rob Cavallo). "It's really like a Buckingham-Nicks record with this power trio backing," says Nicks. She admits to missing Christine McVie, who she hasn't seen in five years. The day after the Grammy awards in January 1998 (where Fleetwood Mac had three nominations but went away empty-handed), McVie packed up, sold her house and car and left for Britain. "I'm not ungrateful to Hollywood but I've lived there for 28 years and I'm homesick," she told this writer shortly before the move. "I want to spend more time with my English family and open a restaurant." She hasn't been back to LA since.

"Chris did not enjoy the experience of being back on the road at all," Nicks says. "And I can understand why she left. She's now 59 and so I'm now the same age she was on that last 1997 tour. It's very hard on a woman to do this. But with her in the band we had a feminine power and I wished she'd stayed."

At 54, and even without make-up, it is still possible to see what it was that once made Nicks one of the most desirable women on the planet when she twisted and twirled her mystical way through "Rhiannon" in her trademark black lace and chiffon. Today, however, she's damaged her hip, and mounts the studio steps gingerly.

"You become more brittle as you get old. But it's all a state of mind— I'm trying to have a young attitude. There's still nobody can dance like me," she says defiantly.

Several of her nine songs on *Say You Will* are equally venerable. In 2001, when she was about to go on tour with her last solo album, she handed over a collection of 17 demos to Buckingham, Fleetwood and John McVie. "I went back through my vaults of tunes and picked all the ones I really liked but which for one reason or another had never seen the light of day" she recounts.

Her colleagues picked five of them for the new album, including "Goodbye Baby" and "Smile At You", written in 1975-76 and which "could easily have ended up on *Rumours*", according to Nicks.

While she was away on tour, the "power trio" of Fleetwood, John McVie and Buckingham rented a house in Bel Air, installed Buckingham's home studio and worked on the songs. "When I came back off tour I was happy with what they'd done. But I listened and I said, 'This isn't going to be good unless we have some new material.'"

In December 2001 she went back home for Christmas to the house she has kept in Phoenix for more than 20 years. A month later, she returned to LA with four new songs. "I was totally nervous," she recalls. "I knew *they* wouldn't like the songs. Your self-esteem plummets and you feel you're the worst songwriter in the world. But I played them and they flipped out." One of them, "Illume", was inspired by 9/11, after Nicks had flown into New York the night before and found herself stranded in the stricken city.

"Lindsey had tears in his eyes," she recalls. "He put his hand on my knee and he said, 'How do you do this?'"

In the absence of Christine McVie's sisterly support, Nicks recruited bosom friend Sheryl Crow to guest on two of the new songs, "Silver Girl" and the title track.

"I penned 'Silver Girl' about Sheryl," she says. "It's an ode to a lady rock star who's always on the road and has a very hard time having relationships and settling down. So it's also totally about me."

Although she admits she couldn't give up the lifestyle the band has afforded her, Nicks can't conceal a certain bitterness based on her conviction that being in Fleetwood Mac has forced her to make huge sacrifices in other areas of her life.

"Being a female rock star is great and it's fabulous and you make lots of money. But it makes it very hard to do anything else. As a woman you give up part of yourself to be in a band," she laments. It's not so much self-pity. Simply a statement of fact. "Every relationship I've ever had, great or small, and whether I was going out with a rock star or a lawyer, has been destroyed by this business."

Yet, in many ways, *Say You Will* is primarily Lindsey Buckingham's album. "The focus was led completely by Lindsey," Fleetwood confirms. "Even on Stevie's songs, because she was out on tour, she handed the reins to Lindsey, which was a very trusting thing. None of this would have happened without him."

Most of Buckingham's nine compositions were originally destined for a solo album he began recording in the mid-'90s. "Then we met at Christine's house six years ago and everybody intervened and said to me, 'You've got to stop your solo album and help get the band together and do this tour.'"

Having been "guilted", as he puts it, into the 1997 reunion, his intention was to return to his solo record. "But Mick was playing on my solo stuff. John was playing bass on it. Even Christine was on it on a limited basis. So to all intents and purposes it was Fleetwood Mac doing a Lindsey Buckingham album. Nobody said, 'We've got to make this a Fleetwood Mac LP.' It just grew into that. In the end, all we had to do with my material was for Stevie to add her vocals and it was a Fleetwood Mac record."

Fleetwood confirms that, when he began recording with Buckingham again, it was not his agenda to get the band back together. "I thought I was going to spend three weeks doing overdubs on Lindsey's album. My whole thing is Fleetwood Mac forever. But I prefaced my renewed relationship with Lindsey by saying, 'You know I want Fleetwood Mac back together. But I don't want you thinking that's why I'm here.' But it went so well that it was Lindsey who said maybe we could turn this into a Fleetwood Mac record."

Even without Christine McVie's songwriting, between them Buckingham and Nicks had so many songs that, at one point, *Say You Will* was going to be a double album. "I thought it would be an intriguing thing for a band to return with something that had such ambition. We even got into sequencing it as a double," Buckingham says.

"Eventually we pulled back on that for issues of pricing and so on. But we kept the core and from my point of view it's the best work we've ever done in terms of the execution and sophistication. Which I guess is appropriate for a bunch of people who are all in their fifties now."

The 1997 tour and accompanying live album, *The Dance,* were "as good a job as we could do in going out and restating our body of work", he says. "But for me, this is the beginning of a whole other thing because it's new songs."

With Nicks out on her solo tour, Buckingham particularly enjoyed working in an all-male environment. "There was a lot of bonding between the three of us and it was a good place to start building a reconfigured dynamic between us. It was very difficult for me for years to have to work with Stevie when I didn't want to be around her. And it was always hard for John to rise to his higher self around Christine. There was never a sense that we were in any way crippled without Chris because we've made a record that's at least as potent."

Nicks, meanwhile, seems genuinely pleased that Buckingham's restless spirit appears finally to have found musical and personal satisfaction.

"Hopefully this record will give him back a sense of purpose and delight. He's in a way better space now and it's wonderful for me to see that. I care about him and his life and what he does and if he's happy. I so want him to be OK.

"This record is his baby and I really think he's gone and done that great thing he always wanted to do."

WHEN MICK FLEETWOOD RANG Lindsey Buckingham on New Year's Eve, 1974, and invited him to join Fleetwood Mac, the move seemed born of desperation.

Recently relocated to LA, the band's star had waned since the glory days of Peter Green, and when guitarist, singer and composer Bob Welch had abruptly left what was the group's ninth line-up in eight years, the future looked bleak indeed—particularly as *Heroes Are Hard To Find,* the band's final album with Welch, had barely sold enough copies "to pay Warner Brothers' electric light bill", as Fleetwood puts it.

Across town, prospects for the Buckingham-Nicks duo looked equally unpromising. Born into a wealthy San Francisco family in October 1947, Lindsey Buckingham fell early under the influence of Elvis Presley's guitarist Scotty Moore and folk groups such as The Kingston Trio and Peter, Paul And Mary. He taught himself guitar (he still doesn't read music) and by 1968 found himself playing bass in a local Bay Area band called Fritz.

Buckingham in turn recommended to them a young singer called Stevie Nicks. Although she had grown up in Phoenix, Arizona, Nicks (born in May 1948) had first met Buckingham when she transferred to high school in San Francisco in 1966. Their 'dream team' introduction appeared to make their subsequent relationship inevitable. Buckingham had been playing "California Dreaming" at a party and Nicks simply started singing with him. Two years later, when Fritz needed a singer, she was the first person he called.

Although they opened for Jimi Hendrix and Janis Joplin, a record deal failed to materialise, and it eventually became obvious they were going nowhere fast. By 1971, Fritz had split, and Buckingham and Nicks—by now lovers as well as musical soul-mates—moved to LA. A record deal with Polydor resulted in the 1973 album *Buckingham Nicks*. But with no real marketing or promotion, it died a death. Nicks was reduced to waitressing at Clementine's, a Beverly Hills singles bar, for $1.50 an hour, while Buckingham did a few sessions and lived on her money.

"I believed that Lindsey shouldn't have to work, that he should just lay on the floor and practise his guitar and become more brilliant every day," Nicks explains. "And as I watched him become more brilliant every day, I felt very gratified. I was totally devoted to making it happen for him. And when you really feel that way about somebody, it's very easy to take your own personality and quiet it way down."

But by late 1974, Nicks was "within weeks" of returning to her parents' home in Phoenix, and contemplating a return to college.

"If we hadn't joined Fleetwood Mac would Lindsey and I have carried on and made it?" she asks today. "I was really tired of having no money and being a waitress. It's very possible that I would have gone back to school and Lindsey would have gone back to San Francisco."

Mick Fleetwood, meanwhile, was searching for a new guitarist to replace the departed Welch, when he ran across Buckingham Nicks at Sound City Studios. He was impressed by the song "Frozen Love" from their Polydor album. But Fleetwood Mac already had a female singer in Christine McVie, so his initial invitation was merely to the guitarist.

"He was standing there grooving to this searing guitar solo and he needed a guitar player. That was as far as his thinking went. I had to explain we came as a duo. Stupid me, eh?" Buckingham jokes today.

Fleetwood was so convinced that Buckingham was his man that he swiftly agreed to take them both—although he promised Christine McVie that she had a veto if she disliked Nicks.

Initially, the guitarist had reservations about submerging his musical personality in an already established band—particularly as he had not been a fan of the Bob Welch-era Fleetwood Mac. Nicks swiftly reassured him.

"I said, 'We can always quit. They're going to pay us $200 each a week, so we can save some money and leave in six months with a little nest egg if it doesn't work,'" she recalls today.

The 'audition' took place over dinner in a Mexican restaurant in LA. Christine McVie immediately took to the new girl, declaring Nicks to be "a bright, very humorous, very direct, tough little thing." The 10th, and most enduring, of Fleetwood Mac's multiple line-ups was in place. Yet it was not necessarily the most stable.

WHAT BUCKINGHAM AND NICKS had failed to reveal to their new colleagues was that, although they came as a team, their relationship was already falling apart at the seams. "Lindsey and I were in total chaos a year before we met Fleetwood Mac," Nicks tells *Uncut* almost 30 years on. "I had already moved out of our apartment a couple of times and then had to move back in because I couldn't afford it. Our relationship was already in dire straits. But if we'd broken up within the first six months of Fleetwood Mac there would have been no record and we would have been in big trouble, so when we joined the band we took the decision to hang in there."

Within three weeks of the Mexican restaurant meeting, Fleetwood Mac were in Sound City Studios in LA. The Buckingham-Nicks teaming brought a pile of songs with them and the difference they made to the sound was immediately evident.

Best of all was Nicks' "Rhiannon", a dreamy, bewitching song with an insistent guitar motif from Buckingham that swiftly came to define the new Fleetwood Mac. Not far behind were Nicks' "Crystal" and "Landslide", rescued and reworked from the duo's Polydor album. Buckingham contributed "Monday Morning" and "I'm So Afraid", while they collaborated on "World Turning".

Christine McVie also appeared inspired by the arrival of the newcomers, and contributed two of her most enduring compositions in "Say You Love Me" and "Over My Head", as well as "Warm Ways" and "Sugar Daddy".

The album was finished inside three months—astonishingly fast given the years they would spend labouring over future releases. Upon completion, the band repaired to Hawaii for a vacation.

When *Fleetwood Mac* was released in July 1975, its success was initially modest. But the band toured relentlessly. "There were no limousines and Christine slept on top of the amps in the back of the truck," Nicks recalls. "We just played everywhere and we sold that record. We kicked that album in the ass."

In September 1976, 15 months after its release, the album topped the US charts, having also produced three hit singles in "Over My Head," "Rhiannon" and "Say You Love Me".

By then, Fleetwood Mac had already been back at work for six months, recording the follow-up at the Record Plant in Sausalito, a half-hour drive over the Golden Gate Bridge from downtown San Francisco.

But during the relentless touring of the previous year, the cracks in the Buckingham-Nicks relationship had grown to a volcanic fissure, and the McVies were also in the middle of divorce proceedings.

The ever-affable and gregarious Fleetwood attempted to hold the ring, adding the roles of guidance counsellor and social worker to that of band leader. "Everybody was pretty weirded out," Christine McVie told Cameron Crowe in a landmark 1977 *Rolling Stone* cover story. "But somehow Mick was there, the figurehead—'We must carry on, let's be mature about this, sort it out.'"

It was a typically brave attitude, for the drummer had problems of his own, with his marriage to Jenny Boyd disintegrating.

"By the time we got to *Rumours,* the emotional rollercoaster was in full motion and we were all in a ditch. Everybody knew everything about everybody and I was definitely piggy-in-the-middle," Fleetwood recalls. "But my best friend was also having an affair with my wife and it was all weird and twisted. It was a total mess and that's how we made the album."

Fleetwood concedes that he had just one consolation denied to the other couples. "At least I was spared the in-house, up-front situation. I didn't have to actually work with my ex-spouse."

While it was left to Fleetwood to console a very unhappy John McVie, the two women, who might so easily have been rivals, developed a mutual support society.

"We're totally different, at complete opposite ends of the personality spectrum," Christine McVie told me in Detroit during the 1997 reunion tour. "The one thing we had in common, which bound us together, was a sense of humour through all the pain."

Later on, neither were short of female company as hairdressers, wardrobe mistresses and make-up artists were added to the extravagant Fleetwood Mac touring circus. But initially they were two women alone in a man's world.

"We didn't have anybody else," Nicks says. "We had to end up being close because otherwise it was just hang out with the guys all the time. And because there was this chaos going on with me and Lindsey, the band gave me a friend in this woman and I could hang out with Christine."

WHEN THEY HAD FIRST ARRIVED in San Francisco at the beginning of the year-long process that was the recording of *Rumours,* the Record Plant provided a house for the band's living accommodation. Nicks and Christine McVie spent only one night under the same roof as the band's male members. "That house was like the riot house," Nicks tells *Uncut.* "There were girls everywhere and everybody was completely drunk the whole time. Me and Chris decided we couldn't be there. The next day we moved out and got two matching apartments next to each other."

Some nights after they had left the studio, a stoned John McVie would come looking for Christine. "He'd be walking up and down the corridor, very upset, screaming her name, and she'd be hiding in my room," Nicks recalls. The inside sleeve of *Rumours* symbolically shows Stevie and Christine embracing while the fatherly Fleetwood looks on.

Christine Perfect and John McVie first met at a Fleetwood Mac gig one night in early 1968. At the time, she admits she was more interested in Peter Green. "But John asked me if I wanted a drink and we sat down and had a few laughs before they went on stage. Then after the concert he came over and said, 'Shall I take you out to dinner some time?' I went, 'Whoa, I thought you were engaged or something?' He said, 'Nah, it's all over.' I thought he was devastatingly attractive but it never occurred to me to look at him."

They went out for a short time, before John disappeared off on Fleetwood Mac's first US tour. "By this time I was really crazy about him," Christine recalls. "But I didn't really know what was happening with him."

She, in turn, went off to Germany with Birmingham blues band Chicken Shack, for whom she was keyboardist/vocalist, and had a fling with "a crazy German DJ" who asked her to marry him. She turned him down and instead wrote John a long letter explaining her feelings for him.

When Fleetwood Mac returned from America, McVie proposed. They were married 10 days later and Christine announced in *Melody Maker* that she was retiring to become a housewife. She soon tired of washing the dishes and, a few months later, in August 1970, she took the fateful decision to join her old man in Fleetwood Mac following Peter Green's departure.

"We were very happy for three years and then the strain of me being in the same band started to take its toll," she says. "When you're in the same band as somebody, you're seeing them 24 hours a day and you start to see an awful lot of the bad side. There's a lot of drinking and John is not the most pleasant of people when he's drunk. Very belligerent. I was seeing more Hyde than Jekyll."

Christine had already embarked on an affair with the band's sound engineer, Martin Birch, in 1973. At the same time, the band's guitarist, Bob Weston, was having an affair with Fleetwood's wife Jenny. This complex web of relationships almost split the band, before Weston was sacked and the McVies agreed to give it another chance. But this merely delayed the inevitable, and they broke up for good in the middle of the band's 1975 US tour.

"I was aware of it being irresponsible," Christine admitted to Cameron Crowe two years later. "But I had to do it for my sanity. It was either that or me ending up in a lunatic asylum. I still worry for him, more than I would ever dare tell him. I still have a lot of love for John. Let's face it, as far as I'm concerned, it was him that stopped me loving him.

"He constantly tested what limits of endurance I would go to. He just went one step too far. If he knew that I cared and worried so much about him, I think he'd play on it."

John McVie later wondered if their problems might not have happened if his wife hadn't joined the band. But by the time they went into the studio to record *Rumours,* they weren't speaking to each other.

"We literally didn't talk, other than to say, 'What key is this song in?'" Christine recalled. "We were as cold as ice to each other because John found it easier that way."

A devastated John McVie began drinking and drugging more and more heavily.

"There's no doubt about the fact that he hasn't really been a happy man since I left him," Christine said in 1977. "Sure, I could make him happy tomorrow and say, 'Yeah, John, I'll come back to you.' Then I would be miserable. I'm not that unselfish."

EVEN 20 YEARS LATER, McVIE still appeared to be carrying a torch for her. One night during the 1997 tour we all got drunk together in the hotel bar after a gig and he decided to address the entire room on the subject.

"She's a lovely, lovely lady, my ex-wife, even though she told me to fuck off," he bellowed at bemused fellow guests before he struggled to his feet and knocked over an entire table of drinks.

When sober, he is more philosophical. "You've got the pressure of being on the road and living with each other and seeing each other at their worst," he told me the morning after the night before. "Chris saw me at my worst one time too many. I drink too much and when I've drunk too much, a personality comes out. It's not very pleasant to be around. And bless her heart, Chris said, 'I don't want to be around this person.' It was awful. You're told by someone you adore and love that they don't want you in their life any more."

To make matters worse for McVie, his wife had taken up with the band's lighting director, Curry Grant, whose presence around the band caused intense friction. "Wherever John was, he couldn't be," recalls Christine. "There were some very delicate moments."

John, meanwhile, took what comfort he could from the groupies back at the band house provided by the Record Plant, and described by Fleetwood as "like a bordello with blacked-out rooms, thick shag carpets, deprivation tanks and a very liberal sprinkling of assorted drugs."

Lindsey Buckingham and Stevie Nicks were at least talking—or, rather, ranting and raving at each other. At one point, the highly-strung Buckingham thought of quitting.

"In the middle of it all, one day Lindsey said, 'I don't know whether I can handle this.' He was not a happy camper," recalls Mick Fleetwood. "I gave him a pep talk, saying, 'This whole thing is a compromise. That's what a band is about. But if it's an unhealthy one for you, then you don't have to be here.' From then on he was really focused on making the record."

For Nicks, there were no second thoughts. "Really, each one of us was too proud and way too stubborn to walk away from it," she recalls. "I wasn't going to leave. Lindsey wasn't going to leave. What would we have done—sat around in LA and tried to start new bands? It was just 'grit your teeth and bear it.'"

There were also problems between Buckingham and John McVie, the two jilted partners who found no comfort in each other's company, as their womenfolk had done.

"I came in as the new kid on the block but I was also the kid with the ideas and so John and I used to butt heads quite a bit," Buckingham recalls. "It took me a long time to appreciate his approach."

On one occasion, McVie hurled a glass of vodka in the guitarist's face. "About the only people in the band who haven't had an affair are me and Lindsey," he later grimly joked.

Instead of quitting, Nicks, Buckingham and Christine McVie began writing songs to each other, like pages from their respective diaries. You had to feel rather sorry for John. As Mick Fleetwood observes, "They were all talking to each other in songs and, because he doesn't sing, he couldn't talk back."

For Nicks, Buckingham wrote the album's opener, "Second Hand News" (*"One thing I think you should know/I ain't gonna miss you when you go"*). Nicks responded immediately with "Dreams" (*"Now here you go again, you say you want your freedom"*).

Then Buckingham takes up the conversation again. First in "Never Going Back Again" (*"Been down one time, been down two times, I'm never going back again"*). Then even more forcefully in "Go Your Own Way" (*"Loving you isn't the right thing to do"*), before Nicks responds once more with "I Don't Want To Know" (*"I don't want to stand between you and love, honey, I just want you to feel fine"*).

For John McVie, Christine penned "Don't Stop" a warm-hearted but still painful message to him that he would one day begin to feel better. However, he must have been less than thrilled to play bass on "You Make Loving Fun", written by his estranged wife for the new man in her life, Curry Grant. She wrote "Oh Daddy" for Mick Fleetwood, separated from Jenny Boyd, the mother of his two children. "The Chain", credited to the entire band, was apparently about all of them and the tangled web they had woven.

The album closes prophetically with Nicks' cocaine anthem, "Gold Dust Woman". "At that time, everybody around me was doing it," she says. "Lindsey and I wonder if we hadn't moved to LA would we ever have got into drugs? Drug-taking was methodical when we got to LA. It was, 'Here, try this.' Everybody was so willing to give you stuff and tell you you'd like it. 'Gold Dust Woman' was about how we all love the ritual of it, the little bottle, the diamond-studded spoons, the fabulous velvet bags. For me, it fitted right into the incense and candles and that stuff. And I really imagined that it could overtake everything, never thinking in a million years that it would overtake me."

According to Buckingham, the drugs went with the territory. "It was anything goes and if you were making records you had to function on a certain level and we all did our share. It was music through chemistry."

And although the drugs may have slowed down the process of recording, they played their part in heightening the band's creativity.

"We weren't just singing to each other but screaming and everything was enlarged by the intake of illegal substances," Christine McVie admitted to me over a bottle of red wine in her hotel suite one night during the 1997 reunion tour.

Nicks—although she is today militantly anti-drugs and threatens to shop anyone around the band whom she catches—concedes the point: "We were in the worst shape. But it was helping us make the best music."

Throughout the *Rumours* sessions, a black velvet bag of cocaine held pride of place under the mixing desk. Every so often, one or other member of the band would demand another hit. One day, engineer Ken Caillat substituted a dummy bag full of talcum powder. When it was next called for, he tipped the bag upside down and emptied the contents all over the floor. McVie and Fleetwood were about to kill him when the laughter of producer Richard Dashut, seated alongside Caillat, made them realise they'd been hoaxed.

But such lighter moments were few and far between. It took a year to make the album—"the most intense year of my life", Lindsey Buckingham would later claim. "Trauma," said Christine McVie. "Trau-ma."

Yet even when they thought they'd finished, the drama wasn't over. Having spent a year making the album, the master tapes had been dragged across the machine heads a thousand times. In those pre-digital days, this had led to a marked degradation of the sound quality, particularly at the upper end of the register, and the band had to go back into the studio in LA to redub.

Initially, the group appeared oblivious to the power of what they had gone and done. Buckingham wasn't convinced that they had a hit on their hands at all.

"I was worried that side two had no continuity," he says. "I thought we'd done the best we could but the album was trailing off and lacked that extra song we needed. I really wasn't aware of the compelling drama it had and I remember certain people being very negative about *Rumours*. We're all so insecure and I really didn't know."

Christine McVie, at least in part, concurred in 1997 when she told this writer: "It was John who suggested the title *Rumours* because we were all writing journals and diaries about each other," she says. "But we didn't quite realise that until all the songs were strung together. Then we knew we had something pretty powerful, to a point that transcended everybody's misery and depression. I think we knew that if we'd all been getting on like a house on fire, the songs wouldn't have been nearly as good."

INDEED. HAS melodic MOR soft-rock ever surged with such emotional discharge and human electricity? Has such a highly polished veneer ever been so dramatically juxtaposed with such a cauldron of simmering tensions and seething passions? Buckingham recalls them all sitting in the same booth, harmonising on each other's songs and looking into each other's eyes with emotions raging uncontrollably.

"You can look at *Rumours* and say, 'Well, the album is bright and its clean and it's sunny,'" Buckingham says. "But everything underneath is so dark and murky. What was going on between us created a resonance that goes beyond the music itself. You had these dialogues shooting back and forth about what was going down between us and we were chronicling every nuance of it. We had to play the hand out and people found it riveting. It wasn't a press creation. It was all true and we couldn't suppress it. The built-in drama cannot be underplayed as a springboard to that album's success."

Nicks puts it even more succinctly. "If you took out all the bad stuff in the band, the songs wouldn't have happened. There simply wouldn't have been a *Rumours* if everything had been fabulous."

But if it seems miraculous that they managed to stay intact and functioning during the recording of the album, once *Rumours* started flying, the group found itself bound together by a force far stronger than any emotional dysfunction. Commerce.

"The band was at the pinnacle of its career and we had a responsibility not to break that up for anything as trivial as a divorce," as Christine was later to joke.

Released in February 1977, *Rumours* topped the US album charts for six months. It was punk's 'year zero'. But that didn't prevent *Rumours* topping the charts in Britain, where it remained in the Top 100 for the next eight years. The record sold 10 million in its first year and at its height in America was going platinum (one million sales) every 30 days.

Rumours also produced four US Top 10 singles in "Dreams", "You Make Loving Fun", "Go Your Own Way" and "Don't Stop", and the album ultimately went on to sell 25 million copies.

Upon its release, Fleetwood Mac embarked on an eight-month US tour that became a debauched, cocaine-and-champagne-fuelled odyssey across the continent, which cemented the band's legendary reputation for excess. And the heady cocktail of success, drugs and more money than they knew how to spend left little space for reflection or time to slow down.

Christine McVie bought Anthony Newley's old mansion in Coldwater Canyon and promptly installed her own English pub and a sculpture studio (in her youth she had briefly attended Birmingham Art College). Outside were parked a pair of matching Mercedes-Benz cars with license plates named after her pair of lhasa apsos. She also dumped lighting director Curry Grant for Beach Boy Dennis Wilson, who she claimed "awakened things in me I'd been scared to experience and made me feel the extremes of every emotion."

Fleetwood bought a cliff-top house in Malibu and a fleet of vintage sports cars. Buckingham—who seemed the least impressed by the trappings of celebrity and money—bought a fine LA home which he shared with *Rumours* producer Richard Dashut, while John McVie divided his time between a 41-foot schooner moored at Marina del Rey and a home in Beverly Hills.

Nicks purchased a large, mock-Tudor home above Sunset Boulevard, referred to as "Fantasy Land", and a home in Phoenix, which is still her base. None of the band was reticent about flashing their cash. But she bought into the rich-and-famous lifestyle more enthusiastically than anyone, having been taught to spend money, she claims, during her affair with the notoriously ostentatious Don Henley.

"He was responsible and I blame him every day. The Eagles had it down," she tells *Uncut*. "They had the Lear jets and the presidential suites long before we did and so I learnt from the best. And once you learn to live like that, there's no going back. It's like, 'Get me a Lear jet. I need to go to LA. I don't care if it costs $15,000. I need to go now.'"

Nicks also embarked on a relationship with Mick Fleetwood that further jeopardised the band's already fragile stability. "Never in a million years could you have told me that would happen. That was the biggest surprise. But Mick is definitely one of my great, great loves," she was still claiming years later. "But that really wasn't good for anybody. Everybody was angry, because Mick was married to a wonderful girl and had two wonderful children. I was horrified. I loved these people. I loved his family. So it couldn't possibly work out. And it didn't. It just couldn't."

In an even more bizarre relationship, on January 29, 1983, Nicks married Kim Anderson, the widower of a school friend, Robyn (the subject of her song "Gypsy"), who suffered from leukaemia, and who died three days after giving birth by Caesarean section to a baby boy called Matthew. Within five months, Nicks had become stepmother to the child by marrying the father.

The rest of the band were appalled, and Christine McVie admits she even refused to buy the couple a wedding present. Their misgivings were well-directed. Within eight months the couple were divorced.

Touring for Fleetwood Mac by now meant private jets and all manner of preposterous demands. Hotels would be told to paint rooms pink and install grand pianos. White, like the one on the cover of *Imagine,* of course. If they couldn't be manoeuvred through the door, they had to be winched through the windows.

SOMEWHERE IN THE MIDST of the madness, the group managed to record further albums. Following *Rumours* was never going to be easy and the double album *Tusk*, released in November 1979, met with distinctly mixed reactions. Again it took over a year to record and cost a million dollars—an unprecedented amount of money at the time. The album boldly mixed radio-friendly pop songs from Nicks and Christine McVie with more experimental and non-commercial pieces from

Buckingham, who dominated the sessions and was adamant the band should show more ambition than merely recording 'Rumours Part II'.

"Coming off an album as successful as that, we were being asked to get on this treadmill of clichéd thought and hash out the same thing again," recalls Buckingham. "Punk and new wave had kicked in during the meantime and, although I wasn't directly influenced by that music, it gave me a kick in the pants in terms of having the courage to try to shake things up a little bit. I wanted something that had a little more depth."

Many of the 20 tracks on the album were prepared by Buckingham, working alone at home. "That got me to more esoteric places than I could go in a group situation. Then I'd take the songs back to the studio, and having the band build on it was the basic premise for much of *Tusk*," he recalls.

The title track employed a 112-piece marching band. And the excess was equally gargantuan on a non-musical level. "Recording *Tusk* was quite absurd," Christine McVie later admitted. "The studio contract rider for refreshments was like a telephone directory. Exotic food delivered to the studio, crates of champagne. And it had to be the best, with no thought of what it cost. Stupid. Really stupid. Somebody once said that with the money we spent on champagne on one night, they could have made an entire album. And it's probably true."

Tusk failed to replicate the numbers *Rumours* had done and although it rose to No 2 in Britain, it only made No 18 in the far more lucrative US market. Ultimately, it went on to sell eight million copies. Impressive for a double album, but in comparison to 25 million, a relative failure.

Other band members were not slow to point the finger at Buckingham. "The rest of the band had a cynical view towards the way *Tusk* was made and the reasons why I thought it was important to move into new territory," the guitarist recalls. "It wasn't just negativity. There was open hostility. Then I got a certain amount of flak because it didn't sell as many as *Rumours*. Mick would say to me, 'Well, you went too far, you blew it.' That hurt. And so it's gratifying now to hear Mick tell anyone who asks that it's his favourite Fleetwood Mac album."

Indeed, the drummer had expressed this very opinion to me just an hour earlier, although he also added that he still feels it would have been better "condensed" into a single disc.

The initially disappointing sales of *Tusk* were boosted by a mammoth 113-date world tour, on which every date was recorded for a live album. Meant to be a 'cheap' option after the million dollars blown on *Tusk*, with typical excess, *Live,* released in November 1980, was eventually assembled from taping over 400 live shows.

When a battle-weary Fleetwood Mac ended the *Tusk* tour at the Hollywood Bowl in late 1980, they were physically and mentally drained and barely able to stand the sight of each other.

"I used to go on stage and drink a bottle of Dom Perignon, and drink one offstage afterwards," Christine McVie later recalled. "It's not the kind of party I'd like to go to now. There was a lot of booze being drunk and there was blood floating around in the alcohol, which doesn't make for a stable environment."

The band was put on hold as members recharged their depleted batteries. Nicks, Buckingham and Fleetwood all made solo albums. But when only the former was successful, accountants and record company executives were soon agitating for another Fleetwood Mac album, and the band reconvened to make *Mirage*. Released in 1982, it was an unsatisfactory album that lacked either the raw emotion of *Rumours* or the runaway ambition which Buckingham had injected into *Tusk*. It sounded like a record made for the sole and cynical purpose of sustaining the Fleetwood Mac brand.

"The most disappointing thing to me after *Tusk* was the politics in the band," Buckingham admits today. "They said, 'We're not going to do that again.' I felt dead in the water from that. On *Mirage*, I was treading water, saying, 'Okay, whatever,' and taking a passive role. For me, none of the albums after *Tusk* quite had it. I think we lost something after that."

Christine McVie has no doubt what it was they had mislaid. "*Mirage* was an attempt to get back into the flow that *Rumours* had. But we missed a vital ingredient. That was the passion," she confesses bluntly.

IT WOULD BE FIVE MORE years before the band would release another album—and, being Fleetwood Mac, there was plenty more trauma in the intervening years. For Fleetwood, they were the beginning of the 'lost' years, which stretched on into the '90s.

"I wasn't quite Keith Moon but I was working hard on getting there," he says today. Along the way he went bankrupt and was relieved of his duties as band manager. Much of his money went up his nose on drugs, although he insists even more was lost on property deals that went wrong.

"It was a wild trip that didn't stop for nine years," he recalls. "I tried very hard to leave the planet and I nearly did. I don't want to romanticise something that's extremely dangerous. It was fun, but it was a bloody nightmare and I would never do it again. It became boring and sordid."

But the real casualty was the far more fragile figure of Nicks, whose cocaine addiction was escalating desperately out of control. Her use had begun as much as a way of coping as a means of getting high. "I'd never felt so tired in my life" she recalls. "When I joined the band, the rock 'n' roll life was a shock to my system. It's so intense and so heavy and being like Fleetwood Mac was like being in the Army. I was doing a lot of drugs just to get me through to the next thing. I don't remember how much we did. But we spent an awful lot of money on it."

Although the coke worked for a while, there was a high price to pay. "We never stopped, never took vacations. And with coke you can stay up way too late. You don't sleep for three days," she recalls today. "But then it backfired. That's what I tell people. And the payback is a bitch. Nobody should go through what I went through. It's not even that good. There was a little bit of fun. But it wasn't fun enough to destroy your life. It creeps me out to talk about it even now."

By 1986, she had hit rock bottom and checked into the Betty Ford Clinic, where Nicks shared a spartan cubicle with an elderly alcoholic woman. Tammy Wynette was a fellow patient.

"I knew I was going to die and I didn't want to die. So I was on my way," she tells *Uncut*. "I did my 28 days and I came out and I was brilliant. I was as strong as an ox and I felt great. I could feel myself starting to glow again and I was totally excited about my life. When I walked through those doors at Betty Ford and they searched me and took away all my stuff, it was like, 'OK I'm never doing THAT again because I'm never coming back to a place like this.'"

She was true to her word. "I haven't even seen cocaine since 1986. Nobody would ever take it out in front of me because they know I would call the police," she says. Yet although she didn't know it at the time, there was worse to come. Nobody around her believed she could stay clean and her friends collectively intervened to persuade her to visit a psychiatrist. Fatefully—and almost fatally—he prescribed a tranquilliser called Klonopin.

Nicks is still angry to this day about what happened. "I agreed to see this psychiatrist to make everybody happy," she says. "But if I had made a wrong turning and got lost and not arrived at that psychiatrist's office that day, the destiny of my life would have been so changed."

Her account of the addiction which ensued is salutary and frightening. "He gave me two little blue pills. One at morning and one at night. Within a couple of months that turned into four little blue pills. Then it became 15 blue pills. He kept increasing my dose. I was in there every two weeks for an hour and he watched me grow heavier and the light went out in my eyes. If I started to run out, I would start to shake so hard people would stare at me. I thought I had Parkinson's disease. I was sick and high and miserable and overweight. I knew I was going to die."

Finally, one day in the early '90s, she realised she could not go on. "I called up my manager and said come and get me and take me to a hospital because I'm not going to be alive in two weeks."

She spent 47 days in the Daniel Freeman hospital in Marina del Rey and kicking a prescription tranquilliser proved far more unpleasant than kicking her cocaine habit. "My hair turned grey. My skin peeled off. I couldn't sleep. I had a terrible headache. My body felt like it was burning," she recalls. She cannot help an involuntary shudder as she tells the story.

Nicks survived. But she is understandably bitter. "These psychiatrists and the medical community are the worst drug dealers in the world," she says. "These drugs will make you fat, ruin your life, make you miserable and destroy anything you want to do. And nobody tells you that."

The blow that Klonopin dealt to Fleetwood Mac was also almost fatal. By the time the band reconvened to record 1987s *Tango In The Night*,

Nicks had already been addicted to the tranquilliser for a year and was in no fit state to make a record.

With Fleetwood's drug abuse also rendering him largely *hors de combat*, it was left to Lindsey Buckingham to pull the album together. "We had to rise to the occasion," he recalls today. "It was a very difficult record to make. Half the time Mick was falling asleep. We spent a year on the record but we only saw Stevie for a few weeks. I had to pull performances out of words and lines and make parts that sounded like her that weren't her."

Buckingham concedes that Nicks was "the most challenging to deal with." But he excludes nobody from his strictures. "Everyone was at their worst, including myself. We'd made the progression from what could be seen as an acceptable or excusable amount of drug use to a situation where we had all hit the wall. I think of it as our darkest period."

With Nicks managing just two songs and Christine McVie three, Buckingham valiantly contributed six compositions and was required, with some reluctance, to give up songs such as "Big Love," "Caroline" and "Family Man", all of which had already been completed for his projected third solo album. If he had not done so, he recognised there simply wouldn't have been an album.

"The rest of us were totally devoid of any focus," Fleetwood admits.

Thanks to Buckingham's gargantuan efforts, the result was a more than acceptable return to form, the greatest adversity yet again bringing the best out of Fleetwood Mac. Yet there's no doubt that Buckingham was deeply distressed by the whole experience, and particularly disturbed by the condition of his former girlfriend.

"The way people were conducting their lives made it difficult to get serious work done. Mick was pretty nuts then. We all were. In terms of substance abuse, that was the worst it got," he recalls. "And Stevie was the worst she's ever been. I didn't recognise her. She wasn't the person I had once known."

All of this directly contributed to the showdown in August 1987 when Buckingham walked out of the band, seemingly for good. "When I was done with the record, I said, 'Oh my God. That was the worst recording experience of my life.' And compared to making an album, in my experience, going on the road will multiply the craziness by times five. I just wasn't up for that. I needed to pull out of the machine and try to maintain a level of integrity for the work that wasn't about the scale or the sales."

TO REPLACE BUCKINGHAM, the band recruited not one but two guitarists in Rick Vito and Billy Burnette. The new six-piece line-up recorded 1990's forgettable *Behind The Mask* before Nicks and McVie also left. Doggedly, the rhythm section of Fleetwood and McVie—who retain legal ownership of the band name—vowed to soldier on. The resulting album, 1995s' *Time*—with Bekka Bramlett, daughter of Delaney and Bonnie, and former Traffic man Dave Mason added to the line-up—was even less satisfying.

Yet the flame of the *Rumours* line-up refused to die. After Bill Clinton had adopted "Don't Stop" as his presidential campaign song in 1992, Buckingham, Nicks and Christine McVie all rejoined Fleetwood and John McVie to perform at the new President's inaugural ball. Five years later, on the 20th anniversary of *Rumours*, came a reunion tour and *The Dance*, a live album culled from an MTV special.

Although Christine McVie didn't enjoy the touring rigmarole and announced that she had come to the end of the road, the rest of the band found that time had proved a great healer.

"Just the fact that we'd survived gave us something in common," Buckingham says.

"Looking back, it's like listening to war stories," Mick Fleetwood jokes. "But you have to remember there were people yelling in pain with their legs shot away. There's blood and guts and disagreements still to this day. But that's what makes it mean a shit."

This article is based on original interviews by the author with Mick Fleetwood, Lindsey Buckingham and Stevie Nicks in LA in February 2003 and also draws on original interviews with Fleetwood, Nicks, Buckingham, John McVie and Christine McVie conducted in Detroit and Indianapolis in October 1997. Previously published sources consulted include Fleetwood Mac—The First Thirty Years *by Bob Brunning,* My 25 Years In Fleetwood Mac *by Mick Fleetwood and a variety of magazine and newspaper interviews and articles, dating from 1977 to the present day.*

RETURN OF THE NATIVE

Mark Ellen | July 2004 | *The Word* (UK)

The *Rumours* Five Fleetwood Mac are unusual for major rock bands in having had two "quiet ones." The distaff bookend to John McVie is his ex-wife. Christine McVie here explains in detail how she came into a dream job and why she came to spurn it.

WHAT A STRANGE LITTLE slideshow we're getting this afternoon, image after image of madness and tension and glory. Here's just a few of them—Christine McVie living at John Mayall's house in L.A. where the "Brain Damage Club" held its regular meetings; successful members were those who jumped off the third-floor balcony into the pool below without sustaining a head injury. McVie stuffed full of drugs in a tiny studio recording *Rumours* with the husband she was divorcing—along with a guitarist and singer who were divorcing each other, and a drummer who was getting divorced. McVie, with Jack Nicholson and Warren Beatty behind her, inviting the new President to step onstage from behind his bullet-proof screen at Clinton's Inaugural Ball before leading the band into *Don't Stop* (which she now reflects should have been *Little Lies*). McVie being called the night before her wedding by Peter Green, with whom she was infatuated, to be told that it wasn't too late to think again. McVie as the stabilising girlfriend through the spiralling decline of Beach Boys drummer Dennis Wilson. "My secretary called me up and said 'Dennis has drowned'," she remembers, "and I said, Ooh God, is he alright? Shock, I suppose."

ALL OF THESE STORIES have one thing in common: you can't imagine them happening to Christine McVie. She may come across as The Groovy Aunt at the family gathering, but the only real clues as to her last 40 years' employment are this unimaginably costly box-of-glass apartment on the south bank of the Thames—its gold-leafed books and rolled hand-towels suggesting hotel suite more than home—and her rock 'n' roll shoes, shiny silver and purple trainers with those little plastic toggles. She's that rare breed of musician who can enter a room without you noticing. She's not a member of the frontline, the preserve of attention-seeking singers and garrulous guitarists, nor really a member of the backline, characterised by I've-had-a-drink-me drummers. She occupied a dimly-lit middle ground, stationary, almost anonymous, just the way she liked it. And how perfectly the five members of Fleetwood Mac would blend on stage, the American starchildren (Buckingham and Nicks) riding the well-oiled chassis of the English rhythm section, the two-metre bearded loon Mick Fleetwood on drums, the cap-sporting manual labourer John McVie on bass, and this dark-eyed and dependable Brummie stoking the engine from the keyboard.

The long-running "band of gypsies" that hoovered her up in 1970 seems to have left her virtually unscathed. She pads silently across the plump carpets talking about the 16th century house she's restoring in Canterbury—"beams akimbo!"—and its 20 acres of farmland, an operation still funded by the endless thud of royalty cheques through her probably rather ornate letterbox (any variations on the theme 'how much do you earn?' are met with the same unswerving mantra: "I do very well, thank-you"). She bowed out of Fleetwood back after their BRIT Awards performance in 1997 and effectively retired from the business. She never really meant to make the new solo album she's now releasing seven years later, it's just the inevitable result of installing a Pro Tools home studio and having a neighbouring nephew who plays the guitar.

I can still see her now on the back of the first long-playing record I ever bought, *Forty Blue Fingers Freshly Packed And Ready To Serve* by Chicken Shack. There she was—tough, unsmiling, immensely cool and fanciable—alongside the leering Gollum-like countenance of Stan Webb and two other seedy-looking beatniks. As ever, the charts at the time were knee-deep in female stars—Lulu, Cilla, Dusty, Pet Clark—but in the British rock underground there were only two girls: Julie Driscoll and Christine Perfect. You wondered how she survived in this man-made world, the 24 year-old daughter of a faith-healer and college professor stuck in some rank old transit van with Chicken Shack, yet 30 years later the unsung story of this brilliant blues torch-singer was only just winding down. In fact it's just come back for an encore.

"YOU *DID* HAVE TO BE tough," she reflects. "A Transit on the M1 on the way home with five fellas after a couple of eggburgers, not too much fun I can tell you, but in a sense it was quite nice. They spoilt me. They took care of me. If you're the only girl in a band, humping your own equipment around, trying to make ends meet, you do tend to get pampered."

She first came down to London aged 15 with a schoolfriend, a text-book romantic picture of how musicians could get a break in the late '50s. They sold their parents some old yarn about staying at each others' houses, took the train out of Birmingham, arrived at the 2i's coffee bar in Soho, changed into their uniforms—little red sweaters and matching black skirts—and managed to get put on before The Shadows, playing their Everly Brothers songs on acoustic guitars. She began copying the trademarks of Freddie King's keyboard wizard Sonny Thompson and soon joined Sounds Of Blue on piano, along with the future Traffic sax player Chris Wood. Chicken Shack offered her a free transfer and, inevitably, they soon found themselves supporting the fast-rising and uniquely imaginative British blues pioneers Fleetwood Mac.

"Funny guys," she remembers fondly, "really great and funny guys. Peter Green was a cocky bugger and disarmingly charming. He was the one that really attracted me first. Jeremy Spencer was vulgar and rude but funny. Used to come onstage and do things with a . . . well, you know," she wrinkles her nose leaving me to supply the missing word 'dildo'. "He used to do impersonations of Cliff and Elvis, *Viva Las Vegas* in a gold suit. Mick Fleetwood I was terrified of, so tall and thin and imposing. He gave the impression of being quite haughty but he's just a puppy really, and I liked John [McVie]. But it was Peter I really liked in the beginning. When John and I decided to get married Peter rang me the night before and said 'Don't do it, you hardly know the guy'. I never told him I fancied him, I'm not that kind of girl! And he never said if he fancied *me*. You'd have to ask him."

For the underground, as she still calls it, there was only one way to bring your music to the people. Scarcely a single radio programme would touch you, you only appeared on TV if you had a hit, and you only got a hit by playing any fog-filled barroom where a load of heads in trenchcoats were prepared to stump up two-and-six to support you. She remembers Freddie King helping change a tyre on their old Commer van as they trundled round the club circuit, a silk bandana round his head to keep his hair looking sharp. There was a magical moment when a record would get airplay and the act would suddenly appear on *Top Of The Pops*, often without you having the faintest clue as to what they actually looked like. Such was the fate of Fleetwood Mac. "People had heard *Albatross* and just naturally imagined they were going to look like The Shadows, and then were astonished to turn on the television and find these long-haired beatnik types."

Peter Green, of course, left the group soon after, one of the saddest and most mythologised exits in living memory, a symbol of the collision between the naive and idealistic young evangelists and an industry sensing no limit to the profit margins rock music could offer. Green told me once, in agonising detail, the story of the acid trip in Germany that caused him permanent mental damage, to the extent that he used a pistol to try and persuade his accountant not to send him any more money after receiving a royalty cheque for a then-staggering £30,000. Contracted to record and tour regardless, Fleetwood Mac asked McVie to join them and they started back in New Orleans only nine days later.

The group lumbered on from pillar to post before Fleetwood was offered studio time by a producer who'd just finished recording the duo Buckingham Nicks. In a brilliant manoeuvre—part strategy, part sheer good fortune on both sides—they asked their guitarist Lindsey Buckingham to join them, who insisted his girlfriend came as part of the package. McVie still finds it hard to explain the degree of victory they achieved, *Rumours* alone selling 200,000 copies a week for months on end with its world total currently standing at some 26 million. It's partly she believes because, even pre-iPod, few people can take a whole album by one act, but they liked the diversity of three completely different songwriters and singers all framed in the comforting soundbed of the same rhythm section. When I ask her why she always kept refining the same type of song, her answer is so honest it ought to be carved on tablets of stone and extended any one of a hundred pop songwriters operating beyond their capabilities, starting with George Michael. "I can't write about racial prejudice and, you know, Ban The Bomb," she shrugs. "I can't *do* heavy messages in music. I've tried and never even recorded them. I sound like a pretentious twot. I write relationship songs. I just don't know how to write anything else."

The years that followed have merged into one huge psychedelic haze. What did it look like, I wonder, success on such a monumental scale? She narrows her eyes and peers out across the river, eventually downloading a picture of the group in the late '70s playing with Peter Frampton at some gigantic San Francisco open-air festival. "So many people," she says squinting into the light, "probably a hundred thousand of them, incredible pixilated images of little tiny dots of colour." Fleetwood Mac's saga came to embody both the best and the very worst of what success could deliver you, a long sleek limousine ride plagued with engine trouble and the occasional head-on collision.

The death of her boyfriend Dennis Wilson was a case in point. Having invited the illiterate ex-con pimp and burglar Charles Manson and his tribe to live in his empty house and to leech off his bank account, the boorish Beach Boys drug-hoover began orchestrating group sex soirees and taking every narcotic then available on the planet. This is how he died in 1983: swimming off his yacht moored at Marina Del Rey, Wilson drank the best part of a bottle of vodka to try and insulate himself against the 58 degree tide. As he dived he realised the seabed was littered with his own possessions, thrown from this very mooring during a domestic with his second wife some years before. He appeared out of the swell clutching a cracked and mud-stained framed photograph of himself with the girl in question, plunged back down, reappeared briefly as a ghostly figure swimming two feet below the surface, and was never seen alive again. His body was found on the ocean floor 45 minutes later. It's pretty hard for an outsider to see why this man was so attractive.

"Well we'd split up before all that but yes, obviously, I've had to ask myself the same question. Why *do* people stay with people? 'Cos they love them I guess. And I loved him for a while. He was very charismatic, great looking, very charming, very cute—if you can call a guy with a beard and a voice like Satan 'cute'. He used to draw people into his life, strangers off planes and off the streets, and they'd become his best friends. I think I mothered him, to be honest. He used to go off and I wouldn't see him for days and days, and then he'd come back and I'd mother him and get him all nice and sober and then he'd go off and go crazy again. It's one of those things. Opposites attract."

You can imagine why she felt like coming home to rural Canterbury in the end, but the drug musicians claim is the hardest to forsake is the soul-feeding sound of applause. How much do you have to hate the life around the music to give up the music itself?

"For some people that *is* their life, to get on those boards and have the light shining on them, and some people never even reach that point. But for me the day had come. I hated the L.A. earthquake, I hated living out of suitcase, I hated flying—I mean how many paranoias do you want? There were tiny moments onstage when you'd get that feeling of magic but otherwise you were just going through the motions. I just started to feel a little dizzy under the lights, to be honest. The vibration of the boards, the volume and the heat, they started to make me feel a little unwell! I'd just had enough. I just didn't want to have any of that noise any more."

24/7—A WEEK IN THE LIFE

Christine McVie

James Halbert | August 2004 | *Classic Rock* (UK)

This "as told to" feature gives a glimpse into the tenor and pace of Christine McVie's post–Fleetwood Mac life.

AT ABOUT EIGHT IN THE morning I take my dogs for the first of the three long walks I give them every day. I've got two Lhasa Apsos, which are like Pekingese, only with longer noses. I would like to say they're a lot prettier than Pekingese, but I don't want to offend any Pekingese owners. My dogs are twin brothers, both blonds. One of them is called Dougal, after the dog in *The Magic Roundabout,* and the other is called George. They run my life completely, and I think I'm starting to look more like them every day—it must be the shaggy blonde fringe and the ears!

"Recently I've spent a lot of time restoring my house. Had I known it was going to need so much work I probably wouldn't have bought it. I live just a few miles outside Canterbury in Kent, and the house is a rambling red-brick building with thatched barns and lots of out-buildings, cottages and a little recording studio. Is it a stately pile? No! But I think it's bigger than the local village, to be honest. The main part of the house dates from 1664, and I've been getting a lot of the wooden beams replaced. If there are any ghosts they must be very nice ones, because I spend quite some time here alone and that's never fazed me in the slightest.

"Reading-wise I've just finished Robin Hobb's massive fantasy trilogy *The Tawny Man*—three fantastic books, each of them practically the length of *The Bible*.

"I used to draw quite a bit, and I still flirt with the idea, but I'm one of those people who gets nervous in front of a blank sheet of paper. I start out thinking I'm going to create a masterpiece, and of course that always leads to disappointment. I have all the artists' supplies and everything, but if what I'm creating doesn't look brilliant from the outset I abandon it.

"I don't have any famous works of art around the house—nothing by Renoir or Monet, I'm afraid. I do have lots of nice etchings and prints and nice landscapes, though. This house is very traditional and very English, so you can't bugger about with anything too modern or it just looks silly. I have a flat up in London, though, and the decor there is more contemporary and eclectic.

"In the evenings I like a bit of telly, particularly crime dramas. I watch *Law & Order* almost every night, and I like *Homicide: Life On The Street*. Sitcom-wise I love *Seinfeld*. I must have seen every episode of that several times, and Jerry Seinfeld is probably my favourite comedian. I like *Curb Your Enthusiasm*, with Larry David, too, but that's a little bit drier. I had to egg myself on to watch the first couple of those, and then I got really into it. It's definitely a grower once you get used to the way it works.

"Cookery shows are good viewing for me, too, and I'm a big fan of *ER*; George Clooney was definitely the most handsome of the doctors, but I quite fancied the bald guy with the glasses as well. You know, the one who's not in it any more, Dr Green [Anthony Edwards]. The other thing I watch is *Have I Got News For You*. That satirical humour is very English, and the banter between Ian Hislop and Paul Merton is usually very good.

"I love Italian food, and I've actually been on a few Italian cooking courses. And although I say it myself, I'm pretty damn good at everything, really! I'm not tremendously fond of making desserts like tiramisu, but I do them well. I'm happier preparing the main courses—a good risotto, a nice spaghetti with seafood, or a traditional roast with a bit of an Italian influence.

"I eat a pretty healthy diet, but I don't work out as such. Three times a day around the paddock with the dogs, or just going from one end of this house to the other, is quite enough! I do ride a bicycle occasionally, but not those stupid stationary ones you see in gyms. I do have one of those, I must confess, but it's quite literally a pain in the arse so I don't use it.

"The only thing I collect is antique perfume bottles: art deco and cut-glass stuff, or any other odd ones that catch my eye as I hobble past antique shops or antique fairs. I try to get up to London a couple of days a week for a bit of retail therapy, and that usually has the desired effect.

"My most prized possession is an oil painting of St Cecelia, patron saint of music. It's hanging up in my hall landing, and it was painted by a guy called Peter Frampton—not the rock musician, but a turn-of-the-century painter from 1904 or thereabouts. St Cecelia is playing the organ, and she's surrounded by beautiful spring flowers. I don't know if many people have even heard of Frampton, but he's becoming quite collectable. I also love my grand piano. It's still the same one I wrote 'Songbird' on.

"I do own a computer, but as I don't enjoy typing I don't really surf the net. I'll email Mick [Fleetwood] or Stevie [Nicks] from time to time, but other than that I don't want to sit in front of a screen all day. The computer looks very nice on my desk, though [laughs].

"I used to be a late-night person, but these days I'm more of an early bird and so I go to bed about nine in the evening. Usually I'll read for a while, but I'm always asleep by midnight. When I still drank, I'd wind down at the end of the day with a glass of good champagne, but now I find that a cup of tea and a chocolate Hobnob does the trick. Exciting stuff, eh?"

CHRISTINE McVIE, 2004

Robin Eggar

This 2004 interview with Christine McVie was conducted for *S*, the magazine supplement of the *Sunday Express*. This verbatim transcript has never previously been published. Here, McVie discusses in depth *In the Meantime*, her follow-up to her previous solo albums, *Christine Perfect* (1970) and *Christine McVie* (1984).

What is your life like now?
I have a flat in London which is a nice place but I spend more time in Kent because I've got dogs and things. I'm about five miles due west of Canterbury. My brother lives near Faversham. I moved back to England about five years ago. I bought the house in 1990. My father died and I felt I hadn't spent any time with my brother. My brother was working as the director of the National Resource Centre in Greenwich University, so he was based in Kent. So I thought I'd buy a house close to my brother, which is what happened. I bought this rather falling-apart beautiful red brick Kent house. Classic with the turned-up tiles, but it did need a lot of work done to it. Over the last ten years I have been busy restoring it and I left the States for good five to six years ago.

What made you decide it was time to call it quits with Fleetwood Mac?
I had more or less decided when I bought the house, when my pop died. I thought, *None of us are getting any younger. I haven't spent enough time with my brother. I have other family in Birmingham I don't see so much of.* And there was the earthquake in 1994, a massive earthquake

in Northridge in L.A. That was enough for me. I thought, *I have got to get out while I still can. I want to go home now.* We did *The Dance* and a tour for that. I told everyone that would definitely be my last tour with the band.

I was surprised how well we did get on. There was never a problem with that. Obviously we did have our bad moments, but the whole *Dance* tour we really did get on well. We did *Tango in the Night* and then Lindsey actually left the band and we toured with another couple of guys playing guitar. We made a couple of records with those guys and they weren't that great, that successful. As years went by, we had a couple of other people join the band, Dave Mason for a while and Bekka Bramlett, and that was the point when I said, "I want to leave." Fleetwood Mac was going nowhere. There was no love lost between Dave Mason and myself. I did leave then and they went on the road.

To cut a long story short, President Clinton was using "Don't Stop" as his campaign song. His offices in Washington called us and said would we like to perform "Don't Stop" at the Inaugural Ball. Are you going to say no to that, whether you are a Republican or a Democrat? It was very flattering. I thought Bill Clinton was a nice fellow.

You've met a few presidents, haven't you?
I'm not that old. [*Laughs.*] We did a couple of bashes for Governor [Jerry] Brown. He was a bit of a groupie. He loved all the rock stars. It was Clinton that re-formed us, because we had to go in and recut the track. That was the resurrection of the original five with Lindsey. It is corny to say, but the old magic was there. So we decided to get together, make a video, record a couple of new tracks, and tour. We didn't make a whole new record. A lot of it was, to be honest, financial, so it was beneficial all round. Everybody was begging for us to re-form.

I said, "If we do this, I promise you this will be the last of it for me. I want to go back to England."

That is what happened. I sold everything and moved back to the old place in Kent. Selling the house and the car, giving up my green card (well I let it run out—it's redundant now) make it much harder to go back. I left everything behind. Friends too, unfortunately. I still stay in touch. It was the thing to do. I felt it was right. The moment I landed at Heathrow Airport, I knew this is it. I was home. It was this weight lifted off me. I never really wanted to leave England. When we left to try and hack out a career in the States, John and Mick assured me it would only be for six months. We never came back. Twenty-eight years later . . . I have always loved England, but one thing led to another and I didn't manage to come home any sooner. I wish I had.

Are you on the last Fleetwood Mac album?
Those two tracks I did for Lindsey when he was doing his solo record. Those songs are taken from a solo project he's been working on. I went down and [put] some background parts on his version before it had been Fleetwood Mac–ified. He wrote to me and asked, "Do you mind if we keep your voice on?" Not at all, but I didn't record on the Mac tracks.

Did they ask you?
A bit during the recording, but they had already begged me during *The Dance*. I got cornered many times backstage after the gigs: "Are you sure, Chris? Please change your mind." I said, "No, this is definitely it." There is a time when you know it is right. Mick said, "Look, we can sort something out. We can record in England. We can work it out so you can get plenty of time in England." I said no. I felt it was the right time. Once I have made up my mind, it's like my relationships: once they are over, that is it; they are history.

I saw them play when they were touring. It was quite fun, actually. Bizarre too. It was the first time in my musical career I was able to see from the audience's point of view. I walked around the auditorium and saw them all up there with me not there. They sounded great and it was a strange sensation. I have to say that when I went backstage and saw them all, they all looked so tired, so exhausted, and I thought to myself, *I didn't make the wrong move there*. Stevie was so exhausted. She did so much trumping about on stage still. She's not as old as me, but she's not a teenager. I think they did fantastic but I just don't want to do it anymore.

You've never had pangs?

No. Everybody said that to me: "Did you feel a little pang?" To be honest with you, no. I was looking at them on stage, thinking, *Thank God I'm not there. Thank God I made the right decision*, because it would be terrible to be wishing I hadn't left. I should imagine they'd take me back, but it won't happen.

How did your solo album come about?

My album was an accident. I didn't start off with the intention of making a record. I was doing these songs, a lot of it for cathartic reasons. When I write songs, I don't care whether they are good or bad. If that is what you do as a means of self-expression, it can help. It's like knitting a sweater or cooking a meal. It's therapeutic, you know?

I started working with my nephew [Dan Perfect]. He's thirty-eight, he plays guitar, and he is really gifted, but he is an artist—a painter—by profession. He plays great guitar and he's very good with Pro Tools, and so we started working on it in my house. I have a little converted barn which we call the Saloon. It has a mock-up of a bar in there and some gear in the corner and a computer. A lot of people said, "This is sounding really good. Why don't you make a record?" I balked at the thought of having to do this again. This is the bit—no, I lie. This is not the bit that really gets me. It is the touring and the live performances. That is out. I got persuaded into releasing this and the proviso was that nobody expected me do live performances anymore. I have retired.

Enough people said people might like to hear some of this stuff. Otherwise what am I going to do—put it on the shelf? This is a little diary of songs that myself—Dan and I put together very casually over a couple of years. It was a hobby really at that point, and then it got horrifically real when they started doing the cover. For a while I thought, *Do I really want to do this?*

I am very proud of it. I like the songs. It is the first time I have ever done anything like that without having Lindsey around or a producer. It was the equivalent of knitting myself a sweater, kind of, and we really enjoyed it because there was no pressure, no deadline, nothing at the back of my head thinking if I was going to make a record, I had to make it commercial. It was completely self-indulgent.

I was tempted a few times to put on the choirs of angels. Not through lack of trying. We tried everything but the kitchen sink. It is difficult to know when to stop because the temptation is to use the choir of angels. That's when you go too far. It was great trying to do a fake sax.

Your brother's sleeve notes say you can't escape it; sometimes you are a songwriter.
Sometimes it feels like that. You think you can. I am not the most prolific of writers in the world. I can go for a couple of years without thinking about going near a piano and then something will catch in my head, I'll sit down at the piano, and before I know where I am I will have the shell of some kind of idea. That is how it starts. At times I'll get on a roll and it's like writing three songs altogether, which is unbelievable. Then I won't do anything for a month.

What is the track "Calumny" about?
That is my nephew's fault. I had to ask him, "What the hell does that mean?" It means treachery. A lot of people still don't pronounce the word properly.

What prompted your new songs?
I had been through a bad relationship that had broken down with a man. That marriage had already gone. That fellow came along three or so years ago and it didn't work out. Some of the songs were working the thing out, working the demon out.

I'm a pretty basic love song writer. Pretty basic relationship writer. I'd be the last one to say it for myself but I've been told that I have a way of saying the obvious in a nonobvious way. "I love you. You love me. We're happy as can be"—there is a way of saying it without making it that obvious so it becomes more universal and it can apply to many different ways to many different relationships in life.

But you're not that lucky in love?

No. I've been very, very unlucky in love. It's been a real drag. No, I've had my good times. No, both Stevie and I, we were married to Fleetwood Mac. That was what we did and it was a harsh marriage. During those years there was no time for anything else and we used to moan about how we were married to the band. During our thirties and forties that is what we did. There was no time for relationships of our own.

Do you regret not having children?

Sometimes, but not really, no, to be honest. I'm at the point now where I am quite content. I like my life. There was a time twenty or so years ago when it would have been nice. It just didn't happen. Now I am very comfortable, content with what I've got. Cooking and gardening. It does sound pretty trivial, doesn't it? But actually its petty blissful after the chaotic life I've led for the past forty years. It's calm. I have lovely people around me, good friends and people who work for me. I live a very simple life. I have my doggies—Lhasa apsos. They are going to be the most famous dogs in Kent. They are brothers. Very cute, Dougal and George. They are actually on the CD booklet inside. They are very spoiled dogs. It is a very simple life, but the one that I chose. I am content. I have no desire to go abroad. At the moment, I am happy with my lot. How complacent is that? It does sound awful.

For thirty-odd years you didn't have a life of your own.

To an extent, that is true. When you are part of a group like that, you don't belong to yourself. You are public property to a degree and at the mercy and demands of all the other members of the band, the other managers, the other agents. Everybody had their own manager. You can imagine the chaos and the pandemonium that transpired from that. And the rampant out-of-control egos, the rampant out-of-control drug taking in the old days. But I have to say it is like a kindergarten backstage these days.

What do you think of the old days now?

We did what everybody else was doing. It was the norm. Everybody walked around with these beautiful silver cocaine holders as jewelry round their neck, or a beautiful coke spoon with a turquoise or an opal in it. It was fashionable to wear drug-related jewelry. Everybody did it. It wasn't abnormal. When we were recording *Rumours*, the girl behind reception would go into the kitchen and cook up a mountain of hash brownies, which got liberally passed around.

What's the most excessive thing you did?
It would have to be staying up for three days with the white powder, liberally washed down by Dom Pérignon. I almost had a heart attack and soon stopped that idea. I thought, *This is for the birds. I can't be doing this.*

Do you still drink?
No, I don't drink. I gave up smoking three months ago, so I chew nicotine gum. I don't do anything now. I'm really boring. I quit drugs about twenty years ago, the white stuff. I just stopped because I wanted to. I can safely say, for me it did not become addictive. It was purely social. In the old days, Stevie and I, the amount we did was so microscopic compared to the big rails that everybody else was doing. I just decided one day I didn't like what it did to me, so I stopped doing it.

I have flirted with not smoking for a few years now and I am going to crack it this time. It is the hardest drug of all. I did quit for five years once. Then my second marriage broke down, so I started again immediately. You can't stop trying.

Can we go way back?
I'm not sure if I can remember that much.

Your background is very non–rock and roll. Your parents were a college professor and a psychic.
We weren't rich but we were an educated family, academically speaking. I studied classical piano. I went to lessons for a good many years until I discovered Fats Domino in my piano stool at home. It was my brother's. I blame him for everything. He is four years older than me and a sax player, really good. It was after that I gave up classical music

and started to learn to try to play the blues. I wrote my first song when I was sixteen. It was rubbish, but probably better than some of the ones I have written recently. I skirmished with writing, then I stopped.

I wrote a few songs in Chicken Shack, but when I joined Fleetwood Mac it was Mick who encouraged me to write. I wrote a couple of songs on *Future Games* or *Bare Trees*. Mick said, "You should write more because you're pretty good." So I struck at it but I didn't think I would ever set the world on fire. I enjoy it and I've been lucky.

My mum was a healer. She did heal people, I'm certain, because I am one of the people she healed. When I was eleven I had this huge wart under my nose and one night she put her fingers on it and the next morning it was gone. She did other things like wear items of clothing. I was very young at the time, so I don't remember much about it, but they would phone her up and say that thanks to her they were completely healed—very sick people. She was interested in psychic research. She was out of time. She belonged to a local psychic research society. I just wanted her to be an ordinary mum. She was completely conventional— a school secretary—but an extraordinary, wonderful woman who died early on when I was just married to John.

I don't claim any psychic powers for myself. I was not blessed with any powers, nor my brother. Not even my mother had any idea about my future. Who could?

There's a story about you losing weight to enable you to go out with Spencer Davis.

I was definitely overweight, about thirteen stone when I was thirteen. When I went to art college I suddenly realized how cute guys were and I wanted one. I did eat a lot of chocolate when I was at school. Then I started eating salads and it melted off me. I don't consciously eat mountains of chocolate anymore.

What was it like playing in Davis's Sound of Blues?

It was a bizarre thing. There weren't many girls in blues bands then— there aren't that many now—and I don't think I even sang very much. It was mainly Stan Webb that was the lead guy.

How were you treated?

I was never a sex goddess—that is not a description of me I would ever use. No, they treated me very well. I never had a problem in any way with being the only girl in the band. With Fleetwood Mac when Stevie joined, the guys always treated me as one of the guys, but with respect. Like a sister I suppose, but they never excluded me from the boy jokes. I had to get used to that, so I now have a mouth like a sewer. I did get protected from certain other things like guys coming up to me. They were good-mannered blokes. Once the girls were in their room, the boys might go down to the bar. I didn't know. Didn't want to know about that stuff.

Has the attitude to women changed in music? In Fleetwood Mac, you and Stevie were radical.

I don't know whether we were lucky but we, and all the peripheral women around [like] makeup artists, were all treated with respect. It was a big family. There was never any abuse or unkindness or rudeness. The blokes were pretty blooming polite for rock stars, quite gentlemanly. I never made any conscious decision to behave like a rock star. We did what we did because we were there.

What were the defining moments in your career?

To be asked to join Fleetwood Mac. It was not something I was expecting. I had a soft spot for Peter Green in the old days. I used to think he was quite cute. I never did anything about it. It was purely an observation. I had always been a big Mac fan. When Chicken Shack weren't playing, myself and Andy Silvester would hightail it to the nearest Mac gig.

I was going out with John, not married to him. We were touring and Fleetwood Mac were touring. I would never see him. When I got married, I left Chicken Shack and became a housewife. I didn't think much beyond that. They were rehearsing for *Kiln House* in Kiln House. I don't know if you remember the album, over which was cartoon drawings. I did them to add to my many talents. Well, questionable talents. I'd smoked a joint when I did that. They were rehearsing as a four piece and about to go on the road. They weren't happy with the sound and wanted to augment the band with another member. Obviously, I was there. I knew all the songs, was listening to the rehearsals, so they just said, "What do you think about joining the band?" I said, "You must be mad, but yes." It was another twenty-five years before I could escape. An entire lifetime later. It was five years ago that I managed to leave.

Meeting Stevie and Lindsey changed everything. We went from being a fairly competent bunch of musicians to being, in a sense, gods. It was the gelling of two different sorts of music. John, Mick, and myself were inherently blues-based musicians. I was part of the rhythm section. I was never Stevie Winwood. I am not a great keyboard player. I get by, but I nestled in with bass and drums. Lindsey and I got on well musically because we could jam off each other. His licks were very different from Stan Webb's and Danny Kirwan's. He was very Californian. He knew his blues chops and had a unique way of playing. I was able to play around him. He pulled me out of the rhythm section and I got a lot more creative, started writing more songs.

The circumstances of the *Rumours* recording are infamous. How the hell did you ever make that record?

Because we didn't do anything else. That was all we lived for. We went to sleep and came back into the studio again and that was what tied you together: the music. Everything else was falling apart, but the music was good. We felt it was good. We didn't know it was that good. We had faith in that what we were doing was really quite fantastic. The eponymous album was very successful—number one for six months. It took a while to get there because we took off when we started touring. It was such a novelty: two girls in a band, all these relationship crises going on. We had no idea it was going to be as good as it turned out to be. That just rocketed out of the stratosphere. Nobody understood what was going on. We were just in a little bubble.

Can you analyze it now?

No, I still really can't. We were living in this dreamworld, all doing too many drugs and drinking too much, all busy getting divorced and fighting amongst ourselves. There were always pocketfuls of people you could talk to. I had to avoid John McVie like the plague for a few months, unless we were playing, when it was all right.

Looking back I don't know what happened. We must have captured the public's imagination somehow. They fell in love with the idea of this musical soap opera. We were like a band of traveling gypsies, all so different from one another. That was what made it so interesting, because Stevie and I are so different from one another. Stevie was this siren, this magic creature on the stage. I was quite content to be behind the keyboards. I didn't want to compete with that at all. I was very happy with where I was.

Lindsey was a Californian boy. John, who was grounded in Ealing, he was a civil servant for a while. And Mick was a wing commander's son, jolly hockey sticks and all that. It was an interesting, bizarre bunch of people.

How did the band not break up at that point?
There were times when I wanted to leave but I was governed by the demands of the other four members of the band and swept away with all the responsibilities of a huge hit record. "I can't leave—what are the others going to do?" I had to plow on and just get on with it, which is what I did, what we all did. If John and I hadn't been forced to work out our differences face to face, we may never have been friends again. So from that point of view, it was a good thing because we worked out our differences and came out the other end as friends.

A perverse form of therapy really.

"The Americans in Fleetwood Mac just don't have enough sense of humor. They take everything much too seriously. Mick, John, and me always kept smiling, even in the dark days of the group." Discuss.
Yes, that's true. They have a different sense of humor. The British sense of humor is more ironic, satirical. There is a darkness to British humor which the Americans never quite got. When things were going badly, the evil emerges, and that is how we survived: released all of that dark humor. Mick was brilliant at that. It took Lindsey and Stevie a while but they twigged in the end. We used to have some bloody good laughs.

Your romance with Dennis Wilson seems an unlikely relationship.
It was an unlikely relationship. Opposites attract, I suppose. I found him insane. Because of that, I found him very attractive. I found him funny. He wasn't being deliberately funny. I found myself laughing at him for the things he did, his attitude to things. He didn't know he was doing it but he amused me, made me laugh, but he was barking mad.

We'd been split up for maybe four years when he died. I was surprised he survived as long as he did, to be honest. He was asking for it all his life. I was surprised he lived as long as he did.

What about you?
I have had my moments of insanity but, all in all, I am fairly level-headed. I might have gone off the rails a couple of times but generally I am pretty much all right. Dunno where it comes from. I can't say my mum and dad, because they are not around. Maybe I am just boring. I can't answer that, because I don't have a clue. Maybe I have a deep inherent sense of common sense.

The madness was not just Fleetwood Mac; it was everybody. The record companies, the groupies, all the engineers, the road managers. You name it—everybody was like that. If you are allowed to behave in any way you want you do . . . there has got to be an innate something in the back of your head that tells you when you have got to stop, when you have gone too far. Everyone has different thresholds, but maybe I was lucky in that I was able to say, "Enough is enough."

From '83 to '84 John and Mick were drinking a lot.
Stevie was away with the fairies. You could safely say that. They had moved in. Lindsey was smoking a lot of marijuana. He lived in a marijuana cage. He was on another planet from everybody else. There was the drinkers, the drug takers, and everybody had a different plateau of noncommunication. It was very strange. I did a bit of everything. A perfect balance: a little bit of marijuana, a little bit of drink, a little bit of powder. I was never extreme in one particular thing. I just plodded along in between the others, never being too radical.

I had to stay in the band until they had all quit everything and didn't need me anymore. They always used to call me Mother Nature. Was I? No. I think I was the same as the others. I just managed to do a little bit of everything and not too much of anything.

How has your life changed since?
I am much more content—dare I say it, happy. Happiness is not a cheap commodity. I don't think anybody can afford happiness. It is a question. I am sixty. Everybody knows how old I am—who cares?—and for the first time in my life I feel really content, at ease with myself. I like living in England. I love living in Kent. I love being around the people I am around. Life is pretty damn good. Tomorrow I am going to go back to Kent, switch on the telly, and watch some Wimbledon.

I don't garden. I supervise gardening. One does not get one's fingers dirty. [*Laughs.*] In a manner of speaking I am the lady of the manor. Don't take it too seriously, for God's sake! The last thing I want to be is too precious. I did go to the odd cooking school because I got very keen on Italian cooking and for a brief while I contemplated opening a restaurant, until I realized quite how much bloody hard work is involved, and money. I learned what I learned: how to make my own pasta and my own bread, all the Italian stuff, homemade pizzas. You never get a pizza like a homemade one. You never tasted anything so good. I had a brief flirtation with that. I have come out of it being a damn good cook and I love cooking Sunday lunch and meals for people. That is a part-time pleasure of mine. Any roast you can possibly imagine I am great at, she says modestly. Desserts I'm no good at. I just buy a big tub of ice cream. The only thing I don't do is dessert.

Are you going back to live performance?
No. I am too private of a person. I have done forty years of it and I don't want to do it anymore. Most of the time, I enjoyed it. I don't like the travel, like living out of a suitcase; I didn't like the lights; and I didn't like the volume. There isn't much else, is there? I did like the audience response. I wasn't so fussed about being adored. Stevie was always the

one who got tossed the teddy bears and the flowers. I didn't even get books of poetry. Stevie might give me one of her teddy bears.

Towards the end I found it very overwhelming being onstage. The lights were hot and it was deafening, so loud that every year my doctor had to hoick out inches of ear wax. You would be amazed how unhealthy it has to be onstage performing at that volume. I was getting disoriented.

Was it lonely?

On the road, not really. My security guard was a good friend. When I was alone it was because I wanted to be alone.

Fleetwood Mac was your family but it stopped you having one of your own. Was it worth the price?

I have to say, yes, it was worth the price, because I have come out of it fairly unscathed, fairly well adjusted, and in fairly—touch wood—good health, both physically and emotionally. And financially I am fine. I am not Elton John, but who the hell needs to have that much money? I am fine. I have been careful and I am quite content and solvent.

THE GREATEST SONGS EVER

Fleetwood Mac—"Dreams"

Johnny Black | May 2005 | *Blender* (US)

"Now here you go again, you say you want your freedom." So exquisitely starts Stevie Nicks's *Rumours* track "Dreams," an achingly beautiful lament for a lost love. The man tasked with the job of arranging Nicks's creation was none other than Lindsey Buckingham, the subject of the song. The delicate, nay agonizing, psychology behind that scenario is explored in this short but revealing article.

28 YEARS AGO THIS MONTH: MAY 1977

VITAL STATISTICS
SONG TITLE: "Dreams"
ARTIST: Fleetwood Mac
LABEL: Warner Bros.
PERFORMERS:
Stevie Nicks: *vocals/piano*
Lindsey Buckingham: *guitars/vocals*
Christine McVie: *piano/vocals*
Mick Fleetwood: *drums/percussion*
John McVie: *bass*
PRODUCERS: Fleetwood Mac with Richard Dashut and Ken Caillat
RELEASED: April 16, 1977
HIGHEST CHART POSITION: 1

WHO'S WHO
STEVIE NICKS
El Lay rock's original witchy woman, and Fleetwood Mac's most successful solo artist.
LINDSEY BUCKINGHAM
Guitar wiz, arranger, producer, all-round renaissance man and, notoriously, Stevie's first big love.
CHRISTINE MCVIE
The Mac's other female singer-songwriter, composer of several hits and former wife of bassist John McVie.

SOMETIMES inspiration strikes first thing in the morning. Sometimes it strikes over lunch. Fleetwood Mac's first No. 1 single, on the other hand, was born on a black-velvet bed overlooking Sly Stone's cocaine pit.

It was early 1976, and Fleetwood Mac were in Sausalito, California, recording their twelfth album, *Rumours*. It would rocket them to formerly undreamed-of heights of success—and equal depths of despair.

"One day when I wasn't required in the main studio," remembers singer Stevie Nicks, "I took a Fender Rhodes piano and went into another studio that was said to belong to Sly, of Sly and the Family Stone. It was a black-and-red room, with a sunken pit in the middle where there was a piano, and a big black-velvet bed with Victorian drapes."

That room, in Sausalito's Record Plant, is also etched into the memory of drummer Mick Fleetwood: "It was usually occupied by people we didn't know, tapping razors on mirrors."

Founded in swinging '60s London by Fleetwood and bassist John McVie, Fleetwood Mac had already tasted massive success in their homeland, only to have it swept away when their brilliant lead guitarist and songwriter, Peter Green, became one of rock's first high-profile acid casualties, leaving the group and virtually falling off the face of the earth for several decades.

Relocating to America, the band spent years treading water until January 1975, when they took on two new members, the young California duo of Lindsey Buckingham and Stevie Nicks. The pair's prodigious songwriting gifts revitalized the group, but they came with a certain amount of baggage too.

"Lindsey and I were lovers," recalls Stevie, "but we were on the point of breaking up when we joined Fleetwood Mac. For the greater good of the band, though, we decided to put our breakup on hold."

By the end of 1975, the first album by the reconstituted group, *Fleetwood Mac*, had gone gold, and they had their first hit single with "Over My Head."

"We were beginning to become rock stars," recalls Nicks, "and we had to get another album together. Sausalito was as romantic as you could possibly imagine. It was gorgeous up there, right by the ocean, in this fabulous studio with Indian drapes, little hippie girls making hash cookies and everybody having dinner 'round a big kitchen table."

Under such circumstances, it should have been paradise, but Nicks and Buckingham's relationship was quickly coming apart at the seams. "We had to go through this elaborate exercise of denial," explains Buckingham, "keeping our personal feelings in one corner of the room while trying to be professional in the other." Inevitably, their true feelings surfaced in the lyrics of the songs they were writing—most notably "Dreams."

"I sat down on the bed with my keyboard in front of me," recalls Nicks. "I found a drum pattern, switched my little cassette player on and wrote 'Dreams' in about 10 minutes. Right away I liked the fact that I was doing something with a dance beat, because that made it a little unusual for me."

Delighted with her brand-new, 10-minute tune, she took it to the rest of the band, who decided to record it the next day. Nicks says Buckingham didn't openly acknowledge that the lyrics—dire warnings that a man can be driven mad by loneliness in the wake of a broken love affair—were directed straight at his heart. Despite this apparent cool, though, the recriminations would eventually come.

Although a basic track for "Dreams" was completed in Sausalito, recording assistant Cris Morris remembers that "all we kept was the drum track and live vocal from Stevie—the guitars and bass were added later in Los Angeles."

"Dreams" didn't immediately wow the band's other female songwriter, Christine McVie. "When Stevie first played it for me on the piano," she says, "it was just three chords and one note in the left hand. I thought 'This is really boring,' but the Lindsey genius came into play and he fashioned three sections out of identical chords, making each section sound completely different. He created the impression that there's a thread running through the whole thing."

Mick Fleetwood revealed that Buckingham found this process agonizing. "It was most difficult for Lindsey because Stevie was the one who pulled away emotionally. He would say, 'I'm doing this for her and making her music, but I can't have closure.'"

Well aware that Nicks had moved on and was already romancing Don Henley of the Eagles, Buckingham responded with bitterly charged songs like "Second Hand News," declaring, "One thing I think you should know/I ain't gonna miss you when you go."

Nicks insists, however, that "Dreams" was her counterpart to another of Buckingham's songs, "Go Your Own Way." "I told him that, in my heart, 'Dreams' was open and hopeful, but in 'Go Your Own Way,' his heart was closed. That's how I felt. That line, 'When the rain washes you clean,' to me that was like being able to start again, and that's what I wanted for Lindsey. I wanted him to be happy."

The *Rumours* sessions, especially the Los Angeles portion, have become notorious as one of the most drug-fueled and decadent episodes in rock history. But Nicks insists that "'Dreams' was written before it got really bad. As our success grew during the making of the album, we had more money, and we started dabbling more with drugs, but the cocaine didn't really start having its effect on us until later. 1980 was probably the worst. Those first four years of Fleetwood Mac were nowhere near as bad as everybody likes to imagine."

By the time "Dreams" was released, *Rumours* was already a platinum album, and Nicks's song soared to No. 1 on June 18, 1977, quickly establishing itself as her signature track.

"Sometimes you can get tired of singing a certain song over and over again," she says, "but I have never gone onstage, either with Fleetwood Mac or in my solo shows, without singing 'Dreams.' I don't think I could."

THE RETURN OF JEREMY SPENCER

Bill Wasserzieher | October 2006 | Blues Revue (US)

There are several parallels between Peter Green and Jeremy Spencer. Both were Fleetwood Mac members, both were inordinately gifted guitarists, both gave it all up for—to a greater or lesser degree—altruistic reasons, and both subsequently disappeared into a half-life of myth and underachievement.

In 2006 Spencer emerged from the shadows for the purpose of his first record release in three decades. This interview was conducted for *Blues Revue*. A shorter version appeared in the hard copy of the magazine, with this much longer version posted on the publication's website. Generated by a combination of phone calls, e-mails, and face-to-face discussion, it gives an insight into why someone who had fame and fortune at his feet walked away from them.

THE MUSIC-BIZ HEAVIES who serve as doorkeepers for the Rock and Roll Hall of Fame welcomed two very different bands among their 1998 inductees. One group epitomized mega-selling '70s and '80s rock; the other played hardcore blues with a British accent. Both were named Fleetwood Mac.

The more famous version of the band was its Stevie Nicks-Lindsey Buckingham-Christine McVie lineup. Their 1977 album *Rumours* stayed on the pop charts for 134 weeks and had sold more than 18 million copies by the time of the Hall of Fame ceremony.

The other, earlier version of Fleetwood Mac began life in 1967 as "Peter Green's Fleetwood Mac Featuring Jeremy Spencer" and barely lasted into the 1970s before guitarists Peter Green, Jeremy Spencer, and Danny Kirwan left, one by one, each suffering from some combination of mental, spiritual, and emotional breakdowns. Only the rhythm section of Mick Fleetwood and John McVie linked the two bands.

But the stature of that first Fleetwood Mac—the one so steeped in blues that B.B. King regularly shared marquees with them—has continued to grow. The curious can easily find the early Mac's studio albums, various live performances, the essential two-disc *Fleetwood Mac in Chicago 1969* sessions with Buddy Guy, Willie Dixon, and Otis Spann, and such intriguing outtake collections as *The Vaudeville Years, Show-Biz Blues*, and *Madison Blues*.

That night in 1998, both Fleetwood Macs were represented at the Hall of Fame. The Buckingham-Nicks-McVie version performed their hits, and Peter Green jammed with Carlos Santana on 'Black Magic Woman'.

Jeremy Spencer could have been onstage too, but he wasn't. He was half a world away in India, playing charity benefits for the blind. After all, Spencer is the slide guitarist who bolted Fleetwood Mac in 1971 to join a religious commune. Having turned his back on fame, he has wandered the globe, living not only in the U.S. and England but also in France, Brazil, Italy, Greece, Sri Lanka, the Philippines, Japan, Mexico, and Switzerland.

Today he's back in the public eye with a new recording, *Precious Little*, issued domestically in July on Blind Pig Records. Spencer tells his story to *Blues Revue*.

How did you come to record a new album?
The promoters of the annual Notodden Blues Festival asked if I wished to play at their 2005 festival. They presented me with a number of choices for an accompanying lineup, one of which was playing with a group of Norwegian blues musicians. Most of the band had been playing blues together for the last 25 years and were heralded as the best in Norway. I discovered there was more interest in, knowledge, appreciation of, and passion for blues in Norway than I'd encountered anywhere else in the world, to the point that they have as many as 25 blues festivals a year.

Not having heard the band, I was especially concerned about Espen Leland, the 40-year-old backup guitarist, as I did not want a "whiz-flash Harry" who could do anything while reading the newspaper. "You want that Delta crap? Sure, watch this: 'ratatatatatatata.' Want jazz, hip-hop, funk? No problem."

I pushed the envelope and asked if Espen played like T-Bone Walker! They said yes, with a mixture of early B. B. King and Albert Collins thrown in. Fortunately, it turned out to be true. And playing together with the rest of the band flowed so well, like, hand in glove. For the first time in 27 years, I seriously considered recording a studio album.

I tested them with a couple of my personal, sensitive favorites not in the blues or '50s vein, 'Maria de Santiago' and 'Precious Little', and they passed with flying colors. Not only did they just play along, but they also got genuinely excited about the songs. I felt I could pull out anything, and they would handle it with sensitivity. So, recording was a serious consideration.

We recorded the album in five days at the analog 24-track Notodden Juke Joint studio, where, amongst antiquated two- and four-track tape recorders, stood the company's pride and joy: the late-'60s Atlantic studios mixing desk!

What are your favorite songs?
I assume you're talking about [my favorites] on the CD. This is hard to answer, as when I listen to it—which, amazingly, I do quite often, as most of my recorded work in the past has made me cringe—each song has its special thing for me at that moment. Overall, I would say 'Bitter Lemon', 'Maria de Santiago', and especially the title song, 'Precious Little'.

Do you feel that you've gained a deeper feeling over the years as a musician?
It's hard to say that about oneself. But I can honestly say that I have. I think that the feeling for playing with emotion beyond mere frustration improves with age. It seems especially true of the blues, in my opinion. The phrasing, when to "speak" and when not to, etc. It's not something you can do merely by playing cosmetically minimalist, or with an intellectually conscious "less is more" feel.

Did you find yourself asking, "Do I really want to do this again?"
I had been pretty badly burned by the last commercial attempt with Atlantic in 1978 [*Flee*], so the idea of going into a studio to record for a major label did not appeal to me. In the '90s, an Indian label released

a live CD recorded at an outdoor concert in Bombay, but I was far from satisfied with the results. I'm glad it stayed local.

In recent years, however, I felt I just wanted something to be out there for those that are interested, an album that I was musically happy with and that was representative of me now, with no pressure of opinions, preconceived ideas of how I should be "marketed," and trends. Yet the idea of sitting in a studio with a bunch of hotshot "do-anything" musicians didn't appeal to me, either.

That's why I immediately felt at home with the Norwegian musicians. There was a chemistry that made me feel instantly relaxed. Plus, for the last eight years or so, I've had a whole new lease of life on playing slide guitar, to the point that playing straight-style finger lead or rhythm no longer interests me.

The decision to record again must have required courage.
It did take some courage just to do it, regardless of what I imagined people would expect of me in terms of a "comeback" style—you know, big, flashy, and screaming. "Come on, Jer, give us the ol' piss-takes and 'Shake Your Moneymaker'." I wanted it small, simple, and uncluttered. Collectively, including the engineers, it seemed we were always unconsciously thinking small, tasteful. If there was anything I wanted to prove, it was that I could do just that and have a listenable product that the public and even I would enjoy.

Bluestown [Spencer's European record label] gave me a lot of space musically and encouraged me. I don't think a big company in the States and especially England would have been so generous. However, Bluestown couldn't afford to be too generous with *time*, and we had to record it in five days on their analog 24-track. That was good, because we had to get it and like it, and we did. It kept that urgent spontaneity that I like. Analog says "no" for you when you can't say it for yourself. We had no time for ProTools.

These days, do you feel a deeper understanding of the music that so excited you in your youth?
Absolutely. Especially with the heart of *sweet* blues, not the screaming, down-and-dirty, grunge-and-sweat kind of modern blues that seems to

be prevalent today. I still listen to Elmore's 'Sky Is Crying', B.B.'s 'It's My Own Fault', [or] Otis Rush's 'I Can't Quit You Baby', for instance, and appreciate these classics more than ever.

I'll quote an interesting passage from a recent bio of Muddy Waters here. When he was asked why the white guys can't play the blues, he said, "There are some beautiful white bands. But they didn't go to the Baptist church like I [did]. They didn't get that soul down deep in the heart like I have. And they can't deliver the message."

I think he hit the core of it right there. Real feeling in blues—and I don't think it's just grumbling about your lot and complaining, but healing and empathetic emotion—has to come from God. It's not a matter of color, but I think most of those dear ol' black bluesers down in the Delta got the point lots quicker 'n us whitey folks.

What are your expectations for this album? The market for music isn't good these days, and, as always, the emphasis is on youth.
I don't have big expectations for the album. But on my travels in Europe, I have been pleasantly surprised at the reactions of some young people to it, especially, believe it or not, teen girls! I don't know what to attribute that to, as I'm no Robbie Williams or Eminem.

Is it enough to know that it will probably reach only a relatively small audience, but that they will be pleased?
Absolutely. Precious little, precious few. When I meet or hear from the people that have responded to it deeply and sincerely, I am somewhat glad if it stays small. I don't know if the record company will agree with me, of course! Even if I never record again, it's an album I can finally say I'd be happy to leave this world with.

When you were first starting out, what made you want to be a musician?
As a kid, plaintive ballads such as 'Unchained Melody', 'It's Only Make Believe', and 'Young Love' got to me the most, especially when I would hear a solitary guitar in the distance echoing the emotion. That's what got me about Elmore James when I heard 'The Sun Is Shining'—that extension of the voice through the guitar. It was just incredible to me. That's

why, when it comes to blues, I like the singer and the guitarist to be the same person, even if the two elements are maybe not as technically proficient as a separate guitar player and singer in a supergroup-style lineup. Maybe there'll be some disagreement about this, but I like to hear the voice and the guitar "answers" breathing as one, if you know what I mean.

Was playing music an answer to something missing in your life, or just the natural thing for someone young at the time?
I played the piano and organ at the time, but when I began learning slide guitar, it was like I'd discovered a way to express emotion, and it was very fulfilling.

Beyond Elmore James, who excited you?
Homesick James [Elmore's cousin], Otis Rush, Albert King, and early Buddy Guy. I also liked Blind Willie McTell and Sleepy John Estes.

What was it like joining a professionally experienced band like Fleetwood Mac in 1967? Peter already had the beginning of his "Green God" reputation as a guitar player, and John McVie and Mick Fleetwood knew the ropes from their time with John Mayall's Bluesbreakers.
Strangely enough, I did not feel intimidated, as it all just fell into place musically. I did feel a lack of confidence, however, playing without a slide to do riffs to back Pete. That's why I didn't, and he ended up having to recruit Danny [Kirwan] to do that!

Tell us about the early Mac repertoire. Who decided what in terms of the set list? You seem to have had plenty of "play" time onstage and in the studio.
In the beginning, with just the four of us, I chose the Elmore stuff and Pete chose his B.B. King-style material. For sure, I was given a lot of play time at the beginning. Too much, actually, and I wore out that Elmore riff.

Please tell us about the early shows in the U.K. Were the shows as wild as the legend has it?
They were as wild as legend *had* it, but legends have a way of developing over the years.

Did things change after Danny joined?
For Pete, John, Mick, and especially Danny, things changed for the better. Danny and Pete were able to develop together, explore new ideas, and the band took off successfully as a result. For me, it changed for the worse, as I just didn't find myself getting anything new. I tried, but you can't work that sort of thing up. As they say, [success] is 10 percent inspiration and 90 percent perspiration, but without that initial 10 percent, it's dry and futile.

How did your reputation for ribald stage humor come about?
I had—and still have to some extent—a silly streak and a penchant for liking to shock people, especially in those days with the staid British. It certainly wasn't all in good taste, and I'm not proud of a lot of those antics [Fleetwood Mac was banned from London's Marquee Club after Spencer appeared onstage wearing a giant phallus]. But we were a bunch of silly kids, really—boys in the band acting up. Nowadays that type of thing no longer shocks anyone; vulgarity is par for the course for supposedly controversial bands. You know, knighted punk stars cursing at a Royal Command performance.

Tell us a bit about Earl Vince & the Valiants—Mac's alter ego incarnation.
The song 'Someone's Gonna Get Their Head Kicked in Tonight' [released under the pseudonym] was a result of an unfortunate experience when Pete, Mick, and John got beaten up in a club in Northern England. I wrote the song as a stab at the type of characters that spoil the fun for everyone at venues. The sad thing was, it seemed that some people didn't get the point, and it became a favored jukebox play for the very crowd it was spoofing.

What are you comfortable saying about the contrast between your old stage persona and your religious leaning, even then?
I believed in God and was searching the Bible and other spiritual books for the answers. I didn't understand it myself, really, why I was such an irreverent little so-and-so onstage and off, yet had those religious inclinations. I realized later that it was true what Jesus said, that the whole need not a physician, but those that are sick. I was just sick, period.

How did you come to sit out the sessions for 1969's Then Play On *but record your first solo album with Mac in support?*

Pete asked me if I had any new stuff for the album. I said no, only 1950s-style rock 'n' roll stuff, which wouldn't have fit in with the direction he and Danny were going. We thought about putting it on a companion EP to be packaged with the album. The idea grew to be its own full-fledged album, which flopped miserably. But I had fun doing it. Actually, in retrospect, one of the most enjoyable things was working with Danny on it, as it brought out a side of him I hadn't seen.

Tell us about the shock of Peter quitting. How did you and the others create Kiln House *without him?*

That couple of weeks working with Danny on my solo album sort of set the stage for having to work together without Pete later. However, I was still desperately lacking original inspiration. Hence, my contribution to *Kiln House* was more of the same, with the exception of 'One Together'.

What were the dynamics like in the band then in terms of friendships and mutual support?

We did stay friends. We had to! Like the old saying: "We'd better hang together, 'cause if we don't, it's for sure we'll hang separately!"

I believe the rest of the band was concerned about me, and they couldn't figure me out. I couldn't even figure myself out. They tried to encourage me with any shreds of new stuff I had. I was even going to drop 'One Together' from the *Kiln House* album, for instance, but they insisted on keeping it on.

Were manager Clifford Davis and Warner-Reprise pushing hard to "keep the show on the road," so to speak?

I didn't feel that those you mention were pushing, although it was evident that we needed to get down to business in the wake of Pete's departure. We pretty much flopped in England, but an encouraging aspect for us was that *Kiln House* was our biggest-selling album in the States up until that time, and the accompanying tour was surprisingly well received. It seemed that the audiences were unfamiliar with what we'd done before and had bought that album on its own merit.

If you don't mind revisiting what you were feeling then, how bad was the pressure to keep things going after Peter left, and how unsatisfying was it all?

I think we all felt the pressure to keep things going after Pete left. He had been the main creative force. And, as usual, I was merely filling the role of being a showman, but with unoriginal material and parodying, which pretty much became just mimicking Elvis in a gold lamé suit. This was very unsatisfying, to say the least. I can't say it enough, that the lack of creative inspiration for me was devastating. It was practically killing me, along with my questions about life and what was I living for. Nothing seemed to have any purpose. I really did feel like Solomon, that "all is vanity," although I'd gotten to that point at only 22 years old.

I'm guessing that Mick was a road warrior as usual, John content to order another pint, Danny perhaps a bit lost already, and I have no idea how Christine handled things. I can't help but think that performing had become a wearisome job by then.

We all felt incapable. But Mick was a good morale booster and road warrior of the "old gigs-ter" school, having experienced a musician's life of feast and famine. I was amazed at his fortitude in that. Danny was coming up with interesting new stuff, although he would be hard pressed for lyrics. We would sit around and brainstorm song themes and words, and everything sounded trite. Christine was more of a lyricist, so when she joined later, things started to take shape in that direction. Me? I didn't know what to say. And if I did, I didn't know how to say it. And bottom line, I just didn't enjoy playing anymore.

By abandoning the band to join the Children of God [later called the Family], I assume you found something—a foundation—to sustain you. Have you been happy these last 35 years?

On the whole, I have been happy. It's funny when people ask me, "Are you happy?" It kind of stops me, and I wonder, not because I doubt it, as we all have good days and bad days, but I have to say that I am. It was difficult at the beginning of joining Children of God—more for me than most. As Jesus said, "How difficult it is for a rich man to enter the kingdom of God." He didn't say it was impossible, but squeezing a camel through the eye of a needle is a squeeze!

Now I can honestly say that every day, month, and year has gotten better, and I am happier now and more fulfilled than ever. It's quite amazing. And one thing is for certain: I found inspiration within two weeks of leaving FM. I started getting ideas for songs and tunes and, later, melodies on the piano. I have stacks of unused ideas that I can't see getting around to finishing, let alone recording, in this life.

What has it been like to live in exotic places over the years? What are some of your good memories from such places as Brazil, the Philippines, India, et cetera?
This is a big one! It's one thing to visit; it's another thing to live in a foreign country! However, it's come to the point that England is more of a foreign place for me now than almost anywhere! But I would say that, generally, I have good memories of the people of these exotic places, and I enjoy their cuisine much more than Western food, my favorite meal being a good Brazilian *fejoiada*!

The climate hasn't always been to my liking; I'm a "four seasons" man. But I am always impressed by the simplicity and humility of the people of the developing world. "The meek shall inherit the earth," and although some of them may not seem to have much, you can see that this saying is true, in that they have wisdom, virtues, gifts, simple faith, and gratitude through the rough times that the richer nations lack.

Did you continue to play as you moved around?
Yes. Sometimes recording in home studios, sometimes for kids in a park, for friends and neighbors, and a few concerts, such as in India for the National Association for the Blind.

Do you mind recapping how the Columbia and Atlantic albums came about?
The 1972 Columbia album came about as a result of meeting one of the company's representatives, Stuart Love. He liked a demo I presented him

with, and they gave us quite a bit of slack to do what we wanted, which I appreciated. I regret that we fell short on the mixing side of things, going more by our uninformed inclinations rather than professional advice.

Atlantic's *Flee* album in 1978 came from a member of the Family's association with a French fashion designer Arianne Brener, who was a friend of Ahmet Ertegun. This was at a time when FM's *Rumours* was still hitting big. The company wanted to cash in on the ex-FM thing, and although Ahmet was excited about our original material, his subordinates in the company won over and turned most of it into a disco nightmare. For me, the only decent track on it is 'Travelling'.

An interesting aside I enjoy telling about recording this album was about one evening in the New York studio when we were finishing overdubs on the disco numbers. The vocal arranger could tell I was down about the way things were going, and he said to me, "It's hamburgers." I said, "What do you mean?" He answered, "You wanna know how I reconcile myself with this? It's just hamburgers. Look, I hate this shit as much as you do, but I tell myself, just give 'em hamburgers. It doesn't matter. Give the kids the shit they want and don't worry about it."

Were you able to keep track of what was happening with Peter and with Danny?
I was able to at a distance, as I've been mostly abroad since I left FM. During a temporary stay in England in 2002, I saw Pete a few times and met Danny once. I have kept up regular communications with Mick over the years, and it's always a very pleasant time when we get to meet.

Your old band became the biggest act in the world in the late 1970s and early 1980s. Were you glad for them and, at the same time, happy to be out of it?
You are correct. I knew I had left them in the lurch in 1971, but I prayed desperately for them to have success beyond anything they had experienced. They could have taken action against me, but to the contrary, they were supportive even to their own hurt.

346 | FLEETWOOD MAC ON FLEETWOOD MAC

Please recap the recent years. I understand that you are living in Ireland now, doing artwork as well as occasionally performing in public. What are the satisfactions?

In the 1970s I lived in the States, England, France, Brazil, and Italy. In the 1980s I lived in Greece, Sri Lanka, the Philippines, and Japan. In the '90s I lived in Brazil and Mexico. For the last few years I've lived in Switzerland, England, and currently have been basing in Ireland. But my lifestyle is [one] that many have found, one of a pilgrim and stranger, and I have to be ready to go or stay, sometimes at a moment's notice, depending on the needs of my wife and my work. It's not comfortable sometimes, but it is exciting. And it's not as if, because I'm almost 58, God is going to allow me to settle down too long too soon.

I have done the occasional performance, but it is with a great deal of thought and prayer. I don't have the time or the desire to go back to the gigging grind, although I do enjoy playing, especially with Trond [Ytterbo, harpist] and the Norwegian musicians. It's a pleasure. And I hope to record again with them someday.

Comic strip and graphic novel illustrating is a joy for me, too: black ink brush-line work like Will Eisner and Terry and Rachel Dodson. I get inspired with ideas for that, and writing short novels and stories, too. I am *busy!*

Rumors have circulated that the original four- or five-piece Mac lineup might reunite for a tour. Is that possible? Would Peter's fragile mental health allow it, is Danny in any kind of shape to do it, and would you want to be part of such a carnival?

You have asked valid questions about reasons that could make it a possible carnival. At this point in time, I have no desire to be a part of it.

How would you sum up your life to this point? All things considered, have you followed the right path?

I was in Fleetwood Mac for three and a half years and have been in the Family for 35. That's 10 times as long. Unless, as some people accuse me of, I'm in a state of denial, that should speak for itself.

ORIGINAL SKIN

Mac Randall | December 2006 | *Guitar World Acoustic* (US)

As well as being a great songwriter and capable vocalist, Lindsey Buckingham is one of the most arresting guitar stylists in popular music. This feature focuses on his technique, with a little insight into his songwriting processes thrown in.

"I'M NOT A FINESSE GUY," says Lindsey Buckingham. "I'm more damn-the-torpedoes." He's actually referring to the way he deals with others, but you could argue that the same applies to his guitar style. Anyone who's seen the hyper-aggressive way his right hand claws at the strings of his Turner Model I electric would have a hard time describing him as a "finesse" player. At the same time, it's equally difficult to claim that Buckingham's unique fingerstyle approach (he's never used a pick) lacks precision or taste. And it's impossible to deny the dazzling musical results. Just listen to any of the albums he's made during his two tenures with Fleetwood Mac, from 1975 to 1987 and from 1997 to the present. Christine McVie and Stevie Nicks may have written more of the band's biggest hits, but Buckingham's playing—along with his backup singing, arranging and production genius—is the magic ingredient that helped make songs like "Rhiannon," "Say You Love Me," "Dreams," "You Make Loving Fun," "Think About Me" and "Gypsy" so memorable, and so successful.

Of course, Buckingham's own songbook is also studded with gems— "Monday Morning," "World Turning," "Never Going Back Again," "Go Your Own Way," "Second Hand News" and "Big Love," to name just a few. But his pop sensibilities have always coexisted with that "damn-the-torpedoes" spirit, which has propelled him into plenty of left-field ventures. First there were the songs he cut by himself in his home studio and contributed to Fleetwood Mac's *Tusk* (1979), twisted lo-fi rock oddities like "Not That Funny" and "The Ledge." Then there were his solo releases—*Law and Order* (1981), *Go Insane* (1985), and *Out of the Cradle* (1992)—on which he backed up his alternately howling and cooing vocals with an army of varispeeded guitars that sounded like they'd been injected with performance-enhancing drugs.

You won't find anything quite as bizarre on Buckingham's new CD, *Under the Skin* (Reprise), his first solo album in nearly 15 years. (His previous two attempts to make a solo record turned into full-blown Fleetwood Mac projects). The primary instruments are acoustic guitar and voice, and overt studio trickery is shelved in favor of stripped-down songcraft. But stripped-down doesn't mean conservative—Buckingham goes for broke the same way he always has, only more quietly. All 11 tracks have a dark, almost creepy vibe, with lyrics so personal that you feel you shouldn't be listening to them. And yet you're somehow compelled to do so. A big part of the draw is Buckingham's intricate fingerpicking, which he showcases on the hair-raising opener "Not Too Late" and a drastically altered version of Donovan's "Try for the Sun."

Between rehearsals with a four-piece band for a fall tour to promote *Under the Skin*, Buckingham chatted with *Guitar World Acoustic* about his new material. His modesty regarding his own abilities comes as a surprise; his obvious devotion to his art does not.

GUITAR WORLD ACOUSTIC: Why did you decide to make such a predominantly acoustic album? There's hardly an electric guitar to be found on the record.

LINDSEY BUCKINGHAM: Well, there are a couple, but certainly no leads [*laughs*]. It's because I have plans to put out a more rock album in the near future, probably about 10 months from now—a fairly close amount of time and, given my track record, *way* closer than normal. So I've actually been working on a pair of albums. And for this one, I really wanted it to hold a certain line. I've been interested for quite a while in trying to distill my fingerpicking style down to its bare essentials, and the album is very much about keeping the production as minimal as possible while still having it sound like a record.

GWA: You play the great majority of the instruments on *Under the Skin*, but not all of them. Who else was involved?

LB: Mick Fleetwood played percussion on "Down on Rodeo" and "Someone's Gotta Change Your Mind," John McVie played bass on "Down on Rodeo" and David Campbell did some orchestration on "Someone's Gotta Change Your Mind." Those two songs were recorded quite a long time ago, almost 10 years ago, at Ocean Way Studios in Hollywood, and they were under consideration for [the 2003 Fleetwood Mac album] *Say You Will*. But that's really it. The other songs are all from the last three years. I recorded them by myself, either at home or on the road with Fleetwood Mac, and they're mostly guitars and vocals with a little rhythmic support. And lots of echo.

GWA: For sure. One song, among many, with "lots of echo" is "I Am Waiting." How did you get that pretty, filtered delay-type sound on the acoustic guitar?

LB: That's an old Roland synth, driven by one nice-sounding Turner thin-bodied acoustic rather than one of those cruddy Strats that you might normally plug into a Roland. The guitar sound is clean, but the synth gives it a chamber-orchestra effect.

GWA: "I Am Waiting" is a Rolling Stones tune, and you also do a cover of Donovan's "Try for the Sun" on the new album. Any particular reason you recorded those songs?

LB: As far as the Stones song goes, there was actually a point where I went through this whole spate of Stones songs that I loved from a certain period—mainly '65 and '66—and tried recording them. All obscure stuff: "The Singer Not the Song," "Gotta Get Away," which will be on the next album, "She Smiled Sweetly," which was another one I cut with Mick [Fleetwood]. They all turned out fine, but I was looking for vehicles for a certain kind of acoustic playing, and "I Am Waiting" seemed the most successful. It was more about the arrangement than the song itself. And the Donovan song was just something I remembered fondly from when it came out, when I was 14 or 15. Its melodic structure is very generic folk-song, but it was close to my heart, and it was a reference point for what I later ended up writing.

GWA: Your arrangement of it is very different from the original, the most obvious change being that it's in 6/8 time instead of 4/4.

LB: That was to suit my own petty guitar needs. It's funny—one of the guys I work with was also working with Donovan at the time I was cutting it, and he mentioned to Donovan that I was doing one of his songs. When he heard which one it was, he said [*imitating an angry Scotsman*], "'Try for the Sun'? What's he doing that one for?" So if he ever hears my version, he'll probably go, "*He fucked it up!*" I don't know how well I succeeded in putting it together.

GWA: It sounds like you wrote it, which must qualify as some kind of success.

LB: Gotta get away from that 6/8 thing, though. Been doing that too long.

GWA: What about those crazed arpeggios you play throughout the first track, "Not Too Late"? How do you play those?

LB: It's my usual extended Travis picking kind of thing. It sounds rapid-fire, but it's really not that hard to play. I've done it live a couple of times in very small settings, and so far I haven't screwed it up.

GWA: I imagine that it's difficult to sing while playing that part.

LB: No, because first of all, the guitar sticks to the same pattern all the way through, and I'm almost talking through the verse. And the chorus is basically one note. With a lot of these songs, I didn't want to get too coy with bringing more instrumentation in on the chorus and then taking it out for the verse, because if you were sitting around, playing the song on a guitar for somebody, that wouldn't be happening. So I was trying to make the music be produced but more real, if that word even applies in this day and age.

GWA: The chord progression in "Not Too Late" somehow reminds me of music by French Impressionist composers like Debussy and Ravel. Have you listened to a lot of classical music? Many of your songs—"Eyes of the World," for example, and the instrumental segments on *Out of the Cradle*—suggest that you have.

LB: Well, that influence is in there, but I'm far from being well-versed in any kind of classical music. It's more like I heard a piece here and there and got a flavor for it. Someone who's played guitar by himself in his room for years will tend to come across things and find ways to incorporate them into his style. But because I was never formally taught on anything, I'm basically a refined primitive. I don't read music, and I just found my own way on guitar. I'm more knowledgeable about rock music than any other kind, but even there it's only to a point. By no means am I a musicologist.

GWA: The sound of the acoustic nylon-string continues to be central to your music. Are you still using the same Rick Turner guitars?

LB: Yes, and a couple of Chet Atkins models that Rick modified, along with the occasional Taylor. My setup's never been too elaborate. I'm not trying out new guitars or looking at what else is out there. I tend to find things that work and stick with them for a long period of time, as long as I can get to what I want to get to. If it ain't broke, don't fix it.

GWA: Is that rhythm part in "Under the Skin" played on a Taylor?

LB: Can't say for sure, but I think that was recorded on one of those 3/4-size Baby Taylors in a hotel room while I was on tour with Fleetwood Mac. It's in open G, and I use a bunch of maj7 chords.

GWA: The chords sound very high and sparkly, as though the guitar was in Nashville tuning. Were you using a capo?

LB: Yes. It's probably moved up [three frets] to Bb or . . . or whatever. I don't know what key it's in. That's where my skill ends. I'm not someone who can transpose into different keys all over the place. I just have my things that I do. I'm sort of like Irving Berlin in that way. He could play in only one key, so he had his piano customized so that he could turn a crank and change the key even though he was still playing the same chords. It's a little easier to do that with guitars.

GWA: The last tune, "Juniper," has a slight Brazilian feel to it.

LB: My wife calls it the *Love Boat* song. Thank you, dear [*laughs*]. It was originally written in a much slower, straighter tempo, and it wasn't something I'd planned to put on this record. But when I was finishing the album I went back to it, and the lyric struck me as more appropriate than it had been when I wrote it. It was a remembrance of growing up [in Palo Alto, California]. Juniper is the name of a street that ran right into the street my family lived on; we used to ride our bikes down Juniper when I was a kid. Now I'm a father, and when you become a parent you see your own parents differently—you can maybe see them in a wiser light. Also, because it was another maj7 song, I thought it would be a nice mate to "Under the Skin." A lot of people said, "Don't put that on there, it's terrible!" And I thought, Well, okay, maybe it is, but you can get away with a lot when it's the last song on the record.

GWA: Parts of the new album are so self-revealing that they make the listener feel like he's eavesdropping on a private conversation. The lyrics cut pretty close to the bone.

LB: Very much so. But there was certainly a precedent set for that kind of writing during a certain time with Fleetwood Mac, and back then I don't think anyone thought about what the specifics of any given song were or what the overall effect on anyone else would be. The aim was just to make it as true as we could and as skillful as we could, and the same holds true here. My life has changed so drastically since the last time I made a solo record. If you go back three years to the last Fleetwood Mac album, there was such a lag time for my material on that because it was all a holdover from what was supposed to be my own electric solo album. I got that off the books, and started fresh and addressed my life as it is now—I'm finally married after so many years of living in a semi-dysfunctional social world, with three beautiful children and the kind of perspective that gives you, combined with whatever goes on in the mind of someone who can see himself healthily, as a mature artist, not trying to be something he's not. That's what came out on the album. Many of these songs seem more truthful to me than anything I've ever done.

GWA: *Say You Will* wasn't the first Fleetwood Mac album that started out as a Lindsey Buckingham solo project. There's a long history of that kind of band usurpation, starting in the mid-'80s with *Tango in the Night*. It reminds me of Michael Corleone in the *Godfather* movies: Every time you want to go off and do your own thing . . .

LB: They pull me back in! [*laughs uproariously*] Before we got back together for *The Dance* [in 1997], they even performed what might be called an intervention. We were over at Christine [McVie]'s house, and everyone was literally standing around me in a circle saying, "You've got to put the solo work down and do this with us."

GWA: Was there any danger of that this time?

LB: There wasn't in terms of the material getting folded over. There was a little bit of pressure about my carving out a sufficient time frame to do this album, tour it, then finish the other one and, in all likelihood, tour that one too. But I talked to Stevie [Nicks] and everybody about it, and I don't think anyone at the end of the day begrudged me the time to do what I felt I needed to do. The way they're looking at it, I think, is that at least I'll get it out of my system: "He'll be a nicer guy after he finishes this." [*laughs*]

GWA: You mentioned your tendency to allow many years to pass between solo albums. Is that because you find it hard to let things go? You're certainly fond of recycling parts of songs. For instance, some sections of "Not That Funny" and "I Know I'm Not Wrong," both on *Tusk*, are nearly identical; one of the verses in "You Do or You Don't" on *Out of the Cradle* shows up again—words and music—as the bridge in "Bleed to Love Her" from *Say You Will* . . .

LB: And the acoustic guitar line in "Eyes of the World" [*from 1982's* Mirage] came out of an instrumental piece on

Buckingham Nicks [*recorded in 1973 before* the *duo joined Fleetwood Mac*]. That's almost like a running gag, though it's not meant to be. I've never had a problem with taking an element from another song—as long as it's my song and I'm not gonna get sued for it—and reusing it in a different way, if it has its own integrity in the new context. It's like leaving little clues for the people who are really paying attention. Again, I don't set out intentionally to do this. I hate to admit it, but it's about expediency. I say, "Oh, that old bit would be cool there." Some people might think it's not cool to use it again, but my feeling is, as long as you don't do it all the time, who cares?

GWA: So that has nothing to do with some obsessive need you have to keep tinkering with a part until it's perfect?

LB: Oh, not at all. It's more just being lazy. [*laughs*]

GWA: Speaking of *Buckingham Nicks,* will it ever be reissued? At this point, it's got to be one of the most famous albums to have never been released on CD.

LB: I know, isn't it ridiculous? Stevie and I own the 24-track masters, and one of Stevie's managers has them at her *house.* I actually didn't know where they were for a while; that's one of those little power plays that goes on. It's become almost an extension of Fleetwood Mac politics, convoluted as they are. Everyone agrees that the record needs to come out, but everyone also agrees that it needs to come out at a time when there can be some kind of event to promote it, and no one knows what that is. Do Stevie and I go out and do dates as a duo? What are we talking about here? So it's in the ether. But the thing is, we'd better hurry up, because pretty soon it's going to be a little late.

GWA: You're very much a pop songwriter, but at the same time you have this radical experimental streak. Has it been difficult for you to strike a balance between your two selves?

LB: It has been, in the past. Say we'd done *Tusk,* never mind how much it sold or didn't sell, and the rest of the band had been on the same page about the musical results—because believe me, they weren't enchanted with the music, it was only years later that people started to acknowledge that it had some worth—I probably would never have even thought about making solo albums. The palette would've been so wide at that point that we would've felt there was room for everything within Fleetwood Mac. As it was, *Tusk* didn't sell 16 million [*as its predecessor, 1977's* Rumours, *had*], and I'd set the stage for the backlash that occurred within the band to disallow that experimental mindset.

So, to answer your question, yes, that kind of backlash put me in the position of having to be a bit bipolar, and that wasn't always that easy. When I listen to the *Go Insane* album, where you've got all these things right off the Fairlight [synthesizer] like "Play in the Rain"—I love it, but the *gesture* of it is what you notice more than the actual music. What I'm trying to do now is keep the experimentalism in play, but in as much of a personal and centered context as possible. There's a lot of room for experimentation without having to go out and wear it on your sleeve.

GWA: Where do things stand with the other solo record?

LB: I have nine songs that I consider finished tracks, which were done at my house in the last year and a half. And I've also got a ton of new material that hasn't been formally cut. During the next month we'll try to set up a game plan, and then when I get off the road we'll start working on it. After that, we'll hopefully get it out in a remarkably short amount of time, for me. That would be the hook: What's he been doing all this time? Answer: Putting two albums out within the course of a year. And then after that . . . [*sighs*] I think it's just Fleetwood Mac for a while. That's what I'm hearing, anyway. We'll see. Nice to keep busy, though—gotta pay for my kids' private schools and all that!

VISION QUEST

Chris Neal | June 2007 | *Performing Songwriter* (US)

As might be expected with the method-focused *Performing Songwriter*, this Stevie Nicks feature finds her discussing her composing craft. In addition, however, she reflects on her solo career and her conviction that there is no point in a Fleetwood Mac without Christine McVie.

NICKS OF TIME
Since her solo career began in 1981, Stevie Nicks has alternated between going it alone and returning to the Fleetwood Mac fold. Here's a handy guide to what Nicks was doing when.

JULY 1981
First solo album, *Bella Donna,* is released.

JULY 1981
First of several collaborations with Tom Petty, "Stop Draggin' My Heart Around," debuts on singles chart.

APRIL 1982
"Edge of Seventeen" peaks at No. 11.

JUNE 1983
Solo album *The Wild Heart* hits stores.

AUGUST 1983
"Stand Back" reaches No. 5.

NOVEMBER 1985
Solo album *Rock a Little* arrives.

JANUARY 1986
"Talk to Me" peaks at No. 4.

MAY 1989
Solo album *The Other Side of the Mirror* is released.

JULY 1991
Nicks tells interviewers that she has quit Fleetwood Mac following a serious falling-out with Mick Fleetwood.

SEPTEMBER 1991
Timespace: The Very Best of Stevie Nicks is released.

JANUARY 1993
Fleetwood Mac's most well-known line up performs at President Clinton's inaugural ball.

MAY 1994
Solo album *Street Angel* is released.

MAY 1997
The reunited Mac tapes the MTV concert special *The Dance* in Burbank, Calif.

JANUARY 1998
Fleetwood Mac is inducted into the Rock and Roll Hall of Fame.

MAY 2001
Solo album *Trouble in Shangri-La* arrives in stores.

MARCH 2007

Nicks' latest hits collection, *Crystal Visions . . . The Very Best of Stevie Nicks,* is released.

The weather is gray, windy and, as Stevie Nicks notes, "a little creepy" outside her home overlooking the Pacific Ocean.

"I call it the 'amoeba fog,'" she says, looking out from the living room of her Los Angeles home. "It sticks right to the coast. You might as well be in Seattle or London for several months out of the year. It suits me sometimes, but after it's been that way for a couple of weeks, I start to go, 'OK, I'd like to see the blue sky.'"

Nicks is well acquainted with both the clouds and the blue sky of L.A. A native of Phoenix (she also keeps a house there), she moved to L.A. from San Francisco with guitarist and then-paramour Lindsey Buckingham in 1971. On New Year's Eve 1974, both were asked to join Fleetwood Mac—and alongside keyboardist Christine McVie, bass player John McVie and drummer Mick Fleetwood, they helped to turn a British blues-rock warhorse into one of the best-selling and most influential bands in pop history.

Nicks became the group's breakout star, thanks to her striking beauty, dusky alto and magnetic stage presence—but perhaps most of all her talents as a writer. Songs like "Dreams," "Rhiannon," "Sara" and "Gold Dust Woman" rang out as evocative, impressionistic transmissions from a parallel world a little more vivid and romantic than our own. Through a poetic lens, she examined femininity, mythology and love—particularly the disintegration and aftermath of her relationship with Buckingham.

In the spring of 1980, Nicks began work on her first solo album. The intervening years have seen her build a persona, fan base and musical legacy that stands apart from the mighty Mac. Hits like "Edge of Seventeen," "Stand Back" and "Talk to Me" provided a constant reminder that Nicks was a singer and songwriter whose talents went much farther than her contributions to the band she could never completely abandon. Those songs and a bounty of others chosen by Nicks herself are now collected on a new compilation album, *Crystal Visions . . . The Very Best of Stevie*

Nicks. As dusk settled over L.A. and the "amoeba fog" clung stubbornly to the coast, we asked Nicks, 58, to describe her creative process, recount her journey through music and predict the future of Fleetwood Mac.

***This is your second greatest-hits collection. How did you pick the songs for* Crystal Visions?**
When you're doing this kind of package, you go back to the singles. But I tried to make this different. "Landslide" and "Edge of Seventeen" with the Melbourne Symphony Orchestra went on in place of the recorded versions at first. You better have a really good in-place-of if you're not going to use the record version. But then I decided to put the real "Edge of Seventeen" on, too, since I could fit it. So there's "Edge of Seventeen" from the very beginning and "Edge of Seventeen" from last year. I thought that was an interesting turn-the-page from one lifetime to another.

You've talked about your "song vault." Every album you make seems to include at least a couple of songs that go back a few years.
I do try to go back and pick up as many of the standout songs as I can. I was reading the article about John Mayer in your magazine [*November 2006*], and he was talking about the fact that when a song doesn't get recorded, it just goes out into space. Sometimes you later realize that song was a lot better than the one that made the record. So you try to go back and pick that song up at some point.

At this point in your career, there are certain songs that your audience would be disappointed if you didn't perform. Do you ever get tired of those?
After you've been doing this as long as I have, you have a certain repertoire. You know there are certain songs people want to hear. You're not going to throw out "Rhiannon," because people are gonna walk away and go, "I can't believe she didn't do 'Rhiannon.'" So you have to figure out a way to summon that passion. I reach down and pull out the emotion that led me to write the song in the beginning. With that, they're not hard to sing. I can always enjoy them. And if I start to get tired of

one of them, I drop it. There have been times when I've dropped "Gold Dust Woman" or "Dreams." I can't drop all of them, but I can drop one here and there.

Why did you revise the lyrics to "Rhiannon"?
How did I revise them?

There are several differences in the recording and the way you do it live. For example, on the original, Rhiannon is "taken by the wind." By the early 1980s, she was "taken by the sky."
Oh, you know what? I don't think I purposely did that. Sometimes I just go off. Those words probably evolved out of my solo work. When I have my two girls with *me [background singers Lori Perry and Sharon Celani have performed with Nicks on most of her solo albums and tours]*, we do all these things I don't do that much in Fleetwood Mac. That is a difference in Fleetwood Mac and my solo work—I am more flamboyant in my solo work. In the Mac, I'm part of a team, so I try not to stand out as much. I blend in more, because I'm one of the charmed three. In my own work, I'm just me. When Lori and Sharon and I are singing, we're able to be more out there, more spacey, more flamboyant.

Do you generally write on piano?
Pretty much. The piano, for some reason, holds a real fascination for me. I'm not a very good player, and I play in a weird sort of way. I don't really play chords. I sound like a second-grader but play good enough to write. Even the total childlike renderings that I come up with, I can hear them orchestrated in my head. "Rhiannon" is just like (*sings melody*) *dun-dun-dun, dun-dun-dun-dun,* it's this little simple thing. But when I was writing it, I could hear what it could be.

What kind of piano do you have now?
I have a nine-foot white Steinway that was played on the road for years by Billy Preston, Leon Russell and other famous people, I'm told. It has a certain sound that's very Leon Russell-Dr. John, that very tinkly kind of sound. Then I have a Bosendorfer that is like a big black cat. It's a

seven-foot grand. These pianos take up so much room that you can't even have living room furniture, but they're my babies. "Edge of Seventeen," "Stand Back," "Dreams," all of my songs I've pretty much written on these two pianos. Each brings out something different in me, because they sound very different.

Let's go back to the beginning of your solo career. Why did you decide to make your first solo album, **Bella Donna** *[1981]?*
Simply to have another vehicle for my songs. The reason was not ever because I wanted to be a big solo artist. I was very interested in continuing to be in my band. I loved being in Fleetwood Mac. But when there are three writers [*Nicks, Buckingham and Christine McVie each contributed songs more or less equally to Fleetwood Mac*], you can only get three or four songs on a record. For me as a writer, that started to become hard.

What do you recall about the making of the album?
We rented Bill Cosby's house in the Palisades. We worked for about two months with [keyboardist] Benmont Tench, Lori and Sharon in the living room at the grand piano every day. We played and sang all the songs on *Bella Donna* over and over until we had them down perfect. It was so much fun. We were like Joni Mitchell and Crosby, Stills & Nash, living in this great house and making music in [L.A.'s] Laurel Canyon. It was one of those real rock 'n' roll experiences that you can never forget. Then we went into the studio, and the record only took three months because we were so rehearsed and practiced and excited—and not spoiled rotten, not self-indulgent. By the time the record came out, Fleetwood Mac was tapping their feet like, "Where the hell are you?" So I only did 12 shows and flew to Paris the next day to join Fleetwood Mac for [the recording of 1982's] *Mirage*.

What was your attitude going into your second solo album, **The Wild Heart** *[1983]?*
Bella Donna had done really well, so we had more confidence. But during *Wild Heart* I was coming to the end of my [romantic] relationship with [producer] Jimmy Iovine, so that was really sad. I was working

with Jimmy, and that was hard. I had already gone through the whole Lindsey-and-Stevie thing, and now here I was back in another situation where I was working with somebody that I had loved and the relationship had started to fall apart.

Why is that?

Mostly because of drugs. Jimmy was not a drug user or a drinker, and the whole world was turning into a bunch of drug addicts at that point. It was heartbreaking for him, because everybody around him was starting to cave in. *The Wild Heart* was a hard record to do, and by the time we got to *Rock a Little* [1985] he had had it. I didn't blame him. I understood. On *Rock a Little,* we were really slipping into darkness.

How does* Rock a Little *sound to you now?

There are some really good things on *Rock a Little.* There are also parts where I go, "What were you thinking? Did you really think that was *good?*" But that was toward the end of my cocaine habit. Everybody was crazy at that point. When you're rich, famous and a drug addict and you're trying to do your music . . . I was always planning to quit, I was always making plans to change my life, and it just didn't happen because we never had a day off. We were always working. I knew at the beginning of the *Rock a Little* tour that I wanted to go into rehab. I had already booked this seven-month tour, but I knew that the second the tour was over in October that I would be going straight into the Betty Ford Center.

Most people who say, "In seven months I'm going into rehab," wind up never going at all.

Right, they don't. But my poor little nose had fallen apart. I went to a plastic surgeon, and he said, "Your nose is in trouble, and you'd better be careful. You could have a brain hemorrhage and die." I was terrified. But I wasn't gonna cancel my tour, so I decided I was just going to walk a tightrope for the next six months. And I did. I took as good care of myself as I could, and I did as little of that stuff as I could possibly do to get through it. Then when the tour was over I went home, got in the car and drove to Palm Springs. I walked into Betty Ford going, "Here I am, fix me."

How did you feel when you finished rehab?
I came out in great shape. I was happy, drug-free and looked incredible, if I do say so myself. The problem came with the rest of the world saying I should either go to Alcoholics Anonymous or to a psychiatrist. I was saying, "Listen, I'm never gonna go back to being a drug addict, ever. I'm not going to AA, because I'm not an alcoholic, and I'm not going to a psychiatrist because I'm not crazy. Get off my back." But people didn't get off my back. They kept bugging me. So one day I said, "Alright, I'll go see a psychiatrist!' And it's too bad, because if I hadn't gone to see this doctor I would have had a much better life. This guy decided that he was going to be the reason that I wouldn't return to coke. So he put me on a drug called Klonopin [a tranquilizer in the Valium family]. This drug is subtle. You take it and you don't really feel it that much. You feel a little calmer. But over a period of time, it starts to fog your brain.

How did it affect your artistic output?
Lucky me, I had written the songs for *The Other Side of the Mirror* [1989] before the Klonopin kicked in. I was very happy with them, and still am. I really love that record. Somewhere out on that tour the stuff kicked in and brought me to my knees. I folded into the couch. I've read through my writings from that time, and I would just be writing about nothing. Pages and pages of . . . *nothing*. That was a very sad period of my life. This guy continued to up my dose over an eight-year period. I will never quite understand how somebody can do that to another person. If I could have just not gone to that doctor, I figure I could have done two or three more really, really good solo records. Those eight years were totally stolen from me. That was worse than the cocaine years, because at least during those years I did something that I considered valuable.

How did you get off Klonopin?
I walked into the psychiatrist's office for the last time in 1993 and said, "I'm going to a hospital, you asshole." He's going, "I don't think you

should do that. We can drop your dose a bit." I said, "You fuck yourself, you bastard." And I went straight to a hospital. I believe that had I not done that, I would have been dead within a year. I went into rehab for 47 days. I went through the worst detox, and I nearly died in there.

So where does the making of Street Angel [1994] fall in relation to that period?
It was done in the very end of that era of my life. When I came out of rehab, I was listening to this record going, "Oh my god, this cost a lot of money, it's not good and I hate it. We can't put this out." So I went in for six weeks and tried to fix it, but it was like making a dress—you cut it to a certain length, and you cannot put the length back in. You can't get the fabric back. I was screwed. There was really nothing I could do. We put it out. By the time I came off that tour, all the songs from *Street Angel* had been dropped from the set list and I almost never spoke of it again. I don't listen to it. I don't even want to hear it.

By contrast, Trouble in Shangri-La [2001] seems like . . . I'm back! (*Laughs*) *Trouble in Shangri-La* was terrific. My world had fallen apart twice now, and I was trying to put it back together this time. It took about three years to make, but when that record was done I was very proud of it. It took a long time, but it was fun.

After that you returned to Fleetwood Mac yet again. How do you look back on the making of Say You Will [2003]?
On Feb. 2, 2002, I went straight from the *Trouble in Shangri-La* tour into recording with them. It was a nightmare doing that record. It really was Lindsey's vision, and it wasn't very much about the other three of us. And of course it was also the first record we had ever attempted to do without Christine [McVie, who left the band in the late 1990s]. Right there, the whole thing was completely insane. She is the magic mediator in that band and always was. She's the one who made light of everything and made everybody laugh and told us all that we were full of shit. She was the person who made it all work. So when she wasn't there, that sunk the boat. I don't think that my friend Chris ever realized how important

she was. Without her, it's a boys' club. The lack of Christine is a big, hollow hole in my heart.

Would you be willing to attempt another record without her?
Absolutely not. Not in this lifetime. Why? We already tried, and it did not work. My thing is, somebody convince Christine to come back and do this one more time. I don't think she's going to change her mind, but stranger things have happened.

Do you have plans for another solo album?
I'm always writing, so I would be lying to say I wouldn't love to. But I don't have a lot of faith about what's going on in the music business right now. I have a 15-year-old niece who is incredibly talented and beautiful, and she sings and she writes. Is there even a place for her? The idea that all these talented kids are out there writing incredible songs that are never going to see the light of day makes me nauseous. So we have to be really optimistic and believe that there is a god, and God will not have a world without music. Let's all just say a prayer that the music will be saved.

What has sustained you through all these years in such a brutal business?
I love to entertain. If Lindsey and I had broken up and not done that first Fleetwood Mac record, I would have still done my music in my own small way. I'd be playing in clubs now, because music is what I love. No matter what, I would have still been doing this. I'm an entertainer at heart.

INSIDE THE SONG
"RHIANNON"
Nicks wrote "Rhiannon" several months before joining Fleetwood Mac, inspired by a character of the same name in Mary Leader's book *Triad*. The original demo, recorded by Nicks and Lindsey Buckingham, takes the song at a much faster clip than the version that would appear on Fleetwood Mac's 1975 self-titled album and reach No. 11 on *Billboard*'s pop singles chart. "It wasn't exactly the song it is today, but it's similar," Nicks says.

Nicks learned that the name "Rhiannon" dates back to the *Mabinogion,* a medieval Welsh book of wisdom. Nicks says she has written around 20 more songs based on *Mabinogion* myths over the last three decades, around which she hopes to eventually build a fantasy movie musical. "They're these amazing stories of Rhiannon and all the gods and goddesses of her gang," she says. "I've been working on it in my heart ever since I wrote 'Rhiannon.'"

INSIDE THE SONG
"SILVER SPRINGS"

Nicks wrote "Silver Springs" for Fleetwood Mac's 1977 album *Rumours,* but the song was cut at the last minute and tucked away instead as the B-side of the hit "Go Your Own Way." It was a decision that deeply disappointed the song's creator (it was restored on the 2004 *Rumours* reissue). When the Mac's most famous lineup reunited for the 1997 concert album and MTV special *The Dance,* the song was revived and became a hit after 20 years.

Nicks' mother, Barbara, suggested to her that "Silver Springs" be included on her daughter's new greatest-hits album, *Crystal Visions . . . The Very Best of Stevie Nicks.* Perhaps not so coincidentally, Nicks had long ago gifted her mother with the song's publishing rights—so it's Barbara who will collect the songwriting royalties. "I said, 'You are a very smart girl, Mom,'" Nicks recalls with a chuckle. "The reason I really did this is that my mom is 79, and having that song on this package makes her a part of this."

CALIFORNIA DREAMING

Sylvie Simmons | September 2007 | *Mojo* (UK)

Much had changed in the life of Stevie Nicks since Sylvie Simmons interviewed her in 1981 for *Kerrang!*—not just the drug taking and band infighting but the fact that transformed circumstances and altered social mores had made Nicks far freer to talk about them.

THE LIVING ROOM IS DIMLY LIT, COSY. AT one end on the floor, propped against a wall, are some paintings—works-in-progress—that could pass as illustrations for children's books. At the other end is an open fireplace with logs blazing, the California sunset having given way to a chilly ocean breeze. Two tiny dogs, neither much bigger than a hairball, one of them clad in a little pink overcoat, skitter between the stiletto-booted feet of a small woman dressed in a floaty chiffon top and tight black pants, her loose blonde hair hanging down to her waist. The expression on her face is unguarded and, as always, a little bit stunned. She looks less like a major rock star who's one year off turning 60 than someone who just fell out of a little girl's drawing and hadn't quite got her bearings yet. She looks, in fact, inarguably and utterly Stevie Nicks-ian.

IN 1985, WHEN NICKS WAS IN THE BETTY FORD CLINIC being treated for addiction to cocaine, she was set some homework: to write an essay on the difference between being Stevie Nicks real-life human, and 'Stevie Nicks' rock icon. She says it was the hardest thing she's ever had to do. It prompts a story about going to her fortieth high school reunion last month. One of the group of girls she used to hang with in her teens told her, "You know what? You haven't changed a bit. You are still our little Stevie girl." She cried on her way home. "It was the nicest thing anybody had said to me," she smiles. "That I'm still the same. Because I've always tried very hard to stay who I was before I joined Fleetwood Mac and not become a very arrogant and obnoxious, conceited bitchy chick, which many do. I think I've been really successful."

She says all of this guilelessly. For someone who's served nearly 40 years in the crazy world of rock, more than 30 as a major star and indulging in her fair share of the sex and drugs, it's innocence more than experience that comes across. As her close friend Tom Petty (with whom she completed a five-month US tour as unpaid guest singer in 2006) said of her, affectionately, "It's like when you've got a sister in the family that nobody wants to talk about much." Meaning someone you love but who's, well, *different*. "Stevie," he added, "does not live in the real world."

She scoffs, "Tom lives in the same world that I do. Because both of us became huge successes very young, we made a lot of money, and that changes your life *immediately*—and those things change *for* you, you don't even try to change them. They take you out of the real world, but they don't need to change who you are."

But who exactly is she? Besides being one of the most successful women in rock, juggling two careers—solo and with Fleetwood Mac— for more than three decades, she is also one of the most mythologised. Having made MOJO and herself steaming mugs of Earl Grey tea, Stevie Nicks settles in an armchair by the fire as we prepare to find out.

STEVIE NICKS HAS KEPT A DIARY EVERY DAY SINCE she joined Fleetwood Mac—New Year's Eve 1974. The rest has been committed to memory; like her performances at age four with her grandfather, A.J. Nicks, an eccentric would-be country musician who lived in a trailer in the desert. He bought Stevie "a little cowgirl outfit with guns and boots and vest" and took her on-stage with him in Arizona bars. Her parents finally put a stop to it, but "it didn't stop me singing. I sang all the time—to the radio, to anybody, until we moved to San Francisco and I did my own music."

The timing was perfect. It was the mid-'60s; Stevie was in her mid-teens. She was writing songs (her first: I've Loved And I've Lost And I'm Sad But Not Blue) and singing with her girlfriends in Mamas & Papas-type harmony bands. Lindsey Buckingham went to the same high school, and the pair met when she saw him singing California Dreamin' at a social evening and joined in, uninvited, on harmony. Almost two years later he formed a band, Fritz, remembered her and asked her to join. So by day she studied speech communication at college, by night she sang with Fritz.

The group was no great success. At the urging of producer Keith Olsen, they disbanded and Nicks and Buckingham moved to Los Angeles. Lindsey stayed home and wrote, while Stevie paid the bills working at Burger King, waitressing at restaurants, even cleaning Olsen's house. The producer helped broker a deal with Polydor, who released their debut, *Buckingham Nicks*, in 1973. A mellow slice of well-produced Californian rock, nevertheless it flopped.

Meanwhile Mick Fleetwood, who'd moved his band to LA, was shopping for a studio and producer. He met Olsen, who played him *Buckingham Nicks* as a demonstration of his sound and got the job. Fleetwood was also looking for a guitar player—a regular occurrence, what with the band's habit of losing them, often in unfortunate circumstances (Bob Welch left citing exhaustion; Danny Kirwan was fired for refusing to go on stage and was later admitted to psychiatric hospital; Peter Green and Jeremy Spencer both left as a result of drug-related trauma and later joined religious cults). The offer of a job was extended to Buckingham, who agreed, if Stevie could come too.

"I know for a fact I was simply being hired as extra baggage," says Nicks, today, "that they only wanted Lindsey and couldn't get him without me. They already had a girl singer [Christine McVie], they didn't need another one who didn't really play anything. They're not going to say, 'You stand out there and be the star and we'll just play.' But I so wanted to be part of it, I thought I could be their secretary or something, *anything*, and they understood I felt this way and never made me feel unwanted."

Quite what McVie made of Stevie in the beginning hardly bears thinking about. Five years older than Nicks, Christine Perfect, as she was before marrying Fleetwood Mac bassist John McVie, had a distinguished musical pedigree: classically trained, lead singer and keyboard player on Chicken Shack's sole Top 10 hit, I'd Rather Go Blind, she'd topped Melody Maker's Best Female Vocalist poll in 1969, the year before she joined her new husband in Fleetwood Mac.

Stevie nods. "I'm sure there were times when I'm flying around the stage in my gossamer chiffon where she had to think to herself, Wow, what's this? Fairy school? But never once did she make me feel like that, never one comment to the effect of, 'I could really have done without you.' Because she knew from the beginning that I was real sensitive and that anything she'd say to me would cut like a knife."

Nicks herself had "no hesitations" about giving up Buckingham-Nicks for Mac. "They were an established band and our album had flopped, we were bankrupt. And when I met them they were very dry and English and I loved them straight away. They didn't audition us or anything, it was like 'Right, rehearsal starts in four days.' Then we started getting paid: $200 a week apiece for four weeks when we were rehearsing, and $400 a week apiece when we actually started recording. Basically I'd been scraping it together to make $300 a month waitressing to pay our rent, our food and our car, and all of a sudden we were making almost $4,000 a month overnight. I was washing hundred dollar bills and hanging them up with clothes pins! As a member of Fleetwood Mac for two weeks I was still working at the restaurant because I'd given them notice. I didn't just want to walk in there and say, 'I'm going to be a famous rock star so I quit and I never liked your food anyway.' It makes you feel bad later, and I like tying up loose ends. So Fleetwood Mac plucked us straight out of *heavy* obscurity. It was hysterical how fast it all happened."

FLEETWOOD MAC, RELEASED IN SPRING 1975, featured three songs Nicks had written, including the hit single Rhiannon, originally planned for the non-existent *Buckingham Nicks II*. The new line-up's first album together sold five million copies. It was quite a turnaround, not just for Nicks and Buckingham, but for the band too. Months earlier, Mac had been battling in court to keep their name—their manager had put a bogus Mac on the road after Mick Fleetwood pulled out of a tour, having learned that their guitarist, Bob Weston, was having an affair with his wife. Now here they were with their first US Number 1.

They were heady days as Nicks describes them—the excitement of going into the studio, the speed with which they made the album, how thrilled everyone was at how it came out. Lindsey was happy, their relationship was going great. "But by the time we came off the road, which was probably three or four months after the record came out, our relationship was not doing that well." And by the time they started the follow-up, *Rumours,* John and Christine McVie were in the same boat. "It wasn't another woman or another man, it was just the *situation.* The whole hugeness of it all had really hit everybody very hard. And the biggest thing is Chris and I got a lot of attention, because we were the girls, and the boys didn't like that. They didn't like it then; they don't like it now."

Fleetwood Mac's 'Soap Opera' years, in which the members' love lives came under constant public scrutiny, would overlap with the 'Marie Antoinette' years of excess. Says Stevie, "I went to see that film the other night and it reminded me a lot of myself and the people surrounding me when we first started with Fleetwood Mac. The clothes and the champagne and how young they all were—and it really touched me. Because we were young too and there was a tragedy for all of us also, just in what it did to all of our lives and taking them out of 'the real world', as Tom Petty would say"

Dogged by tension and extravagance and distracted by sex and drugs, *Rumours* took the best part of a year to record. But lyrics aside—Christine McVie would later comment that everyone was writing about each other—the cracks didn't show on the record's supple ensemble playing and smooth harmonies. This was classic California pop—the band's British blues element as good as gone—featuring songs like Christine's catchy Don't Stop and You Make Loving Fun alongside Stevie's darker cocaine song Gold Dust Woman and the wistful Dreams. *Rumours* hit Number 1 on both sides of the Atlantic, becoming one of the biggest-selling rock albums of all time. And the band, of course, went back on the road, with the new *frisson* of various members variously hating various other members' guts. So how did someone of Stevie's famed sensitivity manage?

"Mostly because I, like everybody who was in Fleetwood Mac, loved Fleetwood Mac the entity, and nobody wanted to leave. People would be, '*You* leave, I'm not leaving.' Lindsey didn't want to quit, I didn't, John didn't, Chris didn't and Mick certainly didn't; he just sat back and watched it. So you went up on-stage and tried to keep your problems off that stage and then went back to separate dressing rooms and hotels and didn't go to the bar after the show, because you didn't even want to take a chance of having a run-in in front of people. So we stayed really very cloistered, especially Chris and I, because the boys could go out but Chris and I couldn't, so we hung out together, drank tea and watched movies and stayed away from the rest of the guys."

It didn't always work. On-stage in New Zealand once, Buckingham got mad at Nicks . . ."I think I was singing through one of his solos or something, and he walked across the stage and kicked me and then went back to his microphone and we just sort of went on with the show. Me being pretty much the ultimate professional, I'm like, OK, that didn't just happen, it was just a joke everybody. Then he threw his guitar at me, *swwwosh!* I saw it coming and ducked. And he would have killed me if it had hit me; a Les Paul weighs about 30lbs. When the song was over he raced off the stage but Chris was so mad she was at the dressing room two seconds after he got there. And she grabbed him—she was going to kill him—then the bodyguards came in and dragged us all apart."

But the show, as they say, had to go on. "Let's just say he was told by everybody, from tour manager to everybody involved, if you ever throw anything at her or kick her again, the crew will attack you and kill you, so you'd better think about it. It never happened again." She pauses a moment. The wind is whipping up now; through the large window you can see it bullying the trees hung with fairy lights in her garden. She continues: "But Lindsey and I have had many things happen on-stage that's *not* a long time ago. We have a very hard time with each other, and he has a very hard time with me because he didn't go after a solo career and I did. He should have and he didn't and it's not my fault. But he blames me."

The idea for Nicks' solo career was cemented during talks with Eagles manager Irving Azoff while Mac were recording *Tusk,* reputedly the most expensive rock album ever made. There was plenty of time to set up a label for her records, Modern, during the 13 months *Tusk* took to make. "That's a long time to go into one room every day, six days a week, but it happened. And it happened because everybody was so busy doing drugs that nobody was organised, and you do things that you would think were just marvellous and the next day you'd come back in and it wasn't, so you'd have to do it again."

Bella Donna, her 1981 solo debut, with its mix of earthy and ethereal (the sexiness of Edge Of 17 and After The Glitter Fades; the chiffon delicacy of How Still My Love and After The Rain) was in contrast "very quick, because we rehearsed for months and really knew our stuff when we went into the studio." "We" being Stevie and the two women who still sing with her, Sharon Celani and Lori Perry, with guest appearances by Tom Petty, Don Felder and members of the Heartbreakers and Bruce Springsteen's E Street Band. "It only took three months. Then I did 12 shows, about a month and the last show at the Beverly Wilshire Theatre, which is on the DVD, you can kind of see in my face that it was over, and I didn't really know if I would ever be able to come back to my solo career. I went scurrying back to Fleetwood Mac as fast as I could." By her own reckoning, her solo career, chronicled on the forthcoming *Crystal Visions* CD/DVD retrospective, has actually helped Fleetwood Mac to stay together, her sabbaticals allowing the Mac to take a holiday and keep off the punishing album-tour-album treadmill while also providing her with a needed outlet.

"When you're in a band with three writers and you do a record every two or three years, that's four songs over three years, and for somebody that writes as much as me that's not very much." And she does appear to write all the time—if not songs then poetry, short stories, fairytales, her diary. She refers to that as her "sanity life", of which, frankly, there didn't seem a lot in the period that led to her going into rehab in 1985: an affair with Mick Fleetwood; a short-lived marriage to Kim Anderson, the widower of her best friend, Robin Anderson, who had died of leukaemia; a coke habit that "ate away my nose. I curse the day I ever did cocaine."

She says she was the first in the band to go to the Betty Ford Clinic, and possibly one of the first LA rock stars. "I don't know many other people that went because Betty Ford is not Malibu Promises. It's boot-camp. I adore Betty Ford, the lady, because she saved my life, but her facility is very tough. They couldn't give a shit that you are a rock star. In 28 days I gave up a 10-year coke habit and I could feel myself just coming back to myself. I also felt, I will *never* have to come back to rehab for cocaine."

Mention that she later spent 47 days in hospital to treat an eight-year addiction to prescription tranquillisers, and it's the only time MOJO sees her bristle. After Betty Ford's, everyone encouraged her to join Narc Anon or at least see a doctor. When she finally gave in, the man she chose turned out, she claims, to be a "rock star groupie". "I can forgive all the miserable cocaine dealers because they were completely screwed up and trying to get enough money to buy food, but this guy was rich and had no reason except that he wanted to keep me coming to his office a couple of times and tell him about what was going on in Hollywood. And I'm lucky to be sitting here today. I could have OD'ed on anything, being that bleary. I could have been Anna Nicole Smith! I don't hate anyone, but I *hate* him."

Hate is not a word that surfaces very often during a conversation with Nicks. She admits the simmering tension that exists between Buckingham and herself, but there appear to be no hard feelings towards ex-lover Mick Fleetwood. An argument over her decision to use her song Silver Springs on her 1991 solo retrospective *TimeSpace,* and not, as he wanted, on Fleetwood Mac retrospective *The Chain,* blew over . . . but then, both were massive sellers. In fact, Stevie's initial Best Of also featured a new song, Desert Angel, dedicated to the American military serving in Opera-tion Desert Storm, which resulted in another turning point in her life.

In 2004 a Washington DC Army hospital approached her to ask if she'd be willing to make personal visits to the bedsides of young veterans injured in the war on Iraq. Stevie's eyes light up when she talks about it. She's set up a fund, she says, and planned her whole solo tour around being able to go back as often as she can. Wasn't she nervous about get-ting so closely involved—after all, didn't she once attract a stalker who was convinced she could cure him of homosexuality with mystical spells? She looks puzzled. "I never heard that one. But you know people keep the really weird stuff away from me, so a lot of that stuff I don't really hear."

Yet she seems aware enough, in general, of the myths that surround her, of people's fantasies of who 'Stevie Nicks' is. If in the past she might have played into those fantasies of the ethereal Californian pop enchantress, you sense there are limits now. She declares, for instance, that she "won't have a face lift". "The idea of looking like a caricature of myself is horrible," she winces. "I feel that if you stay animated from within, that people don't see the age, so I try to forget about it. I deal with it by just being me." And she has been used to being "me" for quite some time, her short-lived marriage aside; she says she "never had children [because] I didn't want to compromise my art".

As a parting shot she also admits to being happy as a workaholic. "I do have this crazy world where I pretty much continually work all the time," she smiles. "I can break real easily if I don't get back a little bit of the love that I try to put out but I'm happiest when I'm working. The other stuff I try to laugh about. Sometimes I'll wake up and I'll go, So what *is* going on in the fabulous life of Stevie Nicks today? And when I do find myself getting tired or complaining, I get really mad at myself and say, You have no right to complain, Stevie. You are a lucky, lucky girl."

A TONIC FOR THE TROOPS

In 2004, a US military hospital invited Stevie Nicks to visit its wounded young soldiers. She's been going ever since. Here she explains why.

"WE WERE playing Washington DC and my manager said Walter Reed Army Medical had asked if I would like to visit. What could I say? I was there from two in the afternoon until almost one o'clock that night. Basically you go in—and believe me, I never thought that this would be anything I would ever do—and you put on a gown and gloves and they say, 'Well this guy's name is John Jones and he was injured in a blast and lost both legs, he's had a bad day but he's very excited to see you.' You go in and I just say, My name's Stevie Nicks, what happened? Because they would like to talk about it. I don't sing to them, just talk. And then the USO comes in and takes a Polaroid and then it's on to the next room and, 'This [is] a girl, Amanda, who was in a blast and lost one leg and a hand,' and you just suck it all up and sit and talk to Amanda for 15 minutes. You don't even have time for a cup of coffee, you just keep going—and when I walked out of that hospital, after having seen about 40 guys and girls who've lost arms and legs, I was so completely blown away by it all and by how these kids' lives would never be the same.

"So I said, I'm going to have to do something about this. I have to do something for them. I thought, maybe I can buy gym equipment for their physical therapy, and then I had an idea. I could take them music. I could give them iPods and fill them up with songs from all different artists and I can take them music. So I called everybody I knew and said I'm starting a foundation and I'm going back in two months, and that's how my Stevie Nicks Soldier's Angel Foundation started.

"I'm very, very dedicated to this. I'm not a mother but I feel incredibly motherly to all these kids—they are so young, 18, 20, 22, and a lot of them are there for anywhere between a year and 18 months—and they love the music. I sign everything—the iPods, the box they come in, the T-shirts we take them. A lot of my girlfriends have started doing this with me and we have bags of popcorn and a movie, so it's fun. They've just built a place in San Antonio, Texas, specifically for amputees and burn victims, and so I'm going there—in fact I've planned my whole tour around it so I can hub out of San Antonio and go there and figure what they need.

"I'm so happy that that one time they invited me to go I actually went, because I feel like it's probably the best thing I've ever done."

Find out more about the Soldier's Angel Foundation at http://www .nicksfix.com/

LINDSEY BUCKINGHAM

"I Was Kind of Poised to Put Out a Solo Record"

Steven Rosen | November 2008 | UltimateGuitar.com (US)

One of the most striking sights in popular music is that of Lindsey Buckingham peeling off glittering electric guitar runs without the aid of a plectrum. Buckingham's 2008 solo album *Gift of Screws* was the electric bookend to his aforementioned acoustic album *Under the Skin*. As such, this promotional interview for it provided an opportunity for discussion of Buckingham's remarkable "axman" gifts.

Lindsey Buckingham doesn't always get the recognition he deserves. He is not an over-the-top player burning up the fretboard with mighty runs at incalculable speeds. In fact, he is not pursuing any sort of guitarist's mantle. Rather, this gifted songwriter/musician quietly offers up his fingerpicking style with a little band called Fleetwood Mac and on his own various solo albums.

He recently recorded Gift Of Screws, a sublime collection of his unique songsmithing abilities matched up with an extraordinary blend of nylon string and steel string acoustics and his sort of slippery, eel-like guitar style that brings to mind Mark Knopfler and other players of subtle persuasion.

At the start of the interview, I was instructed that I'd have somewhere between ten and fifteen minutes. Which is nowhere near long enough to fully explore the multifaceted Buckingham but that's all the time there was. I told Lindsey we should dive right in because we didn't have much time.

"How much time did she give you?" he asked.

I jokingly replied, *"I think she gave me eight minutes."*

"Eight minutes," he exclaimed. *"OK, we'll see how much we can push the envelope."*

Indeed, Lindsey did allow me a few more minutes at the end and seemed to fall right into the groove from the very beginning of our talk.

Ultimate Guitar: Some of the songs originally slotted for the Gift of Screws CD actually ended up on Fleetwood Mac albums?

Lindsey Buckingham: Well, you know, in 2001, I was kind of poised to put out a solo record; this is sort of a pattern that has, I guess you could say, developed. It certainly happened a number of times where there's been an intention and it's gotten, shall we say, intervened upon, by the band and that's fair enough. If you're part of a band and you think of yourself that way, you have to be responsive to the bigger idea or the idea of the whole, shall we say. So, uh, yes, in 2001, I had these songs pretty much finished and the band called up, or Mick called up and said, We want to make a studio album. I said, Alright and probably the bulk of that material that was to be a solo album ironically entitled Gift of Screws was folded over into the 2003 album that Fleetwood Mac did called Say You Will.

So, those songs that were leftover kind of sat on the shelf for a while; they were not really songs that were appropriate for the album I did two years ago, Under the Skin. Because that was really more of an acoustic, finger style album. And so when I started working on Gift of Screws, what ended up being Gift of Screws, I was not actually expecting it to be as rock as it ended up being but it kind of wanted to go that direction and I let it. And once that had been established, I realized that these songs, these couple of stragglers had finally found a home.

What were the stragglers?

Well, the title track, Gift of Screws which has Mick Fleetwood and John McVie playing on it; also another one called Wait For You which also has John and Mick on it. And then, what was the other one? Umm, it's called The Right Place to Fade; it doesn't have John, it's got a different bass player but it does have Mick playing on it. Those three; everything else was written in the last two years.

Does that mean a song you would write for a solo record is interchangeable with a track you'd write for Fleetwood Mac? Do you approach them from a different place in the head and the heart, so to speak?

I think that, you know, it's all from the place; I think that what defines one song as a solo song or a Fleetwood Mac song is more about what you're doing at the time. And I mean the fact that I was able to fold three-quarters of the material from what was going to be an album of mine over into a Fleetwood Mac album without much change except for maybe Stevie on singing a little bit and having John put a different bass part on, there wasn't really much else to do. So, it's more about what project you're doing at the time. And beyond that, I guess that the only thing that would define it is obviously there is sort of a group sensibility that will either be receptive or not to be to a particular song. And something may not make it onto a Fleetwood Mac album because you know, even though you like it, it may not be something that they are embracing. But beyond that, it's pretty much all from the same place.

What about in terms of guitar exploration? On Gift of Screws, for example, are you able to indulge the instrumental side more than you'd have the chance to on a Fleetwood Mac album?

Well, you know, I think there is a little more of that. Because basically what's happening when you work on solo work, or when I work on solo work, is I tend to sort of sit in the studio and play different instruments and try stuff out. And, to some degree, the song itself does not need to be as fleshed out as a song; you can have a rough idea of what you think it might be but you feel pretty comfortable not having it too well-defined because you can kind of assume that the recording process and the writing process can become one large thing. Sort of like painting where you're slopping the paint on the canvas and it'll eventually take you off in a direction if you're willing to be an antenna for that.

Yes, I think the answer is yes. I mean obviously in today's Fleetwood Mac climate, there is more opportunity to do that than there was years ago. For example, when we first joined the band, we had done this one album, Stevie and I (Buckingham Nicks) and probably a lot of what you would hear on that album is closer to the things I would do on solo albums now. In terms of having the guitar cover a lot of ground, finger style guitar co-existing with lead guitar. When we joined the band, there was not a lot of space for me to play on a lot of these things because Christine (McVie) had a style that was pre-existing; John had a fairly melodic bass style which took up a lot of space. And I had to take the space that was left; it was certainly a lesson in adaptation.

Over the years, however, that has sort of been modified and there's been more leeway so it's sort of a role I've reclaimed, shall we say.

You talk about slopping the paint on your music; can you describe how you go through the songwriting process? Your son Will actually helped you with the lyric? If you look at the first song on the album, Great Day and use that as an example, how would you talk about it?
I don't think that most of the time I have that much of an overall vision. With Great Day, that was interesting because I was in the studio one day and my son was hanging out on the couch; he's ten now, he was probably eight at the time. He starts singing, Great day/great day and I said, What is that? And he said, Well, I don't know, I just made it up. So I said, I'm going to try and make that into a song. That was really the center, the fact that my son had come up with this chorus with the lyrics already there and I thought, Oh, that's kind of a gift. And, so, from that, I think probably the first thing I did was to make a drum pattern. And the way I did that was to, it's not a kit of drums on there, it's basically, I think I was beating on the console or beating on the chair, and then I was pulling beats from that and running them through an array of different effects. Because I knew I didn't want the track to have drums on it.

So I started with a pattern on the drums and a chorus idea and everything else, I didn't know what I was going to do. So, I think probably you hear these sort of bluesy kind of dropped-D guitars. By the way, there's a left and right and they're not playing the same thing by a long shot.

So it is a kind of impressionistic cluster of, which is part of what I like about it. And then I'm thinking, OK, I can't do that every time so what am I gonna do? Maybe something lighter. So you get the sense of give and take, call and response, then you've got the do-do-do-do (sings the fragile electric part). Somewhere along the line your melody idea fits into point A and point B, you're trying to anchor one thing to another; and they're all sort of becoming clear to you. Not in a linear fashion but in a kind of a, OK, maybe this can go here. And then maybe you tried that but that didn't work so you tried something else; it's all pretty random. And eventually you get the sense, Well, OK, it seems to be taking shape.

Again, I can't get away from the analogy of the painting where you probably end up painting over a corner you didn't like and you try something else; part of it stays, part of it doesn't. And eventually it begins to take shape; maybe I had some original idea that I wanted to take Will's chorus idea and elaborate on it by making it vocally counterpoint. Of course, getting into some rapid fire soloing. It's funny, the song ended up almost being like a capsule report of everything else on the album. Little bytes in a sort of almost cubistic manner of everything else you're going to hear: a little acoustic playing, lead playing, and counterpoint, and weird drums, and everything all in one.

You mentioned the dropped-D tuning as one of the tools in the arsenal.

Sometimes, yeah; you've got to do it sparingly. Otherwise people will think you're playing the blues or something which I don't. It's not something I'm interested in doing beyond a certain point. You want to use the reference but you don't want to dwell on it.

On the inside cover of Gift of Screws, you're pictured with a Fender Strat. That is not your main instrument, is it?

No, it isn't; my wife was taking pictures that day and you know how things go in photo sessions? I might have been futzing around with it for a specific idea. But my main guitar on stage are the ones Rick Turner designs for me. But oddly enough, most guitars become less useful in the studio because they're sort of across-the-board useful on the stage and sometimes they're great for lead in the studio but they're not specific enough. So I find myself using things that sort of define themselves a little bit more in the studio. I don't know I had the Strat at that particular point in time; I couldn't tell ya.

What are some of the instruments that become more defined in the studio?
Well, I think if you go back to Great Day, you've got those dropped-D parts on a gut string that I have that goes direct. I think it probably is the Strat doing those little response lines.

And the solo?
The solo is probably the Turner. It's probably run through a Roland Synth with an extreme fuzz kind of thing. Umm, I use an old D18, that I've had for a long time, that I use for acoustic layering. There's just a lot of different things; I have a lot of Taylors; I like Baby Taylors, those work really well. Umm, you know, again it's not so much what you got, it's what you do with what you got. You've got to sort of have an idea and then it's pretty easy to find a way to get to what you hear in your head, I guess.

In talking about what you hear in your head, your vocals and your melodies are very ephemeral, very fragile. They tend to drift on top of the music track. Where do those ideas come from?
Well, I don't know; it's probably sort of half and half. A lot of times you have a melody that is completely clear in your mind; sometimes that melody gets modified a little bit but it remains the same and everything else becomes subservient to that. There are plenty of other times where you haven't really begun the track with that in mind. I'm trying to think of a song that would represent that—the second song is called Time Precious Time and it's an arpeggio piece. That's an example of the melody coming last. The idea for that came from, I was watching Terence Malick's film, New World, and there's a piece that he uses over and over throughout that which is sort of an atypical Mahler, not Mahler, Wagner piece. And it's orchestral and it's very liquid and the strings are

swirling up and up and then back down. I was thinking, Gee, how could I do something like that on the guitar?

So I actually found a tuning where the top four strings were maybe a step to a step-and-a-half apart; they were tuned fairly close together so I could arpeggiate like that and find different inversions of the same notes without having to do big stretches. It was all in service of this one idea. A tuning which would be pretty useless for anything else. And then you apply the back-and-forth thumb and three fingers to sort of run up and down those strings and on the low two strings you find the root notes you need to support those figures and that became the song; that became the structure. And it was completely done before there was any melody over it.

So sometimes the sense that there's this kind of, as you say, fragile or ethereal or whatever thing going on over something, is exactly right. It can actually be, I wouldn't say tentative, but it can be less connected as a melody than some people would normally do. Because it's being based around something which wants to allow what came first to come through (laughs).

That's a beautiful way to describe it. You have Mick Fleetwood and John (Note: The voice of the publicist breaks in on our conversation. She says, Hey, Steven, I'm sorry to interrupt in the middle of a question but we're about out of time. If you could please ask your last question?

I'm deflated at this point because I had only begun my examination of Lindsey's music. And Lindsey, sensing my displeasure, says, We'll try for two.

Because, in my mind, he was enjoying the conversation as much as I was).

Umm, so you have Mick and John McVie on the title track and Wait For You. Obviously those particular players bring something very unique to your music.
It's not that there aren't a lot of great players out there who could've done a great job; and I wasn't looking for anything in particular. That was just a situation in which I happened to be working with Mick and with Rob Cavallo, the producer, and it was just a situation which presented itself.

But having said that, I don't know, it's pretty intangible. One thing I'll say about John is that he's got this, and you'll see this on stage, he stands there and he basically focused on only one thing. Because he knows what he wants to play; he's focused on Mick's kick. And he's not gonna stray from that kick no matter what. And Mick's kick is not always that easy to follow because Mick has a great sort of dose of the Charlie Watts in him. And that's what I love about Mick; Mick is this guy who appreciates the unrefined; he appreciates the connection between the animal and the human in the drumming experience. Especially on, say, Gift of Screws; I think that he was actually not happy that this song ended up on a solo album because I think that he would have liked to go out and play it. I don't know, he's just one of these guys who has this great I mean, he is like me in one way even though he's less refined because I would think of myself as a refined primitive because I don't read music and I didn't take lessons and it's all sort of from the gut. Yet I've sort of injected a good dose of the other side of the brain into my process, too. And Mick, in the best possible sense, he doesn't have a clue about what he's doing and that's what's so great about it; it's just pure feeling. I don't know how else to put it really.

Will Fleetwood Mac be performing songs from your solo album?
Well, that's a good question. We are talking about rehearsing in January and doing some dates in the spring. So I might have to get back to you on that. Politics can be a little bit tricky in Fleetwood Mac from time to time. Certainly there are a number of songs on Gift of Screws which are appropriate to be done by Fleetwood Mac especially since there are the players on there. But I guess we're just gonna have to wait and see where the group sensibility wants us to go.

And quite honestly, we went out in 2004 behind Say You Will without Christine McVie which we are going to do again 'cause she's moved back to England; she just doesn't wanna do this anymore and that's fine. I had a great time in 2004 'cause it gave me like half the material to go out there and be the guy that I am up there. Stevie, I think, you know, I think she has a slightly different objective in mind and I think the important thing for us as a group is to think in terms of the people and enjoying each other as people and appreciating each other's feelings a little more. And any sort of agendas that might have to do with music need to take a backseat, I think, to that, going into this.

So, having said that, I don't have any particular need or even thought of doing anything in particular when we go out. I just want us to have a good time and for the audience to have a good time and I think everything else good will follow from that.

Now that the Gift of Screws CD is completed and has been conceptualized, is this the painting you wanted to do? As a songwriter and a guitar player, does it truly represent who you are here in 2008?
Well, the album from two years ago, Under the Skin, which was all about finger style and was as much about what I didn't do as what I did do, I was very happy with how that turned out. And it did in fact open up a whole other area to explore in terms of how to take one or two guitars doing the work of a whole track and apply production value over it. This album, I wasn't really expecting to be as rocky as it was. But because it did turn out that way, it does seem to represent more of the range of what I do and what I have done. So in some ways it sort of refers back to things that are more familiar; that's probably why Warner Bros. likes it more.

I'm completely happy. The thing is, you do the work, you get it to a point where you feel it's as good as you're gonna do; you can't be objective about it, you just have to let it go at some point. It would be the same with a director trying to edit a film; at some point you've got to say, OK, well, this is it. And you let it go. The validity for me always is gonna come from the experience of doing it; what I learned while doing it; what I did to advance my sensibilities as an artist. And someone who wants to continue thinking of himself as someone who has the freedom and is making the choice to keep pushing his own boundaries. And to challenge people and not thinking in terms of playing any particular game in order to try to sell.

I do have that big machine in Fleetwood Mac; it's a big brand name. It's a great luxury to have both. And I think it's important for me to hold that line and understand that line. And, you know, things come out and you never know what the record company is going to say about it but you don't worry about it. You just assume much fewer people are going to gravitate towards it because it tends to be more esoteric; it tends to be more to the left although that may be a little less true with this one.

You don't expect the company to step up with the level of support for the small machine as they would for the big machine. And it's almost irrelevant; you do what you do hopefully for the right reasons and at the end of the day it leaves you in a place prepared to do the next thing and to be as equally excited about it for the right reasons.

That's terrific. Thank you and

(Last note: Before I can finish my thought, the publicist cuts in one last time: Steven, we're out of time. And the line goes dead).

WELCOME BACK

Lindsey Buckingham

James McNair | November 2008 | *Classic Rock* (UK)

Although this is another interview designed to promote *Gift of Screws*, in it Lindsey Buckingham also gives some interesting insights into Fleetwood Mac's current dynamic and the intriguing, but ultimately scrapped, possibility of a Mac containing Sheryl Crow.

Californian guitarist and singer Lindsey Buckingham is best known for playing with Fleetwood Mac. Together with Stevie Nicks he joined the band in 1975, and along with Christine McVie, John McVie and Mick Fleetwood he found fame with the group's 1977 album *Rumours*, a record that to date has sold more than 30 million copies worldwide. On September 15, Buckingham, 58, released his new solo album *Gift Of Screws*.

You've said that you're clinging to idealism on this record.
I'm talking creative idealism, I guess. With Fleetwood Mac, people wanted us to follow up *Rumours* with more of the same, but we made a left turn and did *Tusk* so that we could subvert the status quo and the expectations that the record company had. I suppose there's some of that going on with *Gift Of Screws*, too.

What is *The Right Place To Fade* about?
It's partly about letting down your guard and finding new ways of thinking. There was a time in Fleetwood Mac where we had to live in

a state of denial to get through making records together. There was a polarisation in the group that left a mark on my psyche. I've dealt with that now through meeting a beautiful woman and having three beautiful children.

What's happening with the Mac right now?

Well, I wanted a three-year break to make and tour two solo albums. I've made those records now [*Under The Skin* came out in 2006], and I'm about to tour the second one. After that, Fleetwood Mac will begin rehearsing again in January 2009. We're not going to record right away, though, we'll play some shows first.

But you will make a new album?

Absolutely. The whole band feels that there is a lot left to say and lot left to be shared. There's a unity and a sense of purpose that hasn't been there since the very beginning.

How has Christine McVie's retirement affected Fleetwood Mac?

When we toured in 2003 as a four-piece, Stevie felt a lot of the feminine side of the band had gone. We weren't doing much of Christine's material.

More recently we heard rumours that Sheryl Crow might step into Christine's shoes.

Stevie brought up the idea of Sheryl playing with us. They'd been friends for a while and I think she thought it might bring back some of that female presence on stage. I wasn't closed to the idea, but I had my reservations. I wondered if bringing in someone else to do Christine's songs would degrade Fleetwood Mac to a lounge act level.

What happened next?

Sheryl brought out an album of her own, and while she was promoting it she announced that she was going to be touring with us as part of Fleetwood Mac. Stevie and Mick were not happy about that, and understandably so. It was not an appropriate time or context for her to bring that up; the matter had not been decided.

So she won't be joining?

After the friction that incident created between her and Stevie, I think Sheryl decided that she should step back from the idea. Continuing as a four-piece might be a challenging way to go, but I think it's more credible.

STEVIE NICKS, 2013

James McNair

This is the first publication of the verbatim transcript of an interview with Stevie Nicks conducted for a *Mojo* magazine feature in 2013.

Nicks discusses the fact that, with Christine McVie's disavowal of the ecstasies of retirement, the *Rumours* Five Fleetwood Mac is potentially back in action. It was a reunion by which millions of music lovers were excited, even if—it transpires—Buckingham wasn't.

Note: The documentary referred to is *Stevie Nicks: In Your Dreams*.

The big news chez Fleetwood Mac is that Christine McVie is back. How involved is she going to be?

She's just reemerged to do one song. It could have been a few songs, but Lindsey's very funny about that. Chris left in 1998 and we didn't start *Say You Will* until 2002. It took us that long to figure out what the hell we were going to do without her—or even if we could do without her.

Lindsey seems almost cross about Christine's return. He said she'd "burned her bridges" and requested that *MOJO* not put a lineup shot with Christine in it on the cover of our *Rumours* issue.

I think his words to us were "She can't just come and go." That's important to him, but it's not quite so important to me. Chris is coming to Dublin when we go into production rehearsal, and she's going to come on and do "Don't Stop" the second two nights in London. Much as Lindsey adores her—and he does; she's the only one in Fleetwood Mac he was ever really willing to listen to—he doesn't want the first-night reviews to be all about Christine's one song rather than the set we rehearsed for two months. But it will be wonderful to have her back up there with us, and from there who knows?

Lindsey also told MOJO, "There are still parts of mine and Stevie's relationship that are unresolved, and it will be interesting to visit that on this next tour."
He's probably referring to what I call "the Talk." About a year and a half ago I told him everything I had wanted to say to him since 1968. I said, "Do you remember how cute we were? How we could walk into the room together and people would be mesmerized because we were so funny and smart?" I said, "Lindsey, if we can't go back to being those people, I'm going to quit." I told him, "I have other people I can work with that treat me with warmth and utter respect, and in my world there's never a harsh word spoken."

And his reaction?
He was very quiet. I said, "The ball's in your park, Lindsey—2013 better be great."

So has it been great? And when the pair of you hold hands onstage now, what's going on there exactly? The hand-holding on the 2009 tour seemed a bit hammy.
That's interesting. My cousin John has known Lindsey and I since 1968. He told me, "When I saw you and Lindsey play with Fleetwood Mac in 2009, there was nothing between you. It was as if you were thinking, *What shall I get from room service tonight? Grilled cheese? Tomato soup?* "Hammy" wasn't the word for Lindsey and I in 2009—it was totally fake. But what you see onstage now is not fake. It is loving, and it is as close to those two people who met as teenagers as you could hope for. Every night I tell the story of "Without You," the poem that I wrote in 1972 before we made the *Buckingham Nicks* album. The story has become longer than the song, and I told Lindsey, "I'm sorry. I'm try-ing to shorten it." He goes, "Don't worry, Stevie—it's charming." Three

years ago he would have been like, "Are you kidding? We could do 'The Green Manalishi' in that time."

OK, let's go back a bit. What were the first records that got under your skin?

I listened to lots of Top 40 R&B radio. I loved the Shirelles and Martha Reeves and the Vandellas, stuff like "(Remember) Walking in the Sand" by the Shangri-Las.

But your grandfather Aaron Jess Nicks was a country singer, right?

Right. Everybody called him A.J. When we lived in El Paso, Texas, he bought me a truckload of records when I was in fifth grade. There must have been 150 singles: country, rockabilly, some Everly Brothers, a song called "Party Doll" [written by Buddy Knox and Jimmy Bowen] that went [smiles and sings] "Come along and be my party doll / and I'll make love to you."

Was A.J. an influence?

Yeah, we'd duet on songs like [Dorsey Burnette's] "It's Late," and A.J. picked up that I was a good harmony singer. But my dad was worried when he saw me getting into music, because he'd watched A.J. go down the tubes trying to make it. At the same time, I'd be in the back seat of my parents' car singing some R&B song and saying, "Quieten down! I'm trying to concentrate!" My folks would look back with this bewildered expression that said "Who *are* you?" I totally had my black self going on too.

Your mother, Barbara, was credited with instilling the love of fairy tales and fantasy that would later feed into your lyrics. Hans Christian Anderson? The Grimm Brothers?

Well definitely those, yes. And Halloween was a big day at our house. Mom was one of those gals that really loved having a little girl and making things magical for her. My aunt told me that when I was twenty and my parents got transferred back to Chicago and I stayed in San Francisco, the light went out of my mom's eyes. She'd gone to this freezing cold place without her daughter.

Your father, Jess, became president of the Greyhound bus company and you had to up sticks a lot because of his job. Growing up, did that make lasting friendships difficult?

It did. When we got transferred from El Paso to Salt Lake City, I was pretty bummed because we'd been in Texas for five years and I'd settled in. I remember my mom saying, "You better learn how to make friends fast, Stevie. Open up a bit; you're too much in your own world."

You first met Lindsey at a party in San Francisco in 1966 when you sang "California Dreamin'" together.

Yeah, he was sixteen and I was seventeen. It was just a one-off, three-minute moment. After that I never saw him for two years until Lindsey's drummer called me and asked me to join their band, Fritz.

What did they sound like?

They were a hard rock band. We were in San Francisco and it was the Age of Aquarius. If they'd been like Sly and the Family Stone, that would have been fine by me too.

Fritz opened for Janis Joplin a few times.

The time I remember most was at Stamford Frost Amphitheater. The band that were on directly before her had ran into her time and she screamed, "Get off my fucking stage right now or I'll kill you!" Boy, they wound it up quick! [*Laughs.*] Then Janis gets up there. She's all red and purple feathers, big hair, and silky bell-bottoms, but she's tiny as a peanut. I learned that, small or not, you could walk onstage with a big attitude. Flamboyance with humility I got from Jimi Hendrix when Fritz opened for him around 1969 and then from Grace Slick of Jefferson Airplane I took slinky and floaty. I liked her look a lot.

What are your memories of shooting the cover for 1973's *Buckingham Nicks*?

I'm actually quite prudish. So when they suggested they shoot Lindsey and I nude, I could not have been more terrified if you'd asked me to jump off a speeding train. Lindsey was like, "Oh, come on—this is art.

Don't be a child!" I thought, *Who are you? Don't you know me?* I went out and spent my last hundred dollars on a beautiful hand-painted chiffon-y blouse that wrapped around and tied, and Jimmy Wachtel, my long-term guitarist Waddy's brother, took a bunch of photos of us with me wearing it. But then it was, "OK—now without the blouse." I couldn't breathe. But I did it because I felt like a rat in a trap.

And when your folks saw the picture?
Well, I'd taken it home to show them because I didn't want them taken by surprise. But then I got sidetracked by an ovarian cyst operation, and I kept the picture under my bed for five weeks while I was back home recovering. When the record came out and I saw my father, it was "Why didn't you just say no, Stevie?" I said, "Daddy, I don't know. I didn't feel like I had a choice—I'm so sorry." He said, "OK—move on. But you always have a choice." I learned a big lesson that day.

Buckingham and Nicks joined Fleetwood Mac on New Year's Eve 1974, but you keep waitressing for a bit, right?
About three more days. Mostly I was thinking, *What if this doesn't work out?* because I'd been supporting me and Lindsey and Richard Dashut [later coproducer on *Rumours* and *Tusk*] for several years. I didn't mind. It got me out of the cave. I could leave the guys working and earn enough to pay the rent and keep our Toyota running. I just wanted to make sure that when we joined Fleetwood Mac, we didn't burn our bridges.

In those early days, did Mick and John talk about the "ghosts" of Fleetwood Mac— about what had happened to Peter Green, to Jeremy Spencer?
Oh yeah. And I loved hearing about all that. I like my haunted castles.

Was there a specific moment when you turned from being Stephanie Lynn Nicks into "Rock Star Stevie Nicks"?
I knew that I was Stevie Nicks after about three weeks of being in Fritz. I would stroll through San Jose State with my guitar case thinking, *Does everybody know who I am? I'm a rock star.* I felt it and I believed it.

Was "Rhiannon" part of that later on? A theme song for a new identity?
Not when I wrote it in 1973, no. I wrote it after reading Mary Leader's book *Triad*, which is about a woman who becomes possessed by another character called Rhiannon. It wasn't until 1978 that I found out about *The Mabinogion* [Welsh medieval prose tales that draw on Celtic mythology] and that Branwen and Rhiannon are in there too and that Rhiannon wasn't a witch at all; she was a mythological queen. But my story was definitely written about a celestial being. I didn't know who Rhiannon was, exactly, but I knew that she was not of this world.

In 1994 you told Sylvie Simmons, "I like being a mystery, and I even think I'm pretty mysterious to the people who know me really well."
There are parts of me that nobody knows about, and that nobody ever will know about. There's stuff in my head; things that I want to do when I'm seventy-five. I might go rent a Scottish castle and write some crazy movie . . . or I might not. I like mysterious people. I'm drawn to them. And I think that, thanks to Instagram and Facebook, today's young women have lost their mystery. You want to film yourself in the bathroom in the morning getting ready for school? Are you crazy? You think that's attractive? Being mysterious is *very* attractive, and that's where my little world has always been.

Received wisdom holds that cocaine impairs judgment of what's good music and what isn't. So how come *Rumours* turned out so great?
Because our drug use was just beginning. We started writing *Rumours* through 1976 and it was an involved process during which we were happy and confident. But even during the recording of *Rumours*, the cocaine hadn't taken us over. It was great until it wasn't, you know? We were extremely messed up romantically, but we were young and creative and we still really cared about the band and we were damn well gonna make another great record. The drugs only got really bad during *Tusk*.

At what point did you realize that you had far more songs than Fleetwood Mac could accommodate?
Pretty much right away. Twelve songs on each album between three writers is only four apiece. I was extremely prolific, so every time we made

a Fleetwood Mac record I'd have twenty songs left over. By 1980 I'd be sitting at the piano and Christine would walk through and go [*drops into theatrically overblown English accent*], "Oh my God—she's writing another song!" I'd chase her and she'd shout, "I love you darling!"

Your 1981 solo debut, *Bella Donna*, reached number one in the US and was certified platinum within three months of its release. Did that change the power dynamic in Fleetwood Mac?

Not much. They weren't that impressed. Anything that I did outside of Fleetwood Mac wasn't that important to them. Chris cared, but not the boys. And it wasn't like Beyoncé and Destiny's Child. I'd told them, "I swear to God I'm not leaving ever," and here I am today. But when I signed my solo deal with Atlantic in 1980, I started this whirlwind thing of being able to flit between two worlds. Fleetwood Mac made *Tusk* and I made *Bella Donna*. Fleetwood Mac made *Mirage* and I made *The Wild Heart*, and on it went. I loved it because I get bored easily. I change hotel suites twice in the same week.

Prince played synth on your 1983 single "Stand Back," which you had written by singing new words and a new melody to his song "Little Red Corvette." What do you remember about the session with him at Sunset Sound?

I remember him playing basketball outside like one of the Harlem Globetrotters. He was spinning the ball on his finger and throwing it backwards into the net. In terms of the actual recording he was super quick. Unfortunately we couldn't keep him locked down there forever. [*Laughs.*]

But he later sent you the backing track for "Purple Rain," asking you if you wanted to write something to it.

It was a cassette—and I've still got it—with the whole instrumental track and a little bit of Prince singing "Can't get over that feeling," or something. But it was ten minutes long with the big guitar solo and I was overwhelmed. I told him, "Prince, I've listened to this a hundred times but I wouldn't know where to start. It's a movie; it's epic." It *was* epic. And it *became* a movie.

So you turned down what became Prince's defining song?

Right. But I always feel like there's a little bit of me in it. The olive branch of him giving me that cassette was huge, but I think he would have liked a romance with me too.

Wow. Were you flattered?

Very flattered. I remember Fleetwood Mac were in Minneapolis on tour one time and Prince came and got me right after the show. I'm still in my chiffon stage outfit and he's in his purple stage outfit. We get in his purple Camaro and bomb out onto the freeway at a hundred miles per hour. I'm terrified, but kind of excited too: "Shit, we're gonna get pulled over!" So we get to his purple house and he has a studio downstairs and we try to write a song together. But I've just done a show and I'm tired, so I go upstairs and sleep on the floor of his purple kitchen. In the morning he wakes me up and I have some coffee and I sing a little part on the song. But I've got to be at the airport by 2 PM to take off with Fleetwood Mac, and you *do not* miss that plane. We get into the purple Camaro again. Prince bombs it down the freeway and right out onto the tarmac alongside our private jet. He comes around to open my door and we hug goodbye, but we both look like crazy people. I get on the plane and the rest of the band are like [*drums fingers, rolls eyes*]. I'm like, "What? Nothing happened."

There's a moving story behind "Has Anyone Every Written Anything for You?" from 1985's *Rock a Little*. You'd taken a drive into the mountains with the Eagles' Joe Walsh and he showed you the little silver fountain he'd built in remembrance of the three-year-old daughter he lost.

Yes, that song was written for Joe and Emma Kristen. The drive was in Boulder, Colorado. I was having a hard time and Joe was opening for me, but I soon realized how little I had to complain about. We made the trip up there and he told me the whole story about how Emma had been killed by a drunk driver, on the way to nursery school. Joe had been married to a woman named Stephanie, but they couldn't survive what had happened and they broke up. My song was for Stephanie too, I think. It was for all of us, actually. It was about the whole tragic story and how the insidious stupidity of some drunk asshole driving into a Porsche tore so many lives apart.

How did Joe react to the song?
He was blown away.

You've said that he was the great love of your life.
It was a long time ago: 1983 to '84. We were very excessive. One day my friend Sharon came and said, "Joe told me to tell you that he's taken a plane to Australia. He says he won't be back for several months and don't try to find him." There was never any closure, so I've never got over it. I did go into rehab about a year and a half later, and that was it for me and coke, but I don't think I ever quite bought Joe's thing that one of us was going to die before the other person had the chance to dial 911. Maybe someday he will tell me the truth about what happened to us.

In the new documentary you remark, "I don't think love changes; it can happen at sixteen or seventy-five." Still time, then?
I'm fine without a man in my life. I'm busy and I love being free. If I say, "I'm off to do forty-seven shows, then I'm gonna be back a few days, then I'm gonna take my niece and four of my best friends to Italy and Paris," what guy is gonna shout, "Have a great time!" as my limo pulls away?

One who really loves you?
Well I've tried every kind of man—rock 'n' roll star, average Joe, tour manager, producer—but eventually they all go, "Are you serious? You're not coming home at all?" If I want a boyfriend, I'll find one tomorrow, but they can't come on the road with me if they don't have a job, because the crew start looking at them like, "Why are you here?" That said, if Mr. Right were to walk around that corner, I'd throw all of that out the window. It has happened.

Will the current Fleetwood Mac tour be the last one?
That won't happen until it's super age-inappropriate. Right now we're doing shows that last two hours, forty minutes and it is *kick-ass*. I've

got pains in my fingers from playing tambourine, so I don't know how Mick does it. The first twenty shows of the current tour we'd be going onstage and I'd whisper to Lindsey, "This is too much for me!" But then the lights go up and . . . *bang!*

You're in the car and "Dreams" comes on the radio. Do you still turn it up?
Oh, totally! [*Laughs.*] If I'm out walking and it comes on down the street, I stop people and tell them, "That's me!" It can be a Christine song and I'll still say it's me. I'm very proud.

YOU MAKE FIGHTING FUN . . .

Adrian Deevoy | December 28, 2013 | *Daily Mail* (UK)

Promoting a new greatest hits album, Lindsey Buckingham, Stevie Nicks, and Christine McVie sparred in separate interviews about incidents in Fleetwood Mac's tempestuous past. One could criticize Adrian Deevoy for focusing on this sort of stuff almost to the exclusion of the music, but the Mac soap opera had defined, and to some extent made, the band. Moreover, as can be seen, the members are always willing to discuss it.

Fleetwood Mac are fighting again. Rock-star fur is flying. But this is no ordinary argument. For one thing, the contretemps is being conducted in three different countries. Stevie Nicks fights her corner from an elegant apartment in Paris, Lindsey Buckingham boxes clever in his Californian study and Christine McVie counterpunches from her riverside penthouse in London.

Founder band members Mick Fleetwood and John McVie are keeping out of it. Fleetwood is licking his wounds after his fourth divorce and McVie is in hospital engaged in a more serious battle, with cancer.

The disagreement, believe it or not, concerns one of Fleetwood Mac's few physical altercations. After 45 years of soft rock's favourite soap opera, it's astonishing that the players haven't come to blows more often.

'I was dancing on stage,' begins Nicks, now 65, in the salon of her rented Parisian pied-à-terre. 'It was the *Tusk* tour, 1980, Auckland, New Zealand. I was doing my thing with my shawl and Lindsey pulled his jacket up over his head and started mimicking me, behind my back. I thought, "Well, that's not working for me." But I didn't do anything. This must have infuriated him, because he came over and kicked me. And I'd never had anyone be physical with me in my life. Then he picked up a black Les Paul guitar and he just frisbee'd it at me. He missed, I ducked—but he could have killed me.'

'I'm not sure that happened,' Buckingham, 64, states flatly at his gated LA estate.

'Oh, it happened, all right,' asserts Christine McVie, 70, drinking in a glorious view of the Thames. 'I threw a glass of wine in his face.'

It was always the friction within Fleetwood Mac that produced the most magical music. The pristine production sheen of 1977's gazillion-selling *Rumours* concealed a cauldron of simmering tensions and churning passions. They were an airport novel come to life, and with a sensational soundtrack.

Famously, during the recording of *Rumours*, chiffoned hippy siren Nicks split with Buckingham, her boyfriend of several years, and, after nearly a decade of marriage, Christine and John McVie stopped talking to each other, except to discuss musical matters. And some of the songs—*Go Your Own Way, You Make Loving Fun, Dreams*—were pretty brutal.

'It was tough stuff,' admits Christine McVie. 'But you had to sing about the emotions you were feeling at the time. It was hands-on-the-table honest.'

'Stevie and I weren't even estranged; we just weren't a couple any more,' recalls Buckingham. 'But none of us had the luxury of time and distance to allow for closure. And that's what a shrink will tell you helps us to heal. So it was difficult on a lot of levels. Very difficult.'

August 7, 1987 was an especially difficult day. According to Mick Fleetwood's memoirs, a meeting was called to discuss Buckingham's decision to quit touring, and Nicks remonstrated aggressively with her former boyfriend. As she set about Buckingham, he screamed, 'Get this bitch out of my way. And f*** the lot of you!'

The fracas, Fleetwood claims, culminated in Buckingham slapping her and bending her over the bonnet of a car, before storming off shouting, 'You're a bunch of selfish b******s.'

'That was in the courtyard of my house,' Christine McVie concurs. 'There was a bit of a physical fight, and she wasn't beating him up. It wasn't nice.'

'There wasn't any physical violence,' contends Buckingham. 'It was an unpleasant situation that day, but you have to ask yourself the question, if someone is beating on your chest because they don't want you to leave, isn't that in a way kind of flattering?'

The level of acrimony the incident suggests begs another question: despite Buckingham and Nicks having put on a united front for their latest UK shows, during which they held hands, hugged and generally behaved civilly towards each other, have they ever actually agreed on anything?

'That's a very funny question,' Buckingham laughs. 'I don't know how much we ever did agree. I'm trying to be tactful here, but there was never a huge set of sensibilities that we had in common.'

Of course, what the members of Fleetwood Mac did have in common—supernaturally inspired songwriting aside—was a fondness for drink and drugs. Cocaine and Champagne was their cocktail of choice.

'Well, they go hand in hand, don't they?' shrugs McVie. 'When we were in Sausalito making *Rumours*, the boys would be doing these huge rails of coke while Stevie and I would be in our own place with our little bottles of coke, with tiny coke-spoons that we'd wear on delicate chains around our necks. Very ladylike—much more refined—and actually fairly acceptable at the time. Inevitably, late at night the boys would run out and come looking for ours.'

And is it true that during their private-jet-and-pink-hotel-suite years, Fleetwood Mac would take cocaine while they were performing on stage?

'Absolutely,' confirms Nicks. 'We thought that's what entertainers did in order to maintain that level of activity and creativity.'

'Mick had this rotating platform covered with beer-bottle caps full of coke so he could snort away as he was playing,' marvels McVie. 'At least us ladies would slip off stage for a discreet toot.'

'You know, I never bought cocaine,' Buckingham sniffs. 'There were other people in the band who may have done that.'

Indeed there were. And they bought it by the boatload. Cocaine became synonymous with the Fleetwood Mac brand (Mick Fleetwood reportedly wanted to give their drug dealer a credit on *Rumours*). But by the mid-Eighties, the comedown had kicked in. 'And,' says Nicks, 'the payback was a complete bitch.'

McVie reluctantly acknowledges that her voice, piano and presence make the band somehow complete. Without her, Fleetwood Mac serve up a satisfying set of ingredients, but she is the sauce that unifies them. 'The gravy?' she suggests. 'I think we all sensed that.'

As for Fleetwood Mac's future recording plans, McVie lets slip that she has recently written new songs for the band. 'I sent them to Lindsey and he loved them,' she reveals. 'You could hear his mind whirring, figuring how he could improve them, Mac them up.'

Then out of the blue, in that honeyed voice, she starts to sing.

'We've only just begun . . . '

FLEETWOOD MAC'S CHRISTINE McVIE IS READY TO ROCK. AGAIN.

Ann Friedman | September 2014 | *Elle* (UK)

The Christine McVie–less *Rumours*-era Fleetwood Mac toured in 2009 on the back of nothing but nostalgia: unless you counted the deluxe version of *Rumours*, there was no new album being promoted. The same lineup's 2013 jaunt was almost as disappointing for product-hungry fans: only the four-track *Extended Play*—an iTunes download—was on offer.

This feature offered hope on two counts, revealing that Christine McVie was permanently coming back to the fold and that—regardless of a shrinking record industry that had seen the band's latest two-CD greatest hits set retail at a paltry twelve dollars—there was to be at some point a new bona fide Fleetwood Mac album.

Christine McVie looks into the camera and asks, "How does it feel being a sex symbol in rock 'n' roll?" Hanging out backstage on Fleetwood Mac's 1977 world tour, McVie, the band's keyboardist, looks as if she's had a few vodka tonics (and if this night was like most on the *Rumours* tour, probably a fair amount of cocaine, too). She pauses for the perfect comedic beat, then delivers: "I don't know; ask Stevie Nicks." Her blond shag and shiny caftan shake as she emits a husky laugh. "Oh, listen, Stevie's gonna know I'm kidding," she says in her proper English accent. The two women of Fleetwood Mac have always been friends. There's no need for competition when their roles are so clear: Nicks in front, twirling seductively in her shawls; McVie in back, stealthily ruling the keyboards. If Nicks is the band's witchy goddess, McVie is its warrior queen, strong and steady. She's also one of its key creative forces, having written half the songs on the band's *Greatest Hits* album.

And so in 1998, McVie sent Fleetwood Mac into a midlife crisis of sorts when she announced she was quitting the band. After 28 years of late nights, she was done living out of a suitcase, finished with recording studios and sold-out arenas. She was also increasingly scared to fly. A few years earlier, she'd bought a rambling old manor in the English countryside, and, at age 54, the quiet life beckoned. "I did my last show, got everything shipped out from the house in L.A., went to catch my last flight back to London," she says, "and didn't look back."

Until now. At age 71, after almost 20 years out of the spotlight, McVie has returned. She'll crisscross North America with Fleetwood Mac on a 40-city megatour this fall, playing Katy Perry–size venues from Boston to Portland. "*Serendipity* is the only word I can think of to describe it," she tells me over coffee and salmon-and-cream-cheese sandwiches at her London pied-à-terre. It's in a modern building overlooking the Thames but made cozy with an overstuffed sofa, a leather chair, lots of Persian rugs, and keyboards pushed up against the floor-to-ceiling windows. McVie looks decades younger than her years and exudes well-earned rocker cool. She wears a simple tank top and jeans with a silver-plate belt and a tangle of bracelets. Her shaggy blond hair is almost identical to her *Rumours*-era cut, her skin so tan it's as if she never left California.

"Since she's been back, I'm already feeling the steadying effect of her presence," says Mick Fleetwood, Fleetwood Mac's drummer and jovial father figure. "There is no doubt that there was a void in the chemistry of the band. The band rose successfully to the creative withdrawal, but emotionally . . . the balance was challenged."

Though the band has had a rotating cast throughout its history, the five who will tour this fall—McVie, plus Nicks, Fleetwood, Lindsey Buckingham, and John McVie—are what Christine McVie calls "the *Rumours* Five," a group so tight-knit they describe themselves as a family, albeit an incestuous one: McVie was married to bassist John McVie for eight years and had an affair with the band's lighting director—who later had an affair with Nicks, who was Buckingham's ex-girlfriend and who also had an affair with Fleetwood.

All of this is ancient history, but the champagne-drenched drama did inspire Fleetwood Mac to create its most haunting harmonies and driving guitar anthems. Today it's almost impossible to imagine an album inciting the frenzy that *Rumours* created upon its release in 1977. It sold 10 million copies in its first year, becoming the top-selling album in history at that time. The group toured for a solid year, playing to sold-out 10,000-seat arenas each night. And perhaps because of the suddenness of it all, the band also closed ranks, each buying mansions in Bel-Air and Malibu and mainly hanging out with one another. For Christine McVie, some 5,000 miles from her family in England, Fleetwood Mac was her whole world.

And yet, once her mind was made up, McVie says it wasn't that hard to put the rock 'n' roll life behind her—at first. She dug into her new life and kept busy remodelling the crumbling manor. "You get into your wellie boots and your Range Rover and, walking around with six inches of mud on your shoes, you get to forget about that more polished lifestyle," she says. McVie's second marriage, to fellow keyboardist Eddy Quintela, ended shortly after she left the band, so it was just her and her dogs knocking around that big house.

"It worked out all right for awhile, but then you start to think, Okay, now what? Start to bake some cookies for the—what is it? The YMCA?" she says with that throaty laugh. "I just started getting bored." She made a solo album, 2004's *In the Meantime*, with her nephew Dan Perfect, a musician who lives nearby. But McVie didn't tour to promote it: Her once minor fear of flying had become a full-blown phobia. The very thought of getting on an airplane made her heart race and palms sweat. It was a fear of losing control, she says now, acknowledging the irony: The inability to fly, in turn, confined and controlled her.

Still, "She seemed happy in her life," Fleetwood says. "But I did always find it odd and somewhat worrisome that someone as creative as Chris was so utterly divorced from music in general." While she continued to jot down ideas for songs, for years she barely touched the piano. Then, she realized, "If I don't do anything about this flying business, I'm never going to go anywhere or do anything."

And so the woman who wrote the lyrics "Don't stop thinking about tomorrow" found herself looking forward once again. She began seeing a therapist to overcome the flying phobia. Now she's oddly nonchalant about what was once so debilitating. After months of talking out her fears, the therapist asked, "Where would you like to go if you could fly somewhere?" "Maui," she replied, which is where Fleetwood now lives. The therapist told her to buy a ticket. She didn't have to get on the plane—just buy the ticket. As it turned out, Fleetwood was coming to London, and they agreed to fly to Hawaii together. "We took off, and the feeling was, 'God, I'm free!,'" McVie says. In Hawaii, she played a small gig with Fleetwood's blues band, then the two of them flew to Los Angeles, where they had a dinner with Nicks, John McVie, and Buckingham—the *Rumours* Five, together again. "That was the beginning of how the whole thing started," McVie says of the upcoming tour. "The chemistry between us is just so magical."

In her absence, the band had continued to play live; they still performed "Don't Stop," which McVie wrote about her divorce from John. But Fleetwood Mac had crossed most of the McVie-written songs off its set list—they just didn't sound the same without her voice. When she returned to England, where no one besides the dogs were waiting, "I thought, No, I've got to make some decisions," she says. "I either sit here and wait for my dogs to die or kick-start my life again." She called—and shocked—each of her bandmates, asking: What if I came back?

Nicks was thrilled. John McVie and Fleetwood were onboard too. Buckingham was cautiously optimistic: Could the out-of-practice McVie deliver night after night? "You would really have to commit," he told her. "You couldn't just be popping in and popping out."

She told him it wouldn't be a problem—and it's clear she's taking the promise seriously. Both McVie and Fleetwood enlisted personal trainers to get them into shape. (Her flat is littered with dumbbells and a large blue exercise ball.) "The aim is to be fit enough to stand up for two and a half hours balancing on one foot, which is what I do," she says, playing an air keyboard to demonstrate her stage position. "I'm all occupied."

Unlike the old days, they'll travel by private jet, and McVie will have a few personal attendants along. "I'm going to have someone that packs for me," she says. Nicks has long had wardrobe assistants, but this is new territory for McVie, who lives in jeans and T-shirts. Also new: "I want to go out and do things [on days off], not just stick around having room service for two days," McVie says. "I feel like I know where I'm going now, and I want to enjoy this."

She's been in the studio writing with Buckingham too. At one point she was stuck on a lyric, and he suggested, "Just write about sex." Today, McVie—quick to insist that she writes about love—has about a half-dozen tunes that have a shot at making it onto Fleetwood Mac's next album (though there's no word yet on when to expect it).

I ask whether any of her songs were inspired by her years in the country. "You mean the nunnery?" she jokes, before clarifying. "I was by no means a nun."

These days she's single, but the sparkle in her blue eyes reminds me of the tales I've read about her past: about the liaison with British musician Spencer Davis, the whirlwind romance with a German DJ, and the multiyear relationship with the Beach Boys' Dennis Wilson, who once dug a heart-shape garden in her backyard to profess his love. So, is there much action in the English countryside?

"Well, not much action," she says. "But some." Enough to inspire six good love songs, at least.

ABOUT THE CONTRIBUTORS

Johnny Black has been writing about music for over thirty years, contributing to magazines including *Q*, *Mojo*, and *Classic Rock*, as well as writing books about Jimi Hendrix, R.E.M., and others. He also devised and curates the website www.musicdayz.com, the world's largest online archive of chronological music facts.

One of the grandees of British music journalism, **Roy Carr** made his name at IPC, working for *New Musical Express*, *Melody Maker*, *Vox*, and *Uncut*. He is credited with pioneering the concept of the cover-mount CD. Among his many books are entries in the Illustrated Record series on the Beatles, the Rolling Stones, David Bowie, and Elvis Presley. He is also the coauthor of *Fleetwood Mac: Rumours 'n' Fax*.

Adrian Deevoy is a London-based journalist who works for *GQ*, the *Guardian*, and the *Mail on Sunday*. He is the only writer of his generation to have conducted extensive interviews with Bob Dylan, Prince, Freddie Mercury, Madonna, and the late Daevid Allen of Gong.

Bill DeMain is a music journalist, musician, and Grammy-nominated songwriter. He is owner of the Walkin' Nashville walking tours.

Dave DiMartino is the executive editor of *Yahoo Music* in Los Angeles. He is a former editor of *Creem* and was West Coast bureau chief of *Billboard* and a senior writer at *Entertainment Weekly*. In 1995 he became executive editor of *Launch*, a CD-ROM magazine and Internet music site that was purchased by Yahoo in 2001 and redubbed *Yahoo Music*.

As press officer at RCA records, **Robin Eggar** was allowed to answer the phones the day Elvis died. He then managed punk band the Members and record producer Steve Lillywhite before becoming the *Daily Mirror*'s rock writer. He has written for the *Sunday Times, Esquire, You, The Face, Time Out, NME,* the *Observer, The Word,* and *Rolling Stone,* plus books on everything from fitness, adventure sports, and Chinook helicopters to sixties sex gods.

Mark Ellen worked at the *New Musical Express, Smash Hits, Q, Select, Mojo,* and *The Word* and now writes, broadcasts, and lectures (mostly about music). His memoir, *Rock Stars Stole My Life!,* is published by Hodder.

Ann Friedman is a writer whose work appears frequently in *New York, ELLE,* the *New Republic,* and more. She lives in Los Angeles.

David Gans is a Califonia-based musician and journalist. He served as senior editor (West Coast) for *Record* magazine in the '80s in addition to other music-magazine posts. After he published his first book, *Playing in the Band: An Oral and Visual Portrait of the Grateful Dead,* he migrated into radio, creating the nationally syndicated *Grateful Dead Hour.* His most recent book is *This Is All a Dream We Dreamed: An Oral History of the Grateful Dead.*

Writer, editor, columnist, and publisher **John Grissim** cut his journalist's teeth at *Rolling Stone* in the sixties before his principal interest turned to the ocean. The author of ten books on subjects as diverse as country music, pool hustlers, surfing, and sunken treasure, he lives with his family in the Pacific Northwest. He is currently editing a book about the Kennedy assassination.

James Halbert wrote for *Classic Rock* in the mid to late noughties. He now works as a landscape gardener in Normandy. His favorite Fleetwood Mac track is "Albatross," mainly for the words.

Amy Hanson is a freelance author whose works include biographies of Smashing Pumpkins, Nick Cave, and the liner notes for Mute Records' Nick Cave reissue series. She has contributed numerous articles and reviews to such publications as *Goldmine, All Music Guide, Experience Hendrix, Biblio*, and many others. Domiciled in Delaware with her cats, she was most recently sighted in the *Chicks Dig Gaming* anthology.

Blair Jackson has been writing about music professionally for four decades at *BAM, Mix*, and many other publications. He has penned dozens of liner notes. He is the author of *Garcia: An American Life* and (with David Gans) *This Is All a Dream We Dreamed: An Oral History of the Grateful Dead*.

Norman Jopling wrote for the British music press from 1961 to 1972, during which time he was instrumental in granting exposure to the UK R&B boom. His 2015 book, *Shake It Up Baby!*, revisited his experiences during that seminal period.

Now a professional chemist, **John Kordosh** used to be a writer and editor for *Creem* magazine. He lives at the US-Mexican border with his wife, Alice, and their cat, the Good One.

James McNair was born in Glasgow and lives in London. He currently writes for *Mojo*, the *Independent*, and the UAE-based broadsheet the *National*. In the next life he would like to be able to play guitar like Peter Green.

Chris Neal freelanced for a variety of outlets such as the *Village Voice*, Salon.com, *Nashville Scene, Performing Songwriter*, and *American Photographer*. He spent ten years with *Country Weekly* before helping launch *M Music & Musicians*, where he was senior editor. He died in 2012 at age forty.

Author and music journalist **Alan di Perna** is a longtime contributing editor to *Guitar World* and *Guitar Aficionado* magazines and has also written for *Musician, Billboard, Creem*, Grammy.com, *Rolling Stone*, and the *San Francisco Examiner Magazine*. His books include *Guitar Masters: Intimate Portraits* and *Green Day: The Ultimate Unauthorized History*.

Mac Randall is the author of two books, *Exit Music: The Radiohead Story* and *101 Great Playlists*, and has written about popular music for a variety of publications, including the *New York Times, Rolling Stone, Mojo, Q,* and *Musician*. Currently editor in chief of the music education magazine *Music Alive!,* he lives in New York City.

After spending her youth writing for *Crawdaddy, Rolling Stone, Circus, Creem,* and *People,* **Salley Rayl** grew up. Under the byline A. J. S. Rayl, she authored her swan song to rock and roll, *Beatles '64: A Hard Day's Night in America,* before going on to cover geniuses of a different kind for the likes of *OMNI, Air &Space, Discover,* and *Smithsonian*. She is currently president of GRoK Technologies, which she founded to place into the mainstream the discoveries of one of those geniuses.

Steven Rosen has been writing about the denizens of Rock-and-Roll World for the past forty years. During this period, his work has appeared in a myriad of publications, including *Guitar Player, Guitar World, Guitarist, Rolling Stone, Playboy, Creem, Circus, Musician, Classic Rock, Q, Mojo,* and a host of others.

Since starting with the *New Musical Express,* **Chris Salewicz** has written for quality newspapers and magazines across the globe. He is the author of sixteen books, most recently *Dead Gods: The 27 Club*.

Harry Shapiro is the author of biographies of Jimi Hendrix, Eric Clapton, Jack Bruce, Alexis Korner, and Graham Bond. His latest book is the authorized biography of Gary Moore.

Sylvie Simmons is a renowned rock journalist and the author of fiction and nonfiction books, including biographies of Serge Gainsbourg, Neil Young, and her latest, *I'm Your Man: The Life of Leonard Cohen*. In 2014 she signed a record deal and released her debut album.

Brian Smith has written for many magazines and alt-weeklies, and his fiction has appeared in a variety of literary journals. He's an award-winning journalist, first as a staff writer and columnist at the *Phoenix New Times* and then as an editor at Detroit's *Metro Times*. Before writing full time, Smith was a songwriter who fronted rock-and-roll bands. He has penned tunes with lots of folks, including Alice Cooper. His debut collection of short stories, *Spent Saints,* appeared in 2015.

Bill Wasserzieher writes about music and occasionally film, literature, and travel for a wide range of publications. His byline has appeared in the *Village Voice*, the *OC Weekly*, *LA Weekly*, *Crawdaddy*, *Blues Revue*, *ICE*, *Jazz Review*, *Ugly Things*, *Smithsonian Air & Space*, and the *Saturday Evening Post*.

Nigel Williamson, former editor of the *Tribune* and ex-news editor of the *Times*, has written books about Bob Dylan, Led Zeppelin, and Neil Young. He is also author of *The Rough Guide to the Blues* and *The Rough Guide to the Best Music You've Never Heard*. He was for many years a contributing editor to *Billboard* and *Uncut* and is now a contributing editor to *Songlines* magazine. He first saw Fleetwood Mac play in 1969 and accompanied the group on several dates of its reunion tour of America in 1997.

A music journalist and rock historian since the late 1970s, **Dave Zimmer** is the author of *Crosby, Stills & Nash: The Authorized Biography* and editor of *4 Way Street: The Crosby, Stills, Nash & Young Reader*. He was a longtime editor of *BAM: The California Magazine*, penning features on numerous artists, including Fleetwood Mac, Jefferson Starship, Tom Waits, and Neil Young.

CREDITS

"Peter Green—The Guitarist Who Won't Forsake the Blues" by Norman Jopling. First published in *Record Mirror*, August 19, 1967. © 1967 Norman Jopling. Reprinted by permission of the author.

"Rock'n'Blues via Peter Green: The Big Beat Bug Bites Bluesman Peter" by Norman Jopling. First published in *Record Mirror*, March 9, 1968. © 1967 Norman Jopling. Reprinted by permission of the author.

"Big Mac: Two All Gold Albums Special Songs Let-ups Cheesecake Pickles Divorce on a Star-Crossed Success Run" by John Grissim. First published in *Crawdaddy*, November 1976. © 1976 John Grissim. Reprinted by permission of the author.

"Rich Mac, Poor Mac" by Roy Carr. First published in *New Musical Express*, April 2, 1977. © TIME INC. UK. Reprinted by permission of the publisher.

"The Truth Will Tell" by Salley Rayl. First published in *Circus*, March 31, 1977. © 1977 Salley Rayl. Reprinted by permission of the author.

"Ouija Still Love Me Tomorrow?" by Salley Rayl. First published in *Circus*, April 14, 1977. © 1977 Salley Rayl. Reprinted by permission of the author.

"Nation Gripped in Massive Fleetwood Mac Attack!" by Salley Rayl. First published in *Creem*, July 1977. © 1977 Salley Rayl. Reprinted by permission of the author.

"Fleetwood Mac: The Group as Group Encounter?" by Chris Salewicz. First published in *New Musical Express*, January 19, 1980. © 1980 Chris Salewicz. Reprinted by permission of the author.

"Never Break the Chain" by Amy Hanson. First published in *Goldmine*, November 21, 1997. © 1997 Amy Hanson. Reprinted by permission of the author.

"Mick Fleetwood, 2001" by Sean Egan. © 2001 Sean Egan. Printed by permission of the author.

"Nicks of Time" by Brian Smith. First published in *Phoenix New Times*, November 29, 2001. © 2001 Brian Smith. Reprinted by permission of the author.

"The Rumour Mill" by James Halbert. First published in *Classic Rock*, June 2003. © 2003 James Halbert. Reprinted by permission of the author.

"War and Peace and Fleetwood Mac" by Bill DeMain. First published in *Performing Songwriter*, May 2003. © 2003 *Performing Songwriter*. Reprinted by permission of the publisher.

"Five Go Mad" by Nigel Williamson. First published in *Uncut*, May 2003. © 2003 Nigel Williamson. Reprinted by permission of the author.

"Return of the Native" by Mark Ellen. First published in *The Word*, July 2004. © 2004 Mark Ellen. Reprinted by permission of the author.

"24/7—A Week in the Life: Christine McVie" by James Halbert. First published in *Classic Rock*, August 2004. © 2004 James Halbert. Reprinted by permission of the author.

"Christine McVie, 2004" by Robin Eggar. © 2004 Robin Eggar. Printed by permission of the author.

"The Greatest Songs Ever: Fleetwood Mac—'Dreams'" by Johnny Black. First published in *Blender*, May 2005. © 2005 Johnny Black. Reprinted by permission of the author.

"The Return of Jeremy Spencer" by Bill Wasserzieher. First published on the website *Blues Revue*, October 2006. © 2006 Bill Wasserzieher. Reprinted by permission of the author.

"Original Skin" by Mac Randall. First published in *Guitar World Acoustic*, December 2006. © 2006 Mac Randall. Reprinted by permission of the author.

"Vision Quest" by Chris Neal. First published in *Performing Songwriter*, June 2007. © 2007 *Performing Songwriter*. Reprinted by permission of the publisher.

"California Dreaming" by Sylvie Simmons. First published in *Mojo*, September 2007. © 2007 Sylvie Simmons. Reprinted by permission of the author.

INDEX

ALSO AVAILABLE IN THE
MUSICIANS IN THEIR OWN WORDS SERIES

--- ---

BOWIE ON BOWIE
Interviews and Encounters with David Bowie
by Sean Egan

"This is a fascinating journey through the mind of a musician many people claim to 'know' but who proves time and again that his own essence is often foreign to himself. An asset for Bowie fans." —*Library Journal*

Cloth, 432 pages • ISBN-13: 978-1-56976-977-5 • $28.95 (CAN $34.95)

COBAIN ON COBAIN
Interviews and Encounters
by Nick Soulsby

"This fascinating collection offers you a front-row seat to Nirvana's stunning rise and tragic fall. Before the biographies, before the revisionism, before the mythologies, Nirvana's story is revealed by Cobain and his bandmates as it unfolds, without the benefit of hindsight. *Cobain on Cobain* is the closest you can get to a Kurt Cobain autobiography." —Gillian G. Gaar, author of *Entertain Us: The Rise of Nirvana and Treasures of Nirvana*

Cloth, 592 pages • ISBN-13: 978-1-61373-094-2 • $28.95 (CAN $34.95)

COLTRANE ON COLTRANE
The John Coltrane Interviews
by Chris DeVito

"Through these gripping and revealing interviews, Coltrane comes alive. . . . Though many solid books have been written about Coltrane, this compilation of source materials provides an intimate view of the man and his music. Certainly one of the best music books of the year." —*Library Journal*

Trade paper, 416 pages • ISBN-13: 978-1-55652-004-4 • $18.95 (CAN $20.95)

HENDRIX ON HENDRIX
Interviews and Encounters with Jimi Hendrix
by Steven Roby

"This beautifully edited and annotated collection provides abundant insights into the heart and mind of one of the 20th century's most influential artists. . . . Here we have Hendrix in his own words, with all of his confusion, contradiction, vulnerability, beauty, and brilliance intact." —*Guitar Player*

Cloth, 384 pages • ISBN-13: 978-1-61374-322-5 • $24.95 (CAN $27.95)

JUDY GARLAND ON JUDY GARLAND
Interviews and Encounters
by Randy L. Schmidt

"Garland is often seen, nowadays, as a sort of tragic figure, a superstar who achieved great heights and crippling lows, but here we see her perhaps as she would want to be remembered: an eager, supremely talented woman who never stopped dreaming of a brighter future for herself." —*Booklist Online*

Cloth, 480 pages • ISBN-13: 978-1-61374-945-6 • $28.95 (CAN $34.95)

KEITH RICHARDS ON KEITH RICHARDS
Interviews and Encounters
by Sean Egan

"All of the infamous incidents are covered . . . but what also comes through is his still-burning admiration for the Chicago blues musicians who were his greatest influence and his wariness of fame. Great reading for Stones' fans." —*Booklist*

Trade paper, 288 pages • ISBN-13: 978-1-61374-788-9 • $18.95 (CAN $20.95)

LED ZEPPELIN ON LED ZEPPELIN
Interviews and Encounters
by Hank Bordowitz

"This telling is refreshing and does the unthinkable: it makes Led Zeppelin, beloved to the point of worship, actually likeable." —*PopMatters*

Cloth, 480 pages • ISBN-13: 978-1-61374-754-4 • $28.95 (CAN $34.95)

LEONARD COHEN ON LEONARD COHEN
Interviews and Encounters
by Jeff Burger

"This is a must for Cohen fans." —Starred review, *Booklist*

"Burger's discerning editorial hand selects those conversations with Cohen that offer insights into his music. For longtime fans as well as newcomers to Cohen's work." —*Publishers Weekly*

Cloth, 624 pages • ISBN-13: 978-1-61374-758-2 • $29.95 (CAN $35.95)

MILES ON MILES
Interviews and Encounters with Miles Davis
by Paul Maher, Jr.

"Here is Miles Davis's less familiar voice, his speaking voice. . . . Maher and Dorr gather together Davis's greatest hits in Q & A, and they make compelling reading." —Jack Chambers, author of *Milestones: The Music and Times of Miles Davis*

Cloth, 352 pages • ISBN-13: 978-1-55652-706-7 • $24.95 (CAN $27.95)

SPRINGSTEEN ON SPRINGSTEEN
Interviews, Speeches, and Encounters
by Jeff Burger

"This book is a must for any Springsteen lover as it has so much. . . . Journalist-author Jeff Burger's love of the subject comes across in this vast profusion of unexpected material he's discovered, allowing the reader to view Springsteen from many angles, and over the decades." —*American Songwriter Magazine*

Trade paper, 432 pages • ISBN-13: 978-1-55652-544-5 • $17.95 (CAN $21.95)

TOM WAITS ON TOM WAITS
Interviews and Encounters
by Paul Maher, Jr.

"Absolutely required for Waits fans old and new, this pile of interviews is a magic mountain of weird." —*PopMatters*

Trade paper, 480 pages • ISBN-13: 978-1-56976-312-4 • $19.95 (CAN $21.95)

ALSO AVAILABLE
FROM CHICAGO REVIEW PRESS

STORMS

My Life with Lindsey Buckingham and Fleetwood Mac

by Carol Ann Harris

"Carol Ann Harris experienced the brightness and darkness of rock and roll and bring[s] it to life in a passionate classic." —Danny Goldberg, Fleetwood Mac insider; former head of Atlantic, Modern, Mercury, and Warner Bros; and author, *How the Left Lost Teen Spirit*

"A must-read for any fan of Fleetwood Mac." —*Houston Press*

Trade paper, 400 pages • ISBN-13: 978-1-55652-790-6 • $16.95 (CAN $18.95)